MORAL PHILOSOPHY AND

D1581645

1

MORAL PHILOSOPHY AND THE HOLOCAUST

How far can we ever hope to understand the Holocaust? What can we reasonably say about right and wrong, moral responsibility, praise and blame, in a world where ordinary reasons seem to be excluded? In the century of Nazism, ethical writing in English had much more to say about the meaning of the word 'good' than about the material reality of evil. This book seeks to redress the balance at the start of a new century.

Despite intense interest in the Holocaust, there has been relatively little exploration of it by philosophers in the analytic tradition. Although ethical writers often refer to Nazism as a touchstone example of evil, and use it as a case by which moral theorising can be tested, they rarely analyse what evil amounts to, or address the substantive moral questions raised by the Holocaust itself.

This book draws together new work by leading moral philosophers to present a wide range of perspectives on the Holocaust. Contributors focus on particular themes of central importance, including: moral responsibility for genocide; the moral uniqueness of the Holocaust; responding to extreme evil; the role of ideology; the moral psychology of perpetrators and victims of genocide; forgiveness and the Holocaust; and the impact of the 'Final Solution' on subsequent culture. Topics are treated with the precision and rigour characteristic of analytic philosophy. Scholars, teachers and students with an interest in moral theory, applied ethics, genocide and Holocaust studies will find this book of particular value, as will all those seeking greater insight into ethical issues surrounding Nazism, race-hatred and intolerance.

Moral Philosophy and the Holocaust

Edited by
EVE GARRARD
Keele University, UK
and
GEOFFREY SCARRE
University of Durham, UK

ASHGATE

Published by
Ashgate Publishing Limited
Gower House
Croft Road
Aldershot
Hants GU11 3HR
England

Ashgate Publishing Company
Suite 420
101 Cherry Street
Burlington, VT Vermont, 05401–4405 USA

Ashgate website: http://www.ashgate.com

British Library Cataloguing in Publication Data
Moral Philosophy and the Holocaust
   1. Holocaust, Jewish (1939–1945)—Moral and ethical aspects. 2. National socialism—Moral and ethical aspects. I. Garrard, Eve. II. Scarre, Geoffrey.
   179.7

Library of Congress Cataloging in Publication Data
Moral Philosophy and the Holocaust
      p.   cm.
   Includes bibliographical references.
   1. Holocaust, Jewish (1939–1945)—Moral and ethical aspects. 2. Holocaust, Jewish (1939–1945)—Influence. 3. Genocide—Moral and ethical aspect.
   I. Garrard, Eve. II. Scarre, Geoffrey.

   D804.3.M655 2002
   940.53'18–dc21   2002066703

ISBN 0 7546 1415 8 (hbk.)
ISBN 0 7546 1416 6 (pbk.)

Typeset by Bournemouth Colour Press, Parkstone.
Printed and bound in Great Britain by MPG Books Limited, Bodmin.

Contents

Notes on Contributors

Lawrence Blum is Professor of Philosophy and Distinguished Professor of Liberal Arts and Education at the University of Massachusetts, Boston. He works in the areas of ethics and race studies and has recently published *"I'm Not a Racist, But ...": The Moral Quandary of Race* (2002).

David E. Cooper is Professor of Philosophy at the University of Durham. He has written widely on nineteenth- and twentieth-century German philosophy, and on collective responsibility and war crimes. His most recent book is *The Measure of Things: Humanism, Humility and Mystery* (2002).

Michael Freeman teaches Political Theory in the Department of Government, University of Essex. His interests include nationalism, multiculturalism, ethnic conflict and genocide. His most recent work is *Human Rights: An Interdisciplinary Approach* (2002).

Eve Garrard is a lecturer in the Department of Philosophy at Keele University, UK. She has published papers on meta-ethics and applied ethics, and is currently working on a book on the nature of evil.

Norman Geras is Professor of Government at the University of Manchester. His books include *The Contract of Mutual Indifference: Political Philosophy after the Holocaust* (1998); *Solidarity in the Conversation of Humankind: The Ungroundable Liberalism of Richard Rorty* (1995); and *Marx and Human Nature: Refutation of a Legend* (1983).

Frances M. Kamm is Professor of Philosophy, Professor of Medicine (Bioethics), and Law School Affiliated Faculty, New York University. She is the author of *Creation and Abortion* (1992), *Morality, Mortality* (two volumes, 1993, 1996), and of numerous articles in ethical theory and practical ethics. For 2002 she is visiting professor of Philosophy and Public Policy at Harvard University.

Douglas P. Lackey is Professor of Philosophy at Baruch College and the Graduate Center, City University of New York. He is the author of *Moral Principles and Nuclear Weapons* (1984), *The Ethics of War and Peace* (1989) and *Ethics and Strategic Defense* (1990).

Berel Lang is Professor of Humanities at Trinity College, Connecticut. He has taught as Professor of Philosophy at the University of Colorado and the State University of New York, Albany, and he is the author of several books, including *Act and Idea in the Nazi Genocide* (1990), *Heidegger's Silence* (1996), *The Future* *of the Holocaust* (1999) and *Holocaust Representation: Art Within the Limits of History and Ethics* (2000).

Oliver Leaman is Professor of Philosophy and Zantker Professor of Judaic Studies at the University of Kentucky. He has written and edited a number of books in the area of Islamic and Jewish philosophy.

Tom Rockmore is Professor of Philosophy at Duquesne University, Pittsburgh. He is the author of many books, including, most recently, *Marx after Marxism* (2002).

Geoffrey Scarre is Senior Lecturer in the Department of Philosophy, University of Durham. He is the author of *Logic and Reality in the Philosophy of John Stuart Mill* (1989) and *Utilitarianism* (1996), and the editor of *Children, Parents and Politics* (1989). He has also published many philosophical papers, mainly on ethical themes.

Daniel Statman is a full professor at the Department of Philosophy at the University of Haifa, Israel. He is the author of *Moral Dilemmas* (1995), co-author of *Religion and Morality* (1995), and editor of *Moral Luck* (1993) and of *Virtue Ethics* (1997). In recent years he has been working in the field of virtues and has written on various emotions and character traits, such as modesty, hypocrisy and humiliation.

Hillel Steiner is Professor of Political Philosophy at the University of Manchester and a Fellow of the British Academy. He is the author of *An Essay on Rights* (1994) and co-author of *A Debate Over Rights: Philosophical Enquiries* (with Matthew Kramer and Nigel Simmonds, 1998). He is also co-editor of *The Origins of Left-Libertarianism: An Anthology of Historical Writings* and *Left-Libertarianism and Its Critics: The Contemporary Debate* (2000). His current research includes the application of libertarian principles to global, and to genetic, inequalities.

Laurence Thomas teaches in the Philosophy Department and in the Political Science Department of the Maxwell School at Syracuse University, USA. In October 2000 his lecture 'Happiness and moral powers' was delivered in the presence of Queen Beatrix of Orange.

Nick Zangwill is Lecturer in Philosophy at St. Catherine's College, Oxford. He is the author of *The Metaphysics of Beauty* (2001) and a forthcoming book on the nature of art. He has published many papers on meta-ethics, philosophy of mind and aesthetics.

Introduction

Eve Garrard and Geoffrey Scarre

On his arrival at Auschwitz in the winter of 1944, Primo Levi, a young Italian Jewish chemist who had been arrested for partisan activities, was confined with other newcomers in a vacant hut. For several hours, no food or water was provided for the prisoners. Tormented by thirst, Levi looked through the window and saw a large icicle hanging within reach. Then, he relates:

> I opened the window and broke off the icicle but at once a large, heavy guard prowling outside brutally snatched it away from me. '*Warum?*' I asked him in my poor German. '*Hier ist kein warum*' (there is no why here), he replied, pushing me inside with a shove.[1]

In the catalogue of horrors which has come to be known as the Holocaust or Shoah, Levi's being denied an icicle was a very minor item. Yet the guard's response to the prisoner's innocent and natural enquiry might stand as an emblem of the Nazis' anti-Jewish project as a whole. The man's reply to Levi was not a reasonable answer to a reasonable question. It was not, in a sense, even an unreasonable answer to a reasonable question. It was, more frighteningly and profoundly, a denial that, in the world of the extermination camp, ordinary notions of reasons, of evidence, of justifications for action had any place. For Levi, the fundamental non-rationality of the Holocaust made comprehending it impossible. To understand human actions is to map them within the space of reasons, yet the happenings at Auschwitz are for ever beyond that space. As Levi remarked in an Afterword to *If This Is A Man?*: 'War is always a terrible fact, to be deprecated, but it is in us, it has its rationality, we "understand" it'; whereas 'there is no rationality in the Nazi hatred: it is a hate that is not in us; it is outside man, it is a poison fruit sprung from the deadly trunk of Fascism, but it is outside and beyond Fascism itself'.[2]

How far can we ever hope to understand the Holocaust? And if we cannot understand it, or be sure that we have not *mis*understood it, what prospect is there of our being able to make any worthwhile comments on its moral aspects? What can we say about right and wrong, duty and obligation, moral responsibility, praise and blame, virtue and vice, in a place where there is no why? Worse, our position once we try to discuss such issues can seem false from the start. Moral appraisal demands a certain kind of objectivity, and objectivity may require us to take as dispassionate a look as possible at the facts. Yet a dispassionate attitude to the Holocaust itself appears morally objectionable. Ought we to be *analysing* the deaths of six million men, women and children (to refer only to the Jewish victims of the Nazis)? Wouldn't a contemplative, pain-filled silence be much more proper? Interpreting the moral dimensions of the Holocaust may seem to be something that we could not do if we would, and should not attempt if we could.

That this need not be our final conclusion is attested, we hope, in some degree by the present volume. That, despite the cognitive and moral difficulties, it is possible to engage with the terrible reality of the Holocaust and throw light on it from the viewpoint of moral philosophy is the shared belief of the essayists in this book. In part, this possibility is the result of our increasing temporal distance from the Holocaust. As time passes, there are fewer and fewer people alive with first-hand experience of the Nazi camps and ghettos. But given the wealth of documentary evidence which exists from that era, the gradual exit of the witnesses is, from an evidential point of view, less important than the attainment of a longer perspective within which the Holocaust can be framed. If the shock of the Holocaust has not yet worn off (and indeed may never do so), its power to paralyse critical thought and reflection by now largely has. The Holocaust has often been viewed as a (or *the*) defining moral event of the twentieth century, yet its own definition requires multiple references to the conditions, developments, problems and crises of that century. Aristotle thought that we cannot estimate the significance of events within an individual's life until we can see that life whole. World events like the Holocaust likewise need to be grasped in a broad historical context, whose contours become clearer with time. Even if aspects of Hitler's 'Final Solution' should for ever elude our cognitive grasp, we are in some ways better placed to say what the Holocaust *was* than were our predecessors of fifty years ago.

Moreover, it has frequently been held that attempts to comprehend Nazi deeds are tantamount to attempts to excuse them (Levi himself writes that 'to understand is almost to justify'[3]). While the truth of this view is very disputable, it largely explains the laudable delicacy which has long had an inhibiting effect on discussion: writers have not wanted to hurt the feelings of those survivors who believe, even if falsely, that explanations are exculpations. With the thinning of the ranks of survivors, this reticence is increasingly unnecessary. There are signs, too, that we are moving into a new climate of opinion in which respect for Nazi victims is taken to be better shown by subjecting the Holocaust to close scholarly scrutiny than by passing over it in a silence which might, over time, become indistinguishable from oblivion. ('Holocaust Studies', like other fields of research, are not always as sensitive, subtle or politically pure as one might wish, an issue taken up by Lawrence Blum in his essay. But the best manage to combine searching scholarship with a sustained awareness of the tragic nature of their subject-matter.)

Making sense of the Holocaust requires us to do more than identify the reasons behind Nazi actions. We need also to look at the reasons which should have weighed with the Nazis but didn't. When Levi's thirst-quenching icicle was snatched away, the fact that he was a human being in a frightening and painful situation was an irrelevant consideration for the guard. Nevertheless the refusal to rationalize about why Levi should not have the icicle originated in some brutal Nazi logic. In Nazi eyes Jews were defectively human, a degenerate race. Yet Jews patently exhibited the normal characteristics of human persons, including curiosity and rational prudence. Reducing members of the race to what their oppressors thought of as a more fitting plane of existence required them to be stripped of those features which enabled them to ape their betters. So it was essential that Jews should be excluded from the space of reasons in which other people lived. Jewish curiosity should not only go unsatisfied; it would not be tolerated in the first place. Jews were not simply given no answers; they were not allowed any questions. Nor were they permitted to think of themselves as agents, with their own private reasons for action. The systematic frustration of Jewish desires (except, perhaps, the desire for death) was meant to make their very having of desires seem futile. The theory was that Jews would ultimately come to see themselves in the way their oppressors wished them to: as sub-personal beings whose only roles were to work and to die.

In Auschwitz, wrote Levi, 'everything is forbidden, not for hidden reasons, but because the camp has been created for that purpose'.[4] As Bruno Bettelheim (who had experienced imprisonment at Dachau before the war) explained, 'the goal of the system was depersonalisation'.[5] The moral claims which persons make could not be made by non-, or sub-, persons. As Jews failed to attain personhood, they could not expect to be accorded the privileges associated with that status. (The same went also, to a lesser extent, for Slavs, Poles, gypsies, homosexuals and other 'inferior' specimens of humanity.) Hence a large number of 'Why?' questions (along with a good many 'How?' and 'What?' questions) would never be posed. 'How can it be right to send men, women and children to their deaths in gas chambers?' – 'What justifies the exploitation of the Jews in the camps and ghettos?' – 'Isn't it wrong to do X, Y and Z to ends-in-themselves?' Such questions get a grip when it is *persons* we are dealing with. But for the Nazis, the Jews were only pseudo-persons to start with and quickly lost all vestiges of personhood after a period as camp-guests of the Third Reich. Jews were *not* ends-in-themselves and it was sentimental folly to think otherwise. In the rigidly stratified Nazi world-view, no moral questions about the ways in which Germans treated Jews arose, given the fundamental inferiority of the latter to the former.

For us there are some very large *Why?* questions. Why did the Nazis and their followers not ask the questions which to our minds cry out to be asked? Explaining the conditions under which exterminationist anti-Semitism arose is first and foremost a historical task, although one best tackled by a multidisciplinary approach in which the skills of the historian are supplemented by those of other specialists such as psychologists, sociologists, economists and philosophers. But there are specifically philosophical questions too, and among these some for the *moral* philosopher. For instance, given that the Nazis didn't recognize the Jews as persons, what can be said about their moral responsibility for what they did to members of that race? Is it more blameworthy to kill when one has a sense of the value of the victims than when one has no sense of that value? Is blindness to the worth of the victims an exculpatory factor or a sign of moral bankruptcy? Does one have a right to take violent pre-emptive action against people who one believes (rightly or wrongly) pose a threat? Can there be any forgiveness, and if so by whom, of offences as terrible as genocide?

These questions and others like them are the matter of the present book, which represents an attempt by several philosophers working mainly in the analytical tradition to apply their distinctive skills and approach to some of the moral problems posed by the Nazi era. On the whole, and with a few honourable exceptions, analytical philosophers have been fairly silent about the Holocaust. In the first two or three decades following World War II this reticence was largely the consequence of a misguided professional reluctance to engage at all with first-order moral questions. Instead of talking about issues of right and wrong, analytical philosophers preferred to talk about people talking about right and wrong. But even when the exclusive concentration on meta-ethics began to give way in the 1970s, it took moral philosophers some time longer to recognize that the tragic events of the twentieth century constituted a legitimate area of philosophical enquiry. In fact it might be argued that this recognition is even now incomplete.

Berel Lang, in 'Philosophy's Contribution to Holocaust Studies', takes up this issue, and explores some of the reasons for the marginal nature of philosophy's contribution. Inevitably, he points out, history is bound to come before philosophy (or any other discipline) in the study of the Holocaust, and more contingently, there is an ahistorical element in much contemporary, particularly anglophone, philosophical work. Lang points out some key issues on which philosophical work could appropriately be done, including the concept of genocide, and associated issues of group rights; the nature of group and individual intentions, and the consequent attributions of responsibility; classical issues in ethics such as the problem of evil, and the methodological question of the relevance of extreme situations to ethical theorizing; and the troubled problem of how the Holocaust is to be represented – the limits of representation, and problems connected with the social and political functions (if any) of art.

Many of the papers in this book address one or more of these questions; others explore a further range of issues about the Holocaust. David Cooper, in 'Ideology, Moral Complicity and the Holocaust', is concerned with the intellectual context of National Socialism, but his interest is not so much in the views that causally influenced the development of Nazi doctrines as with those that had ideological affinities with it (some of which still have currency). He deploys here the concept of complicity, such that one doctrine is complicit in another if the first either endorses the second, or lacks the resources to condemn it. The 'received view' on National Socialism is that views complicit in it include hostility to Enlightenment rationalism, rejection of modernity, and a Romantic favouring of emotional and mystical insight. Cooper suggests that Hitler himself was more concerned with (perverted) science (especially Social Darwinism) than with mythology, and that he saw Jews as a quasi-biological threat to the German race – parasites, bacilli, poison in the blood, unnaturally individualistic. National Socialism, Cooper argues, was a modernist movement, though of a reactionary kind, rejecting liberal democracy but not reason or techno-science.

However, these ideological tendencies are only complicit in the Holocaust in combination with a naturalistic view of morality, either one which relativizes it to the interests of the race, or one which construes it expressivistically, as not part of the domain of truth. This is compatible with one strand of the Enlightenment understanding of morality: the attempt to ground it in human nature, and the tendency to subjectivize it, construing it as the expression of feeling rather than truth-oriented belief. Cooper argues that each of these conceptions of morality – relativist and expressivist – in conjunction with a racial ideology, is complicit in the

Holocaust. The received view on complicity inclines us to believe that Nazi thought, and ideologies complicit in it, are now outdated. But Cooper's argument suggests that a range of current views about morality, such as sociobiology, expressivism and deconstructionism, are complicit in the Holocaust, either implying an endorsement of it, or lacking the intellectual wherewithal to reject it.

A recurrent and contentious issue concerning the Holocaust is that of its (putative) uniqueness. Many of the papers in the book touch on this issue, and it is the focal topic of at least two of them. Norman Geras's 'In a Class of its Own?' opens by showing how controversial it has been both to deny and to assert the claim that the Holocaust is unique. He goes on to consider whether objections to the claim are compelling. He points out that doubts about the motives of those who claim uniqueness can be separated from the issue of the truth of the claim. The supposition that the claim's legitimacy is entirely context-dependent is not borne out by the argumentative practice of those who make it – they support their claim by referring to features of the event rather than to features of the context of its assertion. The objection that uniqueness claims are, on one level, trivially true (since all events differ from one another in some way) is one whose truth Geras accepts; but he denies that this makes such claims vacuous in all circumstances, since we can legitimately raise the question of whether an event is unique in any *important* respect, which would give point to the drawing of a category boundary between it and other events.

Geras argues that the uniqueness claim is a normative rather than a descriptive one, and is widely taken to be such, in spite of surface denials. However, we are not thereby committed to invidious comparisons of unquantifiable suffering. Geras identifies four characteristics of the Holocaust which might ground the uniqueness claim, each of which is a feature of what was done rather than what was suffered – the focus is on the perpetrators rather than on the victims. Invoking the Wittgensteinian notion of a family resemblance concept, he argues that though no one feature was necessary for uniqueness, none the less the four he has cited jointly constituted a social system for the production of death, and it is this which grounds the claim that the Holocaust is unique.

In 'Knowledge, History and the Holocaust', Tom Rockmore draws a connection between the uniqueness issue and epistemic concerns about whether we can know or understand the Holocaust. He distinguishes between two construals of uniqueness, one on which an event is unique if it is different in all ways from other events, and the other on which it is unique so long as it has some features which it doesn't share with other events, even though it has many features in common with them. He argues that if an event is unique in the first sense then it will be unknowable; but, he claims, the Holocaust is in fact unique in the second sense, and hence, like other historical events, it is knowable, in virtue of its similarities to other events.

Such knowledge, according to Rockmore, will be perspectival, relativized to a conceptual framework. But this is not because of any distinctive features of the Holocaust: *all* historical knowledge, he claims, is indexed to a conceptual scheme. It doesn't follow from this that any interpretation which purports to be historical knowledge is as good as any other one; there is still room for the idea of cognitive objectivity. However, what counts as objectivity will itself be historically relativized: it will amount to conformity to our current standards of knowledge.

Hillel Steiner and Nick Zangwill both focus on the reasons which the Nazis took themselves to have for acting as they did. Steiner's paper 'Persons of Lesser Value' turns to the issue of values which we may share with the Nazis, and the possibility of a 'slippery slope' between our evaluative commitments and the Nazis' dreadful practice. We want, of course, to reject the essential elements in the system of values which informed the actions of the perpetrators of the Holocaust, and in the light of which they sought to justify those actions. Does it follow that *any* value which the Nazis endorsed is one which we should abjure? Steiner points out that we do in fact share some of the values in terms of which the Nazis justified the Holocaust (for example certain broadly eugenic ones). However, it doesn't follow that we should reject these shared values, since it may be the case that what is objectionable about the Nazi justificatory argument is not, or not entirely, a matter of different values. But we cannot locate the objectionability in the obvious alternative of factual error on the Nazis' part (for example, about the nature of their victims), since a widespread reaction to the Holocaust is that it would have been utterly unjustified even if the facts had been as the Nazis claimed. (This reaction is also discussed in Geoffrey Scarre's paper.) Our account of what is wrong with the Nazi justification should not, Steiner feels, undermine this response – the Holocaust-abhorrence response, as he calls it.

Steiner seeks to identify an objectionable feature of the Nazi argument which is neither an appeal to a value we may ourselves endorse, nor a claim which is factually erroneous. A sophisticated Nazi, he proposes, might argue that some people are genuinely of lesser value than others – they are a poison in the body politic – and that all things considered, the rest of humanity has a right to eliminate them (that is, a positive right to promote the interests of humanity). The obvious response to this Nazi argument is that it is mistaken about the moral status of the victims – they are no less valuable than any other members of the human race. But this response implies that had the victims been as the Nazis believed them to be, then there might have been a justification for what the Nazis did. So this implication falls foul of the Holocaust-abhorrence response, which Steiner is treating as a constraint on accounts of the moral nature of the Holocaust.

Steiner argues that the locus of the Nazi argument's failure is not in its erroneous estimation of the victims, but rather in the nature of its appeal to positive rights. A key feature of the Nazi argument is its claim that the positive right to improve the human condition warrants the infringing of each victim's negative right to life. But on a plausible account of rights, negative rights have priority: only the rights-bearer's *choice* to waive the enforceability of her negative rights can create room for positive rights in others. In the absence of consent there can be no justification for violating the negative rights of others. Hence the sophisticated Nazi argument fails. On this basis, we can see that our commitment to certain values, including eugenic ones, which we share with the Nazis is not in itself troubling; it need not take us on to a slippery slope at the bottom of which lies mass murder. Rather, the pursuit of these values is constrained by consent, whose presence acts as a conceptual barrier to our sliding down that threatening slope.

Nick Zangwill, in 'Perpetrator Motivation: Some Reflections on the Browning/Goldhagen Debate', explores the nature of the motivation of the perpetrators, in particular of those ordinary Germans whose participation in the systematic torture and killing of Jews and others is so notable a feature of the Nazi massacres. He focuses on the debate between the historians Christopher Browning and Daniel Goldhagen about the motivation of the members of Reserve Police Battalion 101. This debate turns on whether these men were in general motivated by eliminationist anti-Semitism, as Goldhagen claims, or whether anti-Semitism (often of a less deadly kind than the eliminationist variety) was only part of the motivational story, as Browning argues, claiming that other 'situational' factors such as peer pressure and obedience to authority play a central role in explaining the killings. This debate is often thought of as an either/or choice, but Zangwill suggests that a more nuanced conclusion, drawing on truths from both sides of the argument, is called for.

Zangwill argues that peer pressure, and obedience to authority, are indeed explanatorily relevant in this case, but that they should be construed as entering into conscious motivation, rather than as social mechanisms working outside of cognition. He concludes (with Goldhagen and against Browning) that eliminationist anti-Semitism was indeed a motivationally necessary condition of the men's actions. But unlike Goldhagen, he accepts the case, implicit in Browning's work, for other motivational factors being present and explanatorily relevant.

The next group of papers, those by Geoffrey Scarre, Douglas Lackey, Michael Freeman and Frances Kamm, concentrate on questions of responsibility. In his paper 'Moral Responsibility and the Holocaust' Geoffrey Scarre takes up at a very general level the issue of allocating responsibility for the events of the Holocaust. He argues that the Holocaust-abhorrence response, which Steiner takes as a fixed point in our moral understanding of what the Nazis did, is seriously out of line with our normal approach to moral responsibility. Normally we regard empirical error, or mistaken belief about the moral standing of our actions, as to some extent mitigating our culpability for them. But in the case of the Nazis we often take a different stance – we say that *whatever* they believed to be the case, they are utterly to be condemned. Against this stance, Scarre argues that our normal moral mode of judgement is likely to be more reliable than our intuitions about atypically extreme cases.

Furthermore, Scarre points out, we need to distinguish between the moral status of the acts performed, and the moral standing of the agent who performs them. How the Nazis saw their victims, and what fears they had of them, may help in part to explain their terrible actions, without in any way diminishing the dreadfulness of what was done. However, ignorance, error, and the dominance of a received and deadly ideology may make a difference to the culpability of the agent. We do allow this shift in attributions of moral responsibility in other cases of horrific actions, such as the early modern persecution of witches, so we should, Scarre claims, be prepared to do so in the case of the Holocaust.

Douglas Lackey's paper is concerned with the moral responsibility of the powerful – of those whose orders led to mass killings. In 'Four Types of Mass Murderer: Stalin, Hitler, Churchill, Truman', he claims that the eponymous leaders were all mass murderers and all evil, though in different ways and to different extents. Lackey allows that acting out of necessity or self-defence does make a difference to the culpability of agents; he argues, however, that such defences are not available for any of these four leaders. Stalin, he claims, must have known that collectivization had produced famine; Hitler had no ultimate reason to eliminate all the Jews, but only a bare irrational preference which in fact was against his own interests; Churchill's bombing of Dresden was effective neither in undermining the Nazi war machine nor in destroying civilian morale, and could not, in 1945, be justified in terms of necessity to win a just war; and even if Truman thought the Hiroshima bomb was needed to end the war, and thereby save lives, he was culpably careless in calculating the relevant figures, and was also intentionally aiming to kill many civilians. For Lackey, this is sufficient to categorize these four men as mass murderers, and hence evil.

Michael Freeman, in 'Is Limited Altruism Morally Wrong?', takes up the issue of the responsibility of bystanders to the victims of horrific acts. Unlike Scarre, he thinks that our normal moral judgements are inappropriate for the problems which arise in extreme circumstances. In our normal moral thinking, duties of special relationship (for example the special duties we owe to members of our own families) are a highly significant part of morality. This is sometimes attributed to the (alleged) pervasiveness in human nature of very limited altruism. This in turn is taken to mean that our duty to help strangers is correspondingly limited. Freeman argues, appealing to the fact/value gap, that the psychological thesis of limited altruism can't by itself settle the issue of the duties of bystanders. Furthermore, global as well as local sympathies are also part of our psychology.

Although common-sense morality endorses limited altruism, this is morally inadequate, Freeman claims, for the kind of problem raised by reflection on the Holocaust. The extreme needs of strangers impose obligations on us, even at the expense of some of our obligations to our nearest and dearest – that is, universalist moral considerations here outweigh particularist ones. Although Freeman acknowledges that there is a universalist case for allowing some measure of ethical particularism into our moral scheme of things, none the less altruism needs to be extended to cope with the demands generated by contemporary conditions.

A peculiarly difficult and sensitive question of responsibility arises with respect to the Jews who collaborated with the Nazi selections for transportation and death, in the hope of saving some Jewish lives. In 'Harming Some to Save Others from the Nazis', Frances Kamm draws on recent developments in moral theory, in particular on deontological principles permitting or prohibiting various kinds of lifesaving act, to illuminate the moral issue of collaborating with evil-doing in order to save lives. She analyses the problem into two key questions: first, does the fact of *selection* (of some to be killed rather than others) make what the Judenrate (Jewish Councils) did morally impermissible; second, does the fact of *collaboration* do so? Kamm deploys features of the 'redirection-of-threat' analysis that has been developed in much-discussed cases in the theoretical literature (such as the 'trolley problem', and Bernard Williams's 'Jim and the Indians' case) to try to establish the moral permissibility (or otherwise) of selecting some to be killed in order to save a greater number of lives. She concludes that in certain circumstances, some such cases are indeed morally permissible. Furthermore, she argues, in some cases of collaboration, where the collaborator acts at the behest of an evildoer solely in order to achieve significant good, then moral responsibility for the harm done accrues to the evildoer alone.

Kamm's theoretical approach is relatively abstract and remote from the specificities of the situations she is considering. In strong contrast, Daniel Statman's paper on tragic decisions exemplifies the relevance of detailed empirical research to an adequate treatment of certain moral issues in this field. The question he is concerned with is whether, in the aftermath of the Holocaust, the removal of Jewish children who were looked after by Gentile protectors, in order to return the children to a Jewish context, can be justified. The standard objection to this is that the child's best interests are the only, or at least the paramount, moral consideration in these cases, and that it's not in the child's best interests to undergo (in these cases for a second time) the pain and possible psychological damage of separation from those who have nurtured them.

Statman, however, defends two claims: first that overall, such removal *was* in the children's best interests, or at least did them no harm; and second that the children are not the only ones whose interests matter here – the interests of relatives, the Gentile carers and the Jewish people must also be considered. Statman's defence of the first claim integrates the results of empirical investigation (mainly psychological) into the effects on children of separation from their parents, with philosophical discussion of the connection between personal identity, genetic origins and the psychological sources of a sense of identity. In pursuit of his second claim, he considers the relative weighting which should be given to the biological parents' wishes, which can plausibly be assumed to be in favour of returning the children to a Jewish context, and the interests of the Gentile carers, who had usually risked their own and their families' lives, far beyond the normal call of duty, to protect the Jewish children. Finally he explores the nature of collective rights to underpin the claim that the Jewish people have an interest in the removal of Jewish children from their Gentile carers, which should not be readily dismissed.

The remaining papers, those by Laurence Thomas, Eve Garrard, Oliver Leaman and Lawrence Blum, deal with various aspects of our response to the Holocaust. On any plausible account of it, its perpetrators bear the responsibility for the most appalling and nightmarish crimes. How should we now respond to this? Should we, for example, be prepared to consider forgiving the perpetrators, or are such agents beyond the scope of human forgiveness? Laurence Thomas, in 'Forgiving the Unforgivable?', focuses his discussion of forgiveness on the implications of profound repentance. He argues that we would have reason to forgive even a Nazi war criminal if he were to be sufficiently repentant and contrite over a sufficiently long period of time. He might, in such a case, be worthy of forgiveness; indeed, it might be the only morally decent response to what he now is. But it does not follow, Thomas argues, that the perpetrator would be *entitled* to forgiveness, or even that justice would require it. Thomas distinguishes between the demands of justice and those of righteousness, and suggests that the reasons for forgiveness, and its appropriateness, are visible from the standpoint of righteousness rather than that of justice. And righteousness, he further claims, is a higher ideal than justice.

However, Thomas acknowledges that no actual Nazi war criminal has met the criterion of profound and longstanding contrition that would warrant forgiveness. Hence his case for forgivability does not indicate that we have any reason to forgive actual Nazi war criminals. Eve Garrard, on the other hand, regards repentance as insufficient to provide a reason for forgiveness, given the horror of the perpetrators' actions. Hence, she argues in 'Forgiveness and the Holocaust', we must look elsewhere if we are to reject the quite persuasive view that the perpetrators are beyond forgiveness. Although the standard arguments against forgiveness are on examination not ultimately convincing, she claims, it is still hard to identify any positive reason we might have to forgive these terrible actions. Garrard argues that we cannot find a reason to forgive in Kantian thoughts about respect for moral agency, but that such a reason might emerge from the relationship in which we stand to all other human beings – that is, from ideas about human solidarity. Drawing on the phenomenon of vicarious shame, to be found even in the concentration camps themselves, Garrard suggests that human solidarity, based on our common human nature and predicament, is sufficiently rich to generate reasons for us to act (for example, to prosecute crimes against humanity). Hence on the same basis there may be reasons, weak but none the less genuine, to forgive even the most terrible of human evildoers.

In 'The Holocaust and the Possibility of Art', Oliver Leaman examines Adorno's famous stricture that 'to write a poem after Auschwitz is an act of barbarism'. Leaman is also concerned about the issue of uniqueness, and whether we can have reason to accept Adorno's prohibition even if we do not (as Leaman himself does not) wish to endorse the uniqueness claim. Having analysed a range of arguments which might be thought to support the Adorno view, Leaman concludes that we don't have sufficient reason to accept it as it stands. He suggests, however, that what Adorno is doing is drawing our attention to the real possibility that some disasters are beyond the scope of art: in the case of the Holocaust an aesthetic response to so all-encompassing an evil may simply be vacuous.

In the final paper in the book, Lawrence Blum explores some of the uses to which we put our remembrance of the Holocaust. He focuses on Peter Novick's widely read book *The Holocaust in American Life*, in which Novick criticizes the highly visible way in which the Holocaust currently figures in American culture. Blum is prepared to concur, at least to some extent, with Novick's claim that the salience of the Holocaust in American culture can divert attention from morally more pressing problems for America today. However, Blum is critical of one of Novick's central theses, namely that we cannot learn important moral lessons from the Holocaust. Blum argues that if the Holocaust is to teach us lessons which apply to other events, then we must be able to draw analogies between them. But this is something which we can indeed do. Blum distinguishes two different, though not incompatible, guidelines for analogizing the Holocaust to other events: the criterion of having a morally significant feature in common, and the criterion of being of sufficient moral gravity. Events which meet either of these two criteria are ones to which we may reasonably hope to apply lessons learned from the Holocaust, and Blum points out that Novick's rejection of this possibility is not consistent with his complaint that we have in fact failed to apply the lessons of the Holocaust to events in Bosnia and Rwanda.

The papers in this book range from those presenting the most abstractly theoretical treatments of their topic, to those which provide a rich integration of the empirical data with the philosophical questions which they generate. The contributors often disagree about the issues here examined. All of them, however, attempt to increase our understanding of the moral catastrophe which so tragically disfigured Europe in the middle of the twentieth century, and whose shadow is over us still.

Notes

1. Primo Levi, *If This Is A Man*, in *If This Is A Man* and *The Truce*, tr. Stuart Woolf, London: Abacus, 1987, p. 35.
2. Ibid., pp. 395–6.
3. Ibid., p. 395.
4. Ibid., p. 35.
5. Bruno Bettelheim, *The Informed Heart: Autonomy in a Mass Age*, New York: Free Press, 1960.

Chapter 1

Philosophy's Contribution to Holocaust Studies

Berel Lang

My title is intended as a provocation. Strictly speaking, it ought to be set off by a question mark – 'Philosophy's Contribution to Holocaust Studies?' For surely, to go by the record, I should be questioning, not asserting, the impact that philosophy has had on the study of the Holocaust. To be sure, a more practical question might focus on the *future* role or contribution of philosophy – but the innocence, even naïveté, of that enquiry as undertaken in isolation becomes only too clear in light of the marginal role philosophy has so far had (or sought) in Holocaust Studies.

That this past role *has* been marginal seems indisputable – not in the sense that philosophical issues have not been raised or discussed in Holocaust writings, but that when they have appeared, this has been mainly in the contexts of historical, literary, or theological analysis, and shaped by authors with commitments and methods based in those fields, not in philosophy. I do not mean to imply that such other perspectives cannot be philosophical: it is a long-standing question within philosophy, after all, whether philosophy has either a subject-matter or a method apart from those defined in other, deliberately more restricted disciplines. But it also seems clear that 'professional' philosophers – applying that term as we otherwise recognize 'professional' historians or literary scholars – have contributed relatively little, in quantity or significance, to Holocaust Studies in its now more than half-century history. I would, furthermore, add to this summary description an assessment: insofar as philosophical issues *have* been addressed and/or *might have been addressed* but were not, the treatment of those issues has suffered from the profession's absence.

I propose to say something more about these two assertions before suggesting an explanation for them and then, in conclusion, citing a number of potential, and needed, contributions that philosophy may yet make to the study of the Holocaust: that is, if it can bring itself and its practitioners to the point – and, of course, if what they bring is accepted.

First, then, on its heretofore marginal presence. If we are not to bog down in endless discussion of what counts or not as a philosophical account or contribution, the only practical criterion seems to me an ostensive definition; that is, a definition constituted by naming the philosophers or professors of philosophy (not quite the same, to be sure) with claims on the 'universe of discourse' of Holocaust Studies. Again, the conclusion here seems unmistakable: that given the scope and resources of Holocaust Studies as a field, a notably small part of it represents the work of philosophers. It is true that Karl Jaspers published a brief book titled *The Question of German Guilt* in the early postwar years (1946),[1] and that Jean-Paul Sartre published his also brief *Anti-Semite and Jew* at about the same time.[2] But the former was a summary account of issues that would resonate without much further word from Jaspers himself, and Sartre's essay was extrapolated from his earlier *Being and Nothingness* with – by his own admission – only slight attention to the substantive factors affecting the history of anti-Semitism or the 'Jewish Question.' In the later 'post-Holocaust' period, philosophers who are cited, or better, *re*-cited in the literature of Holocaust Studies, remain scarce; that a list of them can be ventured at all (as I propose to) is itself indicative of this. So, for a first pass, in alphabetical order, and so mingling ideologies and nationalities: Theodor Adorno, Giorgio Agamben, Zvi Baron, Emil Fackenheim, Jürgen Habermas, Philip Hallie, Hans Jonas, Steven Katz, Sarah Kofman, Emanuel Levinas, Alan Milchman and Joan Ringelheim, Alan Rosenberg, Gillian Rose, Nathan Rotenstreich, John Roth, Leo Strauss, Laurence Thomas, Elisabeth Young-Bruehl, Michael Zimmerman (and analphabetically I should, I suppose, add my own name, as well as contributors to the present volume not otherwise cited).

Obviously, other figures appear on the periphery of this circle, some of them large indeed: Hannah Arendt, for example, whose own rejection of the title 'philosopher' would itself justify her inclusion even if there were no other, more substantial reasons for doing so. Jacques Derrida has circled the edges of the Holocaust from a number of directions. A small 'Society for the Study of Holocaust and Genocide,' founded by Alan Rosenberg, convenes regularly at the several annual divisional conferences of the American Philosophical Association – and a diverse group of mainly French and American philosophers who had not otherwise addressed issues bearing on the Holocaust have found in the Nazi history of Martin Heidegger an occasion for considering National Socialism more generally as they assert or deny the relation between Heidegger's biography and his theoretical work. These include, in the USA, Richard Rorty, Tom Rockmore, and Hans Sluga; and in France, Victor Farias, Jean-François Lyotard, and Philippe Lacoue-Labarthe.

These may seem a not insignificant number, and they include some prominent names. But it also needs to be said that the Holocaust has been a minor theme for many even of these figures. One consequence of this is that few of them or of the positions associated with them have made their way into the canon of Holocaust Studies in its still provisional but nonetheless recognizable form. (Such a 'short list' seems to me reducible to Adorno, Arendt, Fackenheim, and Habermas.) I realize that additional or alternative candidates for these lists are likely to occur to many readers. But even if the compilations offered are at best approximate, their limited extent supports the representation of philosophy as marginal to the general field of Holocaust Studies, certainly off-center – as much off-center, at any rate, as the Holocaust has been to philosophy itself.

The question then remains 'Why? How is this mutual exclusion to be understood, and what does it promise for the future?' Obviously, if the marginality (or indifference or professional dissonance) should be endemic, marking the limits of any possible connection between philosophy and the Holocaust, the future will be much like the past, with the philosophical analysis or narrative of the Holocaust then permanently brief. I do not believe, however, that this need or should be the case, for the following reasons.

Even in its own short history, the field that has come to be known as Holocaust Studies followed an evolutionary pattern that has almost certainly not yet ended. Raul Hilberg's *The Destruction of the European Jews* was published in 1961; although certain scholarly works concerning the Holocaust had appeared previously (for example Leon Poliakov's *Brevaire de la haine: le IIIe Reich et les Juifs* (Paris, 1951) and Gerald Reitlinger's *The Final Solution: The Attempt to Exterminate the Jews of Europe* (London, 1953)), Hilberg's book proved foundational in the construction of the field of Holocaust Studies. It was no accident that this initiating moment should be a work in history (and historiography). In scholarly terms – in moral terms as well – the very first question impelled by the enormity of the Holocaust would, *of course*, be historical; that is, the question of what happened – then extending laterally to how, and finally venturing vertically to the more speculative 'why.' Thus began a dominant historical discourse, with history as a discipline continuing to hold center stage even in the constantly expanding circumference of Holocaust Studies – with little dissent from other disciplinary perspectives about either the persistence or the warrant of that centrality. If ever it was necessary to have the facts of the matter fully and accurately gathered, surely it would be for this event; even its moral weight clearly depended first on questions in the elementary form of who did what to whom – when, where, and how.

On the other hand and in sharp contrast: when Hegel wrote that 'The owl of Minerva begins to fly only with the falling of the dusk' (Preface to *The Philosophy of Right*), he evidently intended his use of a gentle metaphor to assert, not so gently, that in *its* relation to the ongoing rush of history, philosophy would always and only appear late in the day. And this, not as a matter of choice or style, but by necessity: the need of reflection or reason to have something present before it to reflect or to reason *about*. If this lag was for Hegel an intrinsic feature of philosophy in its 'take' on everyday circumstance, furthermore, it would be all the more emphatic for complex and extraordinary events, of which the Holocaust is obviously one. Undoubtedly, other modes of analysis or reflection are also characteristically deferred from the flow of immediate experience; historical writing itself is subject to this, as events require the passage of time before resolving themselves into even provisional historical entities. But even allowing for a common lag of this sort between act and word, it seems still undeniable that the primary figure or trope of the first period of Holocaust Studies has indeed been historical – a priority likely to continue not only in contrast to philosophy but also in relation to psychology or sociology, to literary criticism, even to the ever-increasing and popular expressions of the arts – all of these nonetheless dependent on the grist ground in history's mill and the facts of the Holocaust that are still, constantly, virtually every day, coming to light. (Consider how recently valuable information has surfaced about such rudimentary matters as the role of the Wehrmacht in the 'Final Solution' or the implication in the Nazi war effort of the 'neutral' nations.)

To grant all this, however, is not to preclude shifts of direction and nuance in or around the center of historical reference; and there, it seems to me, a basis appears for suggesting what philosophy might have contributed before this but did not, or – more to the point now – for outlining those aspects of the Holocaust that philosophy might yet address and which, left untouched, would indicate probable lacunae or weaknesses in the accounts given. Admittedly, certain institutional factors that have so far obstructed this prospect – from the sides of both philosophy and history – are unlikely simply to disappear. For its part, contemporary philosophy, especially Anglo-American philosophy, has been notably a- or even anti-historical, even in respect of its own history, let alone in addressing 'external' historical events. Admittedly, there has been some movement recently to counteract this tendency – directly, in addressing the figures and concepts of philosophy's past in relation to their historical contexts and not only as 'contemporaries;' indirectly, through efforts in 'applied philosophy' as in bioethics and the philosophy of law which have drawn philosophers (now sometimes appointed to medical or law faculties) into contemporary history in ways that would have seemed improbable a few decades ago. Even here, however, I suggest that there is danger, both from the outside and internally, of the mistaken attribution to philosophers, because they speak *about* ethical principles and values, of special expertise in practical moral judgment; that is, in assessing or themselves making ethical decisions. In any event, even taking account of these potentially fruitful connections between philosophy and the *alltäglich* world, the general claim seems to remain largely unshaken: that contemporary philosophy has yet to overcome its estrangement from history.

From the other side, the writing of history has not been notably receptive to philosophy, even when it could have benefitted from connections between the two. This wariness no doubt reflects to some extent a sense of territoriality: history as the primary mode of discourse in Holocaust Studies might feel entitled to address relevant conceptual questions also when those extend beyond its own 'normal' limits. The *philosophy* of history, after all – reflection on the conditions of historical explanation, the nature of the relationship between description and interpretation and then between them and evaluation – indeed comes close to the center of writing history, including of course the history of the Holocaust. And so historians have indeed presumed on these issues, understandably pleading the urgency of getting on with the task of unearthing and assembling data, but in any event resistant to what philosophers might have had to say about their theoretical frameworks. Even in the recognizably boundary issues of moral judgment, historians – no doubt because the moral questions posed by the Holocaust are so deeply embedded in its history – have at times simply assumed moral authority: an analogue in my view to the assumption of such authority by professional 'ethicists' among philosophers. The marginality of philosophy in Holocaust Studies has thus reflected an alliance of complementary imbalances: a too narrow or purist view of itself by philosophy acting in concert with a too generous or ambitious view of itself by history.

It may be objected that this account is a historical hypothesis in its own right (or wrong); in any event that even so far as it might be accepted for the sake of argument, it says little about what philosophy can in fact contribute to Holocaust Studies even in general terms, let alone by illuminating specific angles of vision. Here, let me for the moment conflate what philosophy might have contributed in the past but did not with the prospect of its future; thus, I outline a number of issues central to Holocaust Studies that also involve substantive considerations of continuing importance to philosophers. Again, I do not mean to claim that philosophy has special authority, let alone a monopoly, in the discussion of such issues – only that by joining its efforts to other modes of discourse, philosophy can add substantially to understanding them. I mention four such topics out of a larger number of possibilities – all four no doubt familiar but also, still, perplexing and unresolved in the context of Holocaust Studies.

1. The Concept of Genocide

When Churchill, in a speech about the unfolding Holocaust (late in 1942), dramatically asserted that 'We are in the presence of a crime that has no name,' he heralded an issue that continues to this day, one which the coining of the term 'genocide' two years after Churchill's speech, by Rafael Lemkin, did something but not enough to resolve. The 1948 UN Convention on Genocide, however important symbolically, left virtually all the basic questions about the structural and moral character of genocide unsettled: the definition of the groups and types of action to which the term 'genocide' is applicable; the role of intention in those actions; the place of genocide in moral history. That 'genocide' as a term has since its first appearance become an all-purpose epithet, in common usage designating the most heinous crime to which a name has been given, only reinforces the need for elaborating its analysis – as the term and concept no doubt apply paradigmatically to the Holocaust but in their occurrences elsewhere as well. Both for this analysis and for its obverse side – that is, the implied assertion of group *rights* as violated by genocide (rights analogous to and yet arguably distinct from individual rights) – moral and legal philosophers have increasingly focused attention on the concepts and practices involved. And if their work on these issues is still exploratory, anyone familiar with that work will, I believe, recognize its usefulness for understanding the concept of genocide in principle as well as in its specific bearing on the Holocaust (for one small but contentious matter, on the 'Uniqueness Question,' concerned with the claim of uniqueness ascribed to the Holocaust).

2. Corporate and Individual Intentions

Although the heat of conflict surrounding the intentionalist and functionalist interpretations of the 'Final Solution' and the related *Historikerstreit* has diminished, the conceptual issues in those disagreements have arguably remained unsettled. What emerged from those discussions is a large middle ground occupied jointly by what might be called 'intentional functionalists' and 'functional intentionalists,' with other smaller groups still remaining at the far ends of the spectrum – an outcome which, however, seems to me the result of practical compromise rather than conceptual clarification. It is, I believe, a matter of record that a common assumption by all parties to this dispute supposed that what intentions *are* – whether for individuals or corporately; that is, for groups – is self-evident, requiring little or no systematic analysis. That a great deal of attention had been paid specifically to the concept of intention and its complexities in twentieth-century philosophy (both in phenomenology and in linguistic philosophy) never, so far as I am aware, entered the discussion. Would such reference have made a difference to analyses which simply assumed that they involved questions of fact, not theory? Perhaps; perhaps not; it may be too late now to determine this. What we do know is that the issue of how to ascribe responsibility within the bounds of the Holocaust – the extent and nature of responsibility on the parts of individuals and groups, and the differentiated relation of such responsibility to intentional or non-intentional acts – is very much alive in the retrospective assessment of the events constituting the Holocaust. Few commentators, whether philosophers *or* historians, would defend the claim that where there is no intention, there is no responsibility. But this makes it all the more important to consider how and to what extent intentions are legitimately found or ascribed to individuals or to groups, and then, too, of what the moral varieties are of non- or extra-intentional acts.

3. Classical Ethics

Whether an event with the dimensions of the Holocaust entails revision in considering the nature of ethical values or questions as such is itself a pertinent question. Even if that possibility is rejected, furthermore, the status of the classical – standard – ethical questions as they bear on the Holocaust will still be informative, perhaps also innovative, in respect both of those standard questions and of the Holocaust itself. Beginning with such concrete and immediate issues of judgment as the status of punishment and reparation, revenge and forgiveness, the relation between causes and moral reasons, such analysis eventually makes its way to the 'Question of Evil' that has long bedevilled the Western religious and rationalist tradition – how evil can subsist in a just or divinely ordered world. A specific and more concrete variant of the latter arises in respect of the Holocaust perpetrators in the question of whether evil or wrongdoing can be knowingly willed or chosen. For even the undoubted role of bureaucratic processes in the Holocaust does not preclude a role for consciousness or decision-making, and the specific question cannot be avoided, then, of whether Nazi actions were undertaken in the belief of a good to be realized – or with the agents' own consciousness of wrongdoing. The historical issues here are inextricable from the philosophical one of whether the latter framework is indeed an option – an ostensibly empirical question which has too rarely in the history of philosophy been addressed empirically. And then, too, the Holocaust by its extremity suggests a parallel to 'stress tests' in engineering or medicine: whatever warrant may be found for practice or theory in the context of such an event would, everything else being equal, apply a fortiori in less extreme conditions. Or *would* they? The question arises in response, asking then more generally what relevance extreme situations ever have for ethical enquiry into everyday practice and decision.

4. Holocaust-representation

I use this phrase as a catchall for designating a variety of forms of expression related to the Holocaust and the proportionately large number of issues they engender: from the function – or desirability – of Holocaust memorials and museums, to disputes over artistic depictions of events or figures from the Holocaust (the issue of the relation between form and content in fiction, poetry, and films of the Holocaust); to the more general problem of the connection (or as it may be, disjunction) between historical and (so-called) imaginative representations of the Holocaust. And once again: problems like the relation of fictionality to truth, the comparison (or connection) between art and aesthetic values, on the one hand, and ethical values, on the other – not only what can but what *ought* to be represented; the social or political function of art more generally – all these have long and continuing philosophical genealogies. To be sure, those philosophical accounts have often left the issues they address unresolved. Even at their slightest, however, they have clarified the issues to the extent of defining alternative lines of argument; that progress, too, may be usefully directed to the unusual problem of Holocaust representations, especially to the overriding question of what the *limits* to such representation are.

Again, I claim no special privilege for philosophy in considering the issues assembled under these four rubrics; I noted earlier the consensus that philosophy remains always dependent, if to a greater or lesser extent, on provisions supplied by other of the 'humane' and natural sciences. But the converse relation also holds, in the need of practice for theoretical and conceptual frameworks – frameworks which, as the history of ideas has demonstrated, are never immaculately conceived and thus require constant monitoring, whether as invoked by philosophers or anyone else. We do well here, it seems to me, to recall Kant's severe warning about the interdependence of the empirical and the theoretical: 'Concepts without percepts are empty; percepts without concepts are blind.' And if philosophy, past and present, has often seemed more repetitive than progressive, at times following (or leading) the questions it considers into blind alleys, it has also advanced on them in the broad context – by its very formulation, a distinctive contribution – of a general understanding of reality and of human nature within it. None of this gives philosophers privileged access to the topics mentioned; but it brings them at least even with other investigators who, too often, deploy such general frameworks without even recognizing their archaeology – the layers of meaning and contestation from which they come.

Admittedly, at least one serious, probably intrinsic danger threatens this prospect – the defect of its quality. This is the risk that the abstractive impulse of philosophy will express itself at the price of obscuring historical particularity; specifically, that it may come to present the Holocaust as no more than one of a large number of historical events, all of them subsumable under common and so indistinct denominators. The threat of such flights to the abstract is constant for philosophical reflection, and the central figures in philosophy's history, from Plato to Spinoza to Kant and Hegel, have been notable in good measure just *because* they have not fallen victim to it; any objections to which their *conceptions* of history are open stand quite apart from the intense refraction of historical and concrete experience in their thinking. At any rate, philosophy is certainly not alone in facing such characteristic pitfalls, the danger of what Hannah Arendt in a different context called 'professional deformations.' Whatever this threat amounts to, furthermore, seems to me outweighed by the gaps that would be – I have suggested, have been – left by the absence of philosophy, whether effected by its own hand or that of others.

I mean thus to propose that philosophy, by addressing the Holocaust on its own philosophical grounds, may contribute innovative understanding – innovative even in respect of apparently straightforward historical questions and still more certainly for comprehending historical understanding as such – at the same time that its focus on that complex and only too concrete event may enable philosophy to see more deeply into itself. Hegel, in a letter of 1805, wrote (to his correspondent, Johann Heinrich Voss) that 'I should like to say of my aspirations that I shall try to teach philosophy to speak German.' However we judge this aspiration of Hegel's (or his success in realizing it), there could be little disagreement about the value for both philosophy and history if the Holocaust should teach philosophy to 'speak history.' And of course, if the historians would then listen.

Notes

1. *Die Schuldfrage* (Zurich: Artemis Verlag, 1946, trans. E.B. Ashton, New York: Dial Press, 1948).
2. *Reflexions sur la question juive* (Paris: P. Morihan, 1946, trans. New York: Schocken, 1948).

Chapter 2

Ideology, Moral Complicity and the Holocaust

David E. Cooper

Aetiology and Complicity

Most general books on the Third Reich have a section on the 'intellectual roots' or 'ideological foundations' of National Socialism and its 'annihilatory Judeophobia',[1] while many further books are specifically devoted to exposing these 'roots' or 'foundations'. The present chapter is sufficiently adjacent to such writings for it to be a critique of a popular view expressed in many of them. My concern, nevertheless, is different from theirs – a concern with something for which 'roots' and 'foundations' are infelicitous terms. It is a concern, as I shall put it, with the moral complicity of ideological tendencies in National Socialism and the Holocaust.

The expression 'ideological tendency' is to be read blandly. I do not invest 'ideology' with, for example, the sense given it by Marxists. It is intended to suggest little more than views that are at once relatively 'theoretical' and 'action guiding'. National Socialism exploited hatred of Jews, but that phobia, though it may have fed into and been reinforced by theories, was not *per se* an ideology. Again, perpetrators of the Holocaust appealed to hypotheses in biological science; but only when these were woven into a wider, action-guiding view, deemed to warrant mass-murder, did they belong to an ideology. 'Tendency' is a bland term intended to cover particular doctrines, whole intellectual traditions, and loosely knit 'movements' of thought. Nietzsche's doctrine of 'will to power', German Romanticism, and Social Darwinist thought are all, in this sense, tendencies.

The expression 'complicity' requires rather more attention. The terminology of 'roots', 'origins' and 'foundations' used by many authors indicates their primary concern with aetiology. They are attempting to expose the ideological tendencies that 'led to' and actually inspired the Nazi programme. For a number of reasons, that is not my concern. I lack the historical scholarship to make informed judgements about the actual influence of, say, Gobineau's and Chamberlain's works on race. Even if I possessed that scholarship, however, I am unclear how one assesses such counterfactual claims as 'There would never have been National Socialism without Wagner (or Nietzsche, or Lagarde, or …)' – claims that would have to be true if the writings of these men 'led to' that movement. Nor do I want to become embroiled in 'meta-historical' issues about 'the role of ideas': in, for example, the familiar dispute as to whether Nazi policies followed a clear ideological blueprint or, instead, were pragmatic responses to 'events'. (For the record, sweeping rejections of 'the role of ideas' in the Third Reich strike me as singularly implausible, as directed at 'straw-man' versions of 'intentionalist' or 'ideational' explanations.[2] There is surely a truth in the aphorism 'No Hitler, no Holocaust',[3] and it would be odd to ignore the ideological tendencies palpably attested in Hitler's writings and conversations. Is it seriously to be supposed that they were without any actual impact on subsequent events?)

My concern is with the moral complicity of an ideological tendency, not with its aetiological role. The claim that Nietzsche, say, 'bears responsibility' for Nazism or some of its policies is ambiguous. This is clear from the different ways that such claims get defended or attacked. One author will draw attention to the Nazis' enthusiasm for Nietzsche, while another will stress that Nietzsche's 'will to power' was quite different from what the Nazis had in mind. Clearly, there is shadow boxing here. While one author is concerned with aetiology (the actual impact of Nietzsche's writings), the other is concerned with an ideological affinity to National Socialist thought.

Moral complicity in a programme such as the Holocaust comes in degrees, just as complicity of other kinds typically does. A distinction may be drawn between 'strong' and 'weak' complicity. Roughly, an ideological tendency is strongly complicit in a programme when it endorses or justifies it. It is weakly complicit when, though not endorsing the programme, it is without the resources morally to condemn it. My enquiry is into both strong and weak complicity in the Holocaust of ideological tendencies located in the wide orbit of National Socialist thinking.

Four preparatory remarks about complicity will be helpful for what follows. First, the distinction between endorsement and non-condemnation is fuzzy, and so therefore is the distinction between strong and weak complicity. There can be plenty of 'in-between' cases. Second, my characterization of weak complicity assumes that a programme which an ideological tendency is without the resources to condemn belongs, nevertheless, within the scope of the tendency's concerns. There would be no complicity if, so to speak, the programme belonged entirely outside the terms of reference of the ideology.

Third, the issue of a tendency's moral complicity in a programme is logically independent from that of its aetiological role. It is possible for an ideological tendency to be complicit in a policy but to have played no role in 'leading to' it. The eccentric belief that Hitler was Christ come again, in order to avenge his crucifixion, was complicit in the Holocaust, but played no part in 'leading to' it. Conversely, a doctrine may actually have shaped a policy even though, when properly understood, it entails condemnation of it. A putative example is the critical views of Nietzsche on German nationalism and anti-Semitism that, according to most recent commentators, were twisted into their very opposite by Nazi ideologues.

Fourth, the complicity of an idea in the Holocaust is also independent of some, at least, of the intentions of those who champion that idea. It may well be, for example, that some proponents of Social Darwinism or moral relativism had no intention to endorse the murders, indeed would sincerely have been appalled by them. If, nevertheless, those tendencies do endorse the murders, or are without the resources to condemn them, they are complicit in my sense. (Usually when one speaks of complicity, one has in mind the complicity of people; but it is a legitimate and, for my purposes, convenient extension of our usual talk to speak of ideas, theories and so on as complicit.)

If, to return to the third remark, complicity and aetiology are independent, why focus on the former? Does one not thereby ignore the question that 'really matters', that of the intellectual 'causes' of annihilatory Judeophobia? I make two replies. First, the almost 'received' view I shall be criticizing, while expressed in the aetiological terminology of 'roots' and 'origins', turns out, in the hands of many writers, to be one, rather, about complicity. These writers, at any rate, typically offer no more evidence for the causal impact of tendencies than their complicity in the Nazi programme. When, for example, Wagner is charged with responsibility for later events, this is rarely on the basis of the composer's demonstrated influence, but only on that of his ferocious anti-Semitism. So, in treating the received view as one about complicity, I may ignore its aetiological letter, but not its spirit.

Second, lots of questions 'really matter', not just historical ones. One which does – so we are continually reminded – concerns the 'lessons to be learned' from the Holocaust. If I am right, there were ideological tendencies complicit in the Nazi programme that, in similar forms, remain with us today. It is a lesson that 'matters' to learn that various contemporary, indeed fashionable, '-isms' are as lacking in the moral resources for condemning the Holocaust as were some close ancestors in the years before and during that event.

A Received Image and its Critics

In referring to a received view, I do not imply that there are no dissenting voices. Indeed, some of these will be heard shortly. Nor is it a view that, as I describe it, comes unqualified by those who propose it. Indeed, a peculiarity of some of the works I cite is that, in their detail, they are barely consistent with the received view that they proclaim. One might do better to speak of a received rhetoric or image, one often belied by the texts in which it is prominent.

The *locus classicus* of the received image is George L. Mosse's *The Crisis of German Ideology*, whose subtitle, *Intellectual Origins of the Third Reich*, indicates its aetiological ambition. 'Origin' in the singular might have been more suitable, for Mosse's focus is circumscribed. His book 'analyze[s] the history of Volkish thought', in terms of which, he holds, one may 'define Adolf Hitler's German revolution'. While other elements contributing to that 'revolution' are discussed, the book registers the conviction that it is Volkish thought of the kind explored that was the primary inspiration for the Nazi programme. 'National Socialism,' in short, 'was a Volkish movement.'[4] Long sections are accordingly devoted to the champions of this Volkish romanticism – Lagarde, Langbehn, von List, Treitschke, and a host of lesser figures of the nineteenth and early twentieth centuries.

Four aspects of Volkish thought – two 'negative' and two 'positive' – stand out in Mosse's account. First, its 'repudiation' of 'a European heritage … still alive elsewhere: that of the rationalism of the Enlightenment'. Volkish thought opposed the exaggeration and celebration of human beings' powers of reason, including their capacity rationally to determine universal moral principles. National Socialist thinkers, though they 'pretended to be scientific' and assumed the 'trappings of objectivity', merely continued this repudiation.[5] Second, Volkish thought represented 'the rejection of modernity': a 'flight' not only from modern movements of thought, such as 'social radicalism', but from modern trends in art and, indeed, from 'present reality' itself. Profoundly conservative or reactionary, Volkish thinkers and their Nazi offspring condemned, in their 'fear of the machine', the 'glorification of technology'.[6] More generally, they detested everything with which the term '*Zivilization*', in contrast to '*Kultur*', was invested by Oswald Spengler and other cultural diagnosticians.

By way of a 'positive' replacement for the repudiated Enlightenment traditions and trends of modernity, Volkish and fascist thinkers embraced, first of all, an 'emotional and mystical ideology'. For these 'new Romantics', 'mystical', 'spiritual' or 'intuitive' insight – not objective scientific or philosophical enquiry – provided access to truth. Their ideas on race, for example, 'embraced all those features which had emerged from the romantic preoccupation with the German soul'.[7] And it was, of course, precisely ideas of race and Volk that, within a wider turn towards the 'emotional and mystical', gave Volkish thought its second 'positive' aspect and provided a haven for the 'flight from present reality'. 'Grounded in the mysteries of race, nature, and cultural identity', the perception of the German nation as the continuation of an ancient, but now threatened, Teutonic Volk offered an antidote to the prime carriers of that threat – capitalism, Marxism, and their Jewish agents. It was this perception that enabled Hitler to 'transform' the German revolution into 'an anti-Jewish revolution'; but in so doing, he was only 'fulfill[ing] a concept of life which had permeated much of the nation before he ever entered the scene'.[8]

The image painted by Mosse of Nazi ideology is that, in essence, of an heir to irrationalist, anti-science, anti-Enlightenment, anti-modern tendencies, one that replaced what it repudiated by a 'mystical' romanticism centring on the soteriological conception of a slumbering *Volksgeist* which the German people must arouse. It is an image that figures in many writings. Nazism and the genocide represented 'the greatest defection from reason the West has known in recent centuries' and marked the 'failure of the Enlightenment'. They were made possible because 'the roots of Enlightenment were not strong or deep enough to withstand the onslaught of irrationality', and 'because the Germans had lost belief in the universal human value ... of reason'.[9] That 'hunger for wholeness' to which critics of the Weimar Republic gave voice, and which Hitler succeeded in assuaging, was a 'great regression born from a great fear: the fear of modernity'.[10] The tendencies apparent in Nazism reflected 'the peculiarly German inclination to a "mixture of mysticism and brutality"', incorporating, for example, 'the Romantic idolatry of Nature'.[11]

This received image has certainly been challenged. Of several dissenting voices, I mention two with a greater affinity than most to the argument I shall present. Each of them in effect argues that the ideological tendencies central to the Nazi programme belong to different philosophical or metaphysical constellations from that described by Mosse and his followers.

Ernst Nolte famously characterized National Socialism as 'practical and violent resistance to transcendence'.[12] This is resistance, crudely, to what is seen as 'anti-nature', as an attack on the 'familiar' and 'finite' in the name of 'infinite' aspirations. More fully, it is resistance, first, to a 'practical transcendence' that, inspired by 'abstract' ideals, aims to 'disengage' people from 'traditional ties' and to 'assail' previously unmolested processes of 'nature and history'. It is resistance, second, to a 'theoretical transcendence' that aspires to release people from 'the confines of the everyday world' so as to experience, and aspire towards, an 'absolute whole'.[13] In Nolte's view, Marxism – with its ideal of a stateless, propertyless world of complete freedom and equality – was, for the Nazis, the paradigmatic 'transcendental' endeavour.

Quite what Nolte means by 'resistance to transcendence' need not detain us, for this is sufficiently clear to indicate that he is placing the central ideological tendency of Nazism in a different philosophical constellation from Mosse's Volkish thought. While certain ingredients in Enlightenment thought, such as an 'abstract' ideal of universal rights, are jettisoned, there is no obvious reason why resistance to transcendence should require rejection of scientific enquiry and an empirical, objective approach to morality in favour of appeals to 'myth' and 'mystical' insight. (Nolte mentions Hitler's annoyance at the title of Alfred Rosenberg's Nazi tome, *The Myth of the Twentieth Century*: National Socialism, he insisted, was 'the *scientific* truth of the twentieth century'.)[14] Again, one would not expect resistance to transcendence to manifest a wholesale 'fear of modernity', only a rejection of those modern currents – internationalism, say – that threatened a perceived 'natural', 'familiar' order. The idea of Nature indeed plays a central role in the attack on the 'anti-natural' doctrines of 'theoretical transcendence'; but this is no longer the Nature of the romantic adepts of Volkish thought – 'Spirit spatialized', an 'organic spiritual whole' – but the thoroughly unromantic theatre of struggle among species. As for the Volk itself, that becomes, for the resisters of transcendence, one of the species engaged in that unromantic struggle. If, for Germans, the Volk enjoys some distinction beyond, simply, its being *their* 'species', this is for reasons, ultimately, of biology, not because it is the vehicle of some ancient, ineffable *Volksgeist*.

Nolte, in effect, shifts the central Nazi ideological tendencies away from a romantic constellation of thought towards a naturalistic one. Philippe Lacoue-Labarthe, in *La Fiction du Politique* (strangely retitled *Heidegger, Art and Politics* for the English translation), shifts them in a different direction. When he writes that 'the extermination of the Jews ... follow[ed] *essentially* no logic (political, economic, social, military etc.) other than a spiritual one',[15] he sounds to be endorsing the received image. But this 'spiritual logic' turns out not to be anything peculiar to romantic, Volkish thought; rather it is the spirit of 'the West, in its essence' that 'revealed itself' at Auschwitz. More precisely, the 'treatment' of 'the Jewish question' was 'on the basis of ... the Western ideological project (techno-science) ... The "science" from which National Socialism claimed inspiration ... directly led to Auschwitz.'[16] To the spirit of this 'ideological project' of 'techno-science', Lacoue-Labarthe provocatively gives the name 'humanism'. This term is to be understood roughly as it was by Heidegger, as naming a conception of human beings – one that has become increasingly entrenched in modernity – as 'self-determining', 'self-creating' subjects. For the 'humanist', we are creatures with both the 'theoretical' capacity to determine what is valuable and true, and the 'practical' one, through 'techno-science', to determine the shape of the world and its future. 'Nazism is a humanism in so far as it rests on a determination of *humanitas* which is, in its view, more ... effective ... than any other.'[17]

On Lacoue-Labarthe's account, Nazi ideology, far from being a blanket repudiation of Enlightenment and modernity, incorporated their most 'essential' traits. What distinguished and 'degraded' this ideology was not, primarily, the intrusion of 'mysticism' and 'mythology', but the particular ways in which modern, Enlightenment aspirations were 'concretized'. The 'science' that 'inspired' the Nazi programme may have been perverse, but it was nevertheless in the name of science that some Nazis, at least, sincerely justified the Holocaust. Again, the 'self-determining subject' may have been identified by the Nazis, not with the individual or humanity at large, but with the Volk. Still, it remains that the Volk is conceived, not in pre-modern, anti-humanist terms, but through the 'essential' categories of modern Western 'spiritual logic'.

Both Nolte and Lacoue-Labarthe write at too 'metaphysical' a level for easy assessment of their remarks. But their proposals – to relocate Nazi ideology away from the constellation of romantic, Volkish thought to those of 'naturalism' and 'humanism' – are at least suggestive. In what follows, and at a more 'concrete' level, I shall draw on those proposals. Someone may reasonably wonder if it is possible to exploit them simultaneously, for are 'naturalistic' and 'humanist' tendencies not at odds? I shall suggest, however, that there is room for compromise between the naturalist's 'resistance to transcendence' and the humanist's Promethean emphasis on self-determination. Indeed, they form an unholy alliance.

The Complicity of Volkish Thought?

To reject the received image is not to deny that elements of Volkish thought, on Mosse's characterization, found their way into the Nazis' worldview. During its early years especially, the NSDAP platform reflected a rainbow of tendencies, from bucolic traditionalism to 'National Bolshevism', from cultural conservatism to a technophile militarism inspired by writers like Ernst Jünger. Criticisms of the kind anticipated in the previous section, however, suggest that it is at least one-sided to portray Nazi ideology as a 'repudiation' of the rationalism 'celebrated in the Enlightenment, humanist, and positivist tradition', in favour of 'the power of belief, myth, symbols, and *idées-forces* such as the nation'.[18] Indeed, the criticisms suggest this portrayal is doubly one-sided, in its account both of Nazi ideology and of the traditions allegedly 'repudiated' in that ideology. If National Socialism was a rainbow, the diverse phenomenon known as Enlightenment was still more so. But the criticisms also indicate, more strongly, that the received image obscures the tendencies in Nazi ideology most complicit in genocide and the euthanasia programme.

For an ideological tendency in Nazi thought to be judged complicit, it needs to be established, of course, that it *was* a significant tendency in that constellation of ideas. But before asking if this was, in fact, the case with Volkish thought, I raise the question of its moral complicity. Whether or not Volkish thought *was* a significant tendency in Nazi ideology, could it legitimately be invoked in support or exoneration of the extermination of Jews?

The acknowledged 'father' of Volkish thought, coiner of the notion of a *Volksgeist*, was J.G. Herder at the end of the eighteenth century. Here, certainly, was a robust critic of Enlightenment elevation of reason over 'heart, warmth, blood, humanity, life'. The very idea of an anonymous 'human reason' ignores what is 'individual and unique' – the identity of each people's cultural tradition, whose ineffable 'essence' is 'the perpetuation of thoughts and feelings' through a 'mother tongue' that 'embodies' a distinctive experience of the universe.[19] But if Herder was the father of romantic German nationalism, he was also the inspiration, to speak anachronistically, of anti-colonialism and multiculturalism. A 'primitive' culture, like any other, 'bears in itself the standard of its perfection', and it is criminal, in the name either of supposedly universal ideals or of the norms of one's own culture, to 'subjugate … and plunder' other peoples', each the embodiment of its own *Volksgeist*.[20]

During the nineteenth century, to be sure, Volkish thought was largely divested of Herder's generosity towards 'other cultures'. For one thing, the German *Volksgeist* became portrayed, not simply as 'individual and unique', but as positively superior to that of other peoples. Nurtured in a climate and landscape peculiarly congenial to spiritual depth, German culture – even its language – could claim a precedence that would warrant aggressive dominion over other nations. 'Aristocracy of the spirit' and 'Germanness', wrote Julius Langbehn in his best-selling nationalist tract of 1890, *Rembrandt as Educator*, are 'overlapping terms', and in the name of 'German spiritual life', the 'battle-cry' must be 'Swords to the ready!'[21]

Second, Herder's generosity was to become emphatically witheld from the Jews. Indeed, the peculiar twist given by the *Volksgeist* doctrine to a long tradition of anti-Semitism was that, since the Jews were not a genuine Volk, they could be denied whatever respect was owed even to less 'aristocratic' peoples. The Jews, in Treitschke's famous phrase, were 'our misfortune' in a way that other peoples living within the German empire were not. Without a homeland or living language of his own for two millennia, 'the wandering Jew' was a perpetual alien. 'He always speaks as a foreigner', as Wagner put it in *Jewishness in Music*.[22]

Few Volkish writers before the closing decades of the century, however, inferred from the 'aristocracy' of the German *Geist* and the *Geist*-lessness of the Jews that the latter should be exiled, let alone exterminated. More typical was Treitschke's view, shared by many German Jews, that vigorous steps must be taken to assimilate and 'Germanize' the Jewish population. After the economic collapse of 1873, blamed on Jewish financiers, a more virulent anti-Semitism indeed prospered, and barely disguised calls for expulsion or even extermination were heard. However, in so far as those calls issued from an ideological tendency – and not simply from gut hatred and blind economic desperation – their inspiration was a style of racial thinking already at a considerable remove from the romantic *Volksgeist* tradition. In the years immediately before the Nazi revolution, the continuers of *that* tradition – men like the poet Stefan George and the historian Moeller Van Den Bruck – remained aloof from the movement whose triumph began in 1933.

Nor was this aloofness simply a matter of 'taste'. For it is surely difficult to see how the premises of a special 'aristocratic' German *Geist* and the absence of an authentic Jewish one – even when supplemented by beliefs about the machinations of Jewish financiers and the like – could serve to condone the mass exportation or murder of Jews. To serve that purpose, the premises would have to be yoked to certain views about morality that were never, in my judgement, integral to romantic Volkish thought – not in the way they were to the ideological tendencies I now turn to.

Hitler's Anthropology

The obvious place to locate these tendencies is in the writings of Adolf Hitler. Whether or not one subscribes to 'No Hitler, no Holocaust!', the logic and rhetoric of annihilation are plainly visible in those writings. Readers of *Mein Kampf* with expectations shaped by the received image must be surprised by Hitler's animosity towards those 'running around today under the blanket term "folkish"', one almost as 'vague' and 'useless' as 'religious'.[23] Worse than their vagueness, however, was the older Volkish thinkers' conception of a Volk in merely cultural or political terms, as a nation-state, say. They thereby ignored the fact that cultural and historical 'forces … are based essentially on racial elements'. 'Germanness', insists Hitler, does not 'lie in language [or tradition], but in the blood'. The state is only an instrument that 'primarily serve[s] the preservation of [the] physical life' of the race, of a 'community of … homogeneous creatures'.[24]

Hitler's animosity to romantic Volkish thought endured. Albert Speer records his scorn both for Rosenberg's 'unreadable' *Myth of the Twentieth Century* – which 'relapse[d] into the mysticism of the Middle Ages' – and for Himmler's 'mythologizing'. 'What nonsense!' was Hitler's verdict on the latter – and dangerous nonsense, for by promoting a Teutonic cult, the SS chief diverted attention from the proper role models, the Greeks and Romans.[25] Instructive, too, were the fates of the Strasser brothers, early comrades of Hitler during 'the time of struggle'. Otto, who reiterated the Herderian '*völkisch* idea … [that] affirms the right of every nation … to autonomous control' of its life, broke with Hitler and was exiled. Gregor, who rejected the 'feasibility' and 'value' of the new Volkish concepts of 'people's blood' and 're-nordification', was a victim of the Röhm Purge in 1934.[26]

The source for Hitler's worldview was not romantic Volkish thought at all. In 1900, Alfred Krupp sponsored an essay competition on the question of the application of Darwinism to politics, with prizes going to men who later became prominent advocates of racial hygiene.[27] Chairman of the judges was the author of a best-selling work on materialism whose position more closely anticipated *Mein Kampf* than those focused on by Mosse. Ernst Haeckel was a robust naturalist and Social Darwinist. While, at an 'ultimate' level, all behaviour may be 'referred to the mechanics of atoms', it is in Darwinist terms of natural selection, struggle and survival of the fittest that the human sciences must 'solve all [the] riddles' of life.[28] Haeckel was also an anti-Semite, as was a whole generation of anthropologists, eugenicists and geneticists inspired by his work.

For Hitler, as for Haeckel, there is an 'iron logic of Nature': that of the struggle between species for existence, 'health and power of resistance'. At the human level, these species are races, biologically defined in terms of 'blood'. Nature's logic is 'stern and rigid', so that a 'hard fate ... strikes the man who thinks he can overcome' her, especially the 'crazy ideologist' who dreams of a 'higher existence' without struggle between races. Indeed, 'higher existence' and 'spiritual development' are luxuries to be contemplated only when physical survival and 'health' are ensured.[29]

This 'brutally materialistic concept of human motivation'[30] provided Hitler with a different perspective from romantic Volkish thought on a whole range of issues. For example, his expansionist ambitions reflected less a sense of cultural 'mission' – to initiate 'lower' peoples into a 'higher' German culture – than the imperative of *Lebensraum*. If the German people, flag-bearer of the Aryan race, was to survive, it must break out of the confines of a territory unable to sustain it. Again, when he extols the superiority of the Aryan race, it is rarely in terms of 'high' cultural achievements. It is upon 'gigantic scientific–technical achievements', those of thriving 'industry, technology, and commerce', that he harps: on those, in effect, that best testify to a race's fitness to triumph in Nature's struggle.[31] There is nothing here of that 'fear of modernity' and romanticization of Nature that characterized Volkish thought. (Speer recalls that while Hitler 'frequently admired a beautiful view', he was without a 'love of nature' to match his enthusiasm for huge architectural projects.[32])

It was, however, Hitler's perspective on 'the Jewish problem' that was the most striking product of his 'brutally materialistic' thinking. While he endorsed Wagner's point that the Jews were a people without a culture of their own, this was the least of his accusations against them. The Jews, in effect, represented defiance of the natural order, an attempt to 'buck' Nature's 'stern laws'. Just as the body, to maintain its natural healthy state, requires defence against the germs that attack it, so whole human species – races – must defend themselves against the threat of Jewish 'bacilli' and 'parasites'. The Jews are not so much culture-less as 'culture-destroyers', killers of 'the host people' on whom they 'sponge'. This is for two main reasons. First, through intermarriage, the Jews 'poison the blood' of the host people, rendering it less fit to conduct the struggle for existence and 'health'. Second, the Jew, uniquely among human beings, is 'led by nothing but the naked egoism of the individual'.[33] Unnaturally dispersed around the globe, Jews do not belong to a geographically located racial community, and hence cannot, like other men and women, submit their interests to that of such a community. It is Nature's way for creatures to sacrifice themselves for that whole: the Jews are therefore 'anti-nature' – an 'anti-race', as Goebbels put it – and hence a mortal danger to the communal wholes into which they have, like bacilli, entered. All the recent historical evidence demonstrates, in Hitler's view, that, in these two ways, the Jews have been responsible for a 'catastrophic splintering' and weakening of the German world.

Neither these pronouncements, nor the wider conception of life that many anthropologists and geneticists of the day shared with Hitler, invite blanket description as an 'anti-rational repudiation' of 'Enlightenment and positivist tradition'. Haeckel and his followers in fact prided themselves on their positivism, their opposition to 'intuition', *Verstehen* and other distractions from unsentimental appreciation of hard facts and natural laws. Hitler saw himself, in contrast to the Volkish romantic, as pursuing only 'knowledge and ruthless application of Nature's stern and rigid laws'. As did a figure like Hans Günther, an influential professor of Racial Hygiene in the Nazi period. Once 'Darwin recognized the crucial importance of natural selection for all life-forms', one must 'see human beings not so much as individuals but as carriers of heredity', and empirical research establishes that Nature selects for those peoples where the purity and 'health of the stock' has been best 'maintained'.[34] As for Enlightenment tradition, if there is truth in Hans-Georg Gadamer's observation that a central Enlightenment ambition was the elimination of 'prejudice'[35] – of all obstacles to total objectivity – then Hitler and fellow-thinkers were, in intent, heirs to that tradition. It was, wrote Hitler, no 'ground for renouncing reason' that it enjoins beliefs and actions that may be 'profoundly painful'.[36]

It has become a convention when referring to Nazi 'science', including eugenics, to place the word, as I just did, in scare quotes or to prefix it by 'pseudo-'. This is legitimate if the point is to deny that what was followed was *respectable* scientific method. But it is misleading if it suggests that Günther and others rejected scientific method in favour of some alternative mode of access to truth. We should distinguish the person who misapplies scientific method from the opponent of science. Relatedly, we should distinguish the poor reasoner from the person who abjures the use of reason. 'Anti-rational' is surely appropriate only for the latter.

'Naturalism', 'Humanism' and Moral Complicity

This account of Hitler's anthropology offers some confirmation of Nolte's characterization of National Socialism as 'resistance to transcendence'. If Hitler entertained a utopian vision, it was a naturalistic one of a world in which human beings do not transcend their basic, material motives, but submit to an 'iron logic of Nature' that it is hopeless to defy. The account also endorses Lacoue-Labarthe's perception of a 'modern', 'humanist' direction to Nazi ideology. Within the constraints imposed by nature, human beings should strive for a Promethean reshaping of their world, above all through the opportunities afforded by 'techno-science'. It was no accident that, despite its traditionalist support, the NSDAP increasingly attracted doctors, geneticists, technocrats, architects and those 'Faustian men' *par excellence*, engineers – all fired by an ambition to forge a brave new world. The expression 'reactionary modernist' nicely captures the blend of this ambition with repudiation of the democratic, liberal institutions that earlier thinkers had supposed essential to material progress.[37]

Central to Nazi thinking as Hitler's 'naturalistic' anthropology and Promethean enthusiasms were, should we conclude without further ado that they were morally complicit – in the sense explained earlier – in the Holocaust? Hitler, certainly, moves immediately from 'the discovery of the Jewish virus' to insisting that, in the 'battle' against it, we 'shall regain our health only by eliminating the Jew'.[38] If one queries that move, it is because one can imagine people who, sharing Hitler's racial anthropology, would have rejected, on moral grounds, his drastic recipe for 'regaining health'. (We know, after all, of the opposition, even among committed Nazis, to the euthanasia programme.) To exploit Hitler's own analogy: Jains are perfectly aware of the danger to the body posed by some parasites, yet have their moral reasons not to destroy them. Or one can imagine people who, priding themselves on their 'positivism', eschew all comment on 'policy'. *Their* job – as geneticists, say – is simply to lay out the facts and explain the 'hygienic' techniques available, not to pass judgement on the desirability of employing those techniques.

The point is that the ideological tendencies described will only have been complicit in the Holocaust if conjoined with certain views about morality. It will be that conjunction that is either 'strongly' complicit, through warranting the murders, or 'weakly' so, through lacking any resources to condemn them. (Recall that I am not concerned with aetiology. The fact – which I see no reason to question – that a racial anthropology was among the 'causes' of the Holocaust does not, however, entail that, by itself, it was morally complicit in my sense.) In the case of traditional, romantic Volkish thought, it was unclear that there were the moral ingredients to generate a complicit ideology. In that of Nazi thought, however, it is possible to identify conceptions of morality that, fused with racial science, do entail moral complicity in the Holocaust.

These conceptions should be distinguished from various ingredients in the Nazi moral code – sexual puritanism, insistence on obedience to authority, a celebration of hardness and will – that may or may not have discernible logical connections with one another or with the conceptions themselves. These latter are views *about* morality – the nature of moral principles, for example: they belong at the level of 'meta-ethics'.

A thoroughgoing naturalist, like Haeckel or Hitler, for whom such sciences as biology and anthropology are the sole vehicles of truths about the human condition, typically adopts one or other of two approaches to morality. Either he attempts to integrate morality into the naturalistic picture, to 'naturalize' it; or he treats moral belief as falling outside the realm of truth, as mere expression of 'inner feeling', say. Both approaches, and often a combination of them, may be found in the writings of Hitler or his followers.

The more salient, 'naturalizing' approach took the form of a Social Darwinist account of morality, the effect of which was to relativize the validity of moral values to the peoples or races embracing them. 'Values are based essentially on racial elements', wrote Hitler, which is why no 'ethical idea' has a 'right to existence' if it 'represents a danger for … racial life'. Virtue 'cannot be evaluated … in the frame of the outside world', but solely in relation to 'the nationality involved in each … case'.[39] Or, as an early SA chief put it, '"value" is a relative concept … use[d] here to refer to value measured in terms of … the interests of collective German well-being'.[40] While one might expect certain virtues, such as loyalty, to be universally embraced, when moral codes that are equally serviceable to their respective peoples conflict, there is no sense to asking which is the better one. (Occasionally, Social

Darwinism gets invoked in a different way: to privilege the morality of that race or people which proves the 'fittest' in the struggle for survival.[41])

On this approach, a morality has a status like that of a legal code. It does, at any rate, if one denies – as 'positivist' Nazi jurists like Carl Schmitt emphatically did – that the legality of a code is answerable to 'higher' principles of Natural Justice. Just as the truth of 'X is legal' is relative to a particular legal code, so 'X is obligatory/virtuous' is only true relative to the morality of some people. Recognition of this relativity should no more reduce respect for moral principles than a parallel recognition reduces respect for the laws of the land. If there was a tendency liable to impugn the authority or importance of morality, this belonged to the second of the approaches mentioned above. When Hitler associates 'ethical conceptions' with 'pure expressions of feeling', and contrasts them with 'cold logic',[42] the implication is that moral convictions do not belong in the arena even of relative truth. They are merely 'subjective', a matter only of 'inner experience', and hence lack any intellectual authority over people's actions.

As Hitler's own position indicates, however, this view, while frequently voiced, was typically combined with the first approach. Combination was made possible by distinguishing between different spheres of morality. The distinction recalls Hegel's, between *Sittlichkeit* and *Moralität* (social, institutionalized morality versus 'morality of the heart'), or perhaps Max Weber's one between a personal 'ethics of intention' and a political 'ethics of responsibility'. It makes all the difference, Weber writes, to the 'ethical problems of politics' that 'the specific instrument of politics is power, backed up by *violence*', wielded by 'groups of human beings'. Someone who recognizes this will also appreciate that, in political ethics, what matter are 'the disciplined dispassionateness with which one looks at the realities of life, and the capacity to endure them'.[43] It is difficult, reading these words, not to think of Himmler's notorious 'pep talk' to SS leaders at Poznan in 1943. Here he congratulates his audience on the 'decent', humane, far from 'heartless' sentiments they share with Germans at large. But he congratulates them most on a 'hardness' that has overcome the 'human weakness' which acting towards Jews on the basis of such sentiments would betray – for it is 'a crime against our own blood to worry about [Jews] and to bring them ideals'.[44] Sentiments and ideals are fine in their own sphere – in one's own house or village, say – but are without authority, and must indeed be suppressed, when it is a matter of 'the realities of life' in the sphere of political, racial struggle.

I make three comments on these two approaches that, separately or in combination, were salient in Nazi thinking about morality. First, they do not represent a blunt 'repudiation' of Enlightenment moral thought. To be sure, they are incompatible with the postulation of self-evident 'rights of man' or of a 'moral law' determinable by pure reason. But such postulates represented only certain strands in a much wider Enlightenment fabric. No less 'enlightened' were the many efforts to 'ground' morality in human nature: to regard a sensible morality as an instrument that serves to satisfy basic impulses, like the desire for pleasure, whose necessary dominion only otherworldly idealists and divines could doubt. Equally prominent among Enlightenment moral philosophers was a 'subjectivizing' tendency to expel moral beliefs from the realm of truth altogether. Such beliefs are construed as 'sentiments', manifestations of 'sympathy' and 'repulsion', not as corresponding to facts, for the discovery of facts is the monopoly of the empirical and mathematical sciences.

Second, and relatedly, Nazi conceptions of morality were 'humanist' ones in the sense indicated earlier. Moral principles do not answer to anything outside of human decision and will. Either they do not answer to anything at all, being a matter, merely, of 'pure expressions of feeling', or they are instruments that different groups of human beings have forged in order to prosecute their collective, racial interests in the struggle for survival and 'health'.

Finally, the conjunction of a 'brutally materialistic' anthropology, like Hitler's, with one or both of the two conceptions of morality is evidently complicit in the Holocaust. Given the premises of Hitler's racial anthropology and his 'discovery of the Jewish virus', then, 'measured in terms of ... the interests of collective German well-being', the extermination was morally justified in the only sense of those terms, when mouthed by a German, that – on the Social Darwinist 'naturalization' of morality – they can bear. 'Morally justified', being a 'relative concept', is truly applied by Germans – in the one sense of moral truth allowed – to policies deemed, on allegedly scientific grounds, essential to the survival and 'health' of the German people. What I called the 'naturalizing' approach, then, is 'strongly' complicit in the extermination.

The other, 'subjectivizing' approach, though not 'strongly' complicit, is 'weakly' so, for it yields a conception of ethics without the resources to condemn the Holocaust. On this conception, the denunciations by some Germans of the extermination express nothing more than personal feelings. Even if it is granted that feelings of that general kind have their legitimate place at home, they are – as we saw from Himmler's Weberian pronouncements – without any authority in appraisal of national or racial policy. Only judgements made within the realm of truth – one to which expressions of feeling do not belong – have that authority. This is why decision on the proper 'division of the earth', as Goebbels remarked, is 'simply a matter of power, not morality'.[45]

Coda

An unfortunate effect of the received image is to encourage an impression that the constellation of ideas at the 'root' of National Socialist thought belongs to a bygone age, one already past in the 1930s except in Germany. If this impression is justified in the case of some elements of Nazi ideology, it is certainly not in the case of the conceptions of morality identified in the previous section. Indeed, as predicted in my opening section, a 'lesson' to learn by focusing on the question of complicity is that tendencies in ethics alive and well today are strikingly similar to those complicit conceptions. It is our good fortune, for the present at least, that the champions of these conceptions no longer subscribe to a racial science. If they did, then the terrible policies that this science might suggest are ones to which they would be powerless rationally to object.

Consider, first, today's fashionable 'sociobiological' approach to ethics.

According to E.O. Wilson, ethics awaits inclusion in 'the modern [that is, Darwinian] synthesis': it is to be 'biologicized'. When it is, it will be clear that 'morality has no other demonstrable function' than that of a technique by which 'human genetic material [is] kept intact'. Morality, if it is to be more than pie-in-the-sky, must adjust to the 'biological imperative to maximize genetic fitness'.[46] It is odd that Wilson speaks of ethics still *awaiting* 'biologicization', since the view of morality he expresses is, shorn of the racial twist given by Nazi theorists to the notion of 'fitness', indistinguishable from the 'naturalizing' conception proclaimed by Hitler.

Consider, next, the 'subjectivizing' tendency. In *Humanity: a moral history of the twentieth century*, Jonathan Glover unfavourably compares Nazi philosophers with other German-language philosophers of the period, including the logical positivists of the Vienna Circle. It was these other philosophers who could have 'challenged the Nazi belief system' and encouraged critical 'independence and rationality'.[47] Doubtless, members of the Vienna Circle could and did challenge the credentials of racial science and Hitler's anthropology. But on what grounds would they have raised moral objections to Hitler's policies? According to Rudolf Carnap, a moral judgement is 'merely the expression of a certain wish' – a more sophisticated way, masquerading as a genuine statement, of exclaiming 'Hurrah!' or 'Boo!'. When another positivist describes moral terms as 'purely emotive', he could be quoting Hitler or Goebbels.[48] No doubt the logical positivists all said 'Boo!' to the persecution and murder of the Jews. But their position on the nature of morality left them without any resources whatever rationally to defend their moral 'wishes'.

In more recent times, less crude 'subjectivizing' treatments of moral judgements and principles have been developed than that offered by the logical positivists. Yet the general thought that moral judgements lie outside the realm of truth, that their sole authority for the person making them derives from his or her choice, commitment or 'pro-attitude', dominates not only in moral philosophy but in our wider culture. A historian of Judeophobia writes that 'the deconstructionist logic', already developed by the Nazis, 'that today seeks', *inter alia*, to 'dissolv[e] every moral judgement into mere assertions of subjective perception, must ... be ranked among the dangerous delusions of our chaotic world'.[49] Certainly it would be a delusion to imagine that we today possess, either in this deconstructionist subjectivizing or in a neo-Darwinian biologicization of ethics – or in their combination – a conception of morality innocent of complicity in tomorrow's genocide.

Notes

1. The term is Klaus P. Fischer's in his *The History of an Obsession: German Judeophobia and the Holocaust* (1998), London: Constable, p. 4.
2. Jonathan Glover (2001), *Humanity: a moral history of the twentieth century*, London: Pimlico, p. 395, makes this point against Tim Mason's much-discussed 'functionalist' criticism of 'intentionalist' explanation in his *Nazism, Fascism and the Working Class* (1995), Cambridge: Cambridge University Press.
3. Quoted in Fischer, *History*, p. 5.

4. *The Crisis of German Ideology* (1998), New York: Fertig, p. v.
5. Ibid., pp. 315–16, 302–3.
6. Ibid., pp. ix, 316. In the Preface to the 1998 edition, Mosse concedes that the relation between Volkish-*cum*-Nazi thought and modernity (especially technology) was more complex than he had supposed: p. x.
7. Ibid., pp. 313, 302.
8. Ibid., pp. 299, 294, 301.
9. J.P. Stern (1975), *Hitler: The Führer and the People*, London: Fontana, p. 53; Gordon A. Craig (1984), *The Germans*, Harmondsworth: Penguin, p. 127; Fischer, *History*, p. 189.
10. Peter Gay (1992), *Weimar Culture*, Harmondsworth: Penguin, p. 100. See also Stern, *Hitler*, pp. 53–4.
11. Gay, *Weimar Culture*, p. 101 (the words within double quotation marks are those of the historian Ernst Troeltsch); Stern, *Hitler*, p. 54. Other works that emphasize anti-Enlightenment and anti-modern 'origins' of Nazism include Fritz Stern (1963), *The Politics of Cultural Despair: A Study in the Rise of German Ideology*, New York: Doubleday, and Georg Lukács (1969), *The Destruction of Reason*, trans. P. Palmer, London: Merlin.
12. *Three Faces of Fascism: Action Française, Italian Fascism, National Socialism* (1969), trans. L. Vennewitz, New York: New American Library, p. 529.
13. Ibid., pp. 538, 542–3.
14. Ibid., p. 580, n.13.
15. *Heidegger, Art and Politics* (1990), trans. C. Turner, Oxford: Blackwell, p. 35.
16. Ibid., pp. 35, 49–50.
17. Ibid., p. 95.
18. Roger Griffin (ed.) (1995), *Fascism*, Oxford: Oxford University Press, from 'General Introduction', p. 6.
19. F. Bernard (ed.) (1969), *J.G. Herder on Social and Political Culture*, Cambridge: Cambridge University Press, pp. 200, 198, 164.
20. *Reflections on the Philosophy of the History of Mankind* (1968), trans. T. Churchill, Chicago: University of Chicago Press, p. 98; Bernard, *J.G. Herder*, p. 221.
21. In Griffin, *Fascism*, p. 100.
22. Treitschke and Wagner both quoted in Harold James (1989), *A German Identity: 1770 to the present day*, London: Phoenix, pp. 97, 103.
23. *Mein Kampf* (1974), trans. R. Mannheim, London: Hutchinson, pp. 344–5.
24. Ibid., pp. 353–4, 355, 357.
25. *Inside the Third Reich* (1995), trans. R. and C. Winston, London: Phoenix, pp. 147–9.
26. See Griffin, *Fascism*, pp. 114, 123.
27. See Fischer, *History*, p. 117.
28. On Haeckel, see John Passmore, *One Hundred Years of Philosophy* (1968), Harmondsworth: Penguin, Ch. 2.
29. *Mein Kampf*, pp. 259–61, 357.
30. James, *German Identity*, p. 149.
31. *Mein Kampf*, pp. 246, 385.
32. *Inside the Third Reich*, pp. 85–6.
33. *Mein Kampf*, p. 274.
34. In Griffin, *Fascism*, pp. 124–5.
35. *Truth and Method* (1979), trans. W. Glen-Doepel, London: Sheed & Ward, pp. 239ff.
36. *Mein Kampf*, p. 580.
37. See Jeffrey Herf (1984), *Reactionary Modernism*, Cambridge: Cambridge University Press, and David E. Cooper (1999), 'Reactionary Modernism', in A. O'Hear (ed.),

German Philosophy since Kant, Cambridge: Cambridge University Press, pp. 291–304. On 'Faustian man', see Oswald Spengler (1932), *Man and Technics*, trans. C. Atkinson, London: Allen & Unwin. On participation by applied scientists, including doctors, see Benno Müller-Hill (1988), *Murderous Science: Elimination by Scientific Selection of Jews, Gypsies and others, Germany 1933–45*, Oxford: Oxford University Press. On the mentality of one enthusiastic architect-*cum*-technocrat, see Speer's autobiographical *Inside the Third Reich*.

38. Hugh Trevor-Roper, *Hitler's Table Talk, 1941–4* (1988), Oxford: Oxford University Press, p. 332.

39. *Mein Kampf*, pp. 355, 348, 358.

40. Franz von Pfeffer, quoted in Griffin, *Fascism*, p. 119.

41. See, for example, *Mein Kampf*, p. 365, para. 4.

42. Ibid., p. 261.

43. 'Politics as a vocation', in *Weber: Selections in Translation* (1978), trans. E. Matthews, Cambridge: Cambridge University Press, pp. 219, 221, 216, 223.

44. Quoted in Robert S. Wistrich (1995), *Who's Who in Nazi Germany*, London: Routledge, pp. 113–14. Compare the letter cited by Glover, *Humanity*, p. 347, in which a Nazi doctor, while endorsing the euthanasia programme, apologizes for the 'personal', humane emotions that make him too 'weak' and 'gentle' for such work.

45. Quoted in Griffin, *Fascism*, p. 159.

46. *Sociobiology* (1975), Cambridge, MA: Harvard University Press, p. 4; *On Human Nature* (1995), Harmondsworth: Penguin, pp. 2, 167.

47. Glover, *Humanity*, pp. 365–6.

48. Rudolf Carnap (1935), *Philosophy and Logical Syntax*, London: Kegan Paul, p. 24; A.J. Ayer (1967), *Language, Truth and Logic*, London: Gollancz, p. 108.

49. Fischer, *History*, p. 12.

Chapter 3

In a Class of its Own?

Norman Geras

In what follows I address a long-standing question in the study, and wider public discussion, of the Holocaust, and propose an answer to it that, so far as I know, has not been proposed before. I do so the more tentatively in that the question is an unusual as well as difficult one. By way of trying to answer it, I also consider the meaning of the question itself, a task neglected more often than not, though it is indispensable to any clear treatment of the issues at stake.

Was the Holocaust unique? In the first section of this essay (I) I start by giving instances of a widely held belief that it stands apart, and go on to register the controversy surrounding this belief: the strength of feeling that can be caused by its denial – and equally by its affirmation. In the second section (II) I explore the suggestion that this question is not worth pursuing, subject as it is to the influences of identity and political context and to evaluative judgements that serve them. I reject the suggestion, however. I reject it because, as a quick and easy way out, it fails. A legitimate issue remains even once such influences have been noted and the place of evaluative judgement has been allowed for. My argument to that effect encompasses a preliminary discussion of the nature of the question here: what it means to claim that an event like the Holocaust was unique. The third and final section (III) then sets out the principal reasons generally offered in support of the claim that the Holocaust was unique, and the objections to them. I go on to urge, for my own part, that the subject needs to be freed from the shadow of comparative suffering and competitive victimhood; and that the normative content of the uniqueness claim – disowned by some of its advocates, but misguidedly in my view – is easier to acknowledge once this shadow has been lifted. Resuming the earlier discussion of the meaning of the question itself, I propose that a resolution is possible if we focus on what can sometimes be involved in the existence of a conceptual category boundary.

I

In the television series *The Nazis: A Warning from History*, first screened by the BBC in 1997, the narrator says by way of characterizing the Nazi period, '[D]uring the war Hitler authorized a policy unique in all history, the mechanized extermination of an entire people'.[1] Introducing a book one of whose central purposes is to emphasize the precedents there were for the Nazi genocide in the

murderousness of European colonialism, Sven Lindqvist writes: 'European world expansion, accompanied as it was by a shameless defence of extermination, created habits of thought and political precedents that made way for new outrages, finally culminating in the most horrendous of them all: the Holocaust.'[2] In his *Black Dogs*, the novelist Ian McEwan alludes to the Nazi extermination camps as 'our universal reference point of human depravity'.[3]

Writing about the abuse directed at an Israeli footballer by members of the opposing team, a sports journalist expresses the opinion that 'anti-semitism sets off the deepest revulsion because it speaks of the worst of all human crimes'.[4] Above a newspaper article about the purported memoir of a child survivor, this same crime is referred to as 'mankind's greatest atrocity'.[5] The reviewer of a new edition of Jean Améry's *At the Mind's Limits* says that 'the Holocaust represented a kind of moral full stop'.[6] Even disputing the notion that the extremity of the event puts it beyond our ability to grasp or conceptualize, one writer wants to guard against being misunderstood, insisting: 'As an actual historical project … I believe that the Shoah was, in an almost primal sense, without parallel or precedent.'[7] Likewise, arguing that the record of communist crime in the twentieth century was quantitatively unequalled by any other political system despite the greater notoriety of Nazism, the reviewer of a 'black book of communism' insists with respect to the qualitative comparison, 'My answer is clear: the Holocaust was unique.'[8]

These are just a few examples of the view, common in the discourse of our time and, broadly, place, that the Holocaust was a peculiarly terrible, and hence a singular, crime. Notwithstanding the long historical backdrop to it of violence, oppression, cruelty and mass slaughter, the Holocaust is regarded by many as having been exceptional. Yet this view is not universally shared. It has often been challenged. I briefly summarize two broad types of challenge there have been, in order to illustrate the passions that can be aroused on both sides.

I refer, first, to the controversy of the 1980s known as the *Historikerstreit* – the historians' dispute – which began amongst German scholars, though it was quickly internationalized, drawing contributions from historians outside Germany. In the interests of brevity, I concentrate on a central feature of the arguments of one leading protagonist in the debate, Ernst Nolte, and the responses to it. I leave aside what is less directly relevant to my purpose. The feature in question was Nolte's effort, as is sometimes said, to 'normalize' the treatment of the history of the Third Reich by placing it in a broader context: a context in which the Holocaust could be seen as one terrible crime among many others. Care is needed on this point. Formally speaking, Nolte did make a bow towards the view that the Holocaust was a singular crime, for he said as much. However, as so often in these things, it was a matter of the all-round balance of his position, and Nolte's emphasis, overwhelmingly, was on contextualizing the Nazi genocide: on asserting that it belongs to the same history as the American intervention in Vietnam, the Vietnamese invasion of Cambodia, the exodus from Vietnam of the boat people (a 'holocaust on the water'), the Cambodian genocide, the Soviet invasion of Afghanistan and, above all, the liquidation of the kulaks and the Soviet Gulag. His conclusion: 'The Third Reich should be removed from the isolation in which it still finds itself.'[9]

This plea provoked a sharp critical reaction. The eminent historian of Nazi Germany Ian Kershaw, himself broadly endorsing the reaction, summed it up as follows: 'Nolte's position … has met with extensive rejection from scholars in Germany and almost universal condemnation abroad.'[10] Nolte's arguments were seen as an attempt to 'relativize' the Holocaust – a term which itself implies that the event stands, in some important sense, alone. Jürgen Habermas, who initiated the critical response, would later put the matter like this:

> Auschwitz has become the signature of an entire epoch – and it concerns all of us. Something happened there that no one could previously have thought even possible. It touched a deep layer of solidarity among all who have a human face. Until then – in spite of all the quasi-natural brutalities of world history – we had simply taken the integrity of this deep layer for granted. At that point a bond of naiveté was torn to shreds … Auschwitz altered the conditions for the continuation of historical life contexts.[11]

Whether consciously or not, Habermas was hereby echoing a sentiment of Hannah Arendt's articulated more than twenty years earlier: that the perpetrators of the so-called 'Final Solution' thought they had a 'right to determine who should and who should not inhabit the world'.[12]

Historians responding to Nolte argued that Germany's recent past was associated with an unparalleled enormity, and its identity as a nation therefore stained like that of no other. In Germany itself Eberhard Jäckel, castigating what he described as a 'miserable practice' of insinuation, wrote:

> [T]he murder of the Jews was unique because never before had a state, with the authority of its responsible leader, decided and announced its intention to liquidate as completely as possible a certain group of people, including the aged, women, children and babies, and to implement this decision by means of all the official instruments of power at its disposal.[13]

Quoting this passage, the British historian Richard Evans referred to the genocide of the Jews as 'a gratuitous act carried out by a prosperous, advanced industrial nation at the height of its power', and he went on to characterize the general significance of the uniqueness question thus: 'if the Germans did not commit a crime that stood out from all others in its horror, then they have no more to be ashamed of than any other nation … [they are] unburdened by a historical responsibility without parallel anywhere else in the world'.[14] In the United States Charles Maier, also quoting Jäckel, wrote that 'nowhere else but in German-occupied Europe from 1941 to 1945 was there an apparatus so single-mindedly established to carry out mass murder as a process in its own right'.[15] Maier assessed the broad significance of the issue in a way similar to Evans. If what the Germans did is dreadful as one case of genocide among others, he said, then their country can aspire to the same kind of 'national acceptance' as is accorded the perpetrators of other massacres. 'But if the Final Solution remains non-comparable … German nationhood may remain forever tainted.'[16]

In sum, then: for Nolte, a crime like many others and a country on a footing with at least some of the rest; for his critics, a singular enormity and a nation specially marked by its responsibility for it. However, both the force and the direction of controversy, so to put this, can be reversed. For the idea of the Holocaust as a singular enormity has been resisted quite as vigorously as was its putative equivalence with other historical brutalities refused by Nolte's critics. The issue at the heart of this opposite resistance has been Jewish, rather than German, exceptionalism.

In 1984 Pierre Papazian, contributing to an exchange in the Jewish-American magazine *Midstream*, took as his comparative reference point the Turkish genocide of 1915 against the Armenians. Seeing several obvious parallels between the Armenian and Jewish cases – from the state-sponsored character of the two genocides, to the very high proportions of the Armenian and the Jewish peoples killed and the terrible cruelties perpetrated against them, to the destruction in both processes of the foundations of communal continuity – Papazian held the comparative study of genocides to be an essential task of understanding. He accordingly objected to the tendency of certain writers to place the Holocaust beyond comprehension: 'To portray the Holocaust as a metahistorical, somehow mystical event is to render futile all analysis and commentary.' The uniqueness claim, he also wrote, implied 'diminishing the gravity' of genocides other than the Holocaust; it implied 'that no matter what misfortune befalls another people, it cannot be as serious'.[17]

A more recent essay by David Stannard has enlarged upon this last theme in harsher tones, tones of accusation. The primary, though not the sole, contextualizing reference point for Stannard is the fate of the indigenous peoples of the Americas, and the comparability between what happened to them under European conquest and colonization and to the Jews in Nazi Europe is pressed by him on all counts: the numbers and proportions of the peoples killed; the intention in, and ideological bases of, the genocides; the speed and the means of the destruction processes involved. If belittling the sufferings of other peoples than the Jews is again the criticism, this is no longer an inference from the uniqueness assumption; it is treated as its transparent objective. Stannard speaks of that assumption as the 'product of many years of strenuous intellectual labour by a handful of Jewish scholars and writers'; he speaks of a game played – 'guilefully' – 'to advance the Jewish uniqueness agenda and to diminish the significance of every other people's historical suffering'.[18] In fact, it goes beyond diminishing: 'advocates of the allegedly unique suffering of Jews during the Holocaust ... participate in denial of *other* historical genocides ... *such denial is inextricably interwoven with the very claim of uniqueness*'.[19] As for the impulses at work, this is a case, Stannard writes, of 'cultural egotism driving scholarship before it': the uniqueness thesis is 'fundamentally racist', linked to 'Chosen People self-righteousness' and to 'Israel's territorial expansionism and suppression of the Palestinian people'.[20] There is a similar list of charges, and similarly indignant tone, in Norman Finkelstein's *The Holocaust Industry*. The son of Holocaust survivors, Finkelstein reports that the main lesson his mother taught in these matters was, precisely, comparison: 'to open our hearts to the rest of humanity's suffering'.[21] He protests against the claim that the Holocaust 'cannot be rationally apprehended': that it 'is unique because it is inexplicable', a 'mystery'. If it really was 'incomprehensibly unique', this would undermine its 'universal dimension' – or 'universalist message'.[22] To make out distinctions between 'our' suffering and 'theirs' is 'a moral travesty': as if, '[h]owever terrible, the suffering of others simply does not compare'.[23] Finkelstein, for his part too, identifies the dominant motivation here as Jewish exclusivism: 'The Holocaust is special because the Jews are special.' It is a modern version of the 'chosenness' of the Jews and is of Zionist inspiration. 'Holocaust uniqueness,' he says, 'serves as Israel's prize alibi.'[24]

The points themselves are, of course, separable from the indignation. This is evidenced by Peter Novick's more measured treatment of the same topic (among others) in his *The Holocaust and Collective Memory*. Like Finkelstein an American Jew troubled by the uniqueness claim, Novick pursues some of the same arguments. The claim, he says, cannot be accepted as anything other than 'a claim for preeminence'. It can mean nothing else than that 'your catastrophe, unlike ours, is ordinary'. As with the notion that the Holocaust is 'singularly incomprehensible or unrepresentable' – or 'in some undefined way, sacred' – it is 'deeply offensive'.[25] Novick, however, also goes beyond these arguments, to give space to observations of a more methodological kind. The question under review is, he contends, a bad one:

> Insistence on [the Holocaust's] uniqueness (or denial of its uniqueness) is an intellectually empty enterprise for reasons having nothing to do with the Holocaust itself and everything to do with 'uniqueness'. A moment's reflection makes clear that the notion of uniqueness is quite vacuous. Every historical event, including the Holocaust, in some ways resembles events to which it might be compared and differs from them in some ways. These resemblances and differences are a perfectly proper subject for discussion. But to single out those aspects of the Holocaust that were distinctive (there certainly were such), and to ignore those aspects that it shares with other atrocities, and on the basis of this gerrymandering to declare the Holocaust unique, is intellectual sleight of hand.

In another formulation of the same point, Novick suggests that advocating the uniqueness of the Holocaust amounts to finding exactly what you are looking to find.[26]

His greater methodological reflectiveness also leads him to ponder the fact that, in the framework of the earlier German debate, the very same advocacy may have had a different significance:

> [T]he intention of talking in Germany of the uniqueness and incomparability of the Holocaust is to prevent Germans from evading confrontation with that which is most difficult, painful, and therefore probably most useful to confront. Let us remember the context in which many Germans ... objected to the so-called relativization of the Holocaust in recent years ... Those Germans who insisted on the uniqueness of the Holocaust, who condemned its relativization, did so to block what they correctly regarded as a move to evade confrontation with a painful national past ...

It was the different context that made the difference. As Novick puts it, 'context, as always, is decisive'.[27]

II

On both sides of the issue there is a charge of special pleading: here German, and there Jewish, special pleading. The first was seen as present in the similarity alleged between the Nazi genocide and the atrocities of other nations, and in the lessening of the gravity of the former which this implied. Critics condemned it as an effort of evasion of 'a painful national past'. On the other hand, the Holocaust's proposed incomparability in certain respects, its distinctive difference, has invited condemnation just as sharp: the burden of the condemnation now being that this proposal lessens the gravity of atrocities *other* than the Holocaust and the sufferings they involved. Seen also as antithetical to universalist moral commitments, and as mystificatory – because of the Holocaust-incomprehensibility theme – it is criticized as a Jewish bid for privileged consideration and an apologia for Israeli policy towards the Palestinians.

Taking this all together with the point that 'uniqueness' is itself a vacuous notion, one might feel tempted to be done with the whole business. It is a temptation – to intrude a personal note – with which I have become familiar: thinking about the question over several years; lecturing and debating about it; writing, leaving off, resuming; postponing again; rethinking. Some of the argument and counter-argument here is ugly, and the issues are unpleasant in themselves. George Steiner, though he felt compelled to consider the question, said he found it 'deeply unsettling, even repellent'.[28] If, further, the opposed judgements in play can only be assessed with reference to the framing political contexts, including, prominently, the identities and motives of the authors of those judgements, and if the dispute is empty anyway on account of the vacuity of the notion around which it pivots, then perhaps it would be better to move on. In doing so, one might just note the advice, where it applies, that 'Jews should emphasize the ordinariness of the Holocaust, Germans its uniqueness.'[29]

Tempting as the suggestion may be, it is too quick. On closer inspection, it does not persuade. A first clue as to why it does not lies within the very field of disputational oppositions set out above. For, whatever there may be in this debate of special pleading, evasion or apologia, it will at once become clear from fixing upon the two sets of *critics* of these sorry practices that the motivations we have seen imputed and the substantive viewpoints they are said to motivate come apart. Jürgen Habermas does not fit the figure of Stannard and Finkelstein's outrage; Peter Novick's driving impulse is not the species of miserable insinuation lamented by Eberhard Jäckel. Not only this. The viewpoints themselves come apart. Expressed otherwise: the versions of them at which these critics direct their fire are not the only ones. With all due weight given to the importance of context – a matter to which I will return – there is something else just as important, namely content. It is not collapsible into context, as it is also not collapsible into motivation.

Taking, first, the view of the Holocaust as unique, let it be conceded that the ethno-thematic ensemble which we have before us has not been dreamed up out of nothing. Jewish writers have argued for the singularity of the event, and it is a thesis deployed by defenders of Israel – among other things, to justify a brutally oppressive occupation. It is also to be found connected with notions of inexplicable and transcendent mystery, and it can be pressed in ways that do, willy-nilly, appear to diminish the moral import of the sufferings of other peoples than the Jews. However, what is found connected is also found disjoint. Here are some names associated with the idea of the Holocaust as a singular catastrophe: Jürgen Habermas, Eberhard Jäckel, Richard Evans, Isaac Deutscher, Ernest Mandel, Primo Levi, Raul Hilberg, Saul Friedlander, Yehuda Bauer. The list is not exhaustive, merely indicative. What it is indicative of is that there have been scholars of this conviction who were not Jews, and others who were not the right kind of Jews, in a negative meaning of that expression which I construe from the more aggravated of the polemics reported above. These were – or are – not figures who can credibly be suspected of 'Chosen People self-righteousness', Zionist apologia, tendencies to religious mystification *and* anti-universalist moral beliefs. Even if some amongst them were to fall under suspicion of one or other such inclination, they cannot credibly be suspected of them all.

To the best of my knowledge, nothing of the aforesaid ethno-thematic ensemble applies to any of the first three, Jürgen Habermas, Eberhard Jäckel and Richard Evans. They are secular intelligences untouched by the notion of the Holocaust as a sacred or incomprehensible mystery: Habermas a philosopher world-renowned for an intellectual project to renew and defend the legacy of Enlightenment universalism; Jäckel and Evans historians motivated by the comparativism proper to their discipline and without any ostensible agenda to privilege the Jews as victims; all three focused, in fact, on the genocidal *act*, on what the Germans did rather than on what the Jews suffered. Isaac Deutscher, Ernest Mandel and Primo Levi were all Jews, of course. But the first two belonged to the type, proposed by Deutscher himself, of 'non-Jewish Jews'; and, as Marxists, they were both lifelong adherents of an internationalism inhospitable to the concept of the Chosen People. Mandel not only rejected – expressly and categorically – the incomprehensibility thesis, which was incompatible with the scientific cast of his Marxist outlook; he always took the greatest pains to situate the Holocaust's unique features, as he saw them, in the context of other horrors visited on the peoples of the world by capitalism and imperialism.[30] Deutscher, on the other hand, in speaking of 'the absolute uniqueness of the catastrophe', did reckon on there being some limit to understanding here. But this was no discourse of mystical transcendence. It came from an obstacle he perceived in the specific extremity of the event to the explanatory reach *of the historian*. Perhaps a modern Aeschylus or Sophocles, he wrote, might be able to cope with so baffling a 'degeneration of the human character'; but he personally, in his role as historian, encountered it as a limiting opacity.[31] Deutscher's view in this was strikingly similar to Primo Levi's. Levi found the available historical explanations for what he saw as a unique historical atrocity to be not fully adequate to the 'general atmosphere of uncontrolled madness' it had involved. He preferred, he said, the historiographical humility which confessed to not understanding: not understanding 'the furious anti-Semitism of Hitler and of Germany behind him'.[32] But, again, Levi's was a secular and rationalist mind. He took his distance more than once from any theologizing of the experience he had himself survived, the mere fact of Auschwitz, for him, controverting the basis of religious faith.[33] Moreover, his characterization of the atrocity, though evidently recognizing its anti-Jewish impetus, was generalizing in tendency. In identifying what he saw as unique, it was not of Jewish suffering but of the Nazi 'camp system' that Levi spoke: with its 'monstrous modern goal, that of erasing entire peoples and cultures from the world'; combining 'technological ingenuity, fanaticism and cruelty'.

In turn, Raul Hilberg, Saul Friedlander and Yehuda Bauer are also all Jews. The latter two are even Israeli nationals. The world, however, is an upsettingly complicated place. Hilberg, author of a seminal study massive in its scholarship and detail, has characterized the destruction of the European Jews as '*sui generis*', 'irreducibly distinct from any other historical event or phenomenon'. The inspiration for these judgements? On the face of it, the man's identity, not as Jewish, but as 'empiricist'; or 'from the sheer examination of the evidence itself'. It is Hilberg's view as a social scientist that the Holocaust is not subsumable under any of the more standard explanations of political or military category.[34] Friedlander and Bauer too, as historians, both say what they say in apparently quite secular comparativist spirit. Friedlander, it is true, has for many years voiced his doubts about the adequacy of the prevailing explanations in this domain. But, like Deutscher and Levi, he was pointing to some of the historiographical limits he perceived: for example, to things which elude the historian's 'intuitive comprehension', like the psychology of a lust for mass killing.[35] So far as I am aware, nowhere does Friedlander fall back upon any sacralizing impulse. And the declared basis of his receptivity to the uniqueness argument is, yet once more, not any particularity of Jewish suffering but – in a reference to the judgements of Hannah Arendt and Jürgen Habermas – 'some sort of outer theoretical limit' of criminality attained by the Nazi regime.[36] Yehuda Bauer, finally, has written in explicit caution against losing hold of the Holocaust in an abstract symbolism that is ungrounded in close and detailed historical knowledge: '[T]he Holocaust was an actual occurrence in our century. It was not the product of an inexplicable fate or of a supernatural intervention, but one logical, possible outcome of European history.' Whether persuasive or not, Bauer's reasons for thinking that the event was singular are articulated in perfectly general, non-identity-specific categories, thereby making for a practical conclusion of universal scope: to try to learn, 'so that … we may avoid a repetition. Who can tell who the Jews will be next time?'[37]

It may be noted, before moving on, that Norman Finkelstein treats at least two of these last three writers as authorities on their subject, people to whom respectful reference can be made. Raul Hilberg and Saul Friedlander evidently belong, in his eyes, on the good side of the line which he draws between serious scholarship about the Nazi genocide and its egregious ideological representation.[38] Yet he seems unaware of any issue arising for him from his rendition of the claim which both Hilberg and Friedlander support. By contrast, Peter Novick recognizes where a distinction is needed, commenting that Yehuda Bauer is 'a dedicated secularist', and that his arguments on this matter 'are much more nuanced and qualified than the arguments of those who … are observant Jews'.[39] Novick himself makes no more of it, but let this comment of his be allowed to tie up the general point I have been pursuing. Identity, motivation and substantive argument come loose from the connections we have seen established for them here. The view of the Holocaust as unique can be held by non-Jews, by non-Zionists, by Jews who do not believe in Jewish chosenness. It can be held in secular, non-mystical versions that do not put the event beyond general criteria of assessment and comparative study, and that do not derogate from a commitment to universalist values.

I turn back to the German debate and the standpoint criticized by Habermas, Jäckel and others. I can be much briefer about this, since the nature of the disaggregating exercise I am conducting will by now be clear. There is no question but that these writers properly identified their target: in the arguments of Ernst Nolte and other German scholars on his side of the controversy, a thinly disguised apologia for the genocide conceived and executed by the Nazi regime. Having properly identified it, they equally properly subjected it to criticism. Nevertheless, just as there are people of the belief that the Holocaust was unique who are not Jewish, not Zionist and so forth, so there are people who deny that it was unique and who have no obvious interest in German historical apologia. If this is not already plain from the persons, and voices, of the above-discussed opponents of the singularity thesis, consider the example of the North American philosopher Kenneth Seeskin. Seeskin's concern in questioning the Holocaust-singularity thesis is clearly and straightforwardly expressed. He perceives in it a moral ranking, a judgement of better and worse; and it is his contention that beyond a certain point such judgements cannot or should not be made. In his own words, 'Moral reason … reaches a threshold at which comparisons of this sort either make no sense or are reprehensible in their own right.'[40] Another philosopher, Laurence Thomas – an African American and a Jew – has argued similarly, in comparing the Holocaust with American slavery. Thomas refuses any ranking of better and worse between the two historical experiences, adverting instead to a notion of 'ultimate' evils: though there can be a plurality of these, no discriminatory evaluative ranking of them is possible.[41] It is not worth lingering over the contingency that there might be some hidden motivational agenda here, whether of German apologia or of 'unconscious' anti-Semitism.[42]

So much, therefore, in this instance as well, for positing too fixed a connection between identity and motivation, on the one hand, and substantive viewpoint, on the other. As for the viewpoint itself, it is not difficult to see how Nolte's carried its burden of apologia wholly within, irrespective of his German identity. Leaving aside certain other very telling aspects of it not directly relevant to our topic, the diminishing of the gravity of Nazi crimes is manifest in his comparative list. For, that there is a threshold beyond which judgements of better and worse are to be eschewed or make no sense is a proposition one might either quarrel or concur with; but that there is also a threshold *this side of which* lie events of a lesser moral gravity than the Nazi Holocaust should not be contestable. They would certainly include the Vietnamese invasion of Cambodia and the exodus from Vietnam of the boat people. But it was in the company of such events that Nolte wanted to locate the Holocaust, so as to remove the Third Reich from its reputational isolation. This is a different way of questioning the uniqueness thesis than the argument that between events of genocidal magnitude or other hugely murderous scope, or between these and the enslavement of millions of people, no moral ranking is possible. It would have been a piece of apologia coming from anyone, regardless of nationality.

We are brought up against Peter Novick's suggestion, cited earlier: the suggestion that context is decisive, and that, consequently, it was right or appropriate for Habermas, Jäckel and others to insist on the uniqueness of the Holocaust, as a way of getting their compatriots to come to terms with Germany's Nazi past, where it is not right or appropriate for North Americans, Jews amongst them, to do so. What sort of rightness or appropriateness is this? Is it that the insistence by Nolte's critics on the uniqueness of the Holocaust was valid in its particular – German – context? Or is it that, irrespective of validity, that insistence was politically and morally commendable, psychologically to the point or something else of the kind? I explore the latter possibility first. How does this work? Are we to suppose that Habermas, Jäckel and company instrumentalized their relationship to their own views, thinking to themselves, 'Though the murder of the Jews was not especially unique, we Germans should say that it was, so as to encourage one another to face up squarely to our nation's past'? That is certainly not how it appears. It appears, rather, that they argued the murder of the Jews to be unique because they thought it was unique, and gave their reasons for thinking so. Had they not thought so, they could presumably have written (something like): 'Although the Holocaust was not unique, we Germans shouldn't be the ones to dwell on this. It has a different – apologetic – significance for us to dwell on it, as compared with others, who may. We do better to emphasize how terrible a crime the Holocaust was anyway, in order to make a full accounting of the recent history of our nation.' But though Habermas, Jäckel and others are indeed intent on such an accounting, they do not give it as the reason for asserting the Holocaust's singularity. No, they say that the Holocaust was unique and refer to features *of the event itself* which they take as establishing why it was. Could it be that they are merely feigning a commitment to this view – feigning it, because to give public expression to the tactical considerations which dictate what one thinks one ought to say can detract from the persuasive effect of saying it? I decline to take this hypothesis seriously. Even if it may apply to someone somewhere at some time, it is not a hypothesis that could explain the support for an intellectual position by the generality of its proponents, all of them apparently sincere and in earnest, as critics of the so-called relativization of the Holocaust were during the *Historikerstreit*.

We need to differentiate between two ways in which a view may be said to be dependent on the context in which it is put forward. Since, in the present case, context pretty well comes down to the identities of those whose view it is, I will speak, for short, of context-identity dependence; and distinguish the situation in which it is the cogency or validity of a view that is said to be context-identity dependent, from that in which it is its apt or prudent utterability that is said to be context-identity dependent. In the debate we are considering, it is clear that Nolte's critics in Germany thought it particularly *in*apt for the relativization of the Holocaust to be coming from German scholars. But it is equally clear, clear from the very form of their arguments on the point, that this was not a matter of their objecting, 'Relativization of the Holocaust is, in itself, sound; it is just not aptly utterable in the context – that is, by us Germans.' On the contrary, they deemed it neither sound in itself nor aptly utterable in the context. To paraphrase their objections, what they wrote was: 'Something new and unexpected happened there, at Auschwitz' (Habermas). Or: 'Never before had a state acted in such-and-such a way' (Jäckel). This is not the discourse of 'As Germans you shouldn't be saying it, even though it's true'; it is the discourse of 'It isn't true' – albeit with the subtext, 'and you, particularly, shouldn't be saying it'.

I return to the first of the two possibilities mooted in the paragraph before last. Perhaps Novick's suggestion should be taken to mean that insistence on the uniqueness of the Holocaust was not just commendable in the German context – that is, coming from Germans – it was actually valid in that context. But this possibility fares no better than the other. It is subject to the same difficulty. Although Nolte's critics plainly were concerned with the validity-status of the relativizing claim they impugned, the grounds on which they impugned it are not context-identity-dependent grounds. The language used is about what happened, about the specificity of the crimes perpetrated by the Nazi regime. It is not the language of a claim's being untrue *because* coming from Germans, as might be a fitting response to a German historian arguing, say, 'We were more sinned against than sinning.' It is of its being untrue just in virtue of its content, and *vis-à-vis* its object. And this will raise the question why, if a German philosopher may oppose or support a claim on that basis, the basis of what the claim says about the nature of the event to which it relates, a Jewish historian may not do so on precisely the same basis. Can Saul Friedlander be forbidden the identical judgement about the character of the Holocaust which Jürgen Habermas is permitted? Perhaps Friedlander is not forbidden it as such, not forbidden it *in foro interno*. It is merely that, believing the Holocaust unique for the same reason Habermas believes it, he should refrain from giving expression to this, because to do so could be interpreted as courting some kind of privileged consideration for the people to which he belongs. But what if the putative unique-making reason is not a reason of a privileging kind? And what, come to think of it, of scholars who are neither German nor Jewish?

In any event, the exercise Habermas, Jäckel and the rest appeared to believe they were engaged in was arguing over the content of opposing claims about the Holocaust, claims whose cogency they did not think of as dependent on the identity of their utterers, but as dependent on the character of the historical experience itself in its comparative relation to other experiences in the same broad conceptual field. Maybe they were misguided in thinking of the status of the claims in this way. For Novick, remember, insistence on the uniqueness of the Holocaust is 'an intellectually empty enterprise'. It is probably more sensible, therefore, to read his endorsement of *German* insistence on the uniqueness of the Holocaust according to the meaning I gave it at first: not as a revaluation by him of the intellectual substance (or rather lack of it) of the enterprise itself, but as an endorsement of good moral and political intentions. However, this then simply confirms that context is *not* always decisive. It is not decisive for everything that matters. It may well be crucial with regard to motive, intent and much else. But for the cogency or validity of certain intellectual claims, it is their content in relation to their given subject that counts, and not who puts them forward.[43]

It only remains, in this section, to attend to the idea that advocating the uniqueness of the Holocaust is an intellectually empty enterprise. I will argue that the considerations in light of which Novick comes to this conclusion are germane, but that the conclusion itself does not follow from them. They do serve, all the same, to highlight a central methodological point, one that has too often been neglected by those writing on the subject. Novick's contention is that, because every historical event both resembles and differs from other events in the relevant field of comparison, to concentrate on aspects of the Holocaust that were distinctive and 'ignore those aspects that it shares with other atrocities, and on the basis of this gerrymandering to declare [it] unique, is intellectual sleight of hand'. It is an argument he repeats: 'The claim that an event is unique … can be sustained only by gerrymandering: deliberately singling out one or more distinctive features of the event and trivializing or sweeping under the rug those features that it shares with other events to which it might be compared.'[44]

Now, it should indeed be obvious, as soon as one begins to think about this issue, that there is an uninteresting sense in which any event whatsoever can be said to be unique. Since, trivially, no event is ever exactly like another, the question of whether some particular event is unique demands of those addressing it some initial effort of reflection on what would render a positive answer to it non-trivial. In the case under discussion, we need to know whether there is anything *important* that sets the Holocaust apart. Was it an event with characteristics that could justify categorizing it in a different way from other events located nearby it conceptually: other slaughters, other genocides? Are there grounds for treating it as of a different *kind* from them (since to say it is unique is just to say that it is alone, so far, of its kind)? It is a reasonably familiar principle that, faced with a difficult question, one should examine the question carefully before looking for an answer to it. And yet it is remarkable how little self-conscious deliberation there has been about the nature of the question being posed when it is asked whether the Holocaust is unique. It is rarely even noted how unusual the question is. Think of another sort of case – one alluded to for comparison by Peter Novick himself. Think of wars. We might study the Crimean War, the American Civil War, the Franco-Prussian War, the First World War or the Gulf War and, for any one of these, simply take it for granted that in some respects it was an event similar to other such events, which is what made it a war, while in other respects it was different from them, making it that particular war to which we assign an individuating name. It is rare in most cases of historical enquiry to spend a lot of time debating whether a given event was unique, since the answer will always be that in some ways it was, and in other ways it wasn't. In the case of the Holocaust, however – a genocide among other genocides and other slaughters – not only is the question debated, it is debated with passion and sometimes rancour. But there is not much philosophical deliberation as to what the debate is at bottom about, why the question even arises in this instance.[45] Participants will trade back and forth empirical similarities or differences between the Holocaust and other horrors as if, without more ado, that could either establish or overturn the singularity claim. It cannot suffice. In the nature of the case, it cannot. For any event at all, it is always possible to isolate differences between it and other events, and it is always possible to identify similarities between it and other events. Without some focused, up-front reflection about why the empirical characteristics picked out are especially significant on one or another relevant dimension of significance, both argument and counter-argument will miss their mark.

Novick's conclusion that the advocacy on this issue is intellectually empty does not follow, for all that. It is not that there is no worthwhile question here. It is that he fails to identify what sort of question it is. And this is a question, as I have already intimated, of kind, of how we classify events. When we ask if the Holocaust was unique, we are asking about a putative category boundary. The question is no more vacuous in principle applied to the Holocaust than it is applied to anything else. Consider the uncontroversial difference between a chair and a stool. This is the difference, according to a simple dictionary definition, between a seat with a rest for the back, and a seat without either back or arms. In thinking and talking about furniture, do we in fact need such a distinction? Whether we strictly need it or not, we anyway do have it; as a matter of mere convenience probably, though it is easy to picture a community not having it which possessed both seats with backs and seats without them. However, is it, now, a case of gerrymandering, or intellectual sleight of hand, to have and make use of this distinction? Do we thereby ignore, trivialize or sweep under the rug what chairs and stools have in common – such as being, alike, seats, or (standardly) having legs, or (for some chairs) not having arms? Evidently not. All that matters is that the distinction is of sufficient significance, here day-to-day practical significance, that it proves helpful to us to mark it by a terminological boundary. Nothing pertinent seems to hinge on the uncontested simplicity of the example, on the fact that it concerns mere objects of furniture rather than events of great historical scope, with far-reaching consequences in terms of human suffering. If we move back closer to our subject by returning to the example of wars, it can be seen from amongst those I mentioned that, within the general category, we have one sub-category which we mark by referring to 'civil' wars, and another under which we have come to think of two of the wars of the twentieth century, calling them 'world' wars. Moving closer still, it has become common to pick out by the term 'genocide' a certain type and scale of mass killing from other cases of it – as being relatively distinct because threatening the continued existence of an entire people or ethnic group. Once again, does either having or availing oneself of these distinctions constitute gerrymandering, in the sense of some sort of conceptual funny business or rigging? Does it ignore or trivialize what world wars have in common with other wars so to focus on what distinguishes them by giving them this separate designation? Does it sweep under the rug the fact that massacres also involve cruel violence and killing to assign genocides to a class or sub-class of their own? Of course, particular uses of these distinctions might sometimes carry that intent. But it is not self-evident that all uses of them must; and I submit that they commonly do not.

They commonly do not, moreover, whether the categories in question are held to be purely descriptive or to be evaluative as well. That is to say, one might categorize the wars of 1914–18 and 1939–45 as world wars simply on grounds of scale, without any implication that all such global wars must be worse than other wars. Or one might think that they *are* worse, at least generally, because of the greater number of casualties and scale of suffering. Either way, one can remain properly sensible of the horrors of other wars. That you may be staggered by the carnage of the First World War does not entail that you take lightly what the US did in Vietnam. *Mutatis mutandis* with regard to genocides *vis-à-vis* other episodes of mass killing.

Whether 'genocide' is treated as a descriptive marker only or as encompassing events reckoned in general to be at the worse end of the wider category of mass killing to which they belong, use of the concept does not necessarily mean trivializing other occurrences within the wider category, much less ignoring them or sweeping them under the rug – though, obviously, it is possible for someone to misuse the concept of genocide in this way.

Whether or not the Holocaust was unique is a question governed by exactly the same sort of considerations. It asks if the event belongs in a class of its own. It does this whether or not it is explicitly signalled as doing so. Thus, for example, Yehuda Bauer has proposed the distinction between 'holocaust' and 'genocide' to separate events of the kind of which he thinks *the* Holocaust may so far be the only instance from genocides more generally.[46] But even where there is no sign of such methodological self-awareness on the part of the person posing it, that is what this question is about. For it prompts us to consider whether the Nazi onslaught against the Jews constitutes the only case to date *of its kind*. There is no reason in principle why the question should not be approached in the same way we would approach the other distinctions I have discussed: by examining what there is – if anything – of significance that could suffice to justify assigning the Holocaust to a separate category or sub-category; and according to what criteria, or within what framework, for estimating significance.

It is true, in consequence, that an answer to the uniqueness question calls for a value judgement of sorts.[47] But this will not be a value judgement any different from those applying to other classificatory boundaries. It will be a judgement about relative significance: about what, in the given conceptual context, counts as being important enough for us to want to register it. Not just any proposal for a linguistic boundary will pass. Try disseminating into general usage a special term for wars that begin in January; or for episodes of mass killing in which the victims number no fewer than ten thousand, but no more than twelve thousand. Even though the matter under discussion is one in which a definitive resolution, compelling the agreement of all, is unlikely to be forthcoming, reasons need to be provided, and these will be either more or less persuasive: reasons of principle, appealing to general considerations and in a public way, not trading on the identity or interests of their proponents.

What has gone before may be regarded as a prolegomenon to discussion of the question 'Was the Holocaust unique?' on such a basis, and just such a basis. Its aim has been to set up the examination of reasons one way and the other, for what they say, and dislocated from the attribution or condemnation of motives. I have shown how the opposing arguments on this question *can* be dislocated from the motivations (and identities) sometimes seen as being their real inspiration. If they can be, it is better that they are. The problem itself is a sufficient one.

III

I go on to consider the reasons most generally offered for the Holocaust-uniqueness claim. Note that the term 'unique' will carry throughout here the implicit proviso 'up to now'. For if one were to understand by it, not merely unparalleled hitherto, but unrepeatable, this would not be true either of the Holocaust or of any other great crime, except for a terminal act for the human species. The point has been made more than once before. As Primo Levi wrote, 'It happened, therefore it can happen again.'[48] Some, indeed, have suggested that, once given the precedent, a repetition becomes more likely: there is a model to copy; the barriers are lower.[49] In asking whether the Holocaust was unique, I am asking only if it is (of a kind) without parallel to this point in time.

By the same token, I set aside any thought of ineffable mystery attaching to the event, of the type proffered by certain religious Jewish thinkers, for whom the tragedy of the Jewish people under Nazism escapes or exceeds the boundaries of history.[50] Even though something of this thought is to be found also within a secular outlook – I have in mind expressions of a residual incomprehension in the face of vast evil or horror even when there are explanations for it in place[51] – such a sense of incomprehension is found much more widely than in reactions to the Jewish tragedy. It arises from the discrepancy between any massive human trauma and the normal day-to-day experience of people used to living in peace. The Holocaust was a real occurrence within recent history and should not be put beyond the reach of comparison. It can be compared in principle, compared on any dimension, with other human calamities and excesses.

Between five and six million Jews lost their lives in Nazi Europe, constituting some two-thirds of European Jewry and one-third of world Jewry as a whole. It has been estimated that about half of the Jewish dead perished in the death camps, equipped, these, with installations for rapid, large-scale gassing; another quarter in mass shootings; and the rest as a consequence of the dire conditions and brutalities in the ghettos and the concentration and labour camps, and on the death marches during the final months of the Nazi regime. Approximately half of the victims died during the single year of 1942. Does this historical experience stand apart in some significant way?

Stand apart from what? A grim catalogue of great length could be constructed in response, but I limit myself to a shorter, relatively modern, comparative list. Stand apart from the Turkish genocide against the Armenians in 1915, when some 1.5 million people were massacred as a matter of deliberate state policy and under cover of world war, the victims comprising about two-thirds of the Armenians living on Turkish soil and half the Armenian people overall. From the murder by the Khmer Rouge, under Pol Pot, of a million or maybe more of the people of Cambodia, out of a population of some seven million. From the blood-letting in Rwanda in 1994 when, during three months, eight hundred thousand of the Tutsi people were done to death, clubbed, hacked and shot. From the collectivization of agriculture, liquidation of the kulaks and political terror in the Soviet Union under Stalin, which led, through killing, famine and imprisonment in the camps of the Gulag, to millions of dead, the precise number a subject of dispute, but it could be 15 million or more. From what was done to other victims of the Nazi regime: among them Russian prisoners of war, 58 per cent of whom, numbering 3.3 million men, died in captivity – gassed, shot or starved, perishing from disease and overwork; among them, too, the Roma ('Gypsies'), of whom the Germans murdered between a quarter and a half a million, including two-thirds of those on German soil. And from the Atlantic slave trade. And from what has been called the American Holocaust: that is, the fate of the native peoples of the Americas as a result of European conquest and settlement. For the first of these, it is estimated that two million people died being transported across the Atlantic on the so-called 'middle passage', or within the first year thereafter; and that, in all, perhaps ten million lost their lives as a consequence of New World slavery. For the catastrophe that overtook the indigenous American peoples through settler oppression and violence and the epidemic diseases brought about by the arrival of Europeans, the total figure for the dead may be 30 million. In respect of both these last two cases there are also higher estimates.

One aspect of the above list, obviously, is the numbers it contains, in every instance huge, hard to bring within the compass of ordinary experience.[52] But as well as the numbers, there is also the magnitude of cruelty involved – the pleasure or indifference in brutality and murder – and the magnitude of suffering: of those who died violently and prematurely, and of people, also, who did not, who remained alive, the enslaved, the permanently ill, physically or mentally, those who survived with tormenting, ineradicable, memories of pain and loss. I leave the rich phenomenology of all this unelaborated, assuming the reader knows something of it or has it within the power of her imagination. Contemplating the vast catalogue of human atrocity, is there something importantly distinctive about the Holocaust, to justify its separate categorization as a unique horror?

The claim that there is rests, generally, on one or more of four features perceived to have characterized the event. In enumerating these, I shall not cite all the writers who have commented on them. I construct, rather, a composite account from arguments widely canvassed in the literature, referring directly to particular authors only as convenient. My purpose is not to evaluate the cogency of any single presentation of the case, but to assess an overall viewpoint. A composite treatment seems appropriate to doing this. I stress, therefore, that some of those on whose work I draw put only one of the following ideas to the fore and not another, perhaps even opposing this other, whilst others of them may make use of a couple of the ideas in combination, and so forth.

1. Totality of Intent

It has been proposed by many that what distinguished the destruction of European Jewry from other similar events was the comprehensive intent of those who oversaw it: it is the only case to date of the planned total physical annihilation of every member of an ethnic, national or religious group, every man, woman and child, simply because of who they were *qua* members of that group. In one version of this argument, as I earlier indicated, the comprehensive aim is used explicitly to mark off the concept of holocaust as such from that of genocide more generally, the complete physical destruction of the targeted group being contrasted with a collection of measures, including killing, which threatens the group's viability and separate identity without aiming physically to destroy all the individual members of it.[53] However this may be, there are two linked components within the argument: that there was a plan of total destruction; and, as this implies, that there was a more or less unified agency as the instrument of the plan – the German state. The second component points forward to the next theme.

2. *Modernity*

What I encapsulate under this heading is broader in scope and more variable in emphasis and detail than the argument from total intent, but there is a core common to most versions of it none the less. It is that while massacre, genocide, the obliteration of entire cultures, is historically nothing new, the Holocaust differs from other cases on account of its specifically modern methods, of the bureaucratization and industrialization of the killing process. The picture is of a centralized sovereign state, itself a phenomenon of modernity, making use of the characteristic products of modernity, all the scientific, technical and organizational resources at its command, and bringing these to bear in a planned way for the production of mass death outside warfare. Common here, also, is the notion of a pervasive spirit of instrumental rationality within a complex functional division of labour. Governed by principles and procedures which dehumanize those who are the objects of bureaucratic action, it weakens social impulses of moral concern for others. Further ideas are to be found around this central core, with some differences from author to author. For example, an analogy has been drawn between the labour processes developed by the Germans for the mass production of death and modern labour processes more broadly, the 'alienation of labour' distancing those implicated in the killing system from the results of their work, as the modern labourer typically is from the product of labour.[54] Or it is sometimes noted how many of the positive features of modern civilization were not only no barrier to the genocide but became complicit in it, law, science, medicine and the universities all playing their role; and noted, similarly, that the catastrophe occurred in Europe, in the heartland of the Enlightenment and despite it. There have been, in addition, cogent reflections – notably by Zygmunt Bauman[55] – on social and moral distance as a feature of modern societies and on how this likewise supported the killing process, contributing to the isolation of the victims. Such further ramifications notwithstanding, the basic argument is that the Holocaust was unique because of its characteristically modern methods. It was an industrialized process for the mass destruction of human beings.

3. *'Spiritual Murder'*

I take this term from Gitta Sereny,[56] and let it stand for a line of thought either prominent in, or just beneath the surface of, much writing about the singularity issue. I mean the thought that something else was involved in the murder of the Jews than the aim of their physical destruction only; there was an effort at a kind of moral annihilation as well. Through every form of depersonalization, humiliation, degradation and cruelty, to crush out the humanity of the victims in the process of destroying their lives; through use of the remains and appurtenances of the dead to mock and defile them; by secrecy, a denial of the very act of annihilation, to make nothing of their former existences, their past. Primo Levi has spoken in this connection of 'useless' violence and cruelty, explaining the debased meaning of the epithet in the given context as covering those brutalities that were surplus even to the aims of genocide: violence 'with the sole purpose of creating pain'; violence as 'pure offence'.[57]

4. An End in Itself

And this same idea has been applied to the genocidal project overall. The latter is perceived as having been, in a certain sense, 'for its own sake', self-sufficient as an end and not a means towards some other end. The argument must be read according to a principle of interpretative charity, otherwise it can appear inconsistent with a thesis that usually accompanies it. What I take it to mean is that the murder of the Jews was not in pursuit of any 'normal' economic, political, military, territorial or other such practical objective. It was not a means of war, or for the acquisition of land or other assets, or for extending the sway of an empire, or towards altering the configuration of political power. It was, so far, an end in itself: to get rid of the Jews, no more (though also no less). It was relentlessly pursued, often at the expense of other key aims. In a situation of wartime labour shortage, potentially exploitable labour was killed off unused or underused. Trains that might have been put towards the war effort were given over to carrying people to the death camps. It is true, of course, that certain economic benefits were derived from the 'Final Solution', as with the exploitation of Jewish slave labour and the reallocation ('Aryanization') of Jewish businesses, apartments and other property. But these benefits were incidental, not primary. The overriding objective was the destruction of the Jews.

The justification of this objective was not, then, practical. It was not predicated on some other realistic goal, however noxious it might for its part be. The justification was metaphysical, quasi-religious, pseudo-scientific. It was to cleanse the world of an evil and demonic force, a racial parasite, and in this the goal was tendentially universal, not territorially bound (as, for example, the Turkish genocide against the Armenians is argued to have been). The form of justification, it will be evident, can be recast so that the genocidal aim is *not* for its own sake but a means to an end: that, precisely, of a world cleansed of demonic evil, racial impurity or what have you. But I interpret the argument in a way which renders it internally consistent. I interpret it as saying that the destruction of the Jews was not undertaken with any other real practical or attainable objective in mind, not even a morally dubious one like seizing the territory or resources of the dead. It was done for itself, its basis merely hatred and delusion.

I shall now briefly review these arguments, keeping to the same fourfold schema and considering initially what might be said for and against each one taken separately. In doing so, I continue with the composite approach as before, drawing freely on themes to be found within the relevant literature, though henceforth also supplementing them with suggestions of my own.

A. Totality of Intent

One line of sceptical argument has questioned whether it is even appropriate to characterize so complex an event as the Holocaust in terms of the simplifying purposive category of intention. The multiple causes, decisions and processes that were involved in the destruction of the Jews cannot be subsumed, so this argument goes, under the rubric of a single, originary genocidal intention.[58] The counter-suggestion may be offered to this that, whenever or however it emerged, there was eventually a plan for the annihilation of the Jews, and it was crucial to what ensued, irrespective of the (otherwise pertinent) observations concerning the complexities of the overall process. It was crucial to the character of the genocide as an authoritatively willed and concerted project. There is another, quite different, objection, however: which is that, since the focus of the claim is on the comprehensiveness of the genocidal intention and, measured against the scope of that intention, the Nazis failed, it is unpersuasive to stress just this feature of the Holocaust as determining its singularity.[59] Although they succeeded in destroying two-thirds of European Jewry and uprooted a rich, centuries-old cultural tradition in the process, Hitler and his followers none the less failed to destroy the Jews as a people even in parts of Europe, leave aside in the world as a whole. In the categorization of their crime, is the intention more important than the result?

B. Modernity

There is no doubt that the modernity theme does pick out something significant about the Holocaust, pertinently characterizing many of its prominent features. More contentious is whether what it picks out is significant for how we should classify it in relation to comparable events. Significant in what way? Significant for how we are to understand it, or for how we place it historically, or in terms of its relative moral gravity? As variable in emphasis and detail as the modernity theme may be with its various proponents, a common strand has been that the Holocaust was a case not merely of mass killing, but of a peculiarly cold and efficient system of mass killing, one which turned death into the end point of a virtual production line. Its systemic quality provides the key to grasping why and how it unfolded. It gave the process an impersonality, and produced a dispersal and obscuring of individual responsibility, that were part of its lethal dynamic. And it was dehumanizing as well as murderous, its constitutive procedures and language negating the personhood of the victims, who became no more than objects to be processed. Against this it may be said that the technology of any genocide – broadly construed: its material instruments and other resources, forms of organization, associated mind-set and so on – will necessarily be of its time and place. That the Holocaust was marked by the typical features of modernity is true, but is it to the point in deciding on classificatory boundaries?[60] For example, modes of dehumanization characteristic of modernity may well have been central to it, but the dehumanization of enemies and victims is itself a common historical phenomenon – as is illustrated by anti-Semitism, also of critical importance to what occurred. Furthermore, although a vision of bureaucratized, technological mass murder has widely dominated thinking about the Holocaust owing to the potent imagery of the gas chambers in public consciousness, nevertheless a very large number and proportion of the Jewish dead were killed in quite traditional or 'primitive' ways. They were shot, beaten, tortured, starved. Should we see the event's distinctiveness as a genocide in a way that implicitly marginalizes these victims? In any case, is the use of the most up-to-date methods of killing people worse than more old-fashioned ways of killing them? The imagery of the gas chambers is indeed a terrible one. But is it more terrible than that of the killing by club and machete by which the Tutsis were slaughtered in Rwanda?

C. *'Spiritual Murder'*

It has sometimes been asked why, if the victims were to be murdered in any event, the killers and their accomplices indulged in the many practices of prior reduction that they did, depriving people of all symbols and tokens of their former identity, humiliating them in imaginative ways, imposing incidental forms of extreme suffering. One answer, given by Franz Stangl, the commandant of Treblinka, was that this made the work of the killers more manageable psychologically.[61] The significance of the theme may be thought, anyway, to speak for itself. It is that, added to the intended physical extinction of the Jews, there was the extra pain and horror of a kind of moral death. Advocacy on the other side could point to comparable experiences of other groups of victims. It is a widespread phenomenon of massacre, after all, that it is accompanied by cruelties and humiliations of every sort, since there appears to be a tendency in human beings – or in enough human beings where the conditions facilitate this – to enjoy inflicting pain on others. More exceptional would be the example of massacre carried through with an attitude of respect towards the doomed. Then again, however, it might be said that what was involved in the case of the Holocaust went beyond a general tendency to cruelty or excess on the part of people carried away by blood-lust. There was an elaborate set of procedures, methodically worked out, 'improved' over time, for the sole purpose of dehumanizing the victims, of cancelling their status as persons.

D. *An End in Itself*

In Raul Hilberg's formulation, the Holocaust was 'willed for itself and … accomplished for its own sake'. Is this a difference of importance? Why, it might particularly be asked, is it decisive for those targeted? For them, surely, the reasons for their impending doom would be less important than the fact of it. Perhaps it is not a matter of its being worse for them, only a matter of its explanatory significance: that, as Hilberg argues, the Holocaust cannot be accommodated within any of the more usual frameworks of political explanation.[62] And yet some representations of the point do appear to suggest that it is seen as marking a moral distinction. I have quoted Richard Evans referring to the Nazi genocide 'as a gratuitous act'; and Charles Maier saying that only in Nazi Europe was there 'an apparatus … established to carry out mass murder as a process in its own right'.[63] So are we looking here at something worse or only at something … different?

It seems like an apt moment to recall my earlier admonition. In the effort of trying to answer the Holocaust-uniqueness question, we need to think carefully about the nature of the question itself. Unless we do, the reasons passing to and fro before us risk appearing altogether unanchored. They float free of any express criteria for assessing comparative importance. I have proposed that this question is a question of kind: of appropriate classificatory boundaries. In doing so I also said, however, that responding to it calls for a specification of the framework within which we are to adjudge significance. This does not just go without saying; it needs to be spelled out. Otherwise it is difficult to gauge why any consideration offered this way or that is thought to be relevant, let alone important or decisive. So what finally, what in blunt and simple terms, is the uniqueness debate *about*? Picking up a thread that has run through this discussion from the start, I will contend that the claim that the Holocaust was unique is to be viewed as a normative claim. It is not usefully understood as just a matter of descriptive or explanatory taxonomy.

This may seem obvious to many, too obvious perhaps to be worth the argument. But it is sometimes denied by writers who support the claim. I think their denial should be discounted – though I come back in due course to what I believe it may more loosely reflect. At least three reasons tell against accepting it at face value. The first and most straightforward of them is that in certain cases it can be shown textually that the author of the denial somewhere goes back on it. He may want not to be saying that the Holocaust was worse than other extreme and terrible events, but somewhere he does say it, revealing a moral ranking in his thinking on the issue. Thus, for example, Charles Maier is ostensibly very clear about this, writing: 'The point ... is not that the genocide of the Jews was somehow worse, but that it had its own unique characteristics.' Or again: the National Socialist crime is set apart, he says, 'not necessarily making it "worse" but making it different, and appalling and unassimilable'.[64] The strain in these formulations is manifest, however. Every event within the given field of comparison is different, or has its unique characteristics. Maier needs more, so he adds 'appalling' and 'unassimilable'. But it is still not enough. Of which genocide, great slaughter or massacre could the same thing not be said? He leans towards what, finding it troubling to think, he has denied: some notion of worse. In truth, we already know he has embraced it. For he has said as much on the first page of his book, with the special, irremovable taint there will be on German nationhood if its crime is adjudged to be singular rather than one amongst others of a kind.[65] Another example is Yehuda Bauer. In one of his several discussions of this question, Bauer writes of a continuum of evil leading from mass murder through genocide to holocaust, and he goes on: 'Such a continuum does not imply a value judgement as to the degree of moral condemnation, so that one could argue that "mass murder" is in some way less reprehensible than "genocide" or "holocaust".' He overlooks the fact that he has introduced this very discussion with the opposite thought: speaking of how we differentiate between, and 'grade', types of good and evil; and how we do the same with respect to crimes, seeing these as 'more serious or less so'. And, lecturing on the same topic on another occasion, Bauer has called upon the Jewish members of his audience to think about how and why the Jews came to face 'the most terrible thing any civilization has faced to date'.[66]

Second, and more generally, the whole dispute is permeated by implicitly normative assumptions. We might reconsider, in this connection, the language of 'normalization' and 'relativization' used during the *Historikerstreit*, and since. The charge of normalization itself presupposes the abnormality of the Holocaust; and abnormality, be it noted, not in relation to such relatively unstartling political, economic and social phenomena as elections, cabinet reshuffles, protest demonstrations, interest rate fluctuations, trading pacts, patterns of marriage and divorce, changing trends in fashion and so on; but in relation to events that, like the Holocaust, consumed enormous numbers of lives in conditions of extreme suffering. The same applies to the charge of relativization. One need not be so literal-minded as to infer from it the idea of the Holocaust as an 'absolute' (whatever this would mean), but it does imply, at least, a view of the event as exceptional, not to be swallowed up, or not to be swallowed up entirely, within the general category of other mass calamities. It may be suggested that the implicit notions of a general 'norm', and of the Holocaust's abnormality when set against it, were deployed purely descriptively in these arguments, involving no moral component; and likewise for the Holocaust's exceptionality *vis-à-vis* the general category. But *that* is a suggestion I would feel not worth extensive counter-argument. Those alleging 'normalization' and 'relativization' were plainly writing in morally disapprobatory mode; they condemned, or lamented, what they saw as a deficiency of moral perception. This was not just intellectual criticism of an alternative framework to their own for understanding German history.

Third, only if we take the claim in a moralized meaning will it pass the test of significance. I do not say that this must – logically – be so, merely that it is so on the balance of the arguments actually in play. Let us take the view of Steven Katz in illustration of the point. Like others, Katz professes his support for the uniqueness claim in what he says is a non-moralized version, and he has maintained his position during the better part of two decades, taking the trouble to try to answer the sceptical challenge he has met with on this score. The Holocaust, according to him, is 'phenomenologically unique' – in asserting which, he insists, he is '*not* simultaneously endorsing the injudicious claim that the Holocaust is *more evil* than alternative occurrences of extensive and systematic persecution, organized violence, and mass death'. Again: he is '*not* making a *moral* claim'; for he 'know[s] of no method or technique that would allow one to weigh up, to quantify and compare, such massive evil and suffering'.[67]

Rather than challenging them,[68] let us give Katz the benefit of his own disavowals, to see where they lead. His argument for the uniqueness of the Holocaust is a version of the first of the four themes discussed above, totality of intent. It has to be considered why, consequently, if we take this as a strictly non-moralized differentiation, the intention to kill all the Jews, an intention that went unconsummated, should be seen as uniquely significant. Bear in mind what else occupies our field of attention for the given purpose, the purpose of estimating relative significance: a substantial list of events, all of them encompassing gigantic numbers of violent deaths and horrifying levels of cruelty and suffering. Bear in mind, also, that we are not just trying to identify characteristics of the Holocaust that might be, in a general sense, of note or interest. They must be, rather, of sufficient note and interest to justify our opening a separate category for this single event on the list. If the unconsummated intention (of *no* differentiating moral import) to get rid of all the Jews meets this condition, it is hard to see why one could not also open a separate category for other of the historical episodes within our field of attention, even possibly for all of them. You could open a category for the Rwandan genocide because of the extraordinary levels of mass participation it involved and the resulting speed of it by more or less one-on-one killing methods. You could open a category for the Cambodian auto-genocide because of the anti-urban impulse by which, among other things, it was driven. Not to be misunderstood about this: I highlight features of the Rwandan and Cambodian experiences that are not trivial from an analytic or explanatory point of view, no more than is the Nazi intention to annihilate the Jews a trivial feature of the Holocaust. But if that intention (of *no* differentiating moral import) suffices to justify a separate category for the Holocaust, then it is not clear why the highlighted characteristics of the Rwandan and Cambodian experiences would not equally justify a separate category for each of them. This produces trivialization of the uniqueness claim at a higher level, as it were: with the Holocaust unique, not as (say) the only genocide initiated by Germans against Jews, but because of its comprehensive, though unfulfilled, intent; the Cambodian genocide unique, not as the only genocide presided over by Pol Pot, but because of its anti-urban thrust; the Rwandan genocide unique, not simply because, unlike any other genocide, it took place in Rwanda in 1994, but because of its mass-participant character; and so forth. We would have a whole number of 'unique' genocides in this non-morally differentiated style, each sitting within its own category on account of analytically and explanatorily significant features.[69] I repeat: there is nothing untoward, from a logical point of view, about such a highly pluralized non-moral taxonomy. But it is to be doubted that it would have generated the expenditure of energy in arguing the issue that the debate about the Holocaust in fact has generated. My argument is that when the moral content of the Holocaust-singularity claim is taken as consistently renounced, the discussion simply fragments into a pluralization of separate categories mapping on to a multiplicity of differences, with the Holocaust no more exceptional, no more 'standing apart', than many other cognate experiences.[70] It is the framework of a presumed morally significant differentiation which has lent the singularity claim both its focus and its sensitivity, and it is whether or not there is a morally significant differentiation that we need to consider in coming to a conclusion.

The question is whether the Holocaust was worse than other comparable historical phenomena, and we have therefore to ask: worse in what way, according to what criterion or combination of criteria? One seemingly obvious candidate for an answer is: worse in terms of human suffering. Indeed, I believe it is precisely because this is an answer which suggests itself that so many of those arguing for the uniqueness of the Holocaust are prompted to deny that worse is in fact what they mean. The denial, I hypothesize, is to acquit themselves of a discomfort they would feel at being taken in that sense.[71] Like Steven Katz, but not always as explicitly, they shy away from the idea of a weighing up, a discrimination, between episodes of suffering all so massive. I think their intuition in this is right. There are strong reasons speaking against the idea that the Holocaust was worse in terms of human suffering than comparable historical events.

For supposing, first, that some rough quantification of suffering is an appropriate exercise in this context, one could only conclude that the Jewish tragedy must be dwarfed by experiences where the numbers were much greater, as it itself would

dwarf the smaller-numbered ones. We might come back to the Atlantic slave trade
and New World slavery for an example, with an approximate figure for the dead of
ten million, together with the manifold cruelties which the institution and the
practices of that slavery involved. At the levels of human suffering we are talking
about – generally intense and often terminal – it is hard to see what else to do in
quantifying but to count each victim as one, and conclude that, over the greater
number as well as the longer time span, the suffering in this case must have
exceeded that of the Jews in Nazi Europe.

However, such comparative quantification is, arguably, not appropriate, and the
attempt to aggregate suffering across these very large numbers questionable. We
have to remember that when we talk of the suffering of European Jewry, or of any
other mass-victim population, there is not some single aggregate subject that
experienced the total of Jewish, or other, suffering as a unified quantity of pain and
anguish. There are just a lot of individual experiences of those things – though they
are, of course, interrelated to an extent, in that most of the individual experiences
will include a component of pain at witnessing, or merely knowing about, the pain
of others. But the pains remain, for all that, disaggregated individual experiences.
There is no one supra-individual subject of them all. Real and terrible as all these
individual experiences of pain are, aggregating them therefore yields an abstract
quantity, not the single lived subjectivity of *anyone*.[72] What is more, even if we did
want to compare two such abstract quantities, aggregating them is fraught with
difficulty. Two deaths, for example, however they must be reckoned as of equal
import on a certain scale of value, do not necessarily involve the same amount – the
same duration or intensity – of suffering for the individuals whose deaths they are.
It is common experience, as well, that different people bear the same affliction –
whether illness, injury, assault, restraint – with different degrees of fortitude,
making it hard to know whether, 'from the inside', their suffering from the same
apparent external cause is equivalent. We have no reliable way of overcoming these
difficulties to make a summation across millions of separate human beings. What
we know, all we know, is that, here these millions of individuals, there those (greater
or lesser) millions of individuals, suffered; many of them suffered terribly; and they
suffered, each one, *as* an individual. Both here and there, consequently, millions of
suffering individuals, their combined pain unencompassable as a phenomenological
unity by any mind. Be it these millions or those, in the way of human suffering this
is as bad as we can get to grasp. Or it is, at any rate, more than bad enough.

Unless there is some clear other purpose for doing so, we should not rank the
different experiences on the dimension of total suffering, in order not to diminish by
the ranking. For to say that one experience was worse in terms of suffering is to say
that the other was not as bad; and then, however many saving or qualifying clauses
you enter, you arouse the suspicion of belittling other instances of grave suffering.
Sometimes this may be, indeed, the deliberate purpose of the ranking. But even
where it is not, the logic of the comparison is belittling literally: it purports to show
one quantity littler than another. This is a logic, moreover, of a potentially
irremediable cynicism since, given the scale of the catastrophes that have already
been visited by human beings upon other human beings, and given what these add
up to (loosely speaking) in the way of human suffering, there is not now much, short

of a secular Armageddon, that could not be diminished by the comparative exercise. The discourse of competitive victimhood – and it is obscure what other purpose might be served in the present context by such comparisons – is morally ugly. Whatever may be due to people for the torments they, or those related to them, have endured, the historical episodes within our field of attention all lie well beyond any threshold that could reasonably be suggested as a qualifying one.

If the Holocaust was worse, the judgement that it was must be supported by other reasons than the suffering involved. I propose, in conclusion, what I believe may be a viable basis for that judgement. As I indicated in the introduction to this essay I am not aware of the proposal having been made before. At the same time, I view it as in large part hermeneutical. That is to say, it seeks to give a more exact and rounded sense to intimations that are already there in the literature, to sometimes only brief remarks – from Hannah Arendt, Jürgen Habermas, Saul Friedlander and others – but which have not, as I see it, been adequately supported and explained hitherto. The proposal, in any case, is this: that the perception of the Holocaust as unique does have an objective basis in the character of the event, but in order to identify it, the focus of the discussion must be moved away from the victim to the perpetrator, from the scale of suffering to the nature of the crime, and from any idea that there might be a single decisive differentiating feature to recognizing a cluster of several features. I think it is then possible to explicate a concept and image singularly ominous for humankind, to give sense to what, in Saul Friedlander's words, 'has haunted the human imagination' since this catastrophe occurred.[73]

The key is to give up on the idea that, for the Holocaust to have been unique in a morally significant sense, there must be a single characteristic, some one distinguishing feature, that makes it so. No, there mustn't. (More accurately: no, there needn't.) I marshal in support of this contention an argument that is due to Wittgenstein; I have in mind his remarks in the *Philosophical Investigations* about what games have in common. Wittgenstein writes:

> Don't say: 'There *must* be something common, or they would not be called "games"' – but *look and see* whether there is anything common to all … [D]on't think but look!

There is not in fact one common something that characterizes all games. There are what Wittgenstein calls 'family resemblances': in other words, bundles of shared features from a larger cluster of relevant features, which, in different combinations, connect the activities we call 'games' to one another in the way that members of a family can sometimes be linked by visual resemblances, without any one single feature being observable in them all.[74] Now, this suggestion is not always applicable to the delineation of a concept or category. There are concepts for which we can specify the necessary and sufficient conditions for counting some particular entity as an instantiation of them, and concepts for which we can specify the necessary conditions alone. But for others, like games – and tables and chairs, etc. – we cannot. It is merely a sufficient combination of features from a relevant cluster of them that qualifies a given thing, situation or whatever, for inclusion within the boundaries of the concept in question. Wittgenstein, to be sure, was referring to concepts which have multiple instantiations, where *ex hypothesi* here we are dealing with a putative category with only one instantiation to date. But it does not affect the basic methodological point: which is that a category boundary may be appropriate between the Holocaust and other comparable experiences, though none of the candidate differentiating features alone distinguishes it in a morally significant way – for jointly maybe they do.

This, anyway, is my hypothesis: that just in their combination – of total intent; the bureaucratization and industrialization of killing; spiritual murder or moral annihilation; and the pursuit of the project 'for its own sake' – these features of the Holocaust may have added up to something morally singular, and singularly terrible in the public consciousness of our time. This something I will call an *ongoing, and tendentially permanent, social system for the production of death*. Its nearly perfect institutional expression, even though this was not exhaustive of the experience as a whole, was the death camp – whose historical specificity has not, so far as I know, been challenged. The death camp was a type of place, an established institution, into which people arrived to be divided into those to be killed immediately and others to be put, in Hannah Arendt's telling phrase, 'into a permanent status of dying'.[75] This was death not at the margins of life; or at the point or the scene of conflict between different organizations, societies or cultures; or as an outbreak of temporary violence or a breakdown of social controls. It was death as a veritable system of production, as a regularized order of existence. In the words of one commentator on the significance of Auschwitz, 'Here death ... became a way of life ... This was the worst that has ever happened.'[76]

It is in the nature of the hypothesis I am proposing that no one feature of the four which have been itemized and discussed above suffices by itself to capture the whole specifity of the human catastrophe fashioned by Nazism, and that each of them is, in a certain way, 'imperfect': either incomplete, or not altogether specific to the given historical experience, or both. Still, the catastrophe was determined by them in conjunction, drawing something of its quality as a system for the production of death from each one. The comprehensiveness of the Nazi intent meant there would be in principle, in the 'final' analysis, no escape for those defined as Jews, neither through conversion nor through changing their relationship to the goals of the Nazi polity. The industrial technology – again broadly construed: material instruments and modes of organization – though it was not all-prevailing, was entirely apt to a project so shaped for the mass production of death, giving it regularity, predictability and efficiency, and easing the moral discomforts of those implicated in the process of executing it. The efforts at nullifying the status of the victims as persons were similarly apt to a social system in which some human beings are become merely trash: morally nothing either before or after being disposed of; to *which* anything at all can be done before, and from *which* the physical remains can be taken after, to be put to some utilitarian purpose. And that the whole thing was pursued as an end itself in the sense earlier specified, not for any instrumental reason beyond itself, meant that the negation of the humanity of the Jews was unconditional: it was not an ideological cover or superstructure, whether self-conscious or unconscious, for any material gain or goal. This circumstance may or may not have made the deaths suffered worse than deaths which are suffered for other reasons. I do not believe anyone can say as a generality. However, there is, I detect, a sense some people have that a death inflicted unconditionally – simply for hatred or simply for nothing – is a worse crime by the perpetrator than one for instrumental purposes, and whether these are conscious or whether the hatred is an unconscious cover for them. It is as if the feeling of a need that there be such purposes still acknowledges on some minimal level that the victims are people for whom reasons are needed, and not merely trash for which none are.[77] The Jews, in consequence of Nazi policy as it evolved into the so-called 'Final Solution', had come to represent a human universal in their particularity, so to say. They had come to represent ineluctable victimhood. But though it was as Jews that they did so, it was because of something, simple identity – not words said, deeds performed, obstacles posed – that it can at any time become true of anybody and everybody.

Such, if the arguments here carry weight, was the specificity, the uniqueness, of the Nazi crime. It was not that the Jews suffered, or that they mattered, more than other victim groups or peoples. The singularity was not in the suffering, but in the nature of what was perpetrated. And it bears a moral horror unparalleled by other crimes and disasters, not through any single feature of it, but because of a cluster of features which combined into a frightening precedent, an appalling permanent possibility for the future of our species: the production of death as an order of being, an established system of existence. In that, it touched nearer to the final limit of our species – the wilful destruction of humanity itself – than any other event has done so far. But it could happen again. If it were to, we or others to come would immediately recognize the fraternity of the new horror with the Judeocide.

That it happened to them grants the Jews no moral privilege as a people. It does, however, leave some generations of Germans with a morally unique crime to live down and make amends for. Still, it is some generations only. No taint can stand in perpetuity. Although there is a reality to the identity of nations and the continuities within them, no collective guilt is everlasting or constraining on the distantly unborn.

Notes

1.   *The Nazis: A Warning from History*, BBC2 1997. Ian Kershaw is credited as Historical and Script Consultant to the series.
2.   S. Lindqvist (1996), *'Exterminate All the Brutes'*, London: Granta Books, p. x.
3.   I. McEwan (1998), *Black Dogs*, London: Vintage, p. 37.
4.   P. Hayward (1998), 'The race to free football from poison', *Guardian*, 25 February.
5.   A. Karpf (1998), 'Child of the Shoah', *Guardian*, 11 February. The article was about Binjamin Wilkomirski's *Fragments* (1996, London: Picador), a work which has since been exposed as fraudulent.
6.   N. Lezard (1999), 'Reich of death', *Guardian*, 24 July.
7.   M.A. Bernstein (1998), 'Homage to the Extreme', *Times Literary Supplement*, 6 March.
8.   T. Garton Ash (1998), 'The Black and the Red', *Prospect*, June.
9.   E. Nolte (1988), 'Between Historical Myth and Revisionism?' and 'A Past That Will Not Pass Away', *Yad Vashem Studies* **19**, at pp. 51–61 and 68, 71 respectively. Also in J. Knowlton and T. Cates (trans.) (1993), *Forever in the Shadow of Hitler?*, Atlantic Highlands, NJ: Humanities Press, pp. 2–14 and 19, 22.
10. I. Kershaw (1989), *The Nazi Dictatorship: Problems and Perspectives of Interpretation*, 2nd edn, London: Edward Arnold, p. 173.

11. J. Habermas (1989), *The New Conservatism: Cultural Criticism and the Historians' Debate*, Cambridge: Polity Press, pp. 251–2.
12. H. Arendt (1977), *Eichmann in Jerusalem*, London: Penguin, p. 279.
13. E. Jäckel (1988), 'The Miserable Practice of the Insinuators: The Uniqueness of the National-Socialist Crime Cannot be Denied', *Yad Vashem Studies* **19**, p. 110. See also Knowlton and Cates, *Forever in the Shadow of Hitler?*, p. 76.
14. R.J. Evans (1989), *In Hitler's Shadow: West German Historians and the Attempt to Escape from the Nazi Past*, London: I.B. Tauris, pp. 86–9, 102.
15. C.S. Maier (1988), *The Unmasterable Past: History, Holocaust, and German National Identity*, Cambridge, MA and London: Harvard University Press, pp. 71–84, at p. 82.
16. Ibid., p. 1.
17. P. Papazian (1984), 'A "Unique Uniqueness"?', *Midstream* **30**, April, pp. 14–18.
18. D.E. Stannard (1996), 'Uniqueness as Denial: The Politics of Genocide Scholarship', in A.S. Rosenbaum (ed.), *Is the Holocaust Unique? Perspectives on Comparative Genocide*, Boulder, CO: Westview Press, pp. 163–208, at pp. 167, 182.
19. Ibid., p. 197. Emphasis in the original.
20. Ibid., pp. 190, 167, 194.
21. N.G. Finkelstein (2000), *The Holocaust Industry: Reflections on the Exploitation of Jewish Suffering*, London: Verso, p. 8.
22. Ibid., pp. 44–7, 54.
23. Ibid., pp. 8, 47.
24. Ibid., pp. 48–9, 54.
25. P. Novick (2000), *The Holocaust and Collective Memory: The American Experience*, London: Bloomsbury, pp. 9, 197, 212.
26. Ibid., pp. 9, 196.
27. Ibid., pp. 14–15.
28. G. Steiner (1988), 'The Long Life of Metaphor: An Approach to the "Shoah"', in Berel Lang (ed.), *Writing and the Holocaust*, New York: Holmes & Meier, p. 158. (The essay is reprinted from *Encounter* **68**, February 1987, pp. 55–61.)
29. T. Todorov (1996), *Facing the Extreme: Moral Life in the Concentration Camps*, New York: Metropolitan Books, p. 117.
30. For the sources for, and a discussion of, Mandel's views on this matter see N. Geras (1997), 'Marxists before the Holocaust', *New Left Review* **224**, July/August, pp. 19–38. Reprinted as chapter 4 of N. Geras (1998), *The Contract of Mutual Indifference: Political Philosophy after the Holocaust*, London: Verso, pp. 139–70.
31. I. Deutscher (1968), 'The Jewish Tragedy and the Historian', in his *The Non-Jewish Jew and other essays*, London: Oxford University Press, pp. 163–4.
32. See P. Levi (1987), *If This Is A Man*, and *The Truce*, London: Abacus, pp. 391, 394–6; and P. Levi (1989), *The Drowned and the Saved*, London: Abacus, pp. 9–10.
33. F. Camon (1989), *Conversations with Primo Levi*, Marlboro, VT: The Marlboro Press, p. 68; and Levi, *If This Is A Man*, pp. 135–6.
34. R. Hilberg (1980), 'The Significance of the Holocaust', in H. Friedlander and S. Milton (eds), *The Holocaust: Ideology, Bureaucracy, and Genocide*, New York: Kraus International Publications, pp. 95–6.
35. S. Friedlander (1991), 'The "Final Solution": On the Unease in Historical Interpretation', in P. Hayes (ed.), *Lessons and Legacies: The Meaning of the Holocaust in a Changing World*, Evanston, IL: Northwestern University Press, pp. 23–35 (reprinted in S. Friedlander (1993), *Memory, History, and the Extermination of the Jews of Europe*, Bloomington: Indiana University Press, pp. 102–16). See also S. Friedlander (1984), 'From Anti-Semitism to Extermination', *Yad Vashem Studies* **16**, pp. 1–16 and 48–50; his Introduction to G. Fleming (1985), *Hitler and the Final Solution*, London:

Hamish Hamilton, pp. vii–xxxiii; and S. Friedlander (1993), *Reflections of Nazism: An Essay on Kitsch and Death*, Bloomington: Indiana University Press, pp. 120–27.

36. Friedlander, 'Historical Writing and the Memory of the Holocaust', in Lang, *Writing and the Holocaust*, p. 77.

37. Y. Bauer (1978), *The Holocaust in Historical Perspective*, London: Sheldon Press, pp. 43–9. For these points see, further, Y. Bauer (1980), 'Whose Holocaust?', *Midstream* **26**, September, pp. 42–6; 'The Place of the Holocaust in Contemporary History', in J.K. Roth and M. Berenbaum (eds) (1989), *Holocaust: Religious and Philosophical Implications*, New York: Paragon House, pp. 16–42 (reprinted from *Studies in Contemporary Jewry* **1**, 1984, pp. 201–24); and 'Genocide: Was it the Nazis' Original Plan?', in M.R. Marrus (ed.) (1989), *The Nazi Holocaust 3. The "Final Solution": The Implementation of Mass Murder*, Westport, CT: Meckler, Volume 1, pp. 74–84, at pp. 83–4 (reprinted from *Annals of the American Academy of Political and Social Science* **450**, July 1980, pp. 35–45).

38. See Finkelstein, *The Holocaust Industry*, pp. 3, 7, 12, 71, 96, 98–9, 108, 110, 127–8.

39. Novick, *The Holocaust and Collective Memory*, pp. 331–2, n. 121.

40. K. Seeskin (1988), 'What Philosophy Can and Cannot Say about Evil', in A. Rosenberg and G.E. Myers (eds), *Echoes from the Holocaust: Philosophical Reflections on a Dark Time*, Philadelphia, PA: Temple University Press, pp. 91–100; the statement quoted is at p. 93.

41. L.M. Thomas (1993), *Vessels of Evil: American Slavery and the Holocaust*, Philadelphia, PA: Temple University Press, pp. 6–11, 125, 147, 162–3.

42. A hypothesis put forward by Yehuda Bauer in 'Whose Holocaust?' – see n. 37 above.

43. The same thing emerges more swiftly from Norman Finkelstein's treatment of the same issue. In the closing lines of his book, his tirade against the singularity thesis many pages behind him, Finkelstein evidently feels a need to acknowledge the German argument of the 1980s against 'normalizing' the Holocaust. He makes a brief, two-line movement towards the importance of context: if that argument, he says, may have been valid then, it no longer carries conviction, for the staggering dimensions of the 'Final Solution' are by now well known. He then follows up immediately with a would-be qualification: 'And isn't the "normal" history of humankind replete with horrifying chapters of inhumanity?' Of course, it is replete with them. However, if it is replete with them now, it was also replete with them then, in the mid-1980s, all of 15 years ago – as were the dimensions of the 'Final Solution' already well known. So, whatever momentary impulse it may have been that moved Finkelstein to this gesture of recognition for Nolte's German critics, it turns out to be empty. The context makes no difference to the point of substance. See *The Holocaust Industry*, p. 150.

44. Novick, *The Holocaust and Collective Memory*, pp. 9, 196.

45. An exception to this is A. Rosenberg (1987), 'Was the Holocaust Unique?: A Peculiar Question?', in I. Walliman and M.N. Dobkowski (eds), *Genocide and the Modern Age: Etiology and Case Studies of Mass Death*, New York: Greenwood Press, pp. 145–61, at pp. 145–6, 149.

46. See his 'The Place of the Holocaust in Contemporary History'.

47. See Friedlander, *Memory, History, and the Extermination of the Jews of Europe*, p. 81.

48. Levi, *The Drowned and the Saved*, p. 167. Cf. Bauer, 'The Place of the Holocaust in Contemporary History', in Roth and Berenbaum, *Holocaust*, p. 34: 'because it happened once, it may happen again – to any group if the conditions are right'; and *The Holocaust in Historical Perspective*, p. 37.

49. For instance, Arendt, *Eichmann in Jerusalem*, p. 273; and Cynthia Ozick, 'Roundtable Discussion', in Lang, *Writing and the Holocaust*, p. 281.

50. See A.A. Cohen (1993), *The Tremendum: A Theological Interpretation of the Holocaust*,

New York: Continuum, pp. 1–26; and E. Wiesel (1970), *One Generation After*, New York: Random House, pp. 37, 43, 128, 166.

51. See, for example, R. Nozick (1989), *The Examined Life*, New York: Simon & Schuster, pp. 236–42.

52. 'One day he tried to count the Jewish dead ... By the time he had counted twenty thousand, his mouth was dry and his throat felt swollen and gasping. At forty thousand, his mouth began to crack and bleed. It would have taken him a month of counting to count the first million and he would be struck dumb before that.' R.M. Wilson (1992), *Manfred's Pain*, London: Pan Books, p. 171.

53. See n. 46 above.

54. G.M. Kren and L. Rappoport (1994), *The Holocaust and the Crisis of Human Behavior*, New York: Holmes & Meier, p. 153.

55. Z. Bauman (1989), *Modernity and the Holocaust*, Cambridge: Polity Press.

56. G. Sereny (1991), *Into That Darkness*, London: André Deutsch, p. 101.

57. Levi, *The Drowned and the Saved*, pp. 83–101, at pp. 83–4, 95. And see also E.L. Fackenheim (1985), 'The Holocaust and Philosophy', *Journal of Philosophy* **82**, pp. 505–15; and A. Margalit and G. Motzkin (1996), 'The Uniqueness of the Holocaust', *Philosophy and Public Affairs* **25**, pp. 65–83.

58. Seeskin, 'What Philosophy Can and Cannot Say about Evil', in Rosenberg and Myers, *Echoes from the Holocaust*, p. 97. The point relates to a wider debate about the genesis of the 'Final Solution'.

59. Stannard, 'Uniqueness as Denial', in Rosenbaum, *Is the Holocaust Unique?*, p. 185.

60. Papazian, 'A "Unique Uniqueness"?', *Midstream* **30**, p. 16.

61. Sereny, *Into That Darkness*, p. 101.

62. 'The Significance of the Holocaust', in Friedlander and Milton, *The Holocaust*, pp. 95–6.

63. See text to nn. 14 and 15 above.

64. Maier, *The Unmasterable Past*, pp. 72–3, 75.

65. See text to n. 16 above.

66. Bauer, 'The Place of the Holocaust in Contemporary History', in Roth and Berenbaum, *Holocaust*, pp. 18, 30–31. And *The Holocaust in Historical Perspective*, p. 48 (cf. p. 36).

67. S.T. Katz (1994), *The Holocaust in Historical Context, Volume 1: The Holocaust and Mass Death before the Modern Age*, Oxford: Oxford University Press, pp. 27, 31, 34, and 'The Uniqueness of the Holocaust: The Historical Dimension', in Rosenbaum, *Is the Holocaust Unique?*, p. 19; all emphases in the original. See also 'The "Unique" Intentionality of the Holocaust' in S.T. Katz (1983), *Post-Holocaust Dialogues: Critical Studies in Modern Jewish Thought*, New York: New York University Press, pp. 296, 313, n. 22.

68. As do: Seeskin, 'What Philosophy Can and Cannot Say about Evil', p. 98; and Novick, *The Holocaust and Collective Memory*, p. 197.

69. The argument of this paragraph draws on observations about the uniqueness question made to me by Eve Garrard, whom I thank accordingly. I also take the opportunity to thank her more generally for her encouragement and feedback as co-editor of this volume.

70. Open to the same line of objection is Bob Brecher's suggestion that the Holocaust was unprecedented – he abjures the term 'unique' – because it represented 'a culture's turning on and against itself'; though whether that made it worse is, he says, 'another matter'. See B. Brecher (1999), 'Understanding the Holocaust: The uniqueness debate', *Radical Philosophy* **96**, July–August, pp. 17–28, at p. 24.

71. As we have seen, David Stannard and Norman Finkelstein both prefer to focus on the opposite line of thought: that it is a privileging of Jewish suffering that is the guiding

impulse in this matter. Having recommended forbearance from the attribution and condemnation of motives, I will myself respect that constraint. However, I will not forbear from commenting on the presentational freedoms these two authors, their righteous indignation at the failings of others so strong and so displayed, permit themselves. It is by one of these freedoms that they both take good care to point out to their readers that there are Jewish scholars of the Holocaust who are not associated with the uniqueness thesis, while neglecting to emphasize the fact that there are also non-Jewish scholars who *are* associated with it. It is hard to credit that either writer, having read as far into the question as he has, could be unaware of the latter awkward circumstance for them. Not to have confronted it is a convenient negligence, sparing them the trouble of having to integrate it into their thinking. The way they present things licenses the inference, however – on a question coming out of *this* history – that the Holocaust-singularity thesis is a Jewish thesis. For though not all Jews in their uniqueness-story are bad people, all bad people in their uniqueness-story are Jews. There is no need to speculate about what Stannard's or Finkelstein's motives might be, in order to form a judgement about the intellectual quality of their oversight.

72.   My argument against the notion of a unified subject of suffering is not inspired by any general methodological–individualist commitment. I say only that, in the given case, that of widespread suffering, there is no unified collective entity that can meaningfully be regarded as the seat of a single aggregated experience of pain. There are, however, collective entities not reducible without residue to their individual members and these can be the source of significant social actions.

73.   Friedlander, 'Historical Writing and the Memory of the Holocaust', in Lang, *Writing and the Holocaust*, p. 77.

74.   L. Wittgenstein (1963), *Philosophical Investigations*, Oxford: Basil Blackwell, pp. 31–2e; emphases in the original.

75.   H. Arendt, 'Social Science Techniques and the Study of Concentration Camps', in Rosenberg and Myers, *Echoes from the Holocaust*, pp. 365–78, at p. 370.

76.   O. Friedrich (1994), *The Kingdom of Auschwitz*, New York: HarperCollins, p. viii.

77.   I wonder if this is part of the sense of Habermas's remark concerning 'a deep layer of solidarity among all who have a human face' – see text to n. 11 above.

Chapter 4

Knowledge, History and the Holocaust

Tom Rockmore

The series of events that have come to be called the Holocaust raise a number of issues. Some have been extensively studied, but others have not been treated in depth or are still scarcely known despite the immense literature this theme has generated. A short list might include how to comprehend the relation of the Holocaust to other instances of genocide,[1] most recently in Hutu massacres of Tutsis in Rwanda;[2] how to understand the widespread failure of such intellectuals as Martin Heidegger[3] to come to grips with what, at the start of the new millennium, appears to be a turning point in human history; how to counter infrequent, but unfortunately persistent efforts to deny that the Holocaust took place;[4] the proper approach to those concerned to relativize the Holocaust as merely one event among others;[5] how to understand mawkish reactions[6] culminating in claims that, say, in the Holocaust's wake poetry is no longer possible;[7] and how to counter inexcusable efforts to prevent discussion from taking place through forms of the claim that history as such is entirely unknowable.[8]

Like many others, I believe that individuals of all kinds need to study the Holocaust to become acquainted with the history of our time and, if possible, to learn from it, with the aim of preventing, or at least impeding, any possible repetition of similar human tragedies. This unpopular stance suggests that individuals ought to be responsible for and to other people. We live in a historical moment when, for whatever reason, concern for others is rapidly waning. One explanatory factor is obviously economic. At the time of this writing, the economies of so-called first-world countries in the West were until recently in an expansionary mode, but the social net is shrinking as development is increasingly uncoupled from real forms of freedom.[9] In the advanced industrial world more and more individuals seem to be mainly concerned with themselves. If the responsibility of each individual toward others is a function of who one is, then intellectuals have a special duty to wrestle with the salient events of their historical moment, including the Holocaust.

It is, however, one thing simply to ignore, like Heidegger, the Holocaust, which he could not grasp on the basis of his position,[10] and another to cognize or to know it. Cognition of the Holocaust, or indeed any historical event, must grasp its specificity. This requirement applies to all types of historical writing and other ways of knowing the past. Precisely this problem is at stake in revisionist efforts, which take very different forms. French Holocaust revisionism typically denies that the Holocaust occurred,[11] German revisionism rather relativizes it in a way which makes it commensurable with other events. Some German revisionists,[12] most prominently Ernst Nolte, a former Heidegger student and important student of the history of German Nazism, suggest that National Socialism is bad, but better than Bolshevism, hence a morally acceptable choice;[13] others see it as an apologia for Nazism.[14] Certain types of Holocaust revisionism are intended to wipe away the moral stain by historians and others who are politically unrepentant, in some cases clearly still sympathetic to the NSDAP. I have no intention of denying that this is morally dreadful. But it would be mistaken to reject all forms of revisionism across the board. An example is the necessary effort to grasp the Holocaust within, not outside of, our wider understanding of history in order to study it through the entire range of available historical techniques.[15] Indeed, the writing of history is intrinsically revisionary in that later writers build on what is already known about historical phenomena in offering new, supposedly better descriptions and interpretations.

The moral disadvantage of German revisionism is balanced by the epistemological advantage of treating the Holocaust as commensurable with other events, hence as knowable in the same way and to the same degree as historical occurrences of all kinds. The revisionist approach suggests that the Holocaust is not unknowable but can be known precisely because it is not unique. Now it has often been suggested that the Holocaust, which differs from other events not only in degree, but also in kind, is in fact unique, in basic respects unlike any other event or series of events in human history. It is claimed that, although there have been other examples of genocide in this century, there has been only one Holocaust, which is not merely another case of genocide.

The uniqueness claim is merely the most extreme form of the view that the Holocaust is intrinsically different from any other event, hence cannot be known in the same way and by the same means as other historical events if, indeed, it can be known at all. This claim raises an interesting epistemological issue which is the focus of this essay. It needs to be shown how it is possible for an event, or series of events, which is unique, hence in principle unlike anything else, to be cognizable or knowable. In raising the problem of knowledge of the Holocaust in this way, it is not my intention to pose a transcendental question. It is unclear what it would mean even to begin to elucidate the conditions of the very possibility of understanding the Holocaust. I will limit myself here to something more modest, that is, discussion of the real conditions under which the Holocaust can be known. I will be arguing that although the Holocaust is unique, it is also like other events, and, for that reason, cognizable, not through knowledge of the real, but as a 'construction' or 'reconstruction' of it.

Uniqueness and Historical Knowledge

It seems obvious that each event differs from all others which have already occurred if only because they lie in its past. As concerns the Holocaust, the uniqueness claim is merely the most extreme form of the conviction that it cannot adequately be represented or perhaps cannot even be represented at all. According to George Steiner, 'The world of Auschwitz lies outside speech as it lies outside reason.'[16]

Alice and A.R. Eckhardt claim that the Holocaust is unspeakable.[17] Berel Lang suggests that the Holocaust can only be represented literally but not in any other way.[18] Hayden White claims that as a modern event the Holocaust can only be represented through modernist means.[19]

Lang formulates his claim with care. Yet Steiner could only defend his assertion through some way of knowing what it is that language fails to grasp, through extra-linguistic and extra-rational knowledge of the Holocaust. Left unclarified is what it would mean to know beyond language and beyond reason in order to be able to show that either falls short of its cognitive goal.

A more interesting, even more extreme form of this difficulty is the suggestion, which is only rarely formulated explicitly, but which arguably subtends objections to knowing the Holocaust by ordinary means, or knowing it at all, that since the Holocaust is unique it simply cannot be known at all. A wholly singular event, an event that was really *sui generis*, that had nothing whatsoever in common with any other occurrence, which, for that reason, was strictly incomparable, simply could not be cognized.

We need, to begin with, to know what is meant by 'uniqueness' in this context and to examine whether such a claim prevents or impedes cognition in some central way, for instance by causing difficulties in representing the event or series of events in question. What does it mean to know something like the Holocaust? Whatever is unique is by definition utterly unlike anything else, without common measure, *sui generis*, singular, in a word incomparable. Knowledge claims generally, perhaps always, presuppose comparability, even if only in a negative way, for instance about Socrates's snub nose which distinguishes him from other people but also makes him recognizable. What does it mean to know something which is arguably unlike anything else?

A related problem is familiar in such domains as theology and art, whose objects, understood as singular, surpass the cognitive limits of human beings, hence literally cannot be known. We recall the medieval insistence on 'knowing' a transcendent God through a *via negativa*, which Kant later applies to the art object. Unlike the merely beautiful, the sublime, which surpasses all categories, by definition simply surpasses human understanding. The difference is that while in the Judaeo-Christian tradition there is only one deity, there is in principle no limit on the actual or potential number of sublime art objects.

Yet although perhaps satisfactory for theology or art, such an approach is inherently unsatisfactory as an approach to history, including the Holocaust, for two reasons. On the one hand, if the Holocaust surpasses our ability to comprehend it, it allows no lessons to be drawn from it other than the irreducibly minimal claim that no lessons can be drawn from it. History in that case, or at least the Holocaust, would be reduced to a mere happening deprived of any signification for human beings. On the other hand, this kind of approach, while admitting that the Holocaust existed, simply fails to tell us anything useful about what it was. Now it must arguably be possible to comprehend the relation of the Holocaust to other events, however much it differs from them, since if it were wholly *sui generis* it simply could not be understood at all. And since, in a different way, all events are unique, hence singular occurrences, uniqueness cannot itself preclude truth and knowledge. If it did, no historical knowledge of whatever kind would be possible at all.

In discussing uniqueness, or historical singularity, it is important to acknowledge comparability, hence to provide for the practical possibility of knowing historical events of all kinds, while countering efforts to deny or to relativize moral responsibility. It will be useful to distinguish different senses of uniqueness, or singularity, while conceding that what is unique can also be comparable, or like other things, hence cognizable. The Holocaust is doubly unique in that it is different from, hence unlike, other events, and in that it is a unique, unprecedented type of genocide, which has arguably never occurred before or since it took place. The problem, then, is whether uniqueness as such, for instance the singularity of the Holocaust, creates an epistemological barrier which, like Kant's sublime, simply overflows any conceptual framework, hence precludes knowledge.

Representing the Holocaust

The short answer, which captures the result of the discussion of the relation of uniqueness and cognition, is that if any historical event can be known, then so also can the Holocaust. This minimal claim says nothing about how the Holocaust can be known. In order to respond, it will be necessary to consider the vexed problem of representation.

Since it cannot be grasped directly, say through some form of naive realism, to know the Holocaust means to find a way to represent it. The problem of representing the Holocaust has been extensively studied,[20] most recently by Inga Clendinnen,[21] but not, so far as I have been able to determine, in the context of the wider epistemological problem of knowledge of history. For the purposes of the present paper, by the epistemological problem of history I will mean the nature and limits of historical representation, or the representation of historical events. This is an aspect of the more general, extremely difficult problem of cognitive representation.[22] Clendinnen, who is concerned with literary forms of representation, suggests that the Holocaust can best be represented in a disciplined, rigorous form of historical writing.[23] She is not concerned with the different, conceptually prior problem of whether and how it can be known.

There is a difference between uniqueness claims and their effect on our ability to cognize a given event, such as the Holocaust.[24] Uniqueness claims are often made in unconvincing ways. It is not clear, or at least it is insufficiently clear, that the uniqueness of the Holocaust refers to Jews and not to others, especially gypsies.[25] Steven Katz claims the Holocaust is unique since no state had ever as a matter of policy earlier set out to destroy an entire people.[26] Some possible counter-examples include the Atlantic slave trade, the famine in the Ukraine caused by the Soviet government, the decimation of the Amerindians in North America, and the Turkish slaughter of the Armenians. Thucydides recounts the premeditated destruction of the Melians, a different people, by the Athenians several thousand years ago.[27]

The claim for the uniqueness of the Holocaust as an epistemological impediment is more often asserted than argued. According to Jean-François Lyotard, the French postmodernist philosopher, an epistemological skeptic, the Holocaust cannot be represented, since any act of representing 'betrays' the represented.[28] He claims that in representing we create a memory which is intended to protect against forgetfulness but which has in fact the opposite result.

This obscure claim is difficult to evaluate. Lyotard might be saying that there is inevitably a difference between the representation and the represented, and that the former is not the latter. One could then go on to argue, as Heidegger does, that something essential is covered up, or forgotten, in the act of representing whose aim is rather to prevent that from happening. In this view, representation, which results in memory, inevitably fails since it never overcomes the difference between the representation and the represented. Memory records a representation which is always and necessarily inadequate to its task. Yet this cannot be the whole story since it is obvious that representations are more or less successful in capturing what is to be represented. Some Holocaust films do this better than others. One might, then, argue that Alain Resnais's *Night and Fog* (1956) is comparatively more successful than Steven Spielberg's *Schindler's List* (1993). But with the possible exception of Ranke, who implausibly called for the recovery of what happened as it happened, probably no one ever thought that a representation of historical events should be more than a way of 'holding present' what has already occurred in the form of memory.

Lyotard might also be applying his claim that the historical moment in which grand metanarrative schemes, schemes associated with names like Kant, Hegel and Marx, could reasonably be formulated has ended.[29] This approach undermines the very idea of grasping the real by undoing the conceptual strategy intended to secure the inference between what McDowell has usefully called mind and world.[30] On this reading of Lyotard's position, the Holocaust, which cannot be known, must for ever remain beyond the scrutiny of the observer.

The French postmodernist attack on epistemological foundationalism is roughly congruent with other attacks on the most important single strategy for knowledge in the modern period which, at the time of this writing, is widely thought to fail in any known form and in a way which simply cannot be recovered. Yet if this is his meaning, there is nothing which separates the Holocaust from any other event. The problem is not the supposed uniqueness of the Holocaust, its singularity, but rather the more general difficulty in correctly representing anything, anything at all, without regard to its putative uniqueness.

Aristotle, Hempel and Singular Events

I have suggested that the Holocaust is unique, an occurrence that is one of a kind, or singular, but cognizable. One might object that uniqueness is incompatible not only with knowledge of the Holocaust but also with historical knowledge, even knowledge in general. It is sometimes suggested that uniqueness is simply incompatible with claims for knowledge in all its forms, including historical knowledge.

Aristotle, who raises the theme of knowledge of singular events early in the tradition in a famous comment in passing, was obviously not thinking of the Holocaust. In a passage on poetry he remarks that the poet describes what might happen in the future, hence real possibilities, but the historian only establishes the record of the past. He goes on to claim that poetry, which is universal, is comparatively more important than history, which only concerns singular events.[31]

Aristotle's anti-Platonic support of the importance of poetry is based on its supposed universality as a source of possible lessons, which allegedly cannot be drawn from a singular occurrence.[32] Knowledge requires universality. Since a singular event is not universal, it is not cognizable, and cannot serve as a source of general instruction.

If Aristotle were right, it would not be possible to use the past to help us without respect to the future. In that case, Hegel's claim that no one ever learns anything from history would be justified. Fortunately, we do sometimes learn from history, although not often enough. The Vietnamese War could not be won since it was waged against an entire people united by the desire to throw off colonial bonds without regard to the cost in human lives. In its wake, in the United States it is widely understood that the country needed to avoid involvement in another similar land war. This lesson, which was drawn from a singular event or series of events, has since guided the foreign policy of the US government when the occasion to be involved in ground-based foreign wars again arose in conflicts with Iraq, the former Yugoslavia, and so on.

The observation that there is something in common between historical events suggests that history is like nature in that it can be represented and known through general laws. Modern science partly depends on the idea that an appropriately simplified model for nature can be devised to allow successful predictions. Newtonian mechanics represents the planets as a series of point-masses in order to calculate the planetary orbits on the basis of general laws. According to Wilhelm Dilthey, natural sciences provide explanation, whereas social sciences offer understanding. Hempel, who denies this distinction, suggests that history can be cognized through the same model as nature in his covering law model of scientific understanding for which there are general historical laws.[33] Both domains depend on general laws, where by 'general law' is meant a universal statement which can be empirically confirmed or disconfirmed.[34]

Hempel's controversial, reductionist view of history denies the distinction between nature and history in order to apply methods arguably appropriate for knowledge of the former to the latter.[35] Unlike studies of nature, studies of history must take into account human intentions and concrete situations. Hempel's view simply conflates nature and history. Nature has no history; history, which provides the record of human events, occurs within nature to which it cannot be reduced in order to understand it as if it were a natural science.

Like the Vienna positivists, Hempel espouses a view of knowledge as empirical, law-governed, and empirically verifiable. Empirical confirmation and empirical disconfirmation are inseparably related. Although not all claims that can be empirically disconfirmed can be empirically confirmed, claims which can be empirically verified can also be empirically disconfirmed. The view that claims in natural science can be confirmed or disconfirmed is highly controversial. Popper, who holds that we can ascertain individual facts apart from conceptual frameworks, argues that at best such claims can only be disconfirmed.[36] Holists, who claim that what we call facts are indexed to conceptual frameworks, deny that a theory can be disconfirmed on empirical grounds. Thus W.V.O. Quine, who famously contends that science meets its fate as a corporate body, contends that with enough ingenuity any theory can be protected against empirical disconfirmation.[37] Hence there is reason to doubt that fallibilism applies even to natural science.

I see no reason to accept the view that history can be adequately described in terms of a hypothetico-deductive framework. There are no empirically testable laws of history and Hempel does not cite any instances. Although historical interpretation relies on causal models,[38] even Hempel's followers concede that history must be grasped against the background of thought and action.[39] That historical causality cannot be understood as natural causality undermines the very idea of applying an approach, arguably adequate for natural science, to human history.

The deeper, crucial question is whether there are any historical laws at all. It is sometimes held that history is intrinsically rational, for instance in Kant's view that it reflects divine providence, Fichte's view of history as stages in the development of reason, or Hegel's view of reason in history. Michel Foucault's claim that history consists of discrete *epistemes*[40] suggests there are different conceptual models but no overarching conceptual framework.[41] If Foucault were correct, history would consist of isolated fragments which simply could not be known. Yet this model fails since it presupposes what it rejects, namely unity in history, since discontinuity can only be thought against a background of unity. Hence there is no alternative to maintaining that there is reason in history on pain of accepting that it is uncognizable, and that even such apparently irrational, at least a-rational, events as the Holocaust can be grasped through human reason.

Representing Historical Events

Hempel's reductionist view proposes a theoretical framework to interpret history on the assumption that there is something in common between different events. This is consistent with acknowledging their uniqueness while seeking adequate representation of them. The very idea of representation suggests that representation not only refers to but also in some undefined way describes, correlates with, or depicts the represented object.

There are many forms of representation. Pictorial representation has been seen as problematic since Plato's criticism of the mimetic capacity of art and literature. Plato's suggestion that, under appropriate conditions, some people, selected on grounds of nurture and nature, can directly grasp the real is restated in the modern tradition in direct, or naive, realism. From the present standpoint, the Platonic view is indefensible since, like mystical religious experiences, it results in private assertions which cannot be publicly duplicated or tested in any way. And naive realism, as Descartes points out, is unable to respond to questions of illusion and delusion.

Kant provides the first hint of how to formulate a viable view of representation. The critical philosophy follows from his effort to understand the relation of the representation to the object (*Vorstellung zum Gegenstand*) as described in his famous letter to Marcus Herz (21 July 1772).[42] Kant's solution lies in his dark but brilliant claim that knowledge is possible only on the hypothesis that the subject, in a sense he never satisfactorily explains, 'constructs' what it knows.[43]

This claim can be interpreted in two main ways: as suggesting that the cognitive subject is 'affected' by a mind-independent world which it 'constructs' as the objects of experience and knowledge through the hard-wired categories of the human mind, or as suggesting that the subject is 'affected' by an empirical constraint on the basis of which it 'constructs' the world given in experience and knowledge.

These two ways of reading Kant's Copernican Revolution in philosophy are very different, even incompatible. The first regards the human mind as a kind of filtering device with respect to an already constituted independent real.[44] The second depicts the human mind as constituting what we experience out of raw materials so to speak without taking a position with regard to an independent real. At present I am not interested in adjudicating the difficult interpretative question of which view best represents Kant's core commitment. Suffice it to say that I believe that in different places in his writings he is committed to both of them, and that the difference in emphasis between the first and second editions of the *Critique of Pure Reason* lies in a shift from the idealist to the realist side of the critical philosophy. In the present context, I am only interested in which way of reading Kant's position offers the stronger model for interpreting historical phenomena.

The first model suggests a form of the standard view, central to philosophy from Parmenides to the present, according to which to know is to know the real. On this view, we do not and cannot know mind-independent reality as it is, but we can and do know it as it is given in experience as a result of being 'filtered' through the structures of the human mind.

Since phenomena are appearances of the real, the first model is characterized by a relation of the knowing subject to the real. The second model dispenses with any relation to mind-independent reality in analyzing experience and knowledge of objects as mere phenomena, as distinguished from appearances. According to the second model, what we experience and know results from the activity of the mind in ways governed by the categories of the understanding 'affected' by empirical constraints. The second model is that it makes no assumptions about the existence of mind-independent reality at the evident cost of abandoning any claim that reality appears.

I believe that we must reject the first model. We know that the mind is 'affected' by something other than it, but we do not and cannot know what it is, that it is the real, that there is a real, or that the real appears. In other words, it simply cannot be known that representations in fact represent. Representations cannot, say, be cogently said to represent in the form of signs, as when spots are taken as a sign of measles or in any other way. Since we cannot know the mind-independent world as it is, Kant's effort to understand the relation of representations to objects fails. But it succeeds if it is taken as suggesting that we know what we 'construct' through a relation of representation to represented, not outside of, but rather within, the mind. Representations do not represent if that means mirroring objects, as Bacon thought; and if modern science is an example, they do not even picture in any form whatsoever. Rather, as Ernst Cassirer suggests about natural science, our theories symbolize, or bear a symbolic relation to, the world, which they neither reproduce nor mirror.[45]

Kant's constructivist model suggests we know experience, including the past, hence we know history, as a construction[46] indexed to the context, hence to the historical moment. Our theories about the world and ourselves, which are driven by such problems as how best to model nature, are always contextual. The ineliminable contextual component derives from the inability to ascertain facts in isolation from a conceptual framework, point of view, frame of reference, perspective, angle of vision, conceptual scheme, *Weltanschauung*, *Zeitgeist*, and so on. In making this claim I mean to side with Quine against Donald Davidson.[47] If we could grasp facts directly, then we could indeed dispense with the frame/content distinction. Yet since we cannot, this move, which is intended as a strategic retreat to a suitably updated form of realism or even classical empiricism, in which claims to know could be adjudicated wholly and solely through reference to the world as discovered through a so-called process of triangulation, is blocked. What counts as a relevant fact or even as a fact depends on the conceptual scheme for which it is potentially relevant. As the later Wittgenstein emphasizes in his related views of *Lebensform*, referential system (*Bezugssystem*) and language game (*Sprachsspiel*), specific factual claims are only true or false with respect to conceptual frameworks, which are themselves neither true nor false, in a word devoid of assertoric value.[48]

There are at least two main ways to understand the idea that facts depend, to use Davidson's term, on a conceptual scheme. One is to say that any conceptual scheme is situated within a particular discipline, as in Quine's suggestion that scientific theories are only meaningful within the whole of science. In this view, all knowledge is intra-disciplinary since, as Sellars suggests in employing the definite article, knowledge depends on *the* space of reasons, that is, on no more nor less than a single space of reasons.[49] The other is to say there is no way in principle to distinguish cleanly between a particular discipline and the surrounding world, say between science and what Sellars disparagingly calls folk science.[50] In his idea of different worlds, Kuhn suggests that what can be picked out as an object depends on the context in which it occurs, which is due both to intra- and extra-scientific factors.[51] Ludwik Fleck similarly points out how even within science facts are socially constructed.[52]

Our conceptual frameworks are socially constructed. The problems, the vocabulary, the conceptual tools, the language we speak, and the solutions to our problems are mainly inherited from the preceding context. Advances in even such an austere domain as physical theory cannot be isolated from the context, including the social surroundings. Newton's extra-scientific, theological commitments notoriously affected his conceptions of space and time, and so on.

Many writers, including J.G. Herder, W. von Humboldt, Hegel, Marx, Dilthey, Cassirer, and more recently Saul Kripke, Nelson Goodman, the Edinburgh social theorists, Steve Fuller, Steven Shapin, Richard Rorty, and so on admit that social factors affect epistemological claims. It has not been sufficiently understood that if claims to know are contextual, then they are also historical. The familiar view that to know is to know the real now and for ever, which runs throughout the entire

Western philosophical tradition up to the present, cannot be defended. We do not and cannot know that we know the real. And since conceptual frameworks change, we do not and cannot know that the validity of our knowledge claims, even those of the most extravagant kind, surpass what we currently believe in the present historical moment.

Claims to know are indexed to the particular historical moment in which they are formulated and over which they hold sway. Probably no one now thinks that Kant successfully deduced the univocal list of categories ingredient in all human knowledge or even that a single permanent conceptual framework can be identified. Our views of the world and ourselves depend on what is generally thought at a particular time. Kant's critical philosophy, which was formulated at almost the same time as non-Euclidean geometry was being developed, depends on his belief that there was and in fact could only be one geometry. The discovery of non-Euclidean geometry undermines his main argument for a priori knowledge about what must necessarily hold true for objects of experience and knowledge. If knowledge claims are always linked to the current historical moment, hence to history, then knowledge is intrinsically historical.

Historical Constructivism and the Holocaust

Though he understands knowledge as ahistorical, Kant's critical philosophy suggests a very different historical model potentially useful for the cognition of all kinds of experience, including historical phenomena. I would like now to apply this constructive model, implicit in Kant's critical philosophy, to history in general and specifically to the interpretation of the Holocaust.

I believe that we cannot grasp history directly and can grasp it at all only through an angle of vision, point of view, conceptual scheme, conceptual framework and so on.[53] Despite Heidegger, we cannot somehow go back behind the tradition to grasp the problem of being as it arose in Greek philosophy, but only grasp it better or at least differently, in any case as Hans-Georg Gadamer claims, from the present perspective.[54] We can know any cognitive object, including the Holocaust, only in the way and to the degree that it can be captured by a conceptual framework, hence represented.

It is important to stress that cognition cannot knowingly depict the real as it is. What we call the real at any given time is no more than the result of the ongoing negotiations between different parties to the debate.[55] We cannot know the Holocaust as it occurred outside of any conceptual framework. Any conceptual framework must respect the empirical constraint, in the case of the Holocaust what, on the basis of our different interpretative frameworks, we know about the millions of people assassinated by the Nazi regime. The point worth emphasizing for the Holocaust and anything else in the historical domain is that we grasp our cognitive objects not as they are but as they are 'constructed' and 'reconstructed' on the level of mind.

Since we can never compare our representations of events to what actually occurred, we do not and cannot know how our representations of the Holocaust relate to the 'real,' mind-independent Holocaust. In the same way as religion symbolizes what it cannot otherwise know, our representations of the Holocaust bear no more than a symbolic relation to so-called real, or mind-independent, historical events. Though there are always different ways to depict historical events, some of them, such as certain forms of Holocaust revisionism, which offend our current view of how history should be written or which conflict with what we accept as facts, must be rejected. We need for instance to preserve the distinction between history and pseudo-history by differentiating the former, in which different lines of enquiry converge, from the latter.[56]

Merely to claim that different lines of enquiry converge on the historical events in historical interpretation does not tell us which interpretation is better or best. That question can only be adjudicated by adducing criteria to choose between them, such as interpretative strength, or the capacity to account for more of the known facts. Einstein's general theory of relativity is relatively stronger than Newtonian mechanics in being able to account for the precession of the perihelion of Mercury.

Historical Construction and Historical Interpretation

Constructivism in the present context does not refer to sociological theory,[57] as in Scheler's idea of a relative-natural *Weltanschauung*, which concerns the way we experience the world,[58] as when for an anti-Semite it seems obvious that Jews in general are morally degenerate. It rather refers to a generally Kantian approach to knowledge, including historical knowledge. It would be helpful to indicate how a constructivist approach to historical interpretation functions in historical practice. Writing history, including the history of the Holocaust, requires the construction of interpretative frameworks to take into account the known historical data. In every situation it is always possible to construct more than one interpretation to fit the known facts, and there is always more than one perspective for determining such facts.

I will take as an example one of the best known and most criticized recent books on the Holocaust, Daniel Jonah Goldhagen's *Hitler's Willing Executioners: Ordinary Germans and the Holocaust*.[59] In referring to this work, I am not concerned to pass judgment on its merits. Suffice it to say that his reductionist effort to understand all the dimensions of the Holocaust through so-called eliminationist anti-Semitism has been widely criticized.[60] In referring to Goldhagen, I intend only to note the way in which a conceptual framework structures the discussion of its cognitive object, in this case the Holocaust.

Goldhagen, who is concerned to explain how the Holocaust could occur, adopts a modified form of the intentionalist pole of the intentionalist–functionalist debate about historical explanation. Starting from the idea that anti-Semitism is not well understood,[61] he argues that the correct explanation does not lie simply in the SS but rather in widespread German anti-Semitism. Against functionalists, including economic materialists, who point to economic causes, Goldhagen argues that 'Germans' anti-Semitic beliefs about Jews were the central causal agent of the

Holocaust.'[62] Even before the NSDAP came to power, a virulent form of anti-Semitism was at work in German nineteenth- and twentieth-century society:

> [I]n Germany during the Nazi period an almost universally held conceptualization of the Jews existed which constituted what can be called an 'eliminationist' ideology, namely the belief that Jewish influence, by nature destructive, must be eliminated irrevocably from society.[63]

Goldhagen's explanatory thesis, which he regards as offering a new conceptual framework for analysis, is a form of the Kantian claim that reasons can be causes. He concedes that the Holocaust can be understood from different angles of vision, but denies that any of the available models successfully explains what is known. His model depends on the historical investigator to reproduce an attitude toward others, in this case Jews, which has been socially produced, and which is effortlessly learned by individuals socialized into a given society. Like the Lutheran model of responsibility, his explanatory model suggests that even in the most extreme circumstances each person is able to decide individually.

His explanatory thesis purports to tell us what the Holocaust is, hence how it is to be understood. It pre-selects the kind of data which support its thesis and can be accepted. His model tells us that we cannot understand the Holocaust through the actions of a single individual Hitler, hence we also cannot excuse him for it while making the Holocaust uncognizable since there is in effect no smoking gun.[64] It follows for Goldhagen that the legal brief submitted by Reinhold Maurach at the Nuremberg trials according to which Bolshevism was invented by Jews for Jews, was a mere delusion.[65] Yet since Goldhagen also admits that the Nazi perpetrators sincerely held that Nazism was justified to combat Bolshevism,[66] other analyses, other conceptual frameworks yielding very different views of what happened during the Holocaust, cannot be excluded.

More generally, since it is never possible to know the so-called facts in independence of a conceptual framework, it is always possible to construct another conceptual scheme to yield a different, incompatible view of what has occurred. The point is not to deny there is historical objectivity. It is rather to say that what counts as objectivity is a function of the conceptual framework that cannot be derived from the historical data, that depend in turn on that framework, and that justifies itself in relation to data which appear relevant or irrelevant to it. So Pastor Walter Höchstädter's claim in 1944, during the Holocaust, that the Church must not be silent[67] is matched by the well-known silence of Pius XII.[68] The same silence which for one Christian is problematic is for another exemplary. Perhaps like psychoanalysis, historical interpretation can never be brought to an end.

Conclusion: Historical Constructivism and the Holocaust

I have been developing a historicist, constructivist view of knowledge in order to provide for knowledge of the Holocaust while acknowledging its uniqueness. I have argued that the Holocaust is indeed a unique event or series of events that, to the extent that it is knowable at all, must be similar to other historical events. I have further argued that we never just grasp the empirical facts, but 'construct' representations of the historical events, including the Holocaust, within the dual framework of the prevailing conceptual scheme or schemes and the empirical constraints. Finally, I have argued that we do not and cannot know how our representations of the events relate to the events considered apart from us, to which they bear no more than a symbolic relation.

Three objections to this view spring readily to mind as concerns uniqueness, cognitive neutrality, and the very idea of employing an epistemological approach to the Holocaust. It could be objected that this approach slights the uniqueness of the Holocaust, that it suggests that knowledge claims are inevitably biased or at least not neutral, or again that it substitutes philosophy for historiography. In response to the first objection, it seems obvious that 'uniqueness' claims can be interpreted in different ways. If the uniqueness of the Holocaust is taken to mean not only that there has never been an event or series of events like it but also that it has nothing in common with other historical events, that it is utterly singular, then there is no alternative to admitting that it cannot be known, hence lies beyond the real possibility of human cognition.

The second objection points to the problem of historical relativism. The suggestion that knowledge claims are doubly indexed, initially to the context and then to the historical moment, is misconstrued as suggesting there is no cognitive objectivity since cognitive claims are merely subjective. Since we can never know we know in independence of a historically variable framework, cognitive objectivity needs to be understood as not independent of, but rather as dependent on, the historical moment, in a word as historically relative. By cognitive objectivity we cannot mean we know the real; we can only mean that our knowledge claims respect our current standards of knowledge.

The third objection points to the very idea of studying the Holocaust as a problem of knowledge. It could be objected that such an approach reflects a methodological mistake since concerns about knowing the Holocaust are best resolved through recourse to well-known historical models. This objection amounts to claiming that questions about how to write history take precedence over epistemological ones, since historiography takes precedence over philosophy. Yet historiographical questions about the Holocaust, for instance how to understand what is known about Hitler's actions from, say, intentionalist, functionalist or other perspectives, presuppose an adequate representation of the Holocaust. Since the problem of the practical possibility of representing historical events is prior to the historiographical question about which form of historical representation is the best explanatory model, historiography cannot dispense with epistemology.

I come now to my conclusion. Discussion of the Holocaust presupposes its representation. This paper has studied the real conditions of representing the Holocaust, with special attention to the uniqueness claim. I conclude that although as a special form of genocide it is unique, in other ways the Holocaust is like all other events in that it can be and in fact is known through its 'construction' and 'reconstruction' in consciousness on the basis of various historiographical methods, whose choice is properly left to historians.

Notes

1. See Christian Delacampagne, *De l'Indifférence. Essai sur la banalisation du mal*, Paris: Odile Jacob, 1998.
2. See Josias Semujanga, *Les Récits fondateurs du drame rwandais. Discours social, idéologie et types*, Paris: L'Harmattan, 1998.
3. See Tom Rockmore, *On Heidegger's Nazism and Philosophy*, Berkeley: University of California Press, 1997.
4. Deborah Lipstadt, *Denying the Holocaust: The Growing Assault on Truth and Memory*, New York: Penguin, 1994.
5. See *'Historikerstreit.' Die Dokumentation der Kontroverse um die Einzigartigkeit der nationalsozialistischen Judenvernichtung*, Munich: Piper Verlag, 1989.
6. Blanchot's claim is typical: 'Dans l'intensité mortelle, le silence fuyant du cri innombrable.' Maurice Blanchot, *L'écriture du désastre*, Paris: Gallimard, 1980, p. 80.
7. This claim, which is due to Theodor Adorno, conveniently overlooks great writers who came out of the Holocaust, such as Primo Levi or Paul Celan.
8. A prime offender is de Man, who collaborated with the Nazis, but later argued, in an application of Derrida's view that there is nothing outside the text, that there is no way to distinguish between history and fiction. See Paul de Man, *Blindness and Insight: Essays in the Rhetoric of Contemporary Criticism*, Minneapolis: University of Minnesota Press, 1983, pp. 75, 136.
9. See Amartya Sen, *Development as Freedom*, New York: Knopf, 1999.
10. See 'Heidegger and Holocaust Revisionism,' in *Martin Heidegger and the Holocaust*, edited by Alan Milchman and Alan Rosenberg, Atlantic Highlands: Humanities Press, 1995, pp. 131–46.
11. Robert Faurisson is the leading exponent of French Holocaust revisionism, which simply denies that the Holocaust occurred. This pernicious form of revisionism is accepted even by some of the most philosophically sophisticated French philosophers, such as Jean Beaufret, Heidegger's leading spokesman in France. For Beaufret's support of Faurisson's view, see *Annales d'histoire révisionniste* **3** (Autumn–Winter 1987), pp. 204–5.
12. It has been argued that Andreas Hillgruber, a prominent German historian who is usually considered together with Nolte, is not an apologist of any kind. See Perry Anderson, 'On Employment: Two Kinds of Ruin,' in Saul Friedlander (ed.), *Probing the Limits of Representation: Nazism and the Final Solution*, Cambridge: Harvard University Press, 1992, pp. 54–65.
13. See Ernst Nolte, *Heidegger, Politik und Geschichte im Leben und Denken*, Berlin: Propyläen, 1992.
14. See 'Intention and Explanation: A Current Controversy About the Interpretation of National Socialism,' in Tim Mason, *Nazism, Fascism and the Working Class*, New York: Oxford University Press, 1996, pp. 212–30.
15. For a responsible effort to do this, see Michael Marrus, *The Holocaust in History*, Toronto: Key Porter Books, 2000.
16. George Steiner, quoted in Berel Lang, *Act and Idea in the Nazi Genocide*, Chicago: University of Chicago Press, 1990, p. 151.
17. See Alice and A.R. Eckhardt, 'Studying the Holocaust's Impact Today: Some Dilemmas of Language and Method,' in *Echoes from the Holocaust: Philosophical Reflections on a Dark Time*, edited by Alan Rosenberg and Gerald E. Myers, Philadelphia, PA: Temple University Press, 1988, p. 439.
18. See Berel Lang, 'The Representation of Limits,' in Friedlander, *Probing the Limits of Representation*, pp. 300–317. See also Lang, *Act and Idea in the Nazi Genocide*.

19. See Hayden White, 'Historical Emplotment and the Problem of Truth,' in Friedlander, *Probing the Limits of Representation*, pp. 37–53.

20. See, for example, Friedlander, *Probing the Limits of Representation*. See also Dominick LaCapra, *Representing the Holocaust: History, Theory, Trauma*, Ithaca: Cornell University Press, 1994.

21. 'I want to arrive at a clearer understanding of at least some of those persons and processes to be confident that the whole is potentially understandable.' Inga Clendinnen, *Reading the Holocaust*, New York: Cambridge University Press, 1999, p. 4.

22. See Nelson Goodman, 'Reality Remade,' in *Philosophy Looks At The Arts*, edited by Joseph Margolis, Philadelphia, PA: Temple University Press, 1986, pp. 283–306.

23. See chapter 9: 'Representing the Holocaust,' in Clendinnen, *Reading the Holocaust*, pp. 163–84.

24. For general discussion of the uniqueness claim, see *Is the Holocaust Unique?*, edited by Alan S. Rosenbaum, Boulder, CO: Westview Press, 1996.

25. See Ian Hancock, 'Responses to the Porrajamos: The Romani Holocaust,' in Rosenbaum, *Is the Holocaust Unique?*, pp. 39–64.

26. See Steven T. Katz, *The Holocaust in Historical Context, I: the Holocaust and Mass Death before the Modern Age*, New York: Oxford University Press, 1994. Katz's basic claim, which he curiously regards as phenomenological, is that 'never before has a state set out, as a matter of intentional principle and actualized policy, to annihilate physically every man, woman, and child belonging to a specific people.' Ibid., p. 28.

27. See Thucydides, *The Peloponnesian War*, translated by Rex Warner, Baltimore, MD: Penguin, 1959, V, chapter 7, pp. 358–66.

28. For the claim that the Holocaust is unrepresentable, consider Jean-François Lyotard, *Heidegger et les juifs*, Paris: Galilée, 1988 part 8.

29. See Jean-François Lyotard, *La Condition postmoderne*, Paris: Editions de Minuit, 1979.

30. See John McDowell, *Mind and World*, Cambridge: Harvard University Press, 1996.

31. See Aristotle, *Poetics*, in *The Complete Works of Aristotle*, edited by Jonathan Barnes, Princeton, NJ: Princeton University Press, 1984, II, 9, 1451b5–7, pp. 2322–3: 'Hence poetry is something more philosophic and of graver import than history, since its statements are of the nature rather of universals, whereas those of history are singulars.'

32. Mill notoriously argues for induction on the basis of a single instance. See J.S. Mill, *A System of Logic*, London, 1843, book III, chapters 8–10.

33. See Carl Hempel, 'The Function of General Laws in History,' in *Readings in Philosophical Analysis*, edited by Herbert Feigl and Wilfrid Sellars, New York: Appleton-Century-Crofts, 1949, pp. 459–71.

34. It has been argued more recently that the covering law model describes micro-events but fails to describe macro-events. See Clayton Roberts, *The Logic of Historical Explanation*, College Park, PA: Pennsylvania State University Press, 1996.

35. For criticism of Hempel's version of this positivist model, see Wesley Salmon, *Scientific Explanation and the Causal Structure of the World*, Princeton, NJ: Princeton University Press, 1984.

36. See Karl Popper, *Conjectures and Refutations: The Growth of Scientific Knowledge*, New York: Harper, 1965.

37. See 'Two Dogmas of Empiricism,' in Willard Van Orman Quine, *From A Logical Point of View*, New York: Harper and Row, 1963, p. 41.

38. See Murray G. Murphy, *Our Knowledge of the Historical Past*, Indianapolis, IN: Hackett, 1980, p. 102.

39. See ibid., p. 120.

40. See Michel Foucault, *L'Archéologie du savoir*, Paris: Gallimard, 1969.

41. For a discussion of Foucault's positivist view of history, see Paul Veyne, *Comment on*

écrit l'histoire, suivi de Foucault révolutionne l'histoire, Paris: Editions du Seuil, 1978, pp. 201–42.

42. See Immanuel Kant, *Philosophical Correspondence, 1759–99*, translated by Arnulf Zweig, Chicago: University of Chicago Press, 1967, pp. 70–75.

43. See Immanuel Kant, *Critique of Pure Reason*, translated by Werner S. Pluhar, Indianapolis, IN: Hackett, 1996, B xiii, p. 19.

44. There are many passages which suggest that Kant thought that to know means in fact to know a mind-independent world, especially in the *Prolegomena*. See Immanuel Kant, *Prolegomena to Any Future Metaphysics*, translated by James Ellington, Indianapolis, IN: Hackett, 1977, pp. 33 and 77–9.

45. This is a theme throughout his writings, particularly in the last, unfinished volume of *The Philosophy of Symbolic Forms*. See esp. Ernst Cassirer, 'The Concept of the Symbol: The Metaphysics of the Symbolic', in *The Philosophy of Symbolic Forms, IV: The Metaphysics of Symbolic Forms*, translated by J.M. Krois, New Haven: Yale University Press, 1996, pp. 223–34.

46. For skeptical discussion of social constructivism, see Ian Hacking, *The Social Construction of What?*, Cambridge, MA: Harvard University Press, 1999. For a more sympathetic account, see 'Wittgenstein's Philosophy of Mathematics,' in Michael Dummett, *Truth and Other Enigmas*, Cambridge, MA: Harvard University Press, 1978, pp. 166–85.

47. See 'On the Very Idea of a Conceptual Scheme,' in Donald Davidson, *Inquiries into Truth and Interpretation*, New York: Oxford University Press, 1984, pp. 183–98.

48. See Ludwig Wittgenstein, *On Certainty*, edited by G.E.M. Anscombe and G.H. von Wright, New York: Harper, 1972.

49. See 'Philosophy and the Scientific Image of Man,' in Wilfrid Sellars, *Science, Perception and Reality*, Atascadero, CA: Ridgeview, 1991, p. 169.

50. See ibid., pp. 1–40.

51. See Thomas Kuhn, *The Structure of Scientific Revolutions*, Chicago: University of Chicago Press, 1970, p. 118.

52. See Ludwik Fleck, *Genesis and Development of a Scientific Fact*, translated by Fred Bradley and Thaddeus J. Trenn, Chicago: University of Chicago Press, 1979.

53. See R.G. Collingwood, *The Idea of History*, London: Oxford University Press, 1966.

54. The idea that claims to know are indexed to the historical moment, which he borrows from Hegel, is the central cognitive insight of his theory of hermeneutics. See Hans-Georg Gadamer, *Truth and Method*, translated by Garret Barden and John Cumming, New York: Crossroad, 1988.

55. See Hilary Putnam, 'Sense, Nonsense, and the Senses: An Inquiry into the Powers of the Human Mind,' in *The Journal of Philosophy* **XCI** (9), September 1994, p. 452.

56. See Michael Shermer and Alex Grobman, *Denying History: Who Says the Holocaust Never Happened and Why Do They Say It?*, Berkeley: University of California Press, 2000, pp. 2 and 236.

57. See Peter L. Berger and Thomas Luckmann, *The Social Construction of Reality: A Treatise in the Sociology of Knowledge*, Garden City, NY: Doubleday Anchor, 1966.

58. See Berger and Luckmann, *Social Construction of Reality*, p. 6.

59. New York: Random House, 1997.

60. See, for example, Michael R. Marrus, *The Holocaust in History*, Toronto: Key Porter Books, 2000, p. 18:

> Antisemitism was central because Hitler determined that it should be so. Opposition to the Jews became a leitmotif of the regime, whatever the priority assigned to it in a tactical sense, because for Hitler ideological questions mattered and were treated with desperate seriousness. Beyond

this, neither the existence of anti-Jewish traditions in Germany, the commitments of the Nazi leaders, nor the beliefs of the extensive Nazi following in the German population *required* the murder of the Jews. Put otherwise, antisemitism in Germany may have been a necessary condition for the Holocaust, but it was not a sufficient one. In the end, it was Hitler, and his own determination to realize his antisemitic fantasies, that made the difference. The implication is summed up in the title of a popular article on a related theme: 'No Hitler, No Holocaust.'

61. See Goldhagen, *Hitler's Willing Executioners*, p. 34.
62. Ibid., p. 9.
63. Ibid., p. 48.
64. See David Irving, *Hitler's War*, New York: Viking Press, 1977.
65. See *Hitler's Willing Executioners*, p. 393.
66. For this view, see Nolte, *Heidegger, Politik und Geschichte*, p. 150.
67. See *Hitler's Willing Executioners*, pp. 431–2.
68. Wills thinks of this as simply an instance of historical dishonesty. See Gary Wills, *Papal Sin: Structures of Deceit*, New York: Doubleday, 2000, pp. 11–69.

Chapter 5

Persons of Lesser Value: Moral Argument and the 'Final Solution'

Hillel Steiner

Here are two statements, both from distinguished scholars of the Holocaust, that seem to be at odds with one another. On the one hand, there is Raul Hilberg's claim with which few will feel inclined to disagree:

> The Holocaust is a fundamental event in history – not only because one-third of the Jewish people in the world died in the space of four years, not only because of the manner in which they were killed, but because, in the last analysis, it is inexplicable. All our assumptions about the world and its progress prior to the years when this event burst forth have been upset. The certainties of the late nineteenth and early twentieth century vanished in its face. What we once understood, we no longer comprehend.[1]

An apparently contrary view is expressed by Yehuda Bauer:

> The Holocaust, that is, the planned total annihilation of the Jewish people and the actual murder of close to six million of them, is a historical event; it was perpetrated by humans for human reasons, and is therefore as explicable as any other series of violent acts in recorded history.[2]

Perhaps these judgements are not as opposed as they appear to be. Perhaps to be 'as explicable as any other series of violent acts' is entirely consistent with being 'in the last analysis, inexplicable'. Inexplicability, we might even conjecture – and this may be especially true of the Holocaust – can be due as much to a plethora of explanations as to a paucity of them.

One thing, however, does seem fairly clear: the evil that was the Holocaust is far more widely acknowledged than understood. And there are, of course, many perfectly straightforward reasons for this. A good number of them have to do with the uncertainty of what such understanding would amount to, if we had it. What does it *mean* to understand the evil of the Holocaust?[3]

Perhaps this understanding consists in knowing how the Holocaust was possible, in the sense of how it was brought about. How was this programme of mass extermination conceived? How was it initiated and adopted? How were the personnel variously involved in its implementation recruited and organized? How was the crucial acquiescence of so many and varied bystanders ensured? These complex multifaceted questions are fundamentally ones for historians. And despite the voluminous popular as well as scholarly historical literature responding to them, one is bound to presume that its readership is but a fraction of those who recoil in horror at this genocidal event. The vast majority of us wouldn't regard the moral conviction prompting that reaction as in any way impaired by our deficiencies in this sort of understanding.

There are other ways of interpreting the question of Holocaust understanding. Theologians, psychologists, anthropologists and sociologists have searched for such understanding by exploring the ontology of evil, obedience pathologies, scapegoating syndromes, millennial zealotries, the socioeconomic conditions of racism and so forth. These large literatures, again both popular and scholarly, have also attracted wide audiences and intense discussion. But here too we can safely assume that abomination of the Holocaust extends far beyond those possessing even a passing acquaintance with such writings.

To draw attention to this abundance of Holocaust explanations is evidently not to imply their mutual exclusivity (though, undoubtedly, the truth of some of them limits that of others). For explanations, as we often like to say, operate at different 'levels'. And while there can be, and is, important disagreement as to the ordering of these levels, such disagreement does not itself entail that different explanations are inherently rivalrous ones. Indeed, for a phenomenon as complex as the Holocaust – one composed of so many separate events involving so many diverse actions (and omissions) – the likely potency of any one type of explanation looks to be quite limited.

What I shall do in this paper is discuss yet another explanation – one of a type different from those already mentioned. Specifically, I want to explore the structure of one set of reasons held by some of the key perpetrators of the Holocaust: reasons for thinking that the genocidal enterprise in which they were engaged was, regardless of what most of us firmly believe, morally justifiable. It follows pretty directly from what was said above that I'm entirely uncertain as to the relative explanatory weight of such an account. For, in general, how much understanding of an event is to be gained from an analysis of why its perpetrators conceive it to be morally permissible, and even mandatory, is a question of profound significance and one which I readily leave to others.

Nor is there anything very novel in much of what follows. The broad outlines of the (several) Nazi justifications for the 'Final Solution' are familiar enough. Nevertheless and as I hope to show, subjecting them to yet further analysis is not an unprofitable exercise. For a striking feature of some of these justifications is that they embody moral values which are widely affirmed today, not least among persons whose abhorrence of the Holocaust constitutes an unshakeably fixed point on their moral compass. It is this disconcerting fact that warrants some attention.

Such an exercise might reasonably be expected to enhance our understanding in two ways. In the first place, it would give us a clearer view of the structure of the Nazis' moral argument and, more indirectly, of how they may have managed to convince some of those many persons whose extensive collaborative and acquiescent support their genocidal programme both indispensably required and tragically received. But second, and perhaps more valuably, it may lend a greater degree of precision to our understanding of the structure of our own moral commitments, inasmuch as these both categorically condemn that programme while yet embracing some of the very values deployed in its justification. What I'm thereby suggesting, in other words, is that an understanding of the evil of the Holocaust may be more complex than is commonly supposed.

There is, however, one kind of consideration that could be taken to vitiate this exercise right at the outset. Yes, an objector might allow, of course Nazi justifications invoke certain values which many of us share. It would be rather surprising if they didn't. The structure of any coherent moral justification is constituted by a series of inferences drawn from conjunctions of prescriptive and descriptive claims. And though not inconceivable, it's nevertheless highly unlikely that the values embodied in its most general prescriptive claims would be ones completely alien to most of those who, these affinities notwithstanding, quite consistently reject its practical conclusions. For their rejection of those conclusions need not rest on any rejection of those values and can be based entirely on a rejection of some of the descriptive claims utilized in those inferences. This, our objector might suggest, is pre-eminently the case with regard to the Nazi arguments: many of the statements which they asserted as facts were simply not true. And it is the falsity of these factual claims that renders their abhorrent conclusions untenable.

This is a powerful objection but not, I think, powerful enough. To be sure, many descriptive claims crucially implicated in the Nazi justification are notoriously false and many of them were known to be so even on the basis of contemporary scientific evidence. That said, the argument seems not powerful enough to explain the scale and depth of the moral rejection of the Nazis' practical conclusions. For what this *argument from factual error* (which I'll henceforth refer to with that phrase) evidently fails to reflect is the kind of moral commitment which I described above as having abhorrence of the Holocaust as a fixed point on its moral compass. Such a commitment entails that the Holocaust is evil regardless of whether the Nazis got their facts wrong or not. To explain the assignment of that sort of categorical status to Holocaust-abhorrence is to give the structure of the moral commitment entailing it.

Some of the structural features of such a commitment are not unfamiliar. They seem to be instanced in the following case. During the early seventeenth century, Galileo was persecuted by the Roman Catholic Church for his profession of Copernican heliocentrism, in direct opposition to the prevailing Ptolemaic geocentric orthodoxy. Among persons who hold that this persecution was morally wrong, many would judge it to have been similarly wrong for a community of convinced Copernicans to have persecuted someone for professing Ptolemaic beliefs. That is, for such persons the wrongness of Galileo's persecution is entirely independent of the truth or falsity of the doctrines in whose behalf it was perpetrated. Moreover, it is not an implication of their holding that persecution to have been wrong that their moral commitments cannot extend to embracing the values invoked in its defence. Embracing those values, they could none the less and consistently sustain their anti-persecution stand, by virtue of a differently structured moral commitment. This claim, that the wrongness of a particular persecution is not derived from the erroneousness of the scientific theories it relies upon, will henceforth be referred to as the *Galileo Principle*.

Jews, according to Nazi doctrine, are 'persons of lesser value'. Even a cursory glance at the relevant literature reveals that the warrant for this assessment varied considerably amongst the numerous intellectual progenitors of that doctrine. And not all of their accounts of it are, to say the least, mutually consistent. Moreover, this diversity of inspirational sources, and the tensions between them, were to some extent reflected in divisions within the Nazi leadership itself. Some of these accounts were derived from traditional anti-Semitic elements of Christian theology;[4] others drew upon diverse arcane mythologies, often of an explicitly anti-Christian character;[5] still others deployed the secular frameworks of contemporary social science and modern biology. It is with justifications derived from this latter set of sources that we shall be primarily concerned here.[6]

'How does it happen that people become things?' asks Claudia Koonz at the start of her penetrating discussion of genocide and eugenics:

> The question haunts both memory and scholarship about National Socialist genocide against the Jews during World War II. When we focus mainly on concentration camps, deportations, *Sonderkommando*, and mechanized mass murder, the question defies an answer. Such a teleological vantage point, however, distorts our vision by foregrounding the unique aspects of genocide and obscuring its etiology in more normal times. To complement meticulous examination of the final stages of the 'Final Solution', we need to look at the genesis of genocide within the context of the racial schemes that predated orders for extermination by several years. Studies of Nazi extermination routinely include a chapter or two on eugenics and 'racial science' as way stations on the road to Auschwitz. Often, these background chapters imply an inevitable descent down a slippery slope from eugenics to genocide … Although eugenics programs did institute vital preconditions for later extermination programs, they did not inevitably lead to mass murder … In settings as diverse as the Soviet Union and the United States, scientists created the potential for radical racial policies without producing mass extermination. And not even Nazi Party leaders imagined they could exterminate Jews, Gypsies, the disabled, and other 'inferiors' except under the extreme conditions of war. Yet the universality of eugenics notions – seen against the uniqueness of genocide – inspires us to pause and think about connections.[7]

What are these connections? How does one make the move to the judgement that some persons are of 'lesser value' and, from there, to the chilling conclusion that they are merely 'things' or, in the resonant Nazi phrase, 'lives unworthy of life'? Koonz is certainly correct to deny that eugenics programmes inevitably led to mass murder. But such denials have frequently – not least in today's Germany[8] – been found less than convincing. For it is a commonplace that the failures, of either individuals or governments, to implement certain measures may be due to any of a wide variety of factors. Such failures cannot be taken to show that their values do not imply those measures and would not, in more propitious circumstances, be accorded diligent realization.

Koonz's reference to 'a slippery slope' is, both in this particular context and more generally, highly apposite. The use of 'slippery slope arguments' is an endemic feature of moral and political debate. And it sometimes seems that the number of such slopes that do *not* terminate in a reference to the Holocaust can be counted on the fingers of one hand. So the motivation to escape from these slopes is understandably high. But, frequently, so is the cost.

That cost commonly takes the form of inconsistency. And inconsistency *is* a cost in moral argument because it invites the charge of irrationality against those embracing it and thereby seriously disarms them in the face of their opponents. Under such forensic pressure, the aforesaid escape-motivation is easily transformed into an unwillingness to venture anywhere near the slope in the first place: an abandonment of the unquestionably attractive values inhabiting its summit so as to avoid winding up at its gruesome base. This strategy too, then, involves a cost even if it is one which is greatly preferable to the cost of having to endorse that base. That said, what is obviously wanted in such cases is some *principled* means of escaping the slope at a site acceptably anterior to that base. Specifically, we want to explore the structure of a coherent exit from the slope which, many believe, inescapably connects the values underpinning eugenics to Auschwitz.

At this point, yet another potentially vitiating objection needs to be laid to rest. For who, it might be asked, seriously subscribes to eugenic values anyway? The short and correct answer, I believe, is quite a lot of us. Quite a lot of us believe that procreating couples should exercise significant restraint (with regard to smoking, eating, and so on), both before and after conception, to enhance the health of their gametes, embryos and foetuses. Quite a lot of us believe that genetic counselling, for persons contemplating or achieving pregnancy, is a good thing, as is non-conception or abortion or the use of others' gametes in cases with particularly disastrous prognoses. Most believe that somatic cell therapy, to avert the deleterious effects of proven genetic disorders, is highly desirable. Many (though perhaps somewhat fewer) believe that germ cell therapy, to perpetuate such corrections in the genomes of indefinitely numerous descendants, is at least equally desirable. And consequently, many believe that the research and experimental projects which contribute to improvements in these various diagnostic, prophylactic and therapeutic practices are greatly to be encouraged.[9] Are people holding such beliefs engaging in some form of self-deception if they fail to see themselves as neo-Nazis? What further steps lie between their commitments and the endorsement of Auschwitz?

Actually, quite a few. But some of them, it must be admitted, are less easily avoided than others. Take the case of deeming certain persons to be ones of 'lesser value'. We can certainly make sense of the idea that some genetically predisposed traits are of greater value than others and that some are positively disvaluable. Were this not so, it would be exceedingly difficult to explain why so much effort and sacrifice are devoted to securing whatever nurture – as distinct from nature – can contribute to the cultivation of certain genetically predisposed traits and the suppression or neutralization of others.[10] Equally inexplicable would be the payments often awarded to persons suffering disabilities caused by genetic as well as other factors. Does this undeniable fact, that we *assess* genetic endowments in terms of their factorial contributions to differentially valuable characteristics, imply that we differentially value the persons bearing those endowments?

The answer is unclear. On the one hand we want to say that all persons are of equal value. On the other, we seem to think that it would be better if persons with serious and highly inheritable genetic disorders did not produce genetically related offspring. Doesn't this latter view logically commit us to regarding the healthier offspring they would produce, with the aid of some appropriate gene-modifying procedure, as *better* than the offspring they would produce without it? And, if so, doesn't this in turn commit us to regarding whatever genetically *un*modified offspring they actually do produce as *worse* than offspring lacking the latter's serious genetic disorders? And is there some unbridgeable conceptual gulf separating the 'better/worse' scale from the 'greater value/lesser value' one?

These are not intended as rhetorical questions. But they are intended as indications of the sort of slippery slope on which, it's widely thought, eugenic principles would place us. So although there's still a long distance to be traversed before Auschwitz-endorsement is reached, it's worth pausing to consider each of the moves proposed thus far.

The first of these has to do with the comparative assessment of *hypothetical* offspring: those who would respectively be produced if (what I'll call) 'unhealthy genes' were or, alternatively, were not modified. If we believe that, *ceteris paribus*, it would be better to produce genetically healthier offspring, does this entail that, again *ceteris paribus*, such offspring would themselves be better than their less healthy counterparts? One unpersuasive way to deny this entailment is to argue that our comparative judgements about what it would be better to do don't have a one-to-one correspondence with our comparative evaluations of the results that would thereby be brought about. Of course, unforeseen consequences can often block one-to-one correspondence between a *prospective* judgement as to which action would be better and a *retrospective* evaluation of the result that was thereby brought about: maybe, in the light of what we know now, that chosen action wasn't after all better than some of its rejected alternatives. But the correspondence certainly holds between assessments of prospective actions and prospective results.

An apparently stronger ground for denying that the betterness of producing genetically healthier offspring entails that such offspring would themselves be better than less healthy ones is simply the claim that how good persons would be (and hence whether they would be better than others) is hardly a matter of how healthy they would be. Good persons are good and better persons better, we can all agree, by virtue of their characters and their deeds. And this argument would seem equally efficacious in blocking the proposed move from the hypothetical to the actual: the move whereby an *actual* genetically inferior offspring's being deemed worse is vindicated by reference to the genetically superior offspring who *would have been* produced instead had gene modification occurred.

The problem with this argument, however, is that it casts its dissenting net too widely and, in so doing, seems to fly in the face of reasonably well-established scientific facts. Not that scientists dictate the criteria of 'good' and 'better', of course. It's rather that there is significant scientific evidence linking aspects of not only persons' physical health, but also their characters and deeds, to their genetic endowments.[11] Again, we would not wish to treat persons whose behavioural dispositions tend to have morally undesirable consequences as fully blameworthy if those dispositions are substantially conditioned by factors beyond their control, such as their genetic endowments. But the question of how we should treat them – of what balance should be struck between rehabilitative and restrictive measures – is clearly different from the question of whether it would have been better if persons lacking these dispositions had been produced instead. In acknowledging this point, one does not have to agree with either the reasoning or the recommendation of Oliver Wendell Holmes, who famously expressed the Supreme Court's 1926 decision upholding the constitutionality of compulsory sterilization laws:

> It is better for all the world, if instead of waiting to execute the degenerate offspring for crime, or to let them starve for their imbecility, society can prevent those who are manifestly unfit from continuing their kind ... Three generations of imbeciles are enough.[12]

Persons disposed to engage in behaviours with morally undesirable consequences are evidently worse than those who aren't. And there appears to be no credible basis for resisting the identification of *this* understanding of 'being worse' with 'being of lesser value'. So if there are genetic factors which strongly predispose their bearers to engage in such behaviour, it seems that we are logically driven to enter those bearers into a category labelled something like 'persons of lesser value'.

For some people, acceptance of this conclusion would suffice to place us virtually at the gates of Auschwitz-endorsement, if not inside them. The remainder of the slope looks altogether too slippery, too thickly covered by impeccable claims of simple instrumental rationality, to allow for any escape. Those claims run as follows:

(a) The world is a small place, affording humanity inherently insufficient resources to achieve all its moral ends.
(b) Accordingly, we must prioritize these ends and be prepared to sacrifice inferior ones for the sake of superior ones.
(c) Persons of lesser value are ones whose behavioural dispositions do not reflect this prioritization and thus impede its realization.
(d) To fail to constrain such persons is itself morally irresponsible.
(e) They should be quarantined and/or given any therapeutic treatment that promises to modify their undesirable dispositions.
(f) Moreover, some of those persons are ones whose undesirable dispositions are due to their genetic endowments.
(g) Hence, to allow them to propagate their kind is also morally irresponsible.
(h) Quarantine, therapy, mating restriction and sterilization are practices which consume resources.
(i) In at least some cases, these practices consume more resources than they produce or conserve for the achievement of humanity's prioritized ends.
(j) If, in such cases, the elimination of those persons would consume fewer resources than subjecting them to these practices, then they should be eliminated.

These ten propositions obviously don't form a tight deductive argument. But they probably do provide a pretty fair indication of how such an argument could be constructed. Some of them – (a), (f), (h), (i) – register descriptive claims. Others – (d), (e), (g), (j) – assert moral ones. Of the remaining two, (b) records a standard rational choice requirement and (c) stipulates a definition. Which of these propositions can be rejected?

One strategy is to reject (j) directly, leaving the others intact.[13] I'll return to this proposal presently. An alternative move focuses on (c) and insists that the definition it offers is simply not one which applies to Jews as such. That is, although there may well be persons of lesser value and although it's acceptable so to classify any persons whose genetic dispositions are undesirable in the sense stipulated, there is no scientific basis for claiming that persons who are Jews fit that description *simply because they are Jews*.[14]

The difficulty with this move is that it relies upon the earlier cited *argument from factual error*, an argument which fell prey to the *Galileo Principle*. For the case against the 'Final Solution' that we're interested in constructing here is one which establishes its evil status independently of the erroneous factual claims and scientific theories invoked by its perpetrators' justification of it. A commitment to Holocaust-abhorrence, as a fixed point on our moral compass, is not a commitment that presupposes the falsity of Nazi science, however demonstrably false it was.

Does such a commitment ultimately ask too much of us? In complying with its demand that we dismiss as irrelevant – rather than disprove as false – the charges brought by Nazi doctrine against the Jews, are we not guilty of serious bad faith? How can we condemn persons for their actions if we refuse to entertain their reasons for so acting?

I think we *can* do this in the present case. And I think the way we do it has to go something like this. We begin by rejecting proposition (j) and characterizing the 'Final Solution' as an utterly heinous violation of human rights. But this forthright condemnation can be no more than a beginning.

For, to it, a philosophically astute Nazi might reply, first, by immediately conceding that charge;[15] and second, by readily agreeing that those human rights do have moral significance;[16] but third, by adamantly insisting that respect for those rights has (like any other value) to take its place in the queue of humanity's moral priorities. *This* Nazi argues that

> That queue also includes the vital cultural, medical and economic interests of humanity as a whole, which encompasses but vastly outnumbers the Jews and further comprises the literally numberless human generations of the future. How can the oppression and extermination of even as many as six million persons possibly be accorded greater moral significance than the cultural and physical degradation and economic impoverishment of countless others – a degradation and impoverishment which would surely ensue, so our scientists tell us, from allowing Jews to continue to interact with us? It's not that I'm a utilitarian, you understand.[17] I don't accept for a moment that natural or human rights are merely 'nonsense upon stilts'. But aren't there also *positive* human rights, ones which oblige us to protect those vital cultural, medical and economic interests? And don't future as well as present persons have such rights? Furthermore, although all these considerations might seem to justify only [*sic*] restricting Jews in various ways, rather than their extermination, such less drastic measures require significantly more resources and ones which were liable to be denied to us (by misguided others) before they could be made fully effective.[18]

One rather uncompelling rejoinder to these arguments is that an Aryan supremacist is singularly ill placed to invoke the rights of the rest of humanity in defence of the 'Final Solution'. Asserting the genetic inferiority of all other racial groups and the rectitude of their subordination to Aryan rule, he thereby disqualifies himself from any such appeal.

The reason why that rejoinder doesn't work is the same as the reason why condemning a measure as 'paternalistic' is insufficient to imply its moral impermissibility. For this and many other Nazi ideologues, it is the very superiority of Aryans that enables them to see more clearly and to deal more effectively with the Jewish threat to the well-being of humanity. The various weak and benighted other races, being at best 'culture-bearers' rather than 'culture-creators', are inherently incapable of this appointed mission. So if this essentially *ad hominem* rejoinder won't work against these arguments, what will?

I want to suggest that their Achilles' heel lies in their dependence on an unstated and insufficiently considered (though widely held) conceptual belief. This crucial assumption is that *moral rights can conflict with one another*: that is, that duties correlatively entailed by such rights can be jointly unperformable. It is the profound degree of moral indeterminacy engendered by this assumption that is being traded on in these Nazi arguments, an indeterminacy which readily lends itself to the kind of forensic exploitation we've just observed.

Of course, the idea that the members of any given set of rights may not all be mutually consistent is hardly novel. When it comes to legal rights, most of us, I daresay, entertain just such an idea most of the time and find its daily empirical confirmation in much of the ordinary business of the legal system. What are courts doing if not constantly deciding that some action was not, after all, within the ostensible rights of one litigant and amounted to a violation of the rights of the other? That is to say, these courts – and prior to them, legislators – are forever adjusting the boundaries between persons' ostensible rights, by further specifying or simply reassigning the respective contents of what we may compendiously call their 'permissible action spaces'. Such decisions in effect tell some persons that whatever their rights might nominally entitle them to, they don't do so in fact because, due to this policy or that enactment, some of those entitlements fall within the domains of other persons' rights.

Now, however true this may be about *legal* rights, it's far from clear that the same conceptual space – for a gap between nominal and actual entitlement – can exist in a set of *moral* rights, especially basic moral or human rights. Unlike systems of legal rights, a set of moral rights does not come equipped with the auxiliary machinery of courts and legislators to supply such discretionary adjustments between nominally conflicting rights. Nor can we easily conceive of how any persons could possess the authority to do so, nor of how the demands of values other than moral rights can determine their contents without rendering them normatively superfluous (as Bentham imagined them to be).

If this is so, then it would seem that for any proposed set of (non-superfluous) moral rights to be a *possible* set – to be realizable – its members must be mutually consistent. Any set of rights yielding contradictory judgements about the permissibility of a particular action either is unrealizable or, what comes to the same thing, must be modified to be realizable (let alone replicable in legal systems).

In a recent book on rights, I've investigated the characteristics of sets of rights that satisfy this condition of mutual consistency, or what I there call *compossibility.*[19] And while a rehearsal of that investigation would be out of place here, a report of some of its salient findings is not. These include:

1. Every right entails a correlative duty which is permissibly enforcible (or alternatively, waivable) at the sole discretion of that right's bearer.
2. Any set of compossible rights is exhaustively constituted by a subset of foundational rights, along with all (and only) the rights successively derived from them through their bearers' chosen exercises of the powers and liberties entailed by those foundational and derived rights.
3. Those foundational rights are entitlements to portions of negative liberty. That is, they are *negative rights*, correlatively entailing duties of forbearance which all others owe to their bearers.
4. All foundational rights and the rights successively derived from them are, or are reducible to, discretely specifiable property rights: that is, to non-overlapping claims to physical things.
5. All foundational rights consist of claims to the ownership of persons and to portions of natural resources.
6. Human or natural rights are foundational rights, of universal incidence, to self-ownership and to an equal portion of natural resources (or to compensation in the form of its value equivalent).
7. Members of neither past nor future generations hold any rights against presently existing persons.[20]

I further argue, following the similar claims of Rawls, Nozick and Dworkin, that 'rights are trumps': that is, that duties correlative to rights lexically outrank – impose side-constraints on – the demands of all other moral values. Indeed, I suggest that there are conceptual (that is, non-moral) reasons why this is so and, moreover, that a condition of its being so is that all rights are compossible.[21]

How does all this help us in our quest? Well, one thing it obviously does is to even up the odds a little by eliminating the rights of 'numberless human generations of the future' as claims justifying the forcible imposition of sacrifices on *any* existing persons, let alone six million of them.[22] But second, and decisively, in establishing that moral rights must be compossible and that human rights are negative rights, it implies that whatever *positive* moral rights persons have must be derivative ones: ones created by other persons' chosen exercises of their negative rights. If I *choose* to waive some of the forbearance duties you owe me correlative to my human right of self-ownership, then you may well thereby acquire a positive moral right to be provided with some of my labour services or with some of my body-parts or even with all of them. Otherwise not. Not even if there are a lot of you. And not even if your vital cultural, medical and economic interests depend on it.

Humanity does indeed entertain more moral ends than can be achieved with this small world's resources. And it must, accordingly, prioritize them. But if respect for persons' rights is one of those ends, it comes first in that queue. Coming first, it thus permits any optimal realization of those other ends that is consistent with respect for each person's rights. The 'Final Solution' fails to meet that description. Hence the justifiability of rejecting proposition (j) above.

Moreover, given the order of this queue, it is *Nazis* as violators of human rights who qualify as 'persons of lesser value', as defined by them in proposition (c). For it is they 'whose behavioural dispositions do not reflect this prioritization and thus impede its realization'. Since (all and only) duties correlative to rights are permissibly enforcible, proposition (d) – mandating the constraint of persons of lesser value – cannot be entirely rejected. Nor, however, and for the same reason, can it be applied to those persons of lesser value whose failure to prioritize properly falls short of violating rights. The merits of proposition (e), prescribing the appropriate forms of that mandated constraint, lie beyond the scope of this paper.

Where does this leave eugenic values? The short answer is 'intact, but constrained'. Within this moral structure, the pursuit of eugenic objectives – the breeding of healthier people – is confined, like all other pursuits, to what we may call the *terrain of consent*. Future persons having no rights against present ones, the latter are fully at liberty to modify their own offsprings' genetic endowments and those of their further descendants. And since they are all self-owners, no one is at liberty to force others to do so or to prevent them from doing so. Nor therefore can mating restrictions or sterilization be permissibly enforced. Accordingly, proposition (g) must be rejected. The terrain of consent is thus a plateau adjoining the slippery slope mentioned earlier. It provides those who are attracted to eugenic values with a consistent and principled exit from that slope, and saves them from the stark choice between abandoning those values and endorsing Auschwitz.

What, then, of the very idea of 'persons of lesser value'? Here, regrettably enough, the answer is not short. Value, we can broadly say, consists in the realization of our prioritized moral ends, and greater value consists in their greater realization. Evidently, some persons make greater contributions to that realization than others, and some are net detractors from it. The reasons why some of these contributions are negligible or even negative obviously vary from person to person and may, in many cases, be due to factors beyond their control. Whether they are must clearly be the dominant consideration determining how such persons should be treated. But, for reasons explored previously, that consideration seems an insufficient basis for denying that all net non-contributors may be deemed 'persons of lesser value'. That, at least, is one side of the story.

The other side is this. In a prioritized set of ends, value is assigned proportionally according to the rank of the end achieved and the extent of its achievement. If an end is accorded lexical superiority, the value of its achievement (in whole or in part) is necessarily greater than the value of achieving (to whatever extent) any lower-ranked end or combination of them. I've argued that if a set of moral ends includes rights, they must be accorded lexical superiority over all other ends. The value of achieving any or all of these other ends, whether in whole or in part, is less than the disvalue of any right-violation perpetrated in pursuit of that achievement. Since moral rights are vested in all persons, since all persons share the characteristic that their inviolability (in the form just described) is more valuable than anything else, there seems to be some fairly straightforward sense in which they can each be said to be of equal value.

Kant famously enjoins us to treat others not merely as means to our own ends, but also as ends in themselves. Now, as means to our own ends, people clearly *are* differentially – unequally – valuable. Perhaps, then, it's the undominated value of respect for their rights that is chiefly what can be meant by the otherwise rather opaque notion of persons being ends in themselves.[23]

Notes

1. R. Hilberg, Opening Remarks: 'The Discovery of the Holocaust', in P. Hayes (ed.) (1991), *Lessons and Legacies: The Meaning of the Holocaust in a Changing World* (Evanston, IL: Northwestern University Press), p. 11.
2. Y. Bauer, 'Holocaust and Genocide: Some Comparisons', in ibid., p. 36.
3. And would such understanding excuse? D. Dennett (1984), *Elbow Room* (Oxford: Oxford University Press), p. 32, aptly reports J.L. Austin's incisive retort to the suggestion that *Tout comprendre c'est tout pardonner*: 'That's quite wrong. Understanding might just add contempt to hatred.'
4. Concerning crucifixion guilt, blood sacrifice rituals, and so on; cf. D. Cohn-Sherbok (1992), *The Crucified Jew* (London: HarperCollins).
5. As developed in the writings of Houston Stewart Chamberlain, Madame Blavatsky, Guido von List and Alfred Rosenberg, among many others; cf. L. Poliakov (1974), *The Aryan Myth* (New York: New American Library), and the essays by Mosse, Goldstein and Spielvogel and Redles, reprinted in M. Marrus (ed.) (1989), *The Nazi Holocaust, Vol. 2: The Origins of the Holocaust* (Westport, CT: Meckler).
6. National Socialism was frequently characterized by its proponents as 'applied biology'. Recent years have witnessed an astonishing growth in the literature on this aspect of Nazism and its deep historical roots in the national and international medical and scientific communities. One particularly extensive account is P. Weindling (1989), *Health, Race and German Politics between National Unification and Nazism, 1870–1945* (Cambridge: Cambridge University Press). Others are cited below.
7. C. Koonz, 'Genocide and Eugenics: The Language of Power', in Hayes, *Lessons and Legacies*, pp. 155–6.
8. Cf. P. Singer (1991), 'On Being Silenced in Germany', *New York Review of Books*, 15 August, pp. 34–40; B. Schone-Seifert and K.-P. Rippe (1991), 'Silencing the Singer: Antibioethics in Germany', *Hastings Center Report* **21**, pp. 20–27; U. Wessels, 'Genetic Engineering and Ethics in Germany', in A. Dyson and J. Harris (eds) (1994), *Ethics and Biotechnology* (London: Routledge) pp. 230–58.
9. Good philosophical discussions of the values underpinning *some* eugenic objectives are supplied by J. Glover (1984), *What Sort of People Should There Be?* (Harmondsworth, UK: Penguin), J. Harris (1992), *Wonderwoman and Superman* (Oxford: Oxford University Press), and P. Kitcher (1996), *The Lives to Come* (Harmondsworth, UK: Penguin).
10. As many have noted, the advance of genetic technology is constantly shifting the boundary between 'nature' and 'nurture', contracting the domain of the former; cf. A. Buchanan, D. Brock, N. Daniels and D. Wikler (2000), *From Chance to Choice: Genetics & Justice* (Cambridge: Cambridge University Press).
11. It's fair to say that the claims for this evidence, though currently increasing, have been far less sweeping in the latter half of the twentieth century than in its first three decades; cf. D. Kevles (1985), *In the Name of Eugenics* (Berkeley: University of California Press), passim. And the chastening impact of Nazi eugenics has apparently played as much of a role in this development as the far greater complexity introduced by molecular genetics into the interpretation of Mendelian laws of heritability; cf. E. Keller, 'Nature, Nurture and the Human Genome Project', in D. Kevles and L. Hood (eds)

(1992), *The Code of Codes* (Cambridge, MA: Harvard University Press), pp. 281–8. Recent research does suggest the influence of specific genetic factors in various forms of cognitive and affective retardation and deterioration. T. Dobzhansky (1973), *Genetic Diversity & Human Equality* (New York: Basic Books), p. 12, uncontroversially reports: 'That differences between individuals in whatever qualities the IQ tests measure are genetically as well as environmentally conditioned is now securely established.' E. Wilson (1975), *Sociobiology: The New Synthesis* (Cambridge, MA: Harvard University Press), p. 550, more controversially reports that 'Moderately high heritability has been documented in introversion–extroversion measures, personal tempo, psychomotor and sports activities, neuroticism, dominance, depression, and the tendency toward certain forms of mental illness such as schizophrenia ...'; see also D. Wasserman and R. Wachbroit (eds) (2001), *Genetics and Criminal Behaviour* (Cambridge: Cambridge University Press). A useful philosophical overview is provided in M. Ruse (1979), *Sociobiology: Sense or Nonsense?* (Dordrecht: Reidel).

12. Quoted in Koonz, 'Genocide and Eugenics', p. 156. Holmes's remarks, as well as their practical consequences, were often cited by leading Nazis during the 1930s and at their various postwar trials. On the development of the concept of 'degeneracy' as a term of both clinical and cultural appraisal in the nineteenth and early twentieth centuries, see D. Pick (1989), *Faces of Degeneration* (Cambridge: Cambridge University Press).

13. Whether (d), (e) and (g) should also be rejected is discussed below.

14. A standard view is that unlike, say, the Inquisition which identified Jews confessionally, the Nazis (at least officially) identified them genetically. This is only partially true. According to the 1935 Nuremberg Laws, in particular the First Supplementary Decree of the Reich Citizenship Law of 14 November 1935, a 'full Jew' is any person with at least three Jewish grandparents while persons with only one or two Jewish grandparents are, respectively, 'quarter Jewish' and 'half Jewish'; cf. R. Proctor (1988), *Racial Hygiene* (Cambridge, MA: Harvard University Press), pp. 131–2, and M. Burleigh and W. Wipperman (1991), *The Racial State* (Cambridge: Cambridge University Press), p. 45. However, and quite inconsistently, such grandparents could be deemed to be Jewish on confessional grounds alone; cf. Y. Bauer (1982), *A History of the Holocaust* (New York: Franklin Watts), p. 103.

15. That is, the philosophically astute Nazi distances himself from the tactic, employed by so many of his benighted colleagues, of stipulating a value-laden (rather than biological) definition of 'human' whereby Jews are not humans.

16. That is, the philosophically astute Nazi does not burden himself with the heroic task of arguing that the 'Final Solution' has *no* moral costs.

17. Nor are utilitarians debarred from rejecting proposition (j). But since they must deploy the *argument from factual error* to do so, utilitarianism cannot support the kind of commitment to Holocaust-abhorrence sought in this paper.

18. So Berel Lang and others would be mistaken to say, of *this* Nazi, that his 'willingness to risk losing the more general war in order to carry on that [extermination] campaign' (for example by sanctioning the diversion of military resources from the hard-pressed eastern front) is not 'adequately explained on instrumental grounds alone'. Nor need *this* Nazi's commitment to that campaign extend to an endorsement of the many forms of gratuitous brutality practised in the death camps. Cf. B. Lang, 'The History of Evil and the Future of the Holocaust', in Hayes, *Lessons and Legacies*, pp. 101–2.

19. H. Steiner (1994), *An Essay on Rights* (Oxford: Blackwell), passim.

20. This latter claim is implied only indirectly by the compossibility condition and more directly by the 'Choice (or Will) Theory' of rights: a theory defended in *An Essay on Rights*, pp. 59–73, 92, not least on the grounds that its rival, the 'Benefit (or Interest) Theory', unavoidably underwrites the possibility of mutually inconsistent rights; see

further M. Kramer, N. Simmonds and H. Steiner (1998), *A Debate Over Rights: Philosophical Enquiries* (Oxford: Oxford University Press), pp. 233–301. Claim (1) above expresses the essence of the Choice Theory, and its rejection by the Benefit Theory partly explains how the latter can license enforcible paternalistic interdictions of rights-bearers' waivers.

21. More specifically, I argue that *if* a moral code contains a plurality of primary rules which include a rule enjoining respect for rights (that is, justice), those rights must be compossible and that rule must be lexically prime. This leaves open the possibility of moral codes (for example utilitarianism) lacking such a rule; ibid., ch. 6. Cf. J. Rawls (1972), *A Theory of Justice* (Oxford: Oxford University Press), pp. 42 ff.; R. Nozick (1974), *Anarchy, State and Utopia* (Oxford: Blackwell), pp. 28–33; R. Dworkin (1981), 'Is There a Right to Pornography?', *Oxford Journal of Legal Studies* **1**, pp. 177–212.

22. Doubtless we *do* have moral duties to future persons. But since those duties aren't correlative ones – aren't entailed by rights – they must be fulfilled voluntarily.

23. This paper owes much to conversations with Norman Geras, John Harris, Hartmut Kliemt and Caroline Steiner.

Chapter 6

Perpetrator Motivation: Some Reflections on the Browning/Goldhagen Debate

Nick Zangwill

The Issue

What motivated the perpetrators of the Holocaust? Christopher Browning and Daniel Goldhagen differ in their analysis of Reserve Police Battalion 101 (Browning, 1992; Goldhagen, 1996). The battalion consisted of around 500 'ordinary' Germans who, during the period 1942–44, killed around 40,000 Jews and who deported as many to the death camps. Browning and Goldhagen differ over the motivation with which the men killed. I want to comment on a central aspect of this debate.

There is much that I shall not comment on. I shall avoid issues about whether there was something special about the Germans which led them, as a nation, to the killings they did, on the scale they did, to the people they did. That debate has generated the most controversy. But in fact it is not the only issue, or even the most interesting issue, that these two historians raise. So far as possible, I shall focus on why these particular 'ordinary' German men did what they did.

For the most part, I shall examine and assess the arguments deployed by Browning and Goldhagen over this particular battalion. But I also want to show how, or perhaps more modestly, tell a story according to which, the difference between these two historians over Battalion 101 is an instance of a broader difference over the explanation and justification of human action. Indeed, the difference may be deep enough that it reveals a difference over human nature itself. However, the focus will be primarily on the particular historical case, even though the broader issues are never far away.

The issue seems to be one of empirical psychology: what motivated the men? So what interest might a philosopher have in the issue? Why not leave it to those who have the relevant empirical expertise? However, empirical psychological questions about motivation are not categorically distinct from philosophical questions about the nature and explanation of action. And particularly controversial cases may reveal these differences. One of the good things about the writings of these two historians is the way they bring this out, and do so explicitly at times. They do not superficially drop the names of philosophers or vague philosophical isms; rather recognizably philosophical issues are transparently and honestly aired. Theirs is no mere postmodern posturing or pretentious wordiness, but a serious and honest attempt to explain a particular historical event in the light of more general considerations, and at the same time to think about the more general considerations in the light of the particular historical event.

I would like to mention that I admire the work of both these historians. The issue has become rather partisan, so that it is assumed that one must be cheering for one and booing the other. But if I am right that there are rather large conceptions of human action and human nature underlying the debate, then I think we should become more appreciative of the fact that both have views that have considerable plausibility. And even if we think one of them wrong, then we should do them the credit of thinking them wrong in an interesting way, a way that springs from a deep and attractive, if ultimately misguided, view of the springs of human action.

The target question is: what were the *motives* of the perpetrators of Battalion 101? These perpetrators were almost all Germans and their victims were almost all Jews. Many perpetrators of these kinds of killings of Jews were not German, and many other victims of similar German battalions were not Jews. But in this case, for the most part, perpetrators were Germans and victims Jews.

However, both Browning and Goldhagen do at times appeal to non-German perpetrators and to non-Jewish victims as evidence for their views about the German killing of Jewish victims. This is one way in which, in the course of the debate, the focus gets widened and then narrowed again.

Our question is also restricted in time. The question is: what were the motives of the men *at the point of action*? Historians may appeal to anti-Semitism in Germany in the prewar Nazi period or in the pre-Nazi period as *evidence* for a view about the wartime motivations of the men. Goldhagen and Browning differ on this question. For example, Browning queries Goldhagen's assessment of the extent of 'eliminationist' anti-Semitism during the Nazi and pre-Nazi period in Germany (Browning, 1998, pp. 194–200). And since the men were a representative cross-section of German society, Browning infers that anti-Semitism played less of a role in the minds of the men of Battalion 101 than does Goldhagen. Similarly, the two historians sometimes appeal to what the men said under interrogation after the war. But the hope is to locate the ultimate motivation as they killed. This is another way that the focus gets widened and then narrowed again.

Broadly speaking, the main issue that separates Browning and Goldhagen is the extent to which *anti-Semitism* was a motivating factor in bringing these German conscripts to kill Jews. Roughly, Goldhagen thinks that it was, whereas Browning thinks that it wasn't. But, since it is important that anti-Semitism comes in different forms, the more precise claim at issue is whether the killers were motivated by 'eliminationist' anti-Semitism, where that amounts to thinking that Jews should be got rid of. This might be either by expulsion ('resettlement') or by genocide. 'Genocidal' anti-Semitism is one kind of 'eliminationist' anti-Semitism, which is, in turn, a species of the broader genus of anti-Semitism. Both Browning and Goldhagen cite evidence in their favour, and I shall not attempt to adjudicate. Goldhagen thinks that most Germans in Nazi Germany endorsed eliminationist anti-Semitism, and also that the majority of the men of Battalion 101 did so too, and killed for that reason. Browning disagrees with Goldhagen over whether the majority of Germans in pre-Nazi and Nazi Germany endorsed eliminationist anti-Semitism, and he disagrees over the men of Battalion 101 (Browning, 1998, p. 215). Browning thinks that most Germans held a milder kind of anti-Semitism, which meant that they were passive and did not resist the actions of a minority who held the more virulent form. He writes:

> With a few exceptions the whole question of anti-Semitism is marked by silence ... It would seem that even if the men of Reserve Police Battalion 101 had not accepted the anti-Semitic doctrines of the regime, they had at least accepted the assimilation of the Jews into the image of the enemy. (Browning, 1992, p. 73)

> Influenced and conditioned in a general way, imbued in particular with a sense of their own superiority and racial kinship as well as Jewish inferiority and otherness, many of them undoubtedly were; explicitly prepared for the task of killing Jews they most certainly were not. (Ibid., p. 184)

By contrast, for Goldhagen

> the perpetrators, 'ordinary Germans', were animated by antisemitism, by a particular *type* of antisemitism that led them to conclude that the Jews *ought to die*. (Goldhagen, 1996, p. 14)

For Browning, it is sufficient to explain the killings that (1) a majority of the men had a far less virulent form of anti-Semitism, (2) that a minority had the more virulent eliminationist form, plus (3) crucial 'situational' factors – pre-eminently, peer-pressure and authority mechanisms – that operated on the majority of the men (Browning, 1992, pp. 184–6; see also Browning, 2000, p. 169). I shall say that Browning's explanation is 'situational' and that Goldhagen's is 'evaluational'. Of course, the situation was not black and white. Many complex factors bore on the men. There is obviously *some* truth in both Browning's and Goldhagen's hypotheses. The question is how much weight to give to situationist and evaluationist factors.

Both Browning and Goldhagen are fascinated by the opportunity provided by Major Trapp for opting out of the killing, which was by and large ignored by the men (Browning, 1992, p. 2; Goldhagen, 1996, pp. 213–14). Both seek to explain this absence. Goldhagen's thought is: without the motive of anti-Semitism, surely the men would not have obeyed a weak order, the disobeying of which carried no sanction, unless they morally endorsed it and were motivationally inclined to do it. That certainly seems plausible. Nevertheless, it is also possible that many of the men were not sufficiently motivated to kill in virtue of their less virulent anti-Semitism, but other factors led them to it. That, I presume, is Browning's position. Hence other factors are brought into play and given explanatory salience besides eliminationist anti-Semitism.

So – to conscript Kant's language – for Browning, the men merely acted in accordance with anti-Semitism but not out of respect for anti-Semitism, whereas for Goldhagen the men acted in accordance with anti-Semitism *because* they acted out of respect for anti-Semitism. Goldhagen's explanation is Kantian in that it puts the men's moral conception of their own actions at centre stage. Browning's explanation is more Humean in that it seeks to explain their actions by appeal to various causal factors, which include internal mental dispositions and external 'situational' factors, and which may or may not include a self-directed moral evaluation. Perhaps a Humean can explain how moral evaluation is possible on the basis of attitudes and desires (Blackburn, 1998). But for a Humean, action explanation can proceed without moral evaluation.

Compare a case where Goldhagen's thesis is clearly correct and where Browning would obviously be wrong – as I am sure he would admit. Every one of the leading Nazis executed after the Nuremberg trials went to their deaths with a clear conscience. They say as much. They all believed that they had done the right thing. For example, at the Nuremberg trials, Göring said: 'I will absolutely and gladly take responsibility for even the most serious things which I have done …'[1] And again: 'The only motive which guided me was my ardent love for my people, its happiness, its freedom, and its life.'[2] Obviously, Göring was no amoralist! At one point, he spoke of his 'sense of justice'.[3] There is no plausibility in the idea that Göring was someone who was attracted to evil *qua* evil, as Berel Lang suggested that many Nazis were (Lang, 1990; I argue that the Nazis had moral views that were false but perfectly coherent in Zangwill, 2000).

The leading Nazis believed that they had all put Germany first, in a certain way of conceiving of what 'Germany' means. German Jews, of course, did not count as 'German' in this special conception – indeed they were conceived to be the very antithesis of Germans. There should be no doubts as to the motivations with which leading top Nazis acted. They did not suffer from weak will of any sort. They were not subject to over-riding situational pressures. It is clear that they believed in what they did, and they acted accordingly. Those hanged at Nuremberg went to their deaths believing that they had done the right thing. The word 'Germany' was on all their lips. To deny this would be to deny the evidence of what they themselves said, and much else besides. I take it that it is not controversial to claim that the top Nazis were motivated by anti-Semitism. Of course, even they were not all alike. Anti-Semitism was a priority for Himmler in a way it was not for many other of the leading Nazis. Nevertheless, the others clearly had strong and motivationally significant eliminationist anti-Semitic views and attitudes, which flowed at least in part from their particular brand of German nationalism.

Our question is whether something similar is true of the more 'ordinary' men of Battalion 101. Browning distinguishes between the more fanatical Nazi leaders and the general public (Browning, 1998, p. 201). But, by itself, this doesn't meet Goldhagen's point. For even if there is such a distinction, the question is what the less fanatical form of anti-Semitism consisted in. For it may have been fanatical enough to be the kind of reflectively endorsed eliminationist motivation that Goldhagen thinks the killers had.[4]

The question is: what was going on in the minds of the men as they killed? Goldhagen, in somewhat Hegelian style, thinks that ideology drove at least this segment of history (Goldhagen, 1996, p. 455); Browning, in somewhat Marxist style, thinks that ideology did not drive at least this segment of history.

A similar kind of issue is played out in many areas in the humanities. For example, there is an issue about the kind of explanation supplied in the sociology of art, particularly in its standard Marxist and feminist forms (Bourdieu, 1984; Eagleton, 1984; Wolff, 1984). In so far as it is definitive of the sociology of art to abstract from the conscious mental states of the producers and consumers of art, there is a good case for saying that the whole subject is predicated on an error. For no purely 'structural' or 'functionalist' explanation can match the power of a mentalist explanation according to which people's motivations in making and consuming art are, to a significant extent, *transparent* to them. We need to probe people's conception of their own actions, which they see as flowing from their own desires and evaluations. Moreover, the history of art cannot be understood without taking that perspective on board, and it cannot be understood if it confines itself merely to examining abstract social structures, and the like. (I pursue an argument along these lines in Zangwill, 2002.) The debate over the Holocaust is similar in many ways.

Note that the issue we are addressing is rather indirectly related to a standard issue about the Holocaust, according to which there are 'intentionalist' or 'functionalist' explanations of it. For the 'functionalist' school, the ideological contents of the killers' heads did not matter. Whatever motives or ideology they had would not have made any difference, for it was the social structures that determined the occurrence of the Holocaust. On this view, ideology was epiphenomenal, as it is for many Marxists. For the 'intentionalist' school, the virulent anti-Semitism of the Nazis themselves and their narrow circle drove history. But, as with the functionalist school, the thoughts of the men in the killing fields – the perpetrators – were epiphenomenal. But for Goldhagen, both these views are wrong. He is, as it were, a democratic Hegelian: the ideology of the masses drove history, at least in this case. Goldhagen is nearer the intentionalist school than the functionalist school, for unlike the functionalists, he thinks that ideology was efficacious, but Goldhagen also thinks that the efficacious ideology was not restricted to the Nazis and their immediate circle, but was embraced by the majority of Germans, and in particular by those who carried out the killings. Goldhagen goes as far as to assert the counterfactual that if the men in the Battalion had lacked the ideology, the killings would not have happened.

Goldhagen's explanation is not 'monocausal' as many of his cruder critics carelessly and unfairly alleged. (See some of the essays in Shandley, 1998.) Goldhagen allows that many factors together led to the Holocaust. But Goldhagen does think that anti-Semitism was the only relevant *motivational* factor in leading the men to kill. Goldhagen recognizes that other factors were necessary for the killings, but he insists that eliminationist anti-Semitism, as a real psychological factor in the mind of the majority of the killers, was also an important necessary condition (Goldhagen, 1998, pp. 140–41). He thinks, that is, that it is a condition without which the killings would not have taken place. For Goldhagen, the other necessary but non-motivational factors were that state power was in the hands of those committed to extreme anti-Semitic policies, and the war meant that there was the military power and circumstances in which to execute those policies. But the eliminationist anti-Semitic motivation was necessary as a factor in the minds of most of the men. Browning denies this. I shall end up agreeing with Goldhagen about this motivational necessary condition, but I also think that other motivations were necessary. These other motivations are suggested by Browning's work, even though Browning did not put his conclusions in motivational terms. Hence the eliminationist anti-Semitic motivations of the men are not motivationally sufficient to explain the killings.

Some Inconclusive Arguments

Goldhagen argues that the fact that the men of Battalion 101 were *proud* is evidence against Browning's peer-pressure hypothesis. If Goldhagen is right that the men were indeed proud, it would be significant, for pride is a moral emotion. If the men were proud, then they morally endorsed their actions. But why should we think that they were proud?

Goldhagen adduces the *photographs* taken by members of the Battalion as evidence for their pride (Goldhagen, 1996, pp. 245–7, pp. 405–6). The photographs, Goldhagen maintains, show that they felt pride, not shame, in their work. The men certainly look cheerful and proud in the photographs, and so the photographs seem to suggest that the men were proud of their work and therefore did not act out of peer pressure. If they were proud, then they must have judged that their work was worthwhile.

It is not controversial that the photographs present their soldiers as apparently cheerful and proud of what they are doing. However, inferences from that are controversial. One only has to be a little cautious to think that reading real pride into the men in the photographs is at least not straightforward and at most speculative and risky. First, we can easily imagine a sceptical Browning asking: are these photographs a representative sample of the photographs available? And are the men depicted in the photographs a representative sample or just the extreme minority of the men that Browning concedes were eliminationist anti-Semites? And second, even if the photographs do show a representative sample of the men, posed photographs of this sort are typically the upshot of a deliberate project of constructing history. When one poses for a photo, one often presents the appearance one wants to be 'remembered'. One is fabricating 'memory' as one would like it or as others would like it. Even unposed photographs do not simply 'present' reality in a straightforward way. But in posed photographs the situation is far more complex. For the people who pose are participants in creating the resulting photograph. The idea that there is the photographer, on the one hand, and the posing people, on the other, who are merely recorded in the photograph, is surely an illusion. The posing people are collaborators in the overall photographic enterprise.[5]

This point harms Goldhagen's case, because we cannot take the photograph as reliably recording pride. The men are likely to have been adopting the emotional guise that they thought was deemed appropriate in that context. It does not follow that they really felt that emotion. There is little reason to believe that, on this basis. For these reasons, and perhaps for others, the *apparent* pride in these photographs of these soldiers does not lend much support to Goldhagen's hypothesis. Perhaps it is weak evidence. But by itself, it is not sufficient to justify Goldhagen's evaluational view. The photographs might weakly confirm something we already had evidence for, but they are not enough on which to found a controversial doctrine.

Goldhagen appeals to the *cruelty* of the perpetrators. Here he appeals to victim testimony rather than perpetrator testimony. He appeals to the Jewish victims who report that the perpetrators killed with joy and hatred (Goldhagen, 1998, p. 135). This evidence from victims is stronger than that from photographs since the men clearly did not care what their Jewish victims thought, whereas they did care what would be thought by those they thought would see the photographs. The men apparently *enjoyed* the killing. The cruelty of the killings does seem to speak against Browning's obedience or situational views and for Goldhagen's evaluational view. Goldhagen's thought is: why would one *cruelly* and *enthusiastically* obey orders to kill if one disapproved of the orders or even were evaluatively neutral about them? This cruelty, then, seems to support Goldhagen's evaluational explanation. In Goldhagen's words: 'ordinary Germans were motivated by a virulent form of anti-Semitism that led them to believe that the extermination of the Jews was necessary and just' (Goldhagen, 1998, p. 137).

The debate over cruelty often involves argument by comparison. Goldhagen argues that non-Jewish victims of the Holocaust were treated differently in this respect. Browning replied by disputing this. Browning claims that the Germans were also cruel to non-Jewish victims. He gives the example of the group in charge of killing the mentally handicapped who held a party to celebrate killing 10,000 people (Browning, 1998, p. 208). This seems to show cruelty and pride in their work of the same sort that Goldhagen emphasizes in the case of the killing of Jews. But this particular reply of Browning's is ineffective, for many reasons. For one thing, this was not the work of Battalion 101. But, putting that to one side, the men of Battalion 101 might have had all sorts of other murderous ambitions towards other groups, which they were not able to fulfil. Whether or not they also had other such murderous ambitions, they were able to fulfil their ambitions with respect to the Jews. That they were eliminationist anti-Semites does not mean that they were perfect angels in other respects! Furthermore, that *non*-Germans also killed Jews cruelly is simply irrelevant. It does not make the German killers less cruel. There is also a difficulty with the particular example that Browning uses. That the killing of the mentally handicapped was celebrated shows *callousness*, not necessarily *cruelty*, which is something different. They were celebrating a job well done. They clearly did not care about those they killed. But a cruel act is one in which one *does* care, negatively, about one's victim. However, there may be better examples that Browning could draw on. Perhaps they treated Soviet prisoners of war as they did the Jews. But even if this were so, it would not help Browning, for it just shows that the men were generously catholic with their cruelty. Anti-Semitism can and does coexist perfectly comfortably with all kinds of other negative motivations and evaluations concerning other groups.

Given that the Jews were not just killed but killed cruelly, Goldhagen's explanation certainly seems to have the edge over Browning's more situational explanation. This was not merely *effective* killing, as it was when they killed the mentally ill.

However, the bad news for Goldhagen is that even if he is right about the distinctive cruelty with which the men of Battalion 101 killed Jews, it is far from clear that this supports his evaluational thesis. There is a fundamental objection to Goldhagen's whole argument on this point. There is a familiar and hallowed contrast between pleasure and duty. This contrast has been a feature of the intellectual landscape at least since Plato. The two can be in tension. Stern duty can point us in one direction, while seductive pleasure tempts us elsewhere. Human weakness may make one pursue pleasurable things that we believe are not right. In particular, that one *enjoys* one's work does not mean that one thinks it *right*. Goldhagen asks us to respect the victims' evidence, which seems sensible, but if the victims merely report that the perpetrators *enjoyed* the killing, we cannot make any evaluational inference from that, for the perpetrators may have been motivated by pleasure, not duty. (Joanna Bourke (1999) documents many cases in which men enjoy killing in war.)

There could in principle be victim evidence, which somehow pointed to a specific *type* of pleasure or cruelty, which more obviously spoke of an evaluation or a self-reflective endorsement of the killings. But so far as I know (and I may be wrong about this), neither Goldhagen nor anyone else has offered specific evidence along these lines. (I should say that I think that such an argument would be very interesting, and might have a good chance of succeeding in supporting the evaluational hypothesis.)

The contrast between duty and pleasure can also be taken the other way. One can think something right but take no pleasure in it. One might think one's job a worthy one, but not enjoy it. For example, a rat-catcher might feel this way. This objection to Goldhagen is the flip side of an objection to Browning. Browning often appeals to the *displeasure* of the men in killing Jews, as evidence against Goldhagen's evaluational view (for example Browning, 1998, pp. 211–15). Browning says that the men were 'angry, sickened, depressed and shaken' (ibid., p. 212). Let us assume that Browning is right that the men felt these emotions at the time. Let us take their word for it – despite ample reasons for thinking that they had reasons to play down their wartime activities and their endorsement of the 'work' that they were engaged in. Perhaps they really had these emotions and desires. However, Kant, rightly, in my view, distinguished these kinds of motives from the motive of duty (Kant, 1998). Goldhagen's claim is, or ought to be, that they acted, at least in part, out of the motive of duty. One might think that it is one's duty to kill rats or ants but be 'angry, sickened, depressed and shaken' at the unpleasant nature of the work one must do. One might think that the work is a pressing duty but not want to do it *oneself*, like a gory but essential medical operation. One might find it distasteful, disgusting and so on, but think that it ought to be done. Or one might think that the cockroaches in one's kitchen deserve to die, but one might not at all relish treading on them. One might find killing them repulsive, despite one's positive evaluation of one's action. Similarly, that some of the men of Battalion 101 did not enjoy killing Jews does not show that they were not partly driven to do it by the thought that it was their duty to kill them.

The crucial issue is: did the men think that they were doing the right thing? Not: did they enjoy it? Indeed there is an *ad hominem* point against both authors here. If

Goldhagen is prepared to dismiss some of the men's reluctance to kill as stemming from mere squeamishness as opposed to moral disapproval, then he should also be prepared to grant Browning that some of the pleasure the men felt in killing merely shows a kind of visceral blood-lust pleasure, rather than moral approval. And it is no less true that if Browning wants to appeal to visceral blood-lust, he should allow Goldhagen the appeal to squeamishness. Kant's important distinction between 'inclination' and 'the motive of duty' means that the pleasure the Germans took in killing Jews, or equally the displeasure that led some to refrain from killing, does not establish that they were acting or refraining from acting out of duty – that they judged what they did or did not do to be right.

At one point, in support of his non-evaluational view, Browning quotes the policeman who said after the war: 'Truthfully, I must say that at the time we did not reflect about it at all' (Browning, 1992, p. 72). But that is quite consistent with Goldhagen's evaluational view. For perhaps they 'did not reflect' because it was *obvious* to them that it was right. Browning unwarrantedly projects a non-evaluational interpretation on to these words where there is also a rival evaluational interpretation. Contrast the words of the murderous policeman with the words of a Polish 'righteous gentile' called Stefan Raczynski, who said 'It was the natural thing to do ... when the Jews started coming from the forest and they were hungry, we gave them food and didn't think anything of it.' Somewhat similarly, a Dutch 'righteous gentile' called Arie van Mansun said 'There was nothing special about what I did. I did what everyone should have done.' (Both quoted in a display in the United States Holocaust Museum.) A moral judgement can inform one's behaviour in a fundamental way, even though it is not at the forefront of one's consciousness.

Authority

Let us now turn to the issue of authority and of obedience to the orders of authority.

Both Browning and Goldhagen are impressed by the fact that no German was ever punished for refusing to follow orders to kill Jews. Before the killing began Major Trapp, who was in charge of the entire Battalion, told the men that they did not have to kill – they could opt out with no sanction. And a few men were known to have taken up this offer and indeed suffered no sanction. Goldhagen infers that authority mechanisms (alone) cannot explain compliance with the order to kill. *This* argument (and it is not Goldhagen's only argument, as we shall see in a moment) makes two questionable assumptions. The first is that an authority mechanism needs to be backed by sanctions to work. The second is that the men either approved or disapproved of their actions. Both of these assumptions are questionable. On the first point, an authority mechanism might work even if not backed by sanctions. It is enough that it supplies a pressure to *conform*; positive feedback can work in the absence of negative feedback. On the second, the men might have made no judgement at all, rather than a negative judgement. Hence the authority mechanism might be effective even though no sanction was applied, and even though the men did not think that their actions were right.

However, there is another argument of Goldhagen's concerning authority that I think is effective. I think it is his best card. This is his appeal to the fact that Jews were killed even in the face of orders to keep Jews alive. Here orders were being broken and authority flouted. This seems to show that killing Jews was taken to be a good thing, and killing them had little to do with authority structures (Goldhagen, 1996, pp. 382–3). My judgement is that this argument is a very promising one. The argument does, it must be admitted, make certain assumptions: that disobedience was not merely the activity of an extreme minority; that disobedience was not motivated by the pleasure of killing as opposed to a moral judgement about the action; and that the disobedience did not stem from the obedience of earlier orders which retained a kind of momentum, so that newer orders were overridden. However, I get the impression that these assumptions are plausible, though it would certainly be good to see further explicit discussion of them.

Browning replied to this argument from disobedience by saying that the men also disobeyed orders and killed non-Jews, such as Soviet prisoners (Browning, 1998, pp. 204–9). But this does not show that those killings were not evaluationally driven as well. Perhaps the killers had eliminationist anti-Semitic motivations plus similar motivations directed to Soviet prisoners or other groups.

What happened when men of Battalion 101 disobeyed orders was the very opposite of what Browning should predict if he is drawing on Stanley Milgram's work on obedience to authority (Milgram, 1969). Milgram describes a variation on his famous electric shock experiment where there are *two* authorities who disagree (ibid., pp. 105–12). One authority orders the continuation of the experiment with higher shocks while the other orders a cessation of shocks. Milgram comments:

> It is clear that disagreement between the authorities completely paralyzed action. Not a single subject 'took advantage' of the instructions to go on; in no instance did individual aggressive motives latch on to the authoritative sanction provided by the malevolent authority. Rather action was stopped dead in its tracks. (Ibid., p. 107)

But how different the Holocaust! There, there was just one authority who forbade action, and furthermore there *was* a sanction for disobedience, unlike the variation on the Milgram experiment. Yet action was *not* 'stopped dead in its tracks', but persisted despite orders. This supports Goldhagen's conjecture. Browning would have us extrapolate from the Milgram experiments to the Nazi killing fields. Well, it seems that if we do so, we will have to have recourse to eliminationist anti-Semitic ideology – to a positive moral evaluation of the killings. Otherwise, why were authoritative orders flouted?

On the issue of authority, it is ironic, given the sort of criticism which Goldhagen's book aroused outside Germany, that it is *Browning* not *Goldhagen* who appeals to the German national character! Browning talks of 'The German propensity to follow orders' (Browning, 1998, p. 217; contrast Goldhagen, 1998, pp. 142–3). Goldhagen contests this by appeal to the revolt against the Weimar Republic (Goldhagen, 1996, pp. 381–2). There Germans took to the streets against authority. But Browning replied, with considerable plausibility, that this is the exception that proves the rule, since people were revolting in order to restore an authoritarian undemocratic German tradition. On *this* point, I think that Browning is probably right to insist on the importance of specifically German authoritarianism as *a* factor leading to the Holocaust. However, on Goldhagen's side (contra Browning, 1998, pp. 217–18), this point has nothing to do with 'situational' factors and Milgram experiments, as Browning assumes. Such situational explanations appeal to factors outside of people's cognition. (Browning says that social science introduces 'factors beyond the cognition of the perpetrators' (Browning, 1992, p. 220).) But the German authoritarian culture was something consciously and reflectively endorsed, not a non-mentalistic factor manipulating people like puppets. The German people were more like *willing victims* of a Milgram experiment. As with the anti-Semitism, people *thought* that they were obeying orders that were right and proper. That was their reflectively endorsed political culture, not a mere behavioural regularity.

Browning may have been led astray by one aspect of Milgram's writing. Milgram tends to describe conformity to authority in overly behaviouristic fashion:

> There must be a ... drive, tendency, or inhibition that precludes activation of the disobedience response. The strength of the inhibiting factor must be of greater magnitude than the stress experiences, or else the terminating act would occur. (Milgram, 1969, p. 43)

But this seems to be a very odd description of the situation. It would be implausible to think that there is no mentalistic component to conforming to authority. Rather the subject's *beliefs* about authority are surely crucial. Milgram's own research suggests this. He found that a scruffily dressed 'authority' receives less obedience. As Milgram writes,

> the decisive factor is the response to authority, rather than the response to the particular order to administer shocks. Orders originating outside of authority lose all force ... It is not what the subjects do but for whom they are doing it that count. (Ibid., p. 31)

But if that is so, Milgram should not be describing his entire project as undermining the common-sense idea that

> A person acts in a particular way because he has *decided* to do so. Action takes place in a physical–social setting, but this is merely the stage for its occurrence. The behavior itself flows from an inner core of the person ... (Ibid.)

For if a person is *differentially* responsive to different authorities, the response to authority must stem from a decision, which in turn stemmed from a desire or evaluation of the person.

So when Browning says that social science introduces 'factors beyond the cognition of the perpetrators', he is following one aspect of Milgram in accepting a somewhat behaviourist conception of obedience to authority. Browning cites Himmler's speech to the SS men in which, according to Browning, he said that 'exalting obedience is one of the key virtues of all SS men' (Browning, 1992, p. 74). But this is a value that the SS men were supposed to share and internalize. It was to be a consciously endorsed value, not a mere mechanism.[6]

What is questionable here, at bottom, is the general idea that obeying orders is *content neutral* – that it is the sheer obedience which counts, not what is ordered. What is true is that once one has accepted an authority, it might be true that one obeys particular orders without consciously endorsing them when one acts, just as one drives a car – deliberately – without thinking consciously about what one is doing. But one's general acceptance of that authority, in adults, is not independent of an estimation of the rightness of what the authority orders.

My view is that there needs to be more investigation of the way the different values of the agents interacted. Authoritarian and anti-Semitic motivations and values could in principle conflict with one another, and Goldhagen cites some unusual cases where they did. But in the case of Battalion 101, by and large they did not. Authority was a motive and a value, not just a mechanism. And the same is true of anti-Semitism. For the most part, authoritarian and anti-Semitic motives and values neatly complemented each other.

Coda

The question we have been looking at, in Kant's terms, is: what was the deep and basic maxim of the actions of the men as they killed (O'Neill, 1985)? Well, there were lots of men in the Battalion, and a lot of different actions over the years, and the answer will not be exactly the same for all of them. Still, the relevant question is: for most men, and for most killings, what was the predominant efficacious maxim? Was it 'I must kill Jews' or 'I must obey orders' or 'I must not let my colleagues down'? Or was it a tie?

The indirect and comparative evidence points in both directions. Looking back at political culture in the pre-Nazi and Nazi period seems indecisive. And looking at non-Jewish victims and non-German perpetrators does not help. Cruelty does not favour Goldhagen, for the cruelty may stem from a non-evaluative pleasure and not from a value judgement.

Browning seems to be right, as against Goldhagen, that authoritarianism was as central a factor as anti-Semitism in Germany (Browning, 1998, p. 218). Yet against Browning and for Goldhagen, I suggest that authoritarianism and anti-Semitism were not rival factors but two neatly mutually fitting complementary motives. Hence I side with Goldhagen on the question of whether eliminationist anti-Semitic motivation was a necessary causal factor. The men did not act merely in accordance with anti-Semitism but also out of respect for anti-Semitism. But I don't agree that it is the only relevant motivational factor in play. The virtue of Browning's work is to draw attention to the role of authority in the killings. But Browning should not have followed the social psychologists in thinking of authority as an impersonal 'mechanism', a mere feature of the 'situation'. Instead the commitment to authority was itself part of ideology, and an evaluational matter, part of the tacit or explicit political outlook of the men of Battalion 101. The fact that authority stood for the right things, of which anti-Semitism was one among many, conferred legitimacy on the authority. And the fact that the eliminationist anti-Semitic policies they were executing were ordered by a legitimate authority conferred legitimacy on the policy. These two motives and values were mutually reinforcing. Both sorts of motivations and evaluations are indispensable to explaining the Holocaust, at least as enacted by the men of Battalion 101.[7]

Notes

1. *Trial of the Major War Criminals before the International Military Tribunal*, Nuremburg 1947–49, vol. IX, p. 564.
2. Ibid., vol. XXII, p. 368.
3. Ibid., vol. IX, p. 564.
4. My grandfather heard Hitler on a street corner in Germany in the 1920s, long before he came to power, shouting 'Death to the Jews.' Surely very few in Germany could have been in two minds about whether Hitler and his followers had genocidal intentions. Nevertheless, as Browning reminds us, only 37 per cent of Germans voted for Hitler at their last free election before the war (Browning, 1998, p. 197).
5. W.G. Sebald discusses a photograph of Kafka and two companions in which they are posed behind a comic set that reveals only their faces and gives the appearance that the people in the photograph are doing something unlikely (Sebald, 2000). In the photograph Kafka and his friends appear to be passengers on an aeroplane photographed from outside. According to Sebald, there is good reason to think Kafka was particularly unhappy on the day of the photograph, particularly with his companions, but in the photograph, he is smiling broadly, in accord with the conventions of posing for such photographs. There is also good reason to think that the companions were having a rather merry time that day, but they look very glum in the photograph.
6. Browning writes that 'soldiers can obey orders with which they do not identify' (Browning, 1998, p. 219). Certainly there is such a phenomenon, in some cases. But there is no reason to believe that the 101 killers were like this in more than a minority of cases.
7. Many thanks to Eve Garrard for reading and commenting on drafts of this paper, and to Jonathan Friday, Daniel Goldhagen, Raphael Gross and Bernard Reginster for discussion of the issues.

References

Blackburn, Simon (1998), *Ruling Passions*, Oxford: Oxford University Press.
Bourdieu, Pierre (1984), *Distinction*, London: Routledge and Kegan Paul.
Bourke, Joanna (1999), *An Intimate History of Killing*, London: Granta.
Browning, Christopher (1992), *Ordinary Men*, New York: HarperCollins.
Browning, Christopher (1998), 'Afterword', in *Ordinary Men*, 2nd edn.
Browning, Christopher (2000), 'German Killers', in his *Nazi Policy, Jewish Workers, German Killers*, Cambridge: Cambridge University Press.
Eagleton, Terry (1984), *The Ideology of the Aesthetic*, Oxford: Blackwell.
Goldhagen, Daniel (1996), *Hitler's Willing Executioners*, London: Abacus.
Goldhagen, Daniel (1998), 'A Reply to my Critics', in Robert Shandley (ed.) (1998); originally published in *New Republic*, December 1996.
Kant, Immanuel (1998), *Groundwork of the Metaphysics of Morals*, Cambridge: Cambridge University Press.
Lang, Berel (1990), *Act and Idea in the Nazi Genocide*, Chicago: Chicago University Press.
Milgram, Stanley (1969), *Obedience to Authority*, New York: Harper Torchbooks.

O'Neill, Onora (1985), 'Consistency in Action', in her *Constructions of Reason*, Cambridge: Cambridge University Press.

Sebald, W.G. (2000), *Vertigo*, New York: New Directions.

Shandley, Robert (ed.) (1998), *Willing Germans? The Goldhagen Debate*, Minnesota: University of Minnesota Press.

Wolff, Janet (1984), *The Social Production of Art*, London: Methuen.

Zangwill, Nick (2000), 'Against Analytic Moral Functionalism', *Ratio* **13**, 275–86.

Zangwill, Nick (2002), 'Against the Sociology of Art', *Philosophy of Social Sciences* **32**, 206–18.

Chapter 7

Moral Responsibility and the Holocaust

Geoffrey Scarre

It has become something of a commonplace in studies of the Holocaust that whilst it may be possible to achieve at least a limited understanding of the stimulating conditions of the worst atrocity of the twentieth century, no amount of insight into the *mentalité* of its perpetrators could ever warrant our excusing them for what they did. Not only were the Nazis and their associates creators of tremendous evils for the Jews: they were criminal, wicked agents whose motives and aims merit the most unqualified denunciation. Even writers who have probed the mind-set of the agents with some subtlety have generally been quick to disclaim any intention to deny their subjects' guiltiness. Daniel Goldhagen, for instance, in analysing the complex causes which made the men and women of Hitler's Germany succumb to the lethally false, but in the circumstances credible, ideology about Jews and Jewishness firmly condemns the Holocaust as 'one of the worst crimes in human history'.[1] Similarly Hillel Steiner considers that the perpetrators of the genocide deserve the strongest moral blame 'regardless of whether the Nazis got their facts wrong or not' about the dangers offered to the German people by the Jewish.[2] And in discussing the social, psychological and professional pressures that helped to make possible the cruel practices of the Nazi camp doctors, Laurence Thomas remarks that the truth of such explanations 'does not in any way excuse what the Nazi doctors did'.[3] These examples could easily be multiplied.

In this essay I want to explore a disquieting possibility that has been largely, if understandably, neglected by students of the Holocaust. This is that our approach to the question of Nazi guilt is substantially out of line with our normal thinking about moral responsibility and in particular with our usual notions of 'mitigating circumstances'. As a rule, when a person is charged with some moral or legal offence we are ready to listen to the case for the defence; the accused's deed may be atrocious but we do not automatically infer from the presence of *actus reus* the existence of *mens rea*. Perhaps the agent was misled or deluded about the empirical facts or falsely believed they were morally justified in what they did. Not so with the Nazis. Here we assume a priori that nothing could ever diminish the blameworthiness of the architects and agents of genocide. When all the facts are in about the cultural, social and ideological background to the Holocaust, the false racial theories, the bizarre but entrenched beliefs about 'the Jewish threat', the sense of national insecurity and the fear of enemies both within and without, and the painful attempt to redefine German identity following defeat in World War I, we are left exactly where we started on the issue of Nazi guilt: none of these facts has any tendency to lessen blame; they may help to explain but they do not even partially excuse.

If there is an inconsistency in our attitudes to the Nazis and to other wrongdoers, it can in principle be removed either by toughening up our judgements of the latter or by softening those of the former. Which option should we choose? Here we need to ask ourselves which set of moral responses is likely to be the more reliable: those which have developed in the course of everyday existence or those pertaining to experience of a far from ordinary kind? Habits of praise and blame evolve amidst the complex but familiar circumstances of ordinary life, where both goods and evils are mostly relatively modest in scale. We become practised in responding to 'ordinary' evil because we are confronted by so much more of it. It is harder to think about responsibility in more extreme and unusual situations, where we have difficulty in putting ourselves imaginatively into the shoes of the agents. What excuses we are prepared to accept is heavily dependent on our beliefs about why people act as they do; and when behaviour is as alien as that of the Nazis we are less confident that we are getting the explanations right. Hence, maybe, the attraction of the simplifying solution of reading off the moral character of the agent directly from the qualities of the deed itself, so sweeping under the carpet all troublesome questions about motive and intention. Nazi actions against the Jews were unqualifiedly evil; ergo, Nazi agents were unqualifiedly evil too. Admittedly, there might be an argument that precisely because our ordinary moral judgements have been developed in and for ordinary situations, they are likely to be *less* reliable for extreme moral phenomena. But while we clearly need to be careful in extrapolating from the usual to the unusual, the fact is that we have no better model available than that provided by our ordinary judgements, resting as they do on a tried and tested understanding of the interplay of motives, intentions and beliefs.

But it might be suggested that there is another, better reason why it would be wrong to look for excuses for the Nazis. To do so is to show that we do not take seriously enough the sufferings of the persecuted. The idea that anything could reduce the guiltiness of those responsible for six million Jewish deaths (plus the deaths of millions more non-Jewish people) is outrageously insulting to the victims. Evils of such magnitude are beyond all excuse, and anyone who fails to see that, while possibly well-meaning, possesses a radically skewed moral consciousness. Given the scale and horror of the offences committed by the Nazis against the Jews and others, it is grotesque to worry that we may be being unfair to the perpetrators of genocide. Holocaust-abhorrence, as Steiner has said, forms an 'unshakeably fixed point' in the 'moral compass' of most of us.[4] Anyone for whom this is not so needs to reflect urgently on their compass bearings.

However, I think that there is an important mistake embodied in this line of thought, though our laudable fear of falling short in our respect for the victims of genocide makes it easy to commit it. The error is that of failing to distinguish properly between the wrong character of the deed and the guiltiness of the doer. The historical record shows that some at least of the dreadful things that the Nazis did to the Jews were done because they believed the ideology of the dangerous, threatening Jew and wished to remove an enemy whom they perceived as endangering the very survival of the German race. Acceptance of this lethal ideology went right to the top. Even Hitler and Himmler believed in the absurd concoction of the Tsarist police known as the 'Protocols of the Elders of Zion', which purported to set out the programme by which Jewish leaders would achieve world-dominion.[5] A strong thread of self-defence thus ran through the tangled web which was the Nazi rationale for genocide. (Note that I am not suggesting that *all* the evil things the Nazis did to the Jews can be explained by their false consciousness – an important point I will come back to.) This conviction that the Jews imperilled the Germans was ludicrously at odds with reality; yet most moral traditions concede a right to defend oneself, by (proportionate) violence if necessary, against a dangerous enemy. The Nazis believed that the Jews offered a radical threat to the Germans and Germany and that extreme measures were therefore justified against them. In the context of total war, where cavalier attitudes to life and death prevailed and normal inhibitions against killing slackened their grip, 'extreme measures' could come to mean the Holocaust.

There is a famous Chinese story about General Ts'ao Ts'ao of the Han Dynasty who, while still a young man, fell out with the party in power at court and was forced to flee for his life. Travelling through the country incognito with a single companion, he sought refuge one night at a farm belonging to an old friend of his father. Notwithstanding that Ts'ao Ts'ao was a man with a price on his head, the farmer took in the fugitives, promising them good entertainment for the evening. Since, however, there was no wine in the house fine enough for so distinguished a visitor, the farmer hurriedly saddled his donkey and rode off to a neighbouring village to buy some. Uneasy at their host's hasty departure, the two friends were further alarmed to hear at the back of the house the sound of a knife being sharpened. They quietly stepped out into the straw hut at the rear to listen. What they heard did nothing to allay their suspicions:

> "'Bind before killing, eh?'
> "'As I thought,' said Ts'ao Ts'ao. 'Now unless we strike first we shall be taken.'
> 'Immediately they dashed in and slew the whole household, male and female; in all eight persons. After this they searched the house; in the kitchen they found a pig bound ready to kill.
> "'You have made a huge mistake," said Ch'en Kung, "and we have slain honest folk.'"[6]

The violent slaughter of eight people who have done nothing to deserve their deaths is indisputably a tragic evil, something that makes the world a worse place. But though Ts'ao Ts'ao and Ch'en Kung should have taken more trouble to establish the facts before they acted, it would be unreasonable to ascribe as much moral blame to them as we should to a gang of brigands who murdered a household purely for pleasure in the course of a robbery. The fugitives in the story may have behaved recklessly, but at least they acted in self-defence; their false beliefs about the context of action go some way towards reducing their blameworthiness. Whether one is killed 'for fun' or as a result of the kind of error that Ts'ao Ts'ao made, one ends up dead at another's hand when one does not deserve to. But the moral appraisal of the killers is not the same in each case: identical outcomes need not mean identical culpability.

In so far as the self-defensive violence perpetrated against the Jews remained unjust and unmerited, no excuse that can be made for the disastrous error that prompted it diminishes the moral awfulness of the victims' treatment. The Holocaust remains a moral evil of the first magnitude even if the main driving force behind it was what Goldhagen describes as a 'hallucinatory ideology' which wholly misrepresented Jewish intentions. That the Germans got their facts wrong does not change the Holocaust's status as one of the most disfiguring evils in human history. Innocent people suffered and died as a direct result of the intentional actions of other human beings. The Holocaust was morally appalling for the quantity and quality of its constituent acts, its blindness to the value of human beings and their lives and its exaltation of false ideals of racial purity and strength. It was one of the worst offences ever committed by men against other men, irrespective of what the offenders believed.[7]

Christopher Browning has rightly urged that we discard the 'old clichés that to explain is to excuse, that to understand is to forgive'.[8] There is no good argument to the conclusion that we are rationally obliged to excuse a piece of behaviour just because we can explain it (if this were true then God would be rationally compelled to forgive everything). Nor, on the other hand, must we deem it inexcusable. Once an action is explained, there remains the question whether excusal or forgiveness is merited. Sometimes close investigation of a bad act reveals that its perpetrator was a deeper-dyed villain than we had thought. But often the effort to understand leads us to see as 'human, all too human' behaviour that first appeared beyond the pale; we may even be faced with the humbling realization that (for all our own moral respectability!) had we been in the agent's shoes we would probably, or possibly, have done no differently. Empathetic identification with another agent does not require us to adopt or approve their point of view; we may continue to see it as profoundly mistaken in its factual or value commitments. Nor will we necessarily warm to the subject's personality or attitudes. Yet the more we grasp about the origins of actions, the less likely we are to take a black-and-white view of moral responsibility. Where we thought we saw wickedness, we may now discover ignorance, error, prejudice, thoughtlessness, bad logic, distorted values, fears and phobias, and a host of other factors that lead men to hatred and violence. As Seneca noted long ago in his essay *De Ira*, human life is replete with occasions for going wrong.[9]

Another writer to have emphasized the logical gap between understanding a bad action and excusing it is Inga Clendinnen. Her book *Reading the Holocaust* is one of the best recent studies of the psychology and experience of both victims and perpetrators, deeply felt yet dispassionate and objective in its analysis of motives. Clendinnen rejects the rejection by some writers of any attempt to understand the mind-set of the Nazis on the ground that (in the words of Primo Levi) 'to understand is almost to justify'.[10] Understanding is *not* justifying, Clendinnen insists, and we should stop fearing that the task of trying to grasp the Nazis' motives will morally corrupt us. She also strongly criticizes those who, like Saul Friedländer, have placed the debate 'in a conceptual field inhabited by words like "evil"'; this sort of talk is 'of no use whatsoever when it comes to teasing out why people act as they do' (ibid.).

Before taking up the study of the Nazis, Clendinnen spent several years researching Aztec culture and the Spanish conquest of Central America. Her first book concerned Aztec human sacrifice, which she attempted to understand from the Aztecs' point of view (a project which, she hoped, led no reader to assume that she favoured human sacrifice). Subsequently she turned her attention to the life of a charismatic Spanish missionary friar, Fray Diego de Landa, whose religious zeal caused him to be, successively, a friend and a foe to the native Indians. Clendinnen returns to the case of Fray Diego in *Reading the Holocaust*, citing him as a good example of someone whose actions we can understand without feeling much urge to excuse them. Since Clendinnen believes that Landa's case parallels that of such Nazi ideologues as Himmler, her remarks on the moral character of his actions are of much interest. Yet they are also, for reasons I shall explain, more than a little problematic.

Fray Diego started out as a defender of 'his' Indians from exploitation by secular colonists. Things changed when he discovered that his newly Christianized flock had a regrettable tendency to relapse into 'idolatry'. Landa's response was to organize a private inquisition, employing exquisite tortures to extract increasingly fantastic confessions of satanic practices from the hapless Indians. Eventually the over-zealous friar's no-holds-barred campaign against the Devil got so far out of hand that he was recalled to Spain in disgrace by his Franciscan superiors. Back home he used his enforced leisure to write a deeply sympathetic study of the Indians (Clendinnen comments on this that 'Villains are rarely simple men'). Later Fray Diego enjoyed a full restoration to favour and was sent back to Mexico as Bishop of Yucatan.[11]

Clendinnen admits that it is not easy to comprehend a man like Diego de Landa. To make any headway we need to retrieve his intellectual and social world and grasp the 'characteristic patterns' of his thought and action. Her own understanding took a quantum leap when she began to take seriously Landa's own justifications for what he did. What she had earlier dismissed as 'ejaculations of conventional piety' turned out to be 'at once the stuff of his thought and indicators of emotional intensity'.[12] She suggests that we should be equally careful to listen to the Nazis' rationalizations of their actions, however far-fetched or rhetorical they may seem to be. Yet coming to grasp what Landa thought he was up to does not make Clendinnen any more forgiving of him:

> While I respect him, even have some affection for him, I have not the least impulse to exculpate him. Understanding him better has led me to assess his capacity for harm the more severely, and to decide that I would judge him to be one of those rare beings, a fit subject for assassination. In so far as one can calculate those matters, his premature death would have saved many lives and much misery. (Ibid.)

That Fray Diego was 'a fit subject for assassination' is hard to deny. One could hardly have blamed an Indian hit-squad for bumping off the fanatical friar, that interfering foreigner who had caused their people so much misery. It would similarly have been better for the world if Hitler, Himmler and other Nazi ideologues had been murdered during the 1920s. Yet one might judge a dangerous fanatic to be 'fit' for assassination without necessarily holding them to be beyond moral excuse; one might regard them as following their conscience even while performing disastrous actions. Clendinnen's remark that she has 'not the least impulse to exculpate' Fray Diego appears odd in the light of her own analysis of his motives. The Landa of her portrait is a God-driven man who tortured the Indians' mortal bodies in order to save their immortal souls: in his own eyes, he was simply being cruel to be kind. Whilst we are not compelled to excuse a course of action just because we can explain it, we must recognize that explanations sometimes uncover genuinely exculpating factors; and that surely is the case here. If Fray Diego believed that he was only doing his duty, even *helping* his Indians by treating them so harshly, the case for moral blame looks more slender, terrible though his actions were.

Clendinnen describes Landa as a man of 'terrifying self-righteousness', possessed of an unswerving conviction that he acted in the name of God and true religion.[13] Fanatics, whatever their inspiring ideology, are rarely comfortable figures to have around; they are moral loose cannons, liable to discharge themselves when ordinary individuals will be restrained by their natural sympathies, their moral inhibitions against causing harm or their simple preference for an easy life. Fray Diego was short on tolerance but long on devotion to a cause in which he passionately believed. He too may be seen as a victim of sorts, a morally unlucky man whose character and circumstances combined to make him, if not a monster, then a doer of monstrous acts. It is easy for us from our prevalently secular vantage-point to condemn the immoderate religious fervour of Landa's day as a gross and destructive thing. But Landa could not enjoy our wisdom of hindsight. To condemn him as the worse man for that seems unfair and unreasonable.

Note that it is not my contention that historians should avoid passing value judgements on past people. Though their primary task is an explanatory one, it is neither necessary nor desirable that historians should refrain from moral appraisal of the *dramatis personae*. Virtuous and vicious people can be distinguished in the past, as they can in the present. Feeling our way towards moral judgements about those we encounter, whether in person or in the historical record, is a normal part of the process of getting to know them. We are intrigued not just by what people do but by the adequacy of their justifications. We want to know if they would be swayed by our (sensible, virtuous!) reasons, or whether they are moved by considerations which strike us as alien, shocking or incredible. And sometimes we must acknowledge that even some highly repellent practices can acquire a degree of defensibility from the world-view of their practitioners. Aztec human sacrifice, for example, was supported by the theory that the extremely unprepossessing gods in whom the Aztecs believed would shortly bring about catastrophe if they were not appeased by a regular diet of human blood. The Aztecs were thus engaged in something not unlike utilitarian calculation: they judged it better that a relative few should die in order that the majority should be saved. The chief difference between them and us is that we do not believe in their gods. Human sacrifice may be morally repugnant, but it was hard to see it as wrong from their standpoint. Therefore our moral condemnation should be muted.

Not uncommonly what seem at first to be fundamental differences in value commitments resolve themselves, on further scrutiny, into divergences in empirical belief.[14] Or the contrasting behaviour of two communities turns out to stem not from any deep disagreement about basic moral principles but from more parochial ones about the scope of their application (for example, two societies may both place an abstract value on freedom but not see eye to eye about which categories of people should be free); here too variations in empirical belief may be at work in shaping views about the structure and boundaries of the moral constituency.

But even if two groups of people differed in some quite fundamental value commitment, it could still be possible for each to find a redeeming feature in the other's position. Richard Arneson has noted that 'the capacity to do right can be factored into two components, the ability to decide what is right and the ability to dispose oneself to do what one thinks is right'.[15] He adds: 'One might hold the latter capacity to be the true locus of human dignity and worth' (ibid.). In ascribing moral praise and blame, we should be more concerned with what people bring themselves to do than with what they believe. Conforming one's will to one's conscience often involves a struggle against temptation and contrary desires; one may have to screw one's courage to the sticking-place in order to do one's duty. Arneson thinks that 'Resisting temptation and doing what one thinks is right is noble and admirable even if one's conscience is a broken thermometer.'[16] Even if a person's conscience is sound it can sometimes happen that their 'appreciation of the situation' in which they find themself is not; they falsely believe that their victim is a dangerous enemy, or a servant of the Devil, or someone whose life may or must be taken for the sake of the greater good.[17] Maybe some Aztec priests found it hard at first to rip the hearts from living victims; but they steeled themselves in time to the cruel necessity.

Should we try to see those who do terrible things in the name of duty as 'noble and admirable', as Arneson suggests? This is not so easy when their deeds fill us with loathing. Conscience does not always make cowards of us, as Hamlet thought; it can also turn us into bullies. Even if their humanity lost out in the end to their misguided principles or false beliefs, their ability to feel a pang of sympathetic pain for the people they mistreated would render them more familiar, less inhuman, to us. Appeals to 'duty' are, besides, not always what they seem: though they purport to represent the agent's heartfelt moral convictions they may merely fill a lacuna where moral reflection should have been. 'Dutiful' action is the preserve not only of agents with a lively sense of the categorical imperative but also of the morally indolent, the thoughtless and conventional. Appeals to 'duty' can be a way of passing the buck when one is confronted by a painful moral dilemma ('Don't blame me – I'm only doing what I must'). Or it can be a way of cutting the Gordian knot where one is too lazy to think through the complexities of a moral problem; instead of reflecting on the nuances of the case, one cites an approximately relevant principle and considers it settled. Worst of all, some people prefer a recourse to 'duty' (more precisely, to what others have told them is their duty) as a substitute for doing any moral thinking of their own at all.

Yet what should we say when a person does something terrible because they have decided, after due reflection, that it is their moral duty to do it? Even if our abhorrence of their action makes admiring them impossible, it would be (to say the least) harsh to deny that their intention to do right has some exculpatory force. What more can we reasonably ask of someone than that they should do what, after careful consideration, they decide to be right? We may think their notion of duty mistaken, perverse, even crazy; given the chance, we will try to persuade them to see the world by what we believe to be our own better lights. But whether we think them empirically misguided or morally purblind we must acknowledge that by *their* lights they are acting well. And it is difficult to see how we could fairly refuse to allow that fact to be significantly mitigating. Indeed we may find it hard to justify assigning *any* moral blame to someone who acts strictly according to their conscience.

It should be stressed at this point that nothing that has been said is meant to imply that all those responsible for Jewish suffering during the Holocaust were misguided idealists, at bottom upright and well-intentioned people with a distorted picture of facts or values. Hitler's 'Final Solution' supplied opportunities on an unprecedented scale for all varieties of human badness. The history of the Holocaust is a catalogue of offences staggering in both their quantity and their quality. Many found in the Jews' predicament a chance to satisfy their own vicious desires or advance their own selfish interests. Some whose social position was parlous or underprivileged were pleased to find that there were now others beneath them, on whom they could take out their anger and frustration; sadists delighted in the ready supply of victims to whom they could be cruel with impunity; those wishing to get rich quick discovered that they could line their pockets at the Jews' expense; hard-heartedness, treachery, deceitfulness and ingratitude were rife. But underlying these evils and making them possible was an ideologically driven programme which provided the real *raison d'être* of the tragedy. To be sure, part of what made the ideology seem attractive to some may have been the opportunities for sadistic satisfaction, self-aggrandizement, the discharge of envy and so on that it licensed. Not everyone who came to believe that the Jews were a threat to the German race may have *begun* by thinking like that.[18] But the age-old suspicion and fear of the Jews as the threatening 'other' could sow hatred in the hearts even of quite morally ordinary people – those occupying the vast middle ground between sadists and saints. Thus – to generalize – the Holocaust permitted cruelty rather than being motivated by sadism or *Schadenfreude*, and it allowed full rein to envy and greed without being the fruit of acquisitive instincts. Great though these evils were, they were in the main moral epiphenomena of the 'Final Solution', offences committed by opportunists who found that they could profit from the appalling situation of the Jews.[19]

The Holocaust happened when it did not because twentieth-century Germans were wickeder than the average, but because they lived in a politically and economically dislocated world in which an extreme racialist philosophy might come to seem reasonable. This was a world in which Heinrich Himmler could unblushingly inform his SS subordinates in 1943 that they had moral responsibilities to their own blood and to no one else; honesty, decency, loyalty and friendliness were, he conceded, virtues, but they were out of place in dealings with racial inferiors.[20] Our astonishment that Himmler could contemplate the violent deaths of many millions of Jewish, Russian, Polish and other men, women and children with such equanimity would not have been shared by his audience. A generation later, in a different world, the former commandant of the Natzweiler concentration camp would sob into a tape-recorder as he told his interviewers: 'Today it seems so cruel, inhuman, and immoral. *It did not seem immoral to me then*: I knew very well what I was going to do in the SS. We all knew. It was something in the soul, not in the mind.'[21] The past is indeed a foreign country.

To help us to think critically about our moral responses to the Nazis, it is worth comparing our attitudes to the Holocaust with those we take to another exceptionally violent and ideologically driven episode in European history, the early modern 'witch-hunt'. To the modern educated mind, the notion of a satanic conspiracy of malevolent witches is about as remote and incredible as the bloodthirsty pantheon of the Aztecs. But from the late fifteenth century until well into the seventeenth, belief in the reality of maleficent magic, demonic compact and the anti-Church of Satan was no mere popular superstition but a standard component of the learned world-view in even the most advanced centres of the continent. For some historians, the prosecution of (mostly) elderly women from the lower social strata for black magic and consorting with the Devil represented, in Rossell Hope Robbins's words, 'the blackout of everything that *homo sapiens*, reasoning man, has ever upheld'.[22] Writing in the significant year of 1939, H.C. Lea, author of a monumental survey of learned texts on witchcraft, took a similar view: 'There are no pages of human history more filled with horror than those which record the witch-madness of three centuries, from the fifteenth to the eighteenth.'[23] Even the title of Hugh Trevor-Roper's influential 1969 study, *The European Witch-Craze*, implies an assessment of witch-hunters and witch-judges as irrational fanatics.[24]

Yet by and large historians looking back on the witch-prosecuting centuries have taken, especially in late years, a less condemnatory line. Most scholars nowadays accept that while the belief in maleficent witchcraft was a tragic error, it was not a foolish one. In the intellectual context of early modern Europe, which still owed much more to theology than it did to the infant natural sciences, witch-theory made a great deal of sense. Four centuries ago the universe was still conceived as a battle-ground between good and evil spiritual forces, and if God's final victory over Satan was assured, in the short term the Devil would use every weapon in his considerable armoury to spite God and to procure the damnation of mankind. It was only to be expected that Satan would try to seduce human beings to join his side, and that people in socially disadvantaged positions (women, the poor, the elderly and feeble) would be particularly susceptible to his offers of occult power. Thus historians wary of imposing anachronistic standards of judgement insist that we must appraise the reasonableness of witch-beliefs, and the witch-prosecutions they inspired, by reference to contemporary ideas rather than modern ones. An age which can send men to the moon is unlikely to believe in the flight of old women on broomsticks. But in a pre-technological age, the parameters of possibility were drawn quite differently. When demonology was a more highly regarded science than physics, fear of the Devil and his wiles was neither unusual nor crazy.

With such an enemy in the offing, counter-measures had to be rigorous and uncompromising. If Satan was recruiting witches to harm the Christian faithful and advance his dominion on earth, then witches had to be rooted out by every means available. If so much of the treatment of suspected witches seems to us to manifest a pitiless brutality scarcely seen again until the days of the Nazis, with men, women and sometimes even children being burned at the stake (often following horrific tortures to extract confessions and the names of accomplices), we must remember that inquisitors and witch-judges believed themselves to be combating an immensely powerful, truly terrifying foe.[25] Perhaps 40,000 people (four-fifths of them women) were judicially executed in Europe for witchcraft over the course of three centuries: a figure small in comparison with the number of Holocaust victims but shocking enough when we consider that every one of them died for a purely imaginary crime. (Some of the accused, however, probably *attempted* to perform evil magic, or believed themselves to be witches, and so were guilty at least in intention.)

It is not an entirely new idea that we should avoid anachronistic criteria in evaluating the conceptual and moral reasonableness of witch-prosecution. As long ago as 1865, William Lecky, in his *History of the Rise and Influence of the Spirit of Rationalism in Europe*, was arguing in relation to the witch-hunt that 'Men were so firmly convinced of the truth of the doctrines they were taught, that those doctrines became to them the measure of probability, and no event that seemed to harmonise with them presented the slightest difficulty to the mind.'[26] Had men been prepared to apply their reason more empirically, basing their opinions on the data of experience rather than on 'doctrines that were furnished by the Church', the witch-belief would have been exploded sooner. But such was the prevailing climate that 'there was no such thing as a revolution of the reason against conclusions that were strictly drawn from the premises of authority' (ibid.). In Lecky's view, the few writers who expressed scepticism about witchcraft on the whole showed less ability, learning and dialectic skill than the best of those who maintained the orthodox line. Montaigne (admittedly an exception to this generalization) may have held that 'It is putting a very high price on one's conjectures to roast a man alive for them', but his younger contemporary Jean Bodin, the most brilliant political philosopher of the age, thought the case for witchcraft so assured that the harshest measures against convicted witches were justified. (It was Bodin who urged that the appropriate punishment for witchcraft was to be burned alive slowly over a fire of green wood.)[27]

Moral indignation breaks out in Lecky only when he turns his attention to the Scottish experience of witchcraft, where the Kirk promoted the prosecution of witches 'with a thirst for blood that knew no mercy, with a zeal that never tired'. The extreme cruelty of Scottish investigative procedures was evidence of 'a callousness of feeling which has rarely been attained in a long career of vice'. Even so, Lecky considers that the accusing finger should be pointed not at individuals but at 'the system that made them what they were': a narrow, fanatical, pessimistic and intolerant religious ideology which stifled the growth of the warmer human feelings.[28] In the terminology of the present day, it was moral bad luck to be born into a culture which set such little store on human happiness.

Most of us find it easier to pardon the actions of the witch-prosecutors than those of the Nazis. It is worth asking why. If the witch-prosecutors' cultural climate afforded some excuse for the evil things they did, consistency would seem to demand that we should be ready to recognize extenuating factors in the Nazis' case too. Were the latter not similarly caught in the toils of a false but (in the circumstances) believable theory whose lethal implications did not appear to them a reason for rejection? There may be two plausible reasons why, in spite of the evident parallels, our spontaneous attitudes to the two cases tend to be dissimilar. One is that we no longer inhabit the same ideological planet as the witch-believers and it is relatively easy to maintain a detached and objective response to people, long-since dead, whom we meet only in the pages of history books and sensational novels. (This causal explanation does not in itself imply, of course, that such a response is either right or wrong.) In contrast, the world of the 'Final Solution' is still very largely our world: not only is the Holocaust still within the living memory of many, but inter-racial tensions, punctuated with sharper episodes of violence and 'ethnic cleansing', have continued to the present day. While witch-prosecution is no longer a possibility in Western Europe, recent events in the former Yugoslavia show how far enlightenment has still to go before ethnic hatreds become 'mere' history. Time has healed the wounds left on society by the great witch-hunt but not yet those caused by the Holocaust: neither the injuries inflicted on its immediate victims nor the traumatizing effect on successor-generations.

The second reason is one we have met with already: it is feared that taking a 'soft' line on Nazi guilt insults the millions who suffered at their hands, including the living survivors of the camps and those who lost loved ones in the genocide. But do we then insult the thousands of executed witches when we excuse their persecutors on the ground that they acted justifiably in the light of their own sincerely held but grossly mistaken view of the world? Against this charge it can be pointed out that our ability to pity the victims, or to regard their fate as tragic, is not diminished by our judging that their tormentors were acting in good faith. A sense of what the former lost, and of the evil of their losing it, is quite consistent with a belief that there were factors which reduced (in some cases even to zero) the guilt of the latter: unmitigated evil, mitigated guilt. But if we say this with regard to witchcraft-prosecution, we can and should say it too in relation to the Holocaust. It does not represent the Jewish fate to have been a whit less terrible than it was if the major share of the blame for it is placed on the Nazis' adherence to a 'hallucinatory ideology'. Admittedly it is distasteful to criticize those whose sensitivity to the sufferings of Holocaust victims makes it repugnant to them to allow that anything could ever lessen Nazi guilt. Nevertheless I would argue that their attitude is grounded on a misapprehension of the conditions for respect. What crucially matters here is not how guilty the persecutors were but how innocent the victims. Were we to perceive the analysis of Nazi motives as merely an intriguing historical problem we could rightly be accused of a shortfall in our respectful recognition of the humanity of the persecuted. But the undeserved suffering of the Jewish race under the Third Reich rends our hearts as it challenges our comprehension. One would have to have an exceedingly low capacity for empathy – or be as the Nazis were, in the grip of some theory – to escape being moved by a tragedy of such intensity and scale.

Empathy, of course, requires a certain amount of knowledge of the victims, and we know a great deal more about individuals slaughtered in the Holocaust than we do about persons executed for witchcraft. But occasionally a witch-prosecution is sufficiently well documented to spring into vivid life before the reader's eyes. In such a case our sympathies are straightaway engaged, and neither the passage of the centuries nor the alien nature of the ideas which sustained prosecution prevent our responding with the same mix of pity, anger, horror and incredulity which is raised in us by episodes from the Holocaust.

Recent historical investigations have brought to light many previously forgotten cases which assist us to see, in sharp and searing detail, what the experience of being prosecuted as a witch was like from the subject's point of view.[29] So far this illuminating research has been conducted, on the whole, without the sort of moral coyness that, I have argued, blemishes many approaches to the Holocaust. Contemporary historians try to understand witchcraft trials from the point of view of the prosecutors as well as the prosecuted. This involves examining the erroneous theories which justified, to those who believed in them, a vigorous drive against the agents of Satan. The reluctance of most scholars to level blame at the men (and sometimes women) behind the trials reflects their awareness that it takes a person of rare independence of mind to be critical of the received wisdom of their day: self-confidence and courage too, where allegiance to that wisdom is a condition of inclusion in a Church, state, nation or party. The truth – or truism – that some of the cruellest actions performed by human beings have been done in the name of duty (to God, to morality, to one's country or one's leaders) has not yet been fully grasped, or granted, in relation to the Holocaust, but needs to be if the task of coming to terms with the ethical issues it raises is to be pursued honestly and without prejudice.[30]

Notes

1. Daniel Jonah Goldhagen, *Hitler's Willing Executioners: Ordinary Germans and the Holocaust* (London: Little, Brown & Co., 1996), p. 468.
2. Hillel Steiner, 'Persons of Lesser Value: Moral Argument and the "Final Solution"', reprinted in this volume as Chapter 5, pp. 75–88; p. 77.
3. Laurence M. Thomas, *Vessels of Wrath: American Slavery and the Holocaust* (Philadelphia, PA: Temple University Press, 1993), p. 101.
4. Steiner, 'Persons of Lesser Value'.
5. On the history of this document and its variants, see Norman Cohn, *Warrant for Genocide* (London: Serif, 1996).
6. See C.P. Fitzgerald, *China: A Short Cultural History*, 3rd edn (London: Cresset Press, 1961), pp. 505–6. It is sad to relate that Ts'ao Ts'ao's regret for his mistake was muted. 'I would rather betray the whole world,' he is said to have remarked, 'than let the world betray me.'
7. Jeffrie Murphy has suggested that when we believe that something that was done to us was morally wrong and also that 'because of certain factors about the agent (e.g. insanity), it would be unfair to hold the wrongdoer responsible or blame him for the wrong action', the appropriate response to the offence is sadness, not resentment ('Forgiveness and resentment', *Midwest Studies in Philosophy* 7, 1982, pp. 503–16; p. 506). But we can surely resent the evil that is done to us even where, mustering what objectivity we can, we acknowledge the existence of factors that remove or reduce the agent's guilt. According to the *Concise Oxford Dictionary*, to resent is to '[s]how or feel indignation at or to retain feelings about (insult or injury sustained)'. We might, for instance, be indignant about the injustice of our treatment even if we do not believe that those treating us that way are being deliberately unjust.
8. Christopher Browning, 'German memory, judicial interrogation, and historical

reconstruction: writing perpetrator history from postwar testimony', in S. Friedländer (ed.), *Probing the Limits of Representation: Nazism and the 'Final Solution'* (Cambridge, MA: Harvard University Press, 1992), pp. 22–36; p. 36.

9. L.A. Seneca, *De Ira* [*On Anger*]. So many are the opportunities that none of us escapes doing wrong. 'If we are willing in all matters to play the just judge, let us convince ourselves first of this – that no one of us is free from fault' (Bk II, ch. xxviii). In Seneca, *Moral Essays*, translated by John W. Basore (London and New York: Loeb Classical Library, 1928), vol. I, p. 225.

10. Inga Clendinnen, *Reading the Holocaust* (Cambridge: Cambridge University Press, 1999), p. 88.

11. Ibid., p. 90.

12. Ibid., p. 91.

13. Ibid., p. 90.

14. Yet I do not wish to insinuate that the moral outlook of the Aztecs was indistinguishable from that of Jeremy Bentham. In what Clendinnen has called 'the shadowed world of the Mexica' not pleasure but the 'inimical, fructifying sacred, and mankind's heroic, desolating dependence' was at the basis of the moral vision. This was not a climate in which the pursuit of happiness, general or individual, was an obvious goal (*Aztecs: An Interpretation* [Cambridge: Cambridge University Press, Canto edition, 2000], pp. 263–3). On the 'entanglement of the factual and the ethical' in regard to the Aztecs, see too Hilary Putnam, *Renewing Philosophy* (Cambridge, MA: Harvard University Press, 1992), pp. 105–6.

15. Richard Arneson, 'What, if anything, renders all humans morally equal?', in D. Jamieson (ed.), *Singer and His Critics* (Oxford: Blackwell, 1999), pp. 103–28; p. 120.

16. Ibid., pp. 120–21.

17. On our common failure to appreciate situations properly, see J.L. Austin, 'A plea for excuses', in *Philosophical Papers*, 2nd edn (Oxford: Oxford University Press, 1970), pp. 175–204; p. 194.

18. I owe this important observation to Eve Garrard.

19. Or so, at least, I read the evidence. It is only fair to note that not all students of the Holocaust would agree. Some believe that the proffered ideological justifications represented not so much a serious intellectual commitment as a convenient mask for darker motivations. While this debate cannot be pursued in detail here, I think that the rival interpretation not only underplays the significance of the vast amount of anti-Jewish literature, propaganda, training programmes (including university courses on 'racial hygiene'), and so on that early twentieth-century Germans were subjected to (and perhaps, more broadly, the extent to which patterns of behaviour are determined by ideas and beliefs), but also implies an unwarrantably bleak conception of human nature. On my own, more Socratic, view, much wrongdoing that might at first sight seem to evidence depravity can be put down, on further examination, to delusion. Hard though it is to prove such conclusions, my strong suspicion is that amongst those who pushed women and children into gas-chambers there were far fewer 'moral monsters' than sadly mistaken people (ordinary people, like you or me) who believed that what they were doing was right.

20. This notorious speech has been quoted or referred to in many places. One convenient source is Martin Gilbert, *The Holocaust* (London: Fontana, 1987), pp. 614–16.

21. Tom Segev, *Soldiers of Evil* (London: Diamond Books, 2000), p. 19; italics mine.

22. Rossell Hope Robbins, *The Encyclopaedia of Witchcraft and Demonology* (London: Peter Nevill, 1963), p. 3.

23. H.C. Lea, *Materials Towards a History of Witchcraft* (Philadelphia, PA: University of Pennsylvania Press, 1939), p. xxx.

24. H. Trevor-Roper, *The European Witch-Craze of the Sixteenth and Seventeenth Centuries* (Harmondsworth, UK: Penguin, 1969). Significantly there are many historical parallels between anti-Semitism and the persecution of witches. Both groups were traditionally believed, for example, to consort with the Devil and to practise ritual cannibalism at secret meetings or 'sabbats'. See, among many texts on this theme, Venetia Newall, 'The Jew as a witch figure', in V. Newall (ed.), *The Witch Figure* (London and Boston: Routledge and Kegan Paul, 1973), pp. 95–124. It is a striking sidelight on the world of the Third Reich that Himmler and the SS took a keen interest in early modern witch-hunting, even setting up a special research group to investigate the tactics of prosecution. For the SS 'Hexenkommando' see Gerhard Schormann, *Hexenprozesse in Deutschland* (Göttingen: Vandenhoeck & Ruprecht, 1981).

25. Convicted witches in England were usually hanged, though in Scotland, as on the continental mainland, they were burned.

26. William Lecky, *History of the Rise and Influence of the Spirit of Rationalism in Europe* (London: Longmans, Green, new edn, 1882), vol. 1, p. 67.

27. Conviction breeds conviction, especially when it is the conviction of learned people. As late as the 1660s, Meric Casaubon found it hard to believe that witch-theorists of the eminence of Rémy and Grillandus could have been wrong: 'That so many, wise and discreet, well versed in their subject, could be so horribly deceived, against their wills; or so impious, so cruel, as wilfully to have a hand in the condemnation of so many Innocents; or again, wilfully, in the face of the Sun, and in defiance of God, by so many false relations, to abuse all men, present, and future; what man can believe' (*Of Credulity and Incredulity* [London: T. Garthwait, 1668], p. 38).

28. Lecky, *History*, pp. 135, 134.

29. Some randomly selected examples: P. Boyer and S. Nissenbaum, *Salem Possessed: The Social Origins of Witchcraft* (Cambridge, MA: Harvard University Press, 1974); Carlo Ginzburg, translated by J. and A. Tedeschi, *The Night Battles: Witchcraft and Agrarian Cults in the Sixteenth and Seventeenth Centuries* (London: Routledge and Kegan Paul, 1983); Gilbert Geis and Ivan Bunn, *A Trial of Witches* (London and New York: Routledge, 1997).

30. I am greatly indebted to Eve Garrard and Holger Maehle for very valuable comments on an earlier draft of this essay.

Chapter 8

Four Types of Mass Murderer: Stalin, Hitler, Churchill, Truman

Douglas P. Lackey

The provocative description of these four men as 'mass murderers' might be taken as an attempt to show that they were all equally evil. But it is not my purpose to show that Truman was morally on a par with Stalin or that Churchill was morally the same as Hitler. In fact I do not believe such things. Neither is it my purpose to set up scales to determine which of these four is the worst of the murderers. In the case of Hitler and Stalin, this would involve comparing the number of people killed in Hitler's wars and genocides with the number of people killed in Stalin's famines and purges. Such judgments would require demographic skills that I do not possess. What I hope to demonstrate is that there are different types of mass murder and different types of mass murderers, that there is a small but diverse set of rationales that those with the power invoke to justify killing the innocent. Stalin and Hitler and Churchill and Truman were all evil, but they were evil in different ways.

That the four are properly described as 'mass murderers' I have no doubt. They each made choices that produced the deaths of a great many innocent people, choices that they knew would produce such results. Other non-deadly choices were available; they were not pressured by external force or by competing moral norms into the lethal choices they did make. Despite Truman's inferiority complex, Churchill's megalomania, Stalin's paranoia, and Hitler's pathological capacity for hatred, none of them was mentally ill. The excuses of ignorance, necessity, coercion, or insanity are not available. Neither is the justification of self-defense.

True, none of them ever killed anybody with his own two hands. But when they gave the orders that ultimately produced mass death, they had every expectation that those orders would be carried out. Furthermore, if a subordinate refused to carry out a deadly order, they were committed to finding others who would do the job. Murderers need not be killers, if they can get others to kill for them.

The cases of mass killing I shall discuss – the ones, among others, that implicate Stalin and Hitler and Churchill and Truman as mass murderers – are the Ukrainian famine of 1932–33, the Jewish Holocaust of 1941–45, the bombing of Dresden in February 1945, and the bombing of Hiroshima in August 1945. Estimates of the number of victims in these tragedies differ, but there is no doubt that in the Ukrainian famine and the Holocaust, millions of people died, and in the bombings of Dresden and Hiroshima, tens of thousands of people died. But I am focusing, as I explained, on the quality of evil done rather than the quantity of evil unleashed. So

I suggest, as a thought-experiment, that we consider, of all those who died in these four atrocities, just one victim from each: one Ukrainian, one Jew, one German, one Japanese.

Consider the wife of a farmer from Vinnystia province in the Ukraine who starved to death in the winter of 1932–33. What was Stalin's relation to her death? Consider an elderly Polish Jew gassed at Auschwitz in the fall of 1943. What was Hitler's relation to his terrible end? Consider a young German refugee suffocated at Dresden the night of 13 February 1945: how did Churchill's policy choices relate to her catastrophe? Consider a Japanese child incinerated as he walked to school in Hiroshima that morning of 6 August 1945. How do Truman's choices relate to that child? What could each of these leaders say to their victims? What different types of moral and human relationships bind oppressors and victims together in life and death?

The Famine

In the minds of many people who lived outside the former USSR, the story of the Ukrainian famine of 1932–33 is a story of poor weather followed by a poor harvest followed by starvation: too little food, too many mouths to feed, government help arriving too late. But this famine, like most famines, originated in politics. Bad decisions, not bad weather, were the origin of the catastrophe, and the government as much caused the disaster as failed to cure it.[1]

After Stalin consolidated his power in 1929, he was committed to Lenin's idea that the creation of a new socialist state required the reorganization of Soviet agriculture. Farming in Russia and the Ukraine had for centuries been feudal. With the emancipation of the serfs in 1860, it began to be bourgeois, and the bourgeois trend towards small private farms was ironically accelerated by the flight of many large landowners after the Bolshevik revolution in 1917. Now agriculture was to become socialist. To achieve socialized agriculture, in Stalin's terms, two things were required: (1) the abolition of the private farm, via the combination of private holdings into large collectives; and (2) the abolition of markets for agricultural products.

The creation of the collective farms or kolkhozes was the bloody work of 1930–32. Naturally, the peasants who had prospered under the various post-emancipation regimes objected to the abolition of their family farms. Viewed now as obstacles to progress, the top layer of farmers soon found themselves classified as kulaks or 'rich peasants,'[2] where 'rich' meant something like 'owning more than one cow.' Kulaks so defined were subdivided by the authorities into three groups: (1) those to be shot; (2) those to be transported to collective labor camps in Siberia; and (3) those to be forcibly relocated on collective farms. Public support for these brutal policies was generated and sustained by Soviet propaganda that described the kulaks as enemies of society, parasites on the social organism, disease germs within it, and doomed opponents of historical progress.

Soviet propaganda conveyed the impression that the kulaks were a powerful organized group determined to subvert the building of socialism. In fact the kulaks had never, even at the beginning of the collectivization process, formed an organized political group in opposition to the regime. Unlike the White opponents of the Bolsheviks in 1919–20, the kulaks had no territory, no army, no foreign support, no capacity to wage war. Their protests were purely local and invariably ineffective. By the end of 1932, 80 percent of Soviet agriculture had been collectivized, tens of thousands of kulaks had been shot, hundreds of thousands more had been transported, and the remainder were surrounded by a population encouraged to view them as enemies. We can conclude, not by direct evidence, but by reasonable inference, that Stalin knew by 1932 that the kulaks were no threat to his agricultural policy.

Phase Two of the new Soviet agriculture entailed replacing markets with production quotas. The ideological bases for this move deserve to be laid out. The land and its products under socialism were viewed as the common property of the Soviet people, to be used for the common benefit of present and future generations. Grain was therefore neither the property of a private landowner nor the possession of farmers who had labored to produce it. In discussions of agricultural policy, a particular effort was made to portray the new form of economic organization as a cooperative interchange between the peasant class and the industrial working class, with the farmers supplying grain to the workers, and the workers, in return, supplying the farmers with steel plows, tractors, combines, and electricity – often from massive hydroelectric projects. It was expected that the use of tractors and other machines on large plots of land would substantially increase both total grain yield and the per-hour productivity of each agricultural worker. Such was the message of Eisenstein's brilliant and humorous 1929 film devoted to the new agriculture, *Old and New*.

It is obvious in retrospect that the move to publicly owned collectives and to a command economy in agricultural products could not produce the results that were hoped of it. But in assessing the choices of 1932, it must be acknowledged that it was not obvious how poor the results would be. The move from family farms to 'agribusiness' has been the long-term story of American agriculture in the twentieth century, and large-scale American farming methods, by many standards, are the most productive in the world. The notion that rural backwardness could be cured by hydroelectric power was as much a part of the American New Deal as of Soviet five-year plans, and the idea that mechanization of work would usher in an age of leisure and plenty for both rural and urban workers was present not just in the writings of Lenin and the Bolsheviks but in anti-Leninists like Bertrand Russell.[3] Optimism as regards collectivization was misguided, but not insane.

The theory of collectivization, however, will not tell you, in any particular case, what a production target should be. The Soviets felt by 1932 they had installed a superior system of agricultural organization, much better than the pre-collectivization system of 1929. So the production targets for 1932, assuredly approved by Stalin, were set substantially above the figures for the 1929 harvest. But in fact agricultural productivity since 1929 had gone into a steep decline because (a) many of the most productive farmers, as evidenced by their modest wealth accumulations in the 1920s, had been shot or deported, (b) the radical reorganization of production entailed temporary inefficiencies caused by unexpected bottlenecks and miscellaneous confusion, (c) the tractors and other mechanical support required for increased production had failed to arrive or broke down shortly after arrival, and (d) the lack of personal compensation for hard work, Soviet praise for the Heroes of Labor notwithstanding, produced the usual inefficiency of alienated toil. With productivity in steep decline, the 1932 agricultural target was in fact fantastic. This could have been known before the harvest was in, and it was certainly known soon thereafter.

The Soviets nonetheless proceeded to requisition grain at gunpoint according to the 1932 targets. Needless to report, the targets could not be met, but what grain could be found was taken from the farmers. The result was simple and dreadful: the farmers were left with no grain for themselves, no food to get through the winter and early spring. For millennia farmers had kept enough of their product to feed themselves and sold the surplus (if any) to the cities. In this case, the cities had grain for free, the farmers had nothing. They began to starve.

Early reports of starvation could have produced an end to requisitions. They did not, and requisitions, or at least demands for grain, continued through the winter. Since the demanded quota assumed the grain existed, failure to produce the grain was considered proof that the farmers, or at least the kulak farmers, were hiding grain. If grain was hidden, the farmers could not be starving, and there was no need for emergency aid. The farmers could not demonstrate that they were not hiding food, as proof that it was not hidden in one place produced only the assured judgment that it was hidden someplace else.

The official position of the government into 1933 was that the farmers were hoarding grain. Consequently in early 1933 it could not be admitted that the farmers were starving. The provinces were sealed off; those who spoke of starvation were promptly arrested. Foreign nations could not contribute food; the grain in the cities could not be returned to the provinces; city folk who provided handouts to the desperate peasants staggering in from the countryside were subject to arrest. By the spring of 1933, the livestock had been killed and eaten; the ponds fished out; the bark eaten off of the trees. Hundreds of villages became graveyards. In Vinnystia province in the Ukraine, a farmer and his wife slowly starved to death, dying in their home, surrounded by the bodies of their children.

What was Stalin's relation to that woman's death? To begin, we can infer that Stalin did not want that woman to die. In his mind, she could not be an enemy of the regime, because the enemies of the regime, he thought, were kulaks who were hoarding grain. It follows that those who starved could not have been kulaks. Nor could Stalin have viewed her death as a necessary sacrifice in the move to collectivization. There is nothing in the logic of collectivization that says that some should die so that others may prosper. It was, as the preceding sketch indicates, a win–win plan in which everyone was supposed to come out ahead, even in the short run.

It might be argued that Stalin wanted the death of this woman because killing her was one way to display the power of his regime. But this analysis cannot be correct, because the regime, early and late, never acknowledged that there had been a famine. If you are going to impress people with your qualities as a killer, you must let it be known that there are people you have killed. Furthermore, if you want to demonstrate your power, starving people to death is a poor way to go about it. With a famine, it usually appears to outsiders that natural causes, not brutal human power, have produced the deaths.

It is possible that Stalin, early and late, did not believe the reports of starvation. The arguments for socialized agriculture were not insane, and if you believed in socialized agriculture you believed that productivity would be higher in 1932 than it was in 1929. On this basis, Stalin could plausibly think, at least for a while, that there was more than enough grain for everyone. But as the terrible months of early 1933 proceeded, it was apparent to many people in high positions that the farmers had been left with nothing to eat. People very close to Stalin and involved in agricultural policy, like Nikita Khrushchev, later, much later, admitted that they knew that people were 'dying in large numbers.'[4] Some reports of starvation must have been communicated to Stalin, if for no other reason than to inform the leader of what was being said. If he continued to believe, by February 1933, that there was no famine, his belief constituted a pathological rejection of evidence. We do know Stalin had trouble assimilating bad news: witness his refusal to believe, for two long weeks in June 1941, that Germany had invaded Russia. If he could deny reality in 1941, he could have denied it in 1933.

I do not intend by introducing the word 'pathological' to provide Stalin with an excuse for persisting in the belief that there was no famine. When political leaders make decisions with immense consequences, it is necessary, morally necessary, for them to consider, 'What if I am wrong, and what are the consequences if I am wrong?' In this case, the consequence of being wrong was mass starvation. Given that fact, it was murderously reckless of Stalin not to investigate the effects of imposing the quota he himself had set.

But there is a far more probable story, which is that Stalin initially disbelieved the reports of starvation, but, by early 1933, had come to realize that they were true. Stalin then had to choose between (a) acknowledging that the production targets were too high, and returning some portion of the harvest to the farmers, or (b) refusing to acknowledge that the targets were too high, and letting the farmers starve. He chose (b). If so, Stalin was not a person who refused to take steps to discover that he was wrong. Rather he was a person who discovered that he was wrong but refused to admit it to others. Instead of conceding that the production quota was too high, he blamed the failure to meet the quota on the hapless kulaks, who (the propaganda proclaimed) were sabotaging the system. And this, we have argued, he knew they did not have the power to do.

What sort of motive might Stalin have for continuing to insist that there was no famine? If the production quota for 1932 was wrong, then the ability of the regime and its leader to set agricultural quotas was called into question. But if the regime could not set proper production quotas in agriculture, could it be trusted to set quotas in steel, or coal, or any other vital area of production? To concede a problem with production quotas was to concede a basic problem with socialism itself, at least if one equated socialism with the abolition of markets. By refusing to admit a problem with the production quota, Stalin was protecting socialism from the critics who said that efficient matches of production and consumption could only be set by market means. But what was the point of protecting this part of socialism from criticism if the famine had already demonstrated that the abolition of markets had deep problems? If we assume that Stalin knew about the famine, and let the farmers starve in order to preserve the reputation of socialism, then we have a case of someone who would kill for an idea, and kill for an idea he already knew was false. If the woman from Vinnystia could have asked the Great Leader why she was starving when the cities had more than enough grain, Stalin would have answered, 'You are dying to preserve the idea that production improves with the abolition of markets.' The woman could respond with justice, 'My death is proof that this is not true.'

So of the Ukrainians and others we are considering, as they starved in the winter of 1932–33, it can be affirmed first and foremost that Stalin caused their deaths by approving an absurd production quota. Then he either believed, against all evidence, that they were not starving, or he believed that they were starving, and did nothing about it. He came to the Ukrainians and took their food. Then he sealed them off, refused to hear their cries for help, prevented anyone else from feeding them, and afterwards denied that they had died. They had done nothing to deserve this fate. Even by Stalin's standards, they were not enemies of the state. They did not stand in the way of progress. They were conscripted soldiers whose lives were squandered through the incredible blunders of an incompetent general pursuing a dubious cause.[5]

The Jewish Holocaust[6]

Stalin hated the kulaks, but he had no reason to hate the farmers who starved in the famine. If he could have arranged matters differently, abolishing markets, collectivizing plots of land, without starving the farmers, he would have preferred to do so. This is not the case with Hitler and the Jews. Hitler's hatred of the Jews was not a sham designed to attract anti-Semitic followers for the purpose of gaining political power. Indeed, at crucial points in Hitler's career his anti-Semitism cost him power and political support. In early 1933 the German bourgeoisie supported Hitler for Chancellor despite his anti-Semitism, not because of it, because they viewed him as the best bet to defeat the Bolsheviks. In 1943 and 1944, trains that could have been used to transport vital troops and supplies to the Eastern front were diverted into the campaign to exterminate the Jews. Despite these political and military costs, Hitler never hesitated in his anti-Semitism. For him hatred of Jews was not a tactic but a mode of being.[7]

The particular causes of Hitler's anti-Semitic feelings remain a subject of conjecture,[8] but whatever the causes were they were not special. Anti-Semitic feelings of similar character and intensity were shared by a great many in the surrounding culture.[9] But Hitler was unusual in providing a written summary of his views on 'the Jewish problem.' The anti-Semitic arguments of *Mein Kampf*, although not original, are worth cataloguing as specimens of Hitler's intellectual pathology.[10]

First, Hitler argued, in standard pseudo-Darwinian style, that human races are in a struggle for survival against each other, that Germanic races are in competition with Semitic races, and in particular that Aryans are in competition with Jews, who collaborate worldwide against Aryan interests through control of banks, media, the arts and so forth. It follows from the competitive model that every plus for the Jews is a minus for the Aryans, which makes steps by Aryans against Jews acts of preemptive self-defense.

Second, Hitler held that the Jews were responsible for various crimes in recent history. The surrender of the German military forces to the Allies in 1918, in Hitler's reckoning, was not a necessary step resulting from defeat on the field but a betrayal of the German people by the Social Democratic Party, which in Hitler's mind was in the hands of the Jews. Likewise, Hitler fantasized that the Bolshevik Party was in the hands of the Jews, that the crimes of the Bolsheviks were crimes of Jews and that the threat of Bolshevism was a Jewish threat. If 'the Jews' are responsible for past crimes against Germans, then actions by Germans against Jews are just punishments inflicted on the guilty, assuming that all Jews are guilty for what any Jew does.

Third, Hitler assumes that when Jews perpetrated these and other alleged crimes, they did them because they were Jews; that is, being Jewish implies a hereditary disposition towards evil acts. It follows that even if a Jew has done nothing wrong, he cannot be trusted because he will be inclined to do something wrong in the future. And if he does not do anything wrong in the future, still his children and his children's children will have this tendency to evil.

In sum, the Jews have done evil and will continue to do evil to the Aryan Volk. The only way to stop this from happening is either to quarantine the Jews or to eliminate them from the world. Quarantine was the tactic of the racial legislation of 1935–39; it provoked resistance and occasional deadly anti-Aryan violence. (I am describing matters here from the Führer's point of view.) The alternative and permanent solution was the elimination of the Jewish people. The mental road to this second solution was paved by ferocious anti-Semitic rhetoric, in *Mein Kampf* and in Streicher's pornographic pamphlets, portraying Jews as parasites, vermin, viruses, bacteria, and other disease-causing organisms living in filth and polluting the body of the Reich. Elimination of the vermin was a matter of public health.

I have described at painful length these facts about Hitler's emotions and beliefs to distinguish the situation of the Jews under Hitler from the situation of the Ukrainians under Stalin. Stalin did not want the Ukrainians dead; Hitler wanted the Jews dead. The death of the Ukrainians was an unintended consequence of an absurd policy; the death of the Jews was the intended goal of a policy that was rational relative to its objectives. If Stalin had believed that the collectivization of agriculture could have been better facilitated with a lower production target, he would have chosen it. But the extermination of the Jews was not a side-effect of Nazi efforts towards some other goal. It was the goal itself, inexorably pursued.

It does not help our understanding of this catastrophe to describe *all* of Hitler's beliefs as 'irrational' or 'crazy.' One must locate the point where his thought processes went from mildly pseudo-scientific to utterly evil. The doctrine of the importance of race and inevitable conflicts between races was a doctrine endorsed by many nineteenth- and early twentieth-century social scientists, not all of them Nazis and not all of them anti-Semitic. The idea that 'inferior' specimens of humanity should be prevented from reproducing and 'bred out' of the world was the basis of policy in several countries, including the United States, where thousands of mentally retarded women were involuntarily sterilized in the years before World War II. The idea that the Bolshevik revolution was a Jewish plot was affirmed in the early 1920s in speeches by none other than Winston Churchill.[11] But only the Nazis inferred from these empirically shaky premises the necessity, the acceptability or even the slightest desirability of extermination. Where Nazi policy passed over from mediocre social science and madcap history into irrational pathology was in the move from bad premises to murderous conclusions, an invalid inference facilitated by intense hatred focused on a particular race existing independently of any particular beliefs.

I speak here of 'Nazi policy,' a phrase that does not name responsible individuals. There is a controversy, now a bit stale,[12] about whether the policy of extermination was Hitler's idea, or whether it was Himmler's, carried out largely beyond Hitler's notice. The idea of the death camps, the selection of the methods of extermination, the details of transportation – all these I take to be the work of Himmler and the SS. But Himmler was acting to implement an idea of extermination evident in *Mein Kampf*, and it is inconceivable that Hitler did not approve these choices and their timing. Hitler did not conceive of the Nazi Party and the Reich as something greater than himself; it was his creation and his tool, subject to his personal rule: witness his decapitation of the SA leadership in 1934, and his stupendously incompetent micromanagement of the Wehrmacht after 1941. Every initiative was approved by Hitler; every initiative could be stopped by Hitler. A clear 'nicht nun, Heinrich, erstens das Krieg,' and the program of extermination would have been stopped.

I proceed therefore to my imagined meeting between Hitler and the elderly Polish Jew who dies at Auschwitz. The Jew discovers that he is soon to die, and demands of the Führer, 'Why, why are you doing this to me?' Hitler replies, 'You are a member of an accursed race and the world is a better place if you do not exist.' 'But what have I done to you?' says the Jew. 'In my entire life I have committed no crime.' Hitler replies, 'You stabbed Germany in the back in 1918, and because of this millions of brave German men died for nothing.' 'I was not in Berlin in 1918,' says the Jew. 'I was in Poland, praying that Russia would lose to Germany.' 'You Jews spawned the evil of Bolshevism,' Hitler proceeds. The Jew replies, 'I am a Hasid and we do not profess dialectical materialism, if you know what that is.' 'You harbor criminal tendencies which you will pass on to your children,' Hitler proceeds. 'I am too old to have children and you know it,' says the Jew. 'There is one last thing,' says Hitler. 'You are a Jew, and that alone suffices.' 'You hate me regardless of any facts,' says the Jew. 'How can you hate what you do not know?'

By the end of this dialogue, we have uncovered a hatred based on no reasons at all, a self-sustaining emotion unsupported even by fantasized facts. Such a hatred creates a preference – the eradication of its object – but the satisfaction of this preference does not enhance any recognizable human interest in the person who harbors it. It is as if Hitler had a preference that Neptune be colored red. The sudden satisfaction of this preference via some eruption on Neptune might produce momentary exultation, but it would not make Hitler's life go better. Since the preference for the extermination of the Jews does not point to any interest, the hatred and actions based on it are completely irrational. But they are not irrational in any sense that provides an excuse of insanity. Hitler had not lost the power of cognition, or his ability to choose the means that would indeed produce the ends that his hatred dictated to him. True, Hitler did not choose to have this hatred of the Jews, but most feelings that people have are not feelings that they have chosen to have. What they retain is the ability to choose what they do, despite their feelings. In this Hitler had no less free will than anyone else.

I return again to my theme that for the Nazis killing was not a means but an end. In his public speeches, between ventings of emotion against the Jews and the Bolsheviks, Hitler projected a positive ideal: the redemption of Germany, the unification of das Volk, the establishment of a thousand-year Reich, the creation of a better world. How, we ask the Führer, is the extermination of the Jews going to produce this better world? 'Isn't it obvious?' says the Führer. 'The new world will have the feature of being free of Jews.' Means and ends, cause and effect, have fused together in a spinning circle of hate. Millions died to consummate a tautology.

Dresden

The standard view of the Dresden bombing is that this was a necessary act in a just war. That the war against Hitler was a just war I shall not dispute. That the bombing was necessary, that it was a step towards Nazi surrender, that it had any positive effects at all, this I will dispute.

The British bombing campaign against Germany began in late 1941, with daylight raids on *bona fide* military targets, especially the submarine bases, whose destruction was essential to winning the battle of the Atlantic. The British soon discovered that such raids were costly and fairly ineffective. German military targets were well camouflaged. When located, they were difficult to damage and easy to repair. Daylight raiding opened up bombers to concentrated anti-aircraft fire and deadly fighter attacks, against which British bombers carried few guns. Rates of attrition were high, and it was soon apparent that the British Bomber Command had to choose between (a) continued daylight raids and high losses, (b) forgoing raids altogether except for exceptionally favorable cases, (c) shifting over to tactical support for British air and sea operations, or (d) shifting over to bombing raids at night. (a) was unacceptable from the military point of view. (b) was unacceptable from the diplomatic point of view, as Stalin had to be persuaded that Britain was doing its fair share in the war against the common enemy. (c) was unacceptable to those who sought a distinctive role for the air forces in combat, that is, unacceptable to the airmen themselves. Bomber Command and Churchill opted for (d). It was *something*, and less costly than a second front.[13]

But if you bomb at night you cannot see particular targets and you must bomb 'areas' instead. And the only areas that it was plausible to bomb were cities. Such raids violated the written and unwritten conventions regarding bombardment, but they were consciously brushed aside.[14] But a case might be made in 1942 (indeed, was made, by Lord Cherwell, the Scientific Adviser to the Prime Minister) that the outcome of the war was in doubt, and that against a monstrous opponent monstrous means were necessary.[15] If you blow up Germany bit by bit, Cherwell wrote to Churchill on 30 March 1942,[16] then either there will be nothing left or the residue will surrender. Churchill accepted the argument, and appointed Arthur Harris, a vociferous advocate of area bombing, to head Bomber Command. 'The destruction of factories could be regarded as a bonus,' Harris later explained. 'The aiming points were usually right in the centre of the town.'[17] Through 1942 enormous resources were diverted to the development of Bomber Command. By 1943 whole cities like Hamburg and Lübeck were being destroyed in 1,000-plane area bombings that discarded any pretence of conscious direction against military targets.

Even in 1943, the rationale that area bombing would produce German surrender was strained. Cherwell's idea was that such bombing would destroy vital German military assets and undermine German civilian morale. But the German industrial machine was so prodigious that it was still turning out civilian radios late into 1943; and at no point in the war could it be demonstrated that German ground troops had anywhere run out of supplies or fuel because of British area bombing. (Ball bearings and fuel were in short supply, but as a result of daylight raids by the American Eighth Air Force.) As for civilian morale, the British knew best that area bombing does not undermine morale. German bombing had not destroyed *their* morale during the Blitz. If anything, the bombing would drive anti-Nazi Germans into Hitler's arms, just as the Blitz forced the British Left to bury the hatchet with Churchill. Besides, the attitudes of German civilians could have little effect in a country run by Nazis and policed by the Gestapo.

Whatever arguments, limited, inadequate, morally shallow, could be produced for area bombing in 1943, they had completely evaporated by February 1945. By 1945 it could not be argued that area bombing was needed in *lieu of* a second front, as D Day was long past. By 1945 it could not be argued that area bombing was needed to save needed planes, as there was an oversupply of planes of all kinds. By 1945 it could not be argued that area bombing was necessary to destroy German military assets, as those assets could be more effectively destroyed by American bombers in daylight raids conducted under the protection of long-range P-51 fighters. By 1945 it could not be argued that the outcome of the war was in doubt, as the Bulge had already collapsed and Germany was nearing defeat.[18] Nothing good could come of a raid on a city like Dresden, a cultural center of no industrial or military importance, crammed with refugees fleeing (with good reason) before the Red Army advancing from the East. Yet on the night of 12 February and in the early morning of 13 February, the RAF dropped 650,000 thermite bombs on Dresden, and set the city on fire. Tens of thousands burned to death; ten of thousands more suffocated in basements and shelters from lack of oxygen. The next day American bombers dropped tons of high explosives on the city center, and American fighters strafed crowds fleeing to the countryside.

I turn now to Churchill's role in the Dresden atrocity. I have already noted that Churchill had endorsed the general idea of area bombing, accepting the arguments of Lord Cherwell and rejecting the views of Henry Tizard, Solly Zuckerman, and other prominent science advisors who doubted that area bombing could break German morale. By late 1944 the old controversy about 'precision bombing' versus 'area bombing' broke out again, with Charles Portal, Chief of Air Staff, arguing that

Bomber Command should concentrate on German oil refineries and Air Marshal Harris supporting continued raids on German cities. Harris wrote to Portal on 1 November 1944 that 'in the past eighteen months, Bomber Command has virtually destroyed forty-five of the sixty leading German cities … Are we going to abandon this vast task?'[19] Portal replied, 'I have, I must confess, wondered at times whether the magnetism of the remaining German cities has not in the past tended as much to deflect our bombers from their primary objects as the tactical or weather difficulties [in attacking oil refineries] which you describe … '[20]

Harris never hesitated in ordering city raids. 'I was against putting everything into oil,' he later wrote. 'It was using a sledgehammer to crack a nut.' He threatened to resign, and Portal gave in, at least to the extent of listing as targets 'Berlin, Dresden, Chernitz, or any other cities where a severe blitz will … hamper the movement of troops from the west.' This idea of bombardment to harass German troops in the East was conveyed to Churchill via Sir Archibald Sinclair, Secretary of State for Air. From the Prime Minister Sinclair received this prompt and stunning reply (26 January 1945):

> I did not ask you about plans for harrying the German retreat from Breslau. On the contrary, I asked whether Berlin, and no doubt other large cities in East Germany, should not now be considered especially attractive targets. I am glad that this is 'under examination.' Pray tell me tomorrow what is to be done.[21]

This memorandum, the military historian Alexander McKee writes, 'sealed the fate of Dresden.'[22] It supports Harris's contention in his memoirs that the choice of Dresden as a target came directly from 'higher quarters.'[23] But why did Churchill side with Harris's city raids, and not with Portal's oil attacks or Sinclair's troop bombardments? If Harry Truman, whose leadership was not particularly respected (at least at first), could strike Kyoto off the list of bombing targets in Japan, on the grounds that Kyoto was an artistic and religious center, certainly Churchill, whose leadership *was* respected, could have struck Dresden off the list of targets, for similar reasons. But he did not. Why?

The reason could not have been that Churchill thought future good would come from the raid. Indeed, soon after the Dresden raid produced an outcry in Parliament, Churchill penned a self-serving and self-revealing memo that raids of this sort went against British interests (28 March 1945):

> It seems to me that the moment has come when the question of the area bombing of cities simply for the sake of increasing the terror, though under other pretexts, should be reviewed. Otherwise we shall come into control of an utterly ruined land. We shall not, for instance, be able to get housing materials out of Germany for our own needs because some temporary provision would have to be made for the Germans themselves.[24]

But the production of future good is not the sole rational basis for action. There is also the rationale of retribution, which looks to the past. The Germans had bombed the British, so it was just retribution for the British to bomb the Germans. The Blitz had hardly been a matter of a few British people sleeping some nights in the Underground. Fifty thousand British civilians had been killed in the Blitz; tens of thousands more had been maimed. The anger, intense and deep, of the British public demanded that those who caused this suffering be themselves made to suffer in kind. The Germans destroyed Rotterdam, so the Allies could destroy Hamburg. The Germans destroyed Coventry, so the Allies could destroy Lübeck. The Germans bombed London, so the Allies could bomb Berlin. In the eyes of many British and Americans, the destruction of German cities was just punishment for crimes committed. When Hans Rumpf's study of the effects of Allied bombing was published in English in 1965, the publisher added in a prefatory note:

> This book must be read with care. In the course of his study of aerial bombardment during World War II, Hans Rumpf has described in detail the horror and suffering that visited German civilians and German cities under Allied bombing attacks. But he has devoted no more than passing comment to the equally terrifying experiences inflicted by German air attacks on the people of London, Rotterdam, and Coventry.[25]

'They bombed Manchester, so we can bomb Dresden.' Was there a thought like this in Churchill's mind, when he told Sinclair that 'large cities in East Germany should be considered attractive targets'? One might argue that Churchill, distracted by his preparations for the Yalta Conference (4–11 February 1945), was attending to the pressing diplomatic issues and hardly had retribution in mind when he penned the memo that condemned Dresden. But the focus of the Yalta Conference was the territorial arrangement of Europe after the surrender of Germany, which implies that participants in the Yalta Conference thought of Germany as already defeated. If you think of your enemy as defeated, isn't your next thought going to be how the enemy is to be punished?

If Churchill was thinking about punishing Germany, what might he have thought about appropriate forms of punishment? It is interesting that throughout the war, whenever measures against Germany were considered that ran up against the laws of war, the British under Churchill adhered to legal restrictions except in such cases where they had already been broken by the Germans. The British had poison gas that Churchill considered using on German troops, but he chose not to. The British had anthrax bombs that Churchill considered dropping on Berlin, but he chose not to. The Germans, after all, had not used poison gas or anthrax against the British. But the Germans *had* set London afire on Christmas eve in 1940, and this seems to have dissolved any qualms about British fire raids on German cities.[26] In 1944, the bombing of Britain had recommenced with the advent of unmanned V-1 flying bombs and 1945 brought the V-2. For Churchill, it was an eye for an eye. As he remarked in the radio broadcast of 9 February 1941, 'All through these dark months the enemy has had the power to drop three or four tons of bombs on us for every ton we could send to Germany in return,'[27] and the metaphor of payback appears in a speech on 22 June 1941:

> Here in London, and throughout the cities of our island, and in Ireland, there are seen the marks of devastation. They are being repaid, and presently they will be more than repaid.[28]

Now there is in this Deuteronomic reasoning about bombing an obvious crudity of thought: the rule of an eye for an eye is being applied not to a particular wrongdoer and his particular victim, but to 'the British' and 'the Germans,' collective entities of a philosophically suspicious sort. But Churchill was never scrupulous in distinguishing 'the German people' as a moral agent from individual Germans as moral agents. As the author of a book entitled *A History of the English-speaking Peoples* he was comfortable thinking in collectivist terms.[29] Before the House of Commons, 7 May 1941, he remarks, 'The German name and the German race have become and are becoming more universally and more intensely hated than any name or any race of which history bears record,'[30] and a later speech describes 'Hun raiders,' led by 'clanking, heel clicking, dandified Prussian officers.'[31]

But the bombs at Dresden fell on particular people, including a young farm girl who came into Dresden by train from Breslau after widespread reports of rape by Red Army troops. As she died of asphyxiation in the Dresden train station shelter, one could imagine Churchill explaining to her the rationale of her death. 'You must die,' he might begin, 'so that Stalin will be impressed with my power and I will have bargaining chips at the conference table.' 'The conference ended four days ago,' the girl could say. 'It's a little late for that.' 'My friend Lord Cherwell has spoken highly,' Churchill continues, 'of the psychological effects of "de-housing" the German population.' 'I have already been "de-housed" by the Red Army,' the girl could say. 'Spare yourself the effort of de-housing me a second time.' 'You must die because you German people have hit London with V-1s, and the Germans must suffer for what they have done.' 'I attacked nothing,' the girl says. 'I only tended cows. As for "my people," I am half Polish. I never believed in Das Volk. But apparently you do.'

Hiroshima

As with Dresden, some part of the motivation for the bombing of Hiroshima was revenge. It was not just a matter of getting back at the Japanese for the sneak attack on Pearl Harbor. In February 1945, Americans learned for the first time of the atrocious treatment of American prisoners of war by Japanese military forces in Bataan and elsewhere. In March of 1945 American marines suffered tens of thousands of casualties in the assault on Iwo Jima, thousands more died in the ensuing attack on Okinawa. When fire raids over Tokyo killed tens of thousands of civilians in March and May of 1945, few Americans felt sympathy for the Japanese victims on the ground.

But in all the discussions of the first use of the atomic bomb, the focus was not on exacting revenge but on how to use the weapon to end the war.[32] The basic idea was that the atomic bomb, a new and different weapon of war, would produce a 'shock' that might induce surrender. The alternative, so the discussion went, was to invade Japan, an operation sure to produce a high number of military and civilian casualties.

Truman asked the Interim Committee, formed to advise the president about the bomb, to estimate the number of people that would die in an atomic attack on a Japanese city. He was told to expect 10,000 to 20,000 deaths. He asked his military experts to estimate the number of people who would die in a ground invasion of Japan: he was told to expect 100,000 to 200,000 deaths. From this point on in

Truman's thinking arithmetic took over: it was better to kill 10,000 than to kill 100,000; therefore it was good moral mathematics to drop the bomb on Hiroshima. We have direct and indirect evidence that Truman engaged in these morbid calculations. When it became known that over 100,000 people died in the bombing of Hiroshima, Truman began to say to interviewers that 'he had been told' (by whom?) that 'a million'[33] lives[35] would be lost in the invasion of Japan, a figure that had no basis in reality but which served to keep the hypothetical invasion death count higher than the actual bombing death count.

It was perhaps the simplicity of the arithmetic comparison that prompted Truman to tell *Life Magazine*, by way of celebrating the tenth anniversary of the bombing in 1955, that he never lost a night's sleep over the destruction of Hiroshima. The president never felt that the bombing was wrong; never felt that the bombing needed to be excused. Human life has value; a net saving of 90,000 lives justified the attack. 'My object,' he explained to Senator Richard Russell the day after the bombing, 'was to save as many American lives as possible but I also have a human feeling for the men and women of Japan.'[34] So Truman thought, but he did not think enough.

To begin, if one is going to justify a decision of this gravity by comparing numbers, one must make sure that the numbers are right. The figure of 10,000 deaths Oppenheimer and the Interim Committee provided Truman was absurdly low; incorrect by a factor of ten. The bomb was commonly described by those in the know in early 1945 as a weapon that could 'wipe out' an entire city in a single blow, which would imply 'wiping out' most of the people that lived within the city. If the bomb was as terrible as everyone was saying it was, Truman should have wondered why the projected casualty figures were so low, and raised questions that would have produced better estimates. Similarly the estimate of 100,000 deaths to be expected in a land invasion was open to question. That estimate was derived by assuming that the Japanese would fight for the home islands the way they had fought for Iwo Jima and Okinawa, but the Japanese had fought on to the death at Iwo Jima and Okinawa out of loyalty to the emperor, who had not yet decided to surrender to the Americans. If the emperor and his council surrendered in the face of an invasion, or in the immediate wake of one, resistance on the ground would drop to zero. It does no good to object that Truman did not know whether the invasion would induce such a surrender. Truman did not know that bombing would induce surrender either. In the absence of surrender after a land invasion, the killing would have gone on. In the absence of surrender after Hiroshima and Nagasaki, the bombings, atomic or conventional, would have gone on. The casualty estimate for 'continued bombing' would have converged with the casualty estimate for 'continued invasion.'

Next, Truman should have considered not just the numbers of the dead, but who the dead were. Those who would die in the invasion of Japan would be mainly soldiers, intentionally killed; those who would die in the bombing of a city would be mainly civilians, intentionally killed for the purpose of inducing surrender. Intentionally killing soldiers is morally permissible in pursuit of victory in a just war; intentionally killing civilians is plainly murderous, as the Allies insisted whenever the Nazis did it.[35] The fact the Americans had been engaged in intentionally killing civilians in large numbers in Japan starting in January 1945 is irrelevant; murder does not become more permissible as it becomes more frequent. Besides, the earlier terror bombings did not happen on Truman's watch; he was under no obligation to continue what had been done before.

Next, in considering the bombing choice Truman should have devoted more attention to alternative uses of the atomic bomb. True, the Interim Committee told him that they could see no alternative to using the bomb against a city, as a 'demonstration bombing' might fizzle, as Oppenheimer said, 'like a firecracker over a desert.' But the same scientists who were saying in August 1945 that the bomb would be unimpressive unless dropped over a city were saying, in July 1945, that the explosion of the first atomic bomb over the sands of New Mexico was the most awe-inspiring event they had ever seen. If the bomb over New Mexico could make Oppenheimer exclaim, as he reported in his memoirs, 'I am Shiva, destroyer of worlds,' why would not the emperor of Japan say the same thing, if the bomb were exploded over some uninhabited island in the Sea of Japan?

The choice to use the bomb was portrayed by Truman as a choice between 'bombing or invasion.' In fact there was no such choice, as there was no possibility of a land invasion of Japan before late October 1945. The president could not legitimately think, 'If I do not bomb in August, I must invade in October,' as the bombing could have been deferred for three months without precluding the possibility of invasion. In October of 1945, with the invasion ready, the president might perhaps think, 'Either bomb now or invade now,' but he faced no such dilemma in August 1945.

I say, 'the president might *perhaps* think, "either bomb or invade."' If he did so think, his thinking was mistaken indeed. In fact neither the bombing nor the invasion was necessary in any moral sense. The Japanese from 1931 to 1944 had done atrocious damage to the world. But by August of 1945 Japan was a defeated power, unable to do much harm to anyone. The invasion of Japan would have caused great harm to the Japanese. The atomic bombing of Japan did cause great harm. What is the point, what is the necessity, of causing such great harms if not to prevent further harms on a similar scale? It might be argued that Japan was starving American prisoners of war, and that hastening the end of the war saved their lives. But the number of Americans POWs saved by bombing was tiny compared to the tens of thousands that died at Hiroshima. And the lives of the American POWs interned at Hiroshima, several dozen at least, ended when the atomic bomb fell on their heads.

Why did Truman insist on thinking that his only choice was 'bombing or invasion'? True, the invasion would have involved many murders. Perhaps the bombing might have involved fewer murders than the invasion. But to say that the bombing is justified because it involves fewer murders is like saying that because I did not murder my entire philosophy class this morning I am entitled to murder my chairman this afternoon. What morality demands is not that we do fewer murders but that we do none at all.

Truman could have avoided murder, but he did not. The thinking behind his decision to drop the bomb on Hiroshima, with its false dichotomies and spurious necessities, was superficial, indicative of a morally mediocre man who did not grasp the ethically superior alternatives made possible by the great power that had fallen into his hands. Within hours of Hiroshima, Truman was trying to conceal from the world his lack of justification for the bombing. 'The world now knows,' Truman told the American people in the radio address of 6 August, 'that the first atomic bomb was dropped on Hiroshima, a military base.' This sentence, elided from the text of the address reprinted in David McCullough's admiring biography of Truman,[36] inaugurates the tradition among American presidents of covering up the Hiroshima crime and prevaricating about all things nuclear. Sometimes one can grasp the character of an event by the degree to which people are prepared to lie about it. Certainly a small child, one of thousands walking to school in Hiroshima at 8:15 a.m. on 6 August 1945, might have said to Truman, had he not been blinded, mutilated, and blown to ashes, that his house, his street, his school, and his city, were *not* a military base.

A Final Thought-experiment

I have presented four political leaders, four historical episodes, and four victims. All of the victims were treated murderously, but treated murderously for different reasons. To explore further the differences in these supposed rationales, I supply one final thought-experiment. Imagine, reader, that you are yourself each of the four victims, that you can look your killers in the eye and hear what they have to say.

The first killer says to you, 'I do not think you have done anything wrong, and I bear no personal animosity towards you. It is just that your life has gotten in the way of the plan, or rather that your life has gotten in the way of respect for the plan. Though I like you personally, I am committed to preserving respect for the plan; therefore, regretfully, I arrange your death.'

The second killer says to you, 'When I see something I hate, I want to remove it from the world, and among the things I hate are people like you. When I was young and wandering through Vienna, when I saw Jews, indeed, as I wrote in my book, when I smelled Jews like you, I felt an immediate visceral disgust, an instinctive repulsion. Now I have power, and I destroy what disgusts me. If anything repelled you as much as Jews repel me, you would want to destroy it too.'

The third killer says to you, 'I am in grief because some distant cousins of mine, decent English-speaking people, were killed by distant cousins of yours, who, like you, speak German. Because I am in grief I am entitled to retribution, and since I cannot find those who killed my cousins, I choose to kill you instead. It does not matter that you are not the murderer; what matters is that you happen to speak the same language and live within the same borders, and this transfers my righteous indignation from the killers to you.'

The fourth killer says, 'I am engaged in a calculation of how to save the greatest number of lives. The calculation has a number of steps, and almost every step contains an error that a small child could discover, but my mind is such that I am incapable of discovering my mistakes. My conclusion is that if I do not kill you, I will kill a great many other people. Why I must kill the others is not exactly clear, but I choose to kill you rather than choosing to kill them.'

It is, I think, natural to react to the four killers in four different ways, to think that to die one way is worse than to die another way. But finding arguments to justify these natural reactions is difficult. Are the men who kill you regretfully, like Stalin and Truman, treating you better or worse than the men who kill you with exultation or at least some sense of satisfaction, like Hitler and Churchill? Are the men who murder you intending to produce a better future, like Hitler and Truman, treating you with more or less respect than those who murder you believing that your death does not improve the world, like Stalin and Churchill? Are those who murder you falsely thinking that you are a terrible antagonist treating you with more or less respect than those who murder you falsely thinking your existence is a trivial obstacle? Is the man who kills you in the grip of a foul emotion, like Hitler, treating you better or worse than a man who murders you in the grip of a foul calculation, like Truman? Are those who kill you on the basis of bankrupt collectivist concepts, like Hitler and Churchill, treating you better or worse than Stalin or Truman, who kill you on the basis of bogus scientific estimates? The proceedings of the Nuremberg trials run to dozens of volumes. Addressing these questions would take hundreds. No verdict beyond mass murder is suggested here. But it is a dismal observation about our species that we have produced, not only so many murderers, but so many different kinds of them.

Notes

1. For accounts of the Ukrainian famine and the policy decisions that led to it see R.W. Davies, *The Socialist Offensive: The Collectivization of Soviet Agriculture 1929–1930* (Cambridge, MA: Harvard University Press, 1980); Herbert Ellison, 'The Decision to Collectivize Agriculture,' in *Russian Economic Development from Peter the Great to Stalin*, ed. William Blackwell (New York: New Viewpoints, 1974); Dana Dalrymple, 'The Soviet Famine of 1932–34,' *Soviet Studies* **15** (January 1964) and Robert Conquest, *The Harvest of Sorrow* (New York: Oxford, 1986). The number of people who died in the famine is a matter of controversy, and the totals given by Conquest are perhaps double the most reasonable estimates; cf. Barbara Anderson and Brian Silver, 'Demographic Analysis and Population Catastrophes in the USSR,' *Slavic Review* 1985. Nothing in the present chapter, however, hinges on the precise number of people who died in this famine.
2. In 1940 Stalin arranged to have John Ford's film *The Grapes of Wrath* shown to Russian peasants to demonstrate the advantages of Soviet agriculture over American farming. The screenings were stopped when the peasants declared that Ford's Okies were rich because 'they have a truck.'
3. See Bertrand Russell, *Principles of Social Reconstruction* (London: Allen and Unwin, 1916).
4. *Khrushchev Remembers* (Boston: Little Brown, 1970), p. 120.
5. For a terrifying example of the capacity of history to repeat itself see Jasper Becker, *Hungry Ghosts: Mao's Secret Famine* (New York: Free Press, 1966). *Pace* Marx, this second time around was not farce, but utter tragedy.
6. The discussion presumes a general familiarity with the facts of the Jewish Holocaust. One early guide that remains one of the best general accounts is Raul Hilberg, *The Destruction of the European Jews* (Chicago: Quadrangle Books, 1961). See also Lucy S. Dawidowicz, *The War Against the Jews 1933–1945* (New York: Holt Rinehart and Winston, 1975).

7. For biographies of Hitler see Alan Bullock, *Hitler: A Study in Tyranny* (New York: Harper and Row, 1952); Joachim Fest, *Hitler: A Biography* (New York: Harcourt Brace Jovanovich, 1974); Ian Kershaw, *Hitler*, Vol. I *Hubris* (New York: Norton, 1998); Vol. II, *Nemesis* (New York: Norton, 2000).

8. The best psychiatric (not psychoanalytic) study of Hitler is perhaps Fritz Redlich, *Hitler: Diagnosis of a Destructive Prophet* (New York: Oxford University Press, 1998).

9. For a study of the particular culture of Hitler's youth, see Brigitte Hamann, *Hitler's Vienna: A Dictator's Apprenticeship* (New York: Oxford University Press, 1999).

10. Adolf Hitler, *Mein Kampf*, Engl. trans. Ralph Mannheim (Boston, MA: Houghton Mifflin, 1943).

11. '[The Bolsheviks] believe in the international Soviet of the Russian and Polish Jew.' *Winston Churchill: His Complete Speeches*, ed. Robert Rhodes James (London: Chelsea House Publishers, 1974, III, p. 291).

12. The controversy commences with David Irving's *Hitler's War* (New York: Viking, 1977) and the subsequent furor and literature surrounding this book, including Lucy S. Dawidowicz, *The Holocaust and the Historians* (Cambridge, MA: Harvard University Press, 1981).

13. The official history of British decision-making in the bombing campaign against Germany is Sir Charles Webster and Noble Frankland, *The Strategic Air Offensive Against Germany* (London: HMSO, 1961). Good general accounts include Anthony Verrier, *The Bomber Offensive* (New York: Macmillan, 1969) and Max Hastings, *Bomber Command* (New York: Dial Press, 1979).

14. The argument that 'area bombing' is a euphemism for mass murder was pressed by Dr George Bell, Bishop of Chichester. Of Bell, the historians Peter Calvocoressi and Guy Wint write, 'For keeping these Christian ideas before men's minds in spite of the clatter of arms the Bishop of Chichester was not elevated to the highest Christian office in England when the see of Canterbury, for which many inside the Church and out had considered him pre-eminently qualified, fell vacant at the end of 1944.' *Total War* (New York: Pantheon Books, 1972), p. 490. For Bell's speeches see George Bell, *The Church and Humanity* (London: Longmans, 1946).

15. Even as sensitive a critic as Michael Walzer, in *Just and Unjust Wars* (New York: Basic Books, 1967), succumbs to the excuse of 'supreme emergency,' a phrase he introduces specifically for the crisis years of World War II. Given that morality often requires individuals to give up their lives, one wonders why Walzer rejects the idea that morality might require giving up the life of a nation-state.

16. Cherwell wrote, in part, 'In 1938 over 22 million Germans lived in fifty-eight towns of over 100,000 inhabitants, which, with modern equipment, should be easy to find and hit ... If even half the total load of 10,000 bombers were dropped on the built up areas of these fifty-eight German towns the great majority of the present inhabitants (about one third of the German population) would be turned out of house and home ... ', quoted in Hastings, *Bomber Command*, p. 141. Cherwell neglects to say openly that some Germans might die in the process of being 'turned out' but we can presume that Churchill was capable of drawing the inference.

17. Hastings, *Bomber Command*, p. 146. In public announcements there was little hint that the policy had changed. Churchill always referred to hits on German dwellings as 'near misses:' *Winston Churchill: His Complete Speeches*, Vol. VI, ed. Robert Rhodes James, New York, NY: Chelsea House Publishers, 1974, p. 6589.

18. Apologists for Churchill sometimes argue that the Prime Minister authorized the bombing of Dresden in fulfillment of an agreement made at Yalta to assist the Russian advance into Germany. 'The Russian purpose, explained at Yalta eight days earlier, was achieved: refugees on the roads, fleeing Westwards from the firestorm, disrupted the movement of

German reinforcements seeking to pass through the city to the front further east.' Martin Gilbert, *Churchill: A Life* (New York: Henry Holt and Company, 1991), p. 824. The idea that German armored columns could be slowed down by ragtag stragglers from Dresden is ludicrous, as is the suggestion that Churchill, who for two years after the invasion of Russia had delayed opening a second front in Europe, was worried about Russian troop losses on the way to Berlin. In fact the existence of 'troops moving east' towards Dresden cannot be verified. The 'Russian request' story is also part of the official history of the American Army Air Force in World War II: 'It was this blow [the Dresden bombing] that set off the controversy about terror bombing already described. The Secretary of War had to be apprised of Dresden's importance as a transportation center and the Russian request for its neutralization.' Wesley Frank Craven and James Lea Cate, *The Army Air Forces in World War II* (Chicago: University of Chicago Press, 1948–58), p. 731.

19. Hastings, *Bomber Command*, p. 385.
20. Ibid., p. 386. Harris's rhetoric here, not to 'abandon this vast task', bears an eerie resemblance to the language in Himmler's 1943 plea to commandants at Auschwitz to finish the job, however difficult.
21. Quoted in Alexander McKee, *Dresden 1945: The Devil's Tinderbox* (New York: E.P. Dutton, 1982), p. 102.
22. Ibid.
23. Arthur Harris, *Bomber Offensive* (London: Collins, 1947).
24. Hastings, *Bomber Command*, p. 401.
25. Preface to Hans Rumpf, *The Bombing of Germany*, trans. Edward Fitzgerald (New York: Holt, Reinhart, Winston, 1965). Rumpf's pathbreaking study was originally published in 1961.
26. Churchill was once asked in the House of Commons whether attacks on Berlin and Rome were 'reprisals' for attacks on London. Churchill replied, 'There is not much to be gained from putting Questions of this kind,' *Winston Churchill: His Complete Speeches*, VI, p. 6254.
27. Ibid., p. 6344.
28. Ibid., p. 6423.
29. Churchill's speeches throughout his lifetime abound with collectivist metaphors, for example, 'The Slav and the Teuton are quite different kinds of metal … ' (22 February 1919). *Winston Churchill: His Complete Speeches*, III, p. 2672.
30. Ibid., VI, p. 6392.
31. Ibid., p. 6429 (22 June 1941).
32. For the decision-making leading to Hiroshima see Richard Hewlett and Oscar Anderson, *A History of the Atomic Energy Commission, Vol. I. A New World* (University Park, PA: State University of Pennsylvania Press, 1962); H. Feis, *The Atomic Bomb and the End of World War II* (Princeton: Princeton University Press, 1966); Gar Alperowitz, *Atomic Diplomacy, Hiroshima and Potsdam* (New York: Simon and Schuster, 1965); Gregg Herken, *The Winning Weapon* (New York: Knopf, 1980). These books are listed in increasing order of moral condemnation of the Hiroshima decision.
33. Rufus E. Miles, 'The Strange Myth of a Million Lives Saved,' *International Security* **10** (2) (Fall 1985), pp. 121–40.
34. David McCullough, *Truman* (New York: Simon and Schuster, 1992), p. 458.
35. Cf. Churchill, 12 June 1941: 'The ruins of Warsaw, of Rotterdam, of Belgrade are monuments which will long recall to future generations the outrage of unopposed air-bombing applied with scientific cruelty to helpless populations.' *His Complete Speeches*, VI, p. 6423. Perhaps one argument against bombing Dresden and Hiroshima is that the earlier Nazi atrocities are no longer recalled, having been eclipsed in scale by Allied attacks.

36. McCullough, *Truman*, p. 455. The full text is given in *The Truman Administration*, edited by Barton Jay Bernstein (New York: Harper and Row, 1966). The official text of the quote says 'Hiroshima, an important military base,' but in the actual broadcast, as heard on the recording, Truman omits the word 'important.' Perhaps the president was too embarrassed by the magnitude of this whopper to follow his own script.

Chapter 9

Is Limited Altruism Morally Wrong?

Michael Freeman

1. Moral Dilemmas

A philosopher is sitting at her desk writing a paper on moral philosophy. In her in-tray lies a letter from Oxfam's fund-raising department requesting a donation to aid the destitute victims of a civil war in Africa. There is also a letter from one of her students asking for a reference in connection with his application for postgraduate study, the deadline for which falls very soon. It is her daughter's birthday tomorrow, and she must get to the shops to buy her a much-desired, and promised, present. What should she do? She has promised the paper to the editor of a volume of essays on moral philosophy, and, through the editor, to the publisher. She could postpone the reply to Oxfam, but only to a time when it will almost certainly compete with other obligations. To write references for students is a normal, and normatively required, part of her job, and she has an obligation to the student to make all reasonable efforts to get it done by the deadline. She loves her daughter, of course, and naturally does not wish to disappoint her on her birthday, and, indeed, believes herself to be under an obligation not to do so. She could prioritize the commitments according to the applicable deadlines, but this might still leave her with conflicting obligations, and it might also assign a very low priority to those obligations, such as giving to Oxfam, that carry no particular deadline. It is not clear that temporal priorities would conform with proper moral priorities.

Intuitions may not resolve these dilemmas. The Africans may have the greatest need. To weigh this in the balance with a letter of reference or a birthday present may itself seem immoral. But another intuition 'protects' the daughter's birthday: perhaps the philosopher has a *right* as well as an obligation to carry out such a family function. The other obligations are based on no light principles, for they derive from contracts, from which the philosopher benefits. This intuition might be expressed by suggesting the implausibility of saying to the student, without discomfort: 'I'm sorry I couldn't write your reference on time, but I was sending a cheque to Oxfam (and to Amnesty International, and to Médecins Sans Frontières, and to Greenpeace, and so on).' And perhaps her paper will be a masterwork of moral philosophy.

If our philosopher were a utilitarian, she would have calculated how to maximize overall utility, but would have run into problems, not only of quantifying the relevant utilities, but of identifying all the consequences of her choices. Discounting uncertain benefits might give the birthday a strong priority over Oxfam, but the discounting is itself uncertain, and the outcome not obviously morally correct. If she were a Kantian, she might try to will the appropriate universal laws, but it is far from clear how this would decide priorities. If she were a communitarian, she might put the Oxfam letter at the bottom of the pile, but communitarianism is notoriously unclear as to what communities actually are, and of very little help in determining priorities among different community obligations. The daughter, the student and the editor might all make their claims on 'communitarian' grounds. If she were a 'postmodernist' she might be able to justify *any* choice, but only because she could provide a ('foundational') justification for none.

Conflicting obligations and moral dilemmas are common experiences of everyday life, and many people manage them most of the time by 'muddling through', because they are not burdened by the philosopher's urge for consistency. Only exceptionally are such dilemmas experienced as acute. Moral philosophers reflect on dilemmas, and seek reasoned, systematic and coherent resolutions of them. They offer the layperson, however, a confusing diversity of solutions, thus failing to overcome muddling through, which, whatever its merits, is not a philosophical way to proceed. There is, however, something more deeply troubling about muddling through life's minefield of moral dilemmas. Philosophers who conclude that common-sense morality serves the ordinary person as well as, or better than, academic philosophy often assume that 'common sense' is being applied in 'normal' circumstances in which it is unlikely to do much harm. The Holocaust calls this assumption into question. The 'common sense' of most ordinary Germans was probably not very different from that of other ordinary people in similar circumstances. Even the guard who said 'Here is no why' may have thought it a reasonable thing to say in the circumstances. We need to be clear why it was not.

One of the most challenging moral problems raised by the Holocaust is that of the obligations of 'bystanders': those who were neither direct participants in the process of mass murder nor its victims. Bystanders can be roughly divided into two kinds: those who were sufficiently close to the process to have intervened in some way, but probably at great risk to themselves and perhaps their families; and those more remote from the process, who might nevertheless, especially if they were political leaders, have taken action to disrupt the process. Many people will admire those who took risks to rescue Jews. Many may feel uneasy about both individuals and governments who took no action to prevent the disaster, even when sufficient information about it was available. This is commonly known as 'the bystander problem', and the problem is often thought to be how to persuade or motivate bystanders to intervene or mitigate moral disasters, especially if the risk to themselves is not great. This problem has been debated in relation to recent events such as the massacres in Cambodia, Bosnia, Rwanda and Kosovo. There is, however, a tradition in moral philosophy that suggests that the bystander problem may have been misdescribed. The central concept in this tradition is that of limited altruism. The central argument is that limited altruism is a deep and pervasive feature of human nature, and that any moral philosophy that requires more than limited altruism is doomed to failure, and perhaps potentially authoritarian. There is an affinity between the idea of limited altruism and the morality of special relationships, for those who endorse this idea may well think that it is consistent with strong obligations to those with whom we have close connections. Limited altruism calls into question the obligation to help strangers, and this is precisely what was required if Jews were to be rescued from the Holocaust. It is important, therefore, to investigate the strength of the idea of limited altruism.

2. Universalism versus Particularism

The problem of limited altruism is familiar to many moral philosophers in terms of the distinction between agent-neutral and agent-relative duties. I prefer the terminology of ethical universalism and ethical particularism that is used by some political philosophers,[1] since it expresses more clearly the contrast between obligations based on two different kinds of human relations: those between human beings as such and those between human beings connected by a special relationship. A good example of ethical universalism is provided by Hillel Steiner:

> Here's a simple rights violation. Blue is sitting in her garden and Red, whose garden adjoins hers, points his gun across the fence at her and fires, wounding her. There's no contractual understanding between them, nor any previous violation of Red's rights by Blue, that could make this shooting permissible. So Red's action is a clear encroachment on Blue's self-ownership.
>
> Suppose, instead, that the person Red aims at and hits is White, whose garden is adjacent to the other side of Blue's garden. And suppose that a contractual understanding or previous violation which might license this action is similarly lacking. Isn't Red's action an encroachment on White's self-ownership? Does it make any relevant difference that the fence separating White's garden from Blue's, unlike the one between Red's and Blue's, is an *international boundary*? Clearly not. Red's shooting outsider White is as much a violation of original rights as his shooting insider Blue. Our moral duties to respect other persons' original rights and the rights derived from them don't suddenly evaporate at international boundaries. More generally, they don't end at the borders of whatever local, regional or national jurisdiction we happen to be in. These duties are *global* in scope.[2]

Steiner's universalist conclusion may follow logically from his universalist theory of rights, or it may be based on what he takes to be our universalist intuition that unprovoked killing is always wrong, or it may derive from a combination of the two. Whatever its justification, it can be located in the universalist natural-law tradition. A classic expression of this tradition can be found in Locke's account of 'the state of nature'. In that state, Locke maintained, promises and bargains made between a Swiss and an Indian in the woods of America 'are binding to them … for truth and keeping of faith belongs [*sic*] to men as men, and not as members of society'.[3] This is an uncompromising rejection of 'communitarianism'. We need know nothing of Swiss or Indian cultural attitudes towards truth or keeping of faith. A bargain is a bargain, and bargains are binding on 'men as men'. This conception of universal morality repeats, of course, that of the Stoics, and anticipates a common contemporary conception of universal human rights, which, Jack Donnelly says, are 'the rights that one has simply because one is a human being'.[4]

Onora O'Neill has argued that the numerous disagreements between 'cosmopolitans' and 'communitarians' are not best seen as pitting *universalism* against *particularism* in ethics. Cosmopolitans and communitarians, she maintains, agree that moral principles must have universal *form*; that is, they must hold for all rather than some cases within a certain domain. What makes cosmopolitans distinctive is, rather, their view of the proper *scope* of moral principles, which they extend to include at least all humans, wherever they live.[5] David Miller makes a similar point, but with a significant difference in terminology. He seeks to explain the difference between *ethical universalism* and *ethical particularism*. It is tempting, but misleading, he argues, to express this difference by saying that universalists believe in ethical *impartiality*, whereas particularists believe in ethical *partiality*. However, the ethical particularist, according to Miller, does not advocate partiality. He endorses impartiality, but does not accept that impartiality entails universalism. The ethical particularist may require all members of group G to be impartial towards other members of G, but may not require them to treat outsiders similarly. In discriminating against outsiders, members of G are not displaying partiality.[6] O'Neill's communitarians can have principles that are universal in form, and Miller's particularists can be impartial among a particular group of people. The terminological difference is that Miller does pit universalism against particularism, which O'Neill says is not the best distinction to make. However, on this issue, Miller's view seems the better, for it is surely linguistically odd to consider someone a universalist who believes that a certain principle holds for all people within a certain domain, if that domain is very restricted. If I apply the same rules to all my children, I am impartial among them, as Miller says, but I am hardly thereby a universalist. Yet Miller's treatment of impartiality is not satisfactory. He is correct to say that impartiality may have limited scope: an impartial judge is not impartial *vis-à-vis* everyone in the world. But, in his example, the members of group G surely *are* 'partial' to their fellow group members in discriminating against outsiders. The universalist, therefore, is someone who believes that some moral principles apply to everyone.

Abstract moral philosophies, such as Kantianism or utilitarianism, may be universalist in a fairly clear sense. Apparently universal principles, however, may not be strictly universal. The United Nations' Universal Declaration of Human Rights, for example, states, in Article 1, that all human beings 'are born free and equal in dignity and rights'. This seems to be unqualifiedly universalist. Article 14 says that 'everyone' has the right to seek and to enjoy in other countries asylum from persecution. But 'everyone' does not have this right; only persecuted persons do. If this seems unduly pedantic, we may pass to Article 16, which tells us that men and women 'of full age' have the right to marry and to found a family.[7] If all these principles are 'universal', they do not apply to all human beings, and the sense in which they are 'universal' requires some explanation. A further problem is that universal human rights are often expressed as absolute, but interpreted as limited. For example, Article 19 of the Universal Declaration says that everyone has the right to freedom of expression, but it is widely agreed that this right ought to have *some* limits (for example, prohibitions of incitement to racial hatred are often permitted). It is not clear that the *limits* are universal, and, if they are not, the rights, properly understood, are not unqualifiedly universal.

The concept of ethical universalism is, therefore, not entirely clear, but it can nevertheless be distinguished from ethical particularism. Miller offers a useful definition of the latter:

> Ethical particularism … holds that relations between persons are part of the basic subject-matter of ethics, so that fundamental principles may be attached directly to these relations. It invokes a … picture of the ethical universe, in which agents are already encumbered with a variety of ties and commitments to particular other agents, or to groups or collectivities, and they begin their ethical reasoning from those commitments.[8]

It is noteworthy that the first of these sentences does *not* distinguish ethical particularism from ethical universalism, whereas the second does. Locke's example of the Swiss and the Indian making a bargain in the woods of America shows that universalists can hold that relations between persons are part of the basic subject-matter of ethics, so that fundamental principles may be attached directly to these relations. A bargain is a relation between persons. Locke held that keeping faith was a fundamental principle that might be attached directly to such relations. However, to *begin* ethical reasoning from ties and commitments to *particular* other agents, groups or collectivities would be rejected by universalists because it protects those ties and commitments from ethical evaluation. A person who *began* their ethical reasoning from their commitment to the Nazi Party would appear to be ethically defective to universalists.

The philosopher's dilemma, with which we began, shows, however, that there appears to be ethical merit in particularism, and that it is a legitimate rival to universalism. If it is not plausible to suggest that *any* ties and commitments whatever give rise to fundamental ethical obligations, it *is* plausible to suggest that *some* such ties and commitments do. It would take an extreme universalist to deny that we have *special* obligations to our family, friends, neighbours, fellow members of local, ethnic, religious, national and/or other communities, or to parties to contracts. Locke's Swiss wanderer had a *special* obligation to the Indian with whom he had made a bargain, and this was because keeping faith is a *universal* obligation. Thus, universal principles can support special obligations. In accordance with these obligations, parents ought to care for their children; one ought to help one's friends; be loyal to one's community; and perform one's job to the best of one's ability. Our philosopher, the example assumes, had *some* special obligation to her daughter, her student and her editor, for it is these obligations that create the dilemma, given the ethical claims of needy Africans. Miller's ethical particularism, however, does claim to be able to resolve the dilemmas to some extent, for it allows us to give priority to the claims of our nearest and dearest. One form of ethical particularism could even sort out our philosopher's priorities by allocating the more moral weight the nearer and dearer the claimant. Thus daughter comes before student; student before editor; and editor before Africans. Even this 'nearest and dearest' form of particularism does not entail that we have *no* obligations to distant strangers; only that they have lower priority than our obligations to those who are near and dear.

Ethical particularism, on Miller's account, differs from ethical universalism in that it admits special obligations *at the most fundamental level of morality*. Whereas ethical universalism admits to the foundations of morality only such general principles as 'act in accordance with the categorical imperative', ethical particularism admits such special obligations as those to one's children, friends, co-ethnics and fellow citizens. Ethical particularists claim that this morality is rooted in human nature. Most people act in practice as ethical particularists, giving priority to their nearest and dearest, and individuals whom we would regard as morally decent do this. Even universalist philosophers do this in practice. To condemn this as immoral on universalist grounds would, therefore, be inhuman, fanatical and potentially totalitarian.[9]

Ethical particularism appeals to a common sense that it claims is very wide and very deep, to human psychology, and even to biology.[10] It seems heroic, or mad, for the universalist to deny the considerable moral weight of special obligations. Even relativist, postmodernist or other forms of scepticism would find it difficult to undermine the empirical claim that most people, most of the time, prefer their nearest and dearest, and would therefore find it difficult to reject inference that any ethic that ignored this would be futile. Ethical particularism might, in this sense, be *true*. If it is, does it undermine ethical universalism? A negative answer is possible if ethical universalism can endorse the truth in ethical particularism. This is the approach that Brian Barry takes by distinguishing, in his theory of justice as impartiality, between *first-order impartiality* and *second-order impartiality*. First-order impartiality would require us, in deciding how to act, to treat everyone impartially always. This would have the consequence that the needs of distant strangers would weigh equally with those of our children. It would, therefore, violate the common-sense preference for our nearest and dearest. Second-order impartiality, by contrast, requires only that the principles upon which we act treat all human beings impartially. According to second-order impartiality, I may prefer my own child, but because she is *my* child, and not because she is morally superior to any other child and has more basic rights.

David Miller, while not claiming to argue in favour of ethical particularism and against ethical universalism in general, does try to defeat universalist arguments for special obligations in the context of the question of our obligations to our fellow nationals. He considers, in order to refute, two universalist arguments for special obligations. The first is the argument from *the ethical division of labour*. This argument requires us to recognize that no one can help every needy person in the world. There must be an ethical division of labour, in which different helpers aid different needy persons. Attending to our nearest and dearest, it might be argued, is a good ethical division of labour because everyone will be well motivated to help and will be relatively well informed about what help is needed. Miller argues that this is objectionable because help will not go where it is most needed (according to universalist criteria): Swedes will help fellow Swedes and Rwandans will help fellow Rwandans, which may not be the best way (by universalist criteria) to help needy Rwandans. The second universalist argument for special obligations is based on *the right to freedom of association*. If there is a *universal* right to freedom of association – which most universalists would acknowledge – there must be some special obligations to fellow members of associations. To this universalist argument for special obligations Miller objects that it does not support obligations to fellow *nationals*, since nations are not voluntary associations.[11]

Miller tells us that his argument is not intended 'as a critique of universalism in itself'. A universalist approach to ethics, he continues, 'might still be the correct one'.[12] This argument is surprisingly over-cautious, because Miller defends 'nationality' (his word for reasonable nationalism), and argues that universalism cannot provide a reasoned basis for 'nationality', and that ethical particularism can because it rests on 'well established facts about human identity and human motivation'.[13] His argument is, therefore, an argument for ethical particularism, and against ethical universalism, even if it is explicitly stated not to be generally decisive. However, the limits of Miller's argument leave ethical universalism largely undamaged. Universalists may, for example, support an ethical division of labour without requiring that the division of labour be along national lines. They may hold, for example, that *multinational* institutions should carry the primary obligation to help the world's neediest people. They may support voluntary associations because they are expressions of freedom without claiming that nations are such associations. Universalists may support reasonable nationalism on other grounds or not at all. Miller's arguments from the ethical division of labour and freedom of association neither undermine universalism in general (which he concedes) nor even the possibility of universalist arguments for nationalism.

Miller's argument for 'nationality' is, paradoxically, stronger as a *general* argument for ethical particularism and against ethical universalism, than it is as a more limited argument against the universalist case for nationalism. Miller claims to have shown that 'the ethics of nationality' rest on 'well established facts about human identity and human motivation'. These facts are that identities are formed, first and foremost, in close, intimate groups, and the sentiments that arise in such groups are the strongest motivators of human action. These claims have some intuitive force, but they do not necessarily support nationalism. They suggest that family bonds would typically be strongest, and loyalty to family would not necessarily lead to loyalty to nation: the national origins or religious affiliations of a family, for example, might lead to loyalty to a nation other than that in which a person resided.

3. Limited Altruism

However, if Miller's account of human nature provides weaker support for nationalism than he thinks it does, it undermines universalism more than he thinks it does. For his defence of 'nationality' rests on a Humean meta-ethic of natural sentiments and limited altruism. He tells us that 'Hume *saw* that morality *had to be* understood in relation to natural sentiments, so that the judgements we make about others *must* reflect their (and our) natural preferences for kinsmen and associates'.[14] Miller attributes to Hume moral *knowledge* not *belief*, and this knowledge is of *necessary truths*. This meta-ethical claim is sufficiently strong that it is worth repeating the following passage from Hume that Miller quotes in its support:

> When experience has once given us a competent knowledge of human affairs, and has taught us the proportion they bear to human passions, we perceive, that the generosity of men is very limited, and that it seldom extends beyond their friends and family, or, at

most, beyond their native country. Being thus acquainted with the nature of man, we expect not any impossibilities from him; but confine our view to that narrow circle, in which any person moves, in order to form a judgement of his moral character. When the natural tendency of his passions leads him to be serviceable and useful within his sphere, we approve of his character, and love his person, by a sympathy with the sentiments of those, who have a more particular connexion with him.

Hume's argument is inductive. He derives moral judgement from 'experience'. What experience teaches us is that 'the generosity of men is very limited', and consequently we do not expect the impossible, but form a judgement of a person's moral character by confining our view to that narrow circle in which a person moves. Hume moves from empirical observations about limited generosity to empirical claims about how we make our moral judgements. However, Hume's argument, and Miller's gloss on it, imply that we *rightly* make such judgements. Miller cites Hume in aid of *ethical* particularism, and not in support of a 'value-free' moral psychology.

Miller's implicit *general* case against ethical universalism, therefore, derives from the Humean meta-ethic of natural sentiments and the Humean psychology of limited altruism. The psychology contains much truth: human generosity is limited. The meta-ethic is vulnerable to challenge on two grounds. The first is that *sentiments* can be ethically good or bad, and we need an *independent* ethical theory to discriminate between the two. The second objection to the Humean meta-ethic is that sentiments are, to some extent, *social* rather than *natural*, and thus the appeal to nature is unduly conservative. Nevertheless, the meta-ethic has some force in so far as limited altruism is pervasive and enduring. It may seem plausible to propose that any ethic that flew in the face of limited altruism would break up on the rock of certain enduring realities of human nature. The case for the Humean meta-ethic is that it is 'realistic', and that its denial is 'utopian'.

The Humean principle of limited altruism challenges ethical universalism. It is very doubtful that the project of securing universal observance of human rights could be carried out by persons with very limited generosity that seldom extended beyond their native country. This kind of universalism seems to be *psychologically* incompatible with Humean limited altruism. Miller admits some obligations based on 'common humanity' and the concept of 'basic rights', but, in his argument, our obligations to our fellow nationals have priority over those of distant strangers, and, although we may have some obligation to help the latter, this may involve only a very limited cost to the former.[15] The idea of limited altruism as an *ethical principle* as distinct from a *psychological observation* would allow only a very weak form of ethical universalism. This means that the ethical claims of our nearest and dearest stand in strong potential conflict with those of distant strangers who may be in extreme need. This has important implications for the ethics of the Holocaust and other genocides, for a putative duty to help potential or actual victims of genocide may require considerable sacrifice of special obligations: safe nations may have to incur great risks to aid victim nations. Michael Walzer, to whose political philosophy Miller's is quite similar, holds that 'humanitarian intervention' is justified when it is a response, with reasonable expectations of success, to acts 'that shock the moral conscience of mankind'.[16] The rescuers of Jews during the

Holocaust acted at extreme risk, not only to themselves, but to their families and friends.[17] The psychological thesis of limited altruism implies that such behaviour is extremely rare, which is true, although we must note that it exists, its actual extent is unknown, as is its future potential. Ethical particularism as a normative theory implies that such behaviour may be *immoral*, and that those who collaborated with the Holocaust, out of fear for their own fate and/or that of their nearest and dearest, may have done the right thing. It seems reasonably debatable whether one has an obligation, or even moral permission, to risk the lives of one's family to save those of strangers, especially if the success of the rescue is uncertain. It seems perverse, however, to imply that 'righteous Gentiles' were acting immorally.

The source of the problem may be found in a passage from Locke's account of the state of nature. This state, according to Locke, is a state of liberty, but not of licence. This means that everyone has the liberty to dispose of his person or possessions, subject to the law of nature, 'which obliges every one', and teaches all 'who will but consult it' that no one ought to harm another in his life, health, liberty or possessions. Everyone 'as he is bound to preserve himself', ought, *when his own preservation comes not in competition*, to preserve the rest of mankind, *as much as he can*.[18] Locke here identifies two *universal* and 'natural' obligations: (1) not to harm others; (2) to preserve others. These obligations are, however, *limited* in two ways: (1) the obligation to preserve mankind does not apply when one's own preservation competes with it; (2) the obligation to preserve mankind is limited by one's ability. This seems to mean that one has no obligation to save the lives of others (however many they are) at the cost of one's own life. However, it is not clear otherwise how much sacrifice we are obliged to make for the sake of others. It is not clear, in particular, how far we are obliged to *risk* our lives to save the lives of others, nor which other sacrifices we may be obliged to make to help or protect others. Locke places some limit on the obligation to others for the sake of self-interest, but it is not clear whether Lockean natural law would or would not endorse Miller's principle that *nations* are obliged only to make limited sacrifices for members of other nations. Holocaust rescuers possibly went beyond what Lockean natural law required of them. Millerite nationalism probably requires considerably less.

Miller translates the Humean principle of limited altruism at the level of individual psychology and ethics to the principle of limited sacrifice at the level of the ethical obligations of well-off nations to needy nations. He also implicitly translates the Lockean principle of individual self-preservation to that of the national right to self-determination.[19] The resultant theory of nationality might entail an obligation to act to help foreigners in the event of extreme poverty or of a human-rights catastrophe such as genocide, but this obligation would be limited both by the principle of limited sacrifice and by the right to self-determination of the nation whose members are in need of help. These two principles support familiar arguments against 'humanitarian intervention' on the grounds that it is more often than not (1) ineffective, if not (2) counterproductive, and therefore (3) immoral. Miller's principle of 'nationality' is similar to that of the apparently universalist and cosmopolitan United Nations in that its ideal world consists of liberal, democratic and mutually friendly nations, who help each other in times of need, but not at much cost to themselves and without violating the principle of national self-determination. Whether or not this is a morally attractive ideal, it is not well designed to take seriously contemporary problems that would be highlighted by reflection on the Holocaust, that is, those of genocide and other severe human-rights violations.

Miller holds that 'identity', which is formed to a significant extent, according to him, by 'nationality', entails obligation. It is this entailment – for which Miller provides no argument – which grounds the supposed obligation to give priority to one's fellow nationals. The argument suffers from two principal weaknesses. The first is that, as a proposition in social psychology, the assertion that nationality provides the content of identity is only partially true (and may be hardly true at all for some individuals). The second weakness is that the inference from identity to obligation is logically invalid. 'Identities' can be morally bad and good (for example, Nazis and rescuers), and any obligations that might, in some way, derive from identities would depend on their moral quality. If one's identity were that of a Nazi, one's first obligation might well be to change it. One may, of course, have an identity as 'a citizen of the world', a 'cosmopolitan' or an 'internationalist'. Miller concedes that the priority of obligations to fellow nationals 'seems to cut against *a powerful humanitarian sentiment* which can be expressed by saying that every human being should matter equally to us'.[20] The 'identity' argument is, therefore, decisive neither empirically nor logically. There is evidence that 'identity' is *empirically* linked to *sense of* obligation (this is hardly surprising, since 'identity' is likely to include self-perception of one's moral character), but this may lead to altruistic, universalist behaviour. Rescuers of Jews during the Holocaust often reported to interviewers that they acted 'naturally', that is, that altruistic action flowed 'naturally' from their character and upbringing.[21] Thus, the truth in the identity-obligation thesis can support altruism and universalism. The questions then become to understand why it is relatively rare, which is a problem in social psychology, and how it might be made more common, which is a problem shared by social psychology and ethics.

4. The Ethical Division of Labour

Miller criticized the universalist argument for 'nationality' from the ethical division of labour on the ground that the rich would help their fellow nationals, and the poor would help their fellow nationals, and the outcome would fail to meet the requirements of a universalist conception of justice. The objection to this argument accepts the necessity of an ethical division of labour, but denies the assumption that it has to be based on the priority of obligations to fellow nationals. In other words, the universalist must disconnect the valid principle of the ethical division of labour from the questionable principle of the priority of nationality. If there is an obligation to help those in extreme need – whether because of extreme poverty or extreme persecution – which principles ought to give shape to the appropriate ethical division of labour? I suggest that the following are plausible.

The first principle derives from the maxim that ought implies can. A necessary condition for the obligation to help is the ability to help. I call this *the ability principle*. It may seem obvious. It requires interpretation, however, that may not be straightforward. This is because, while the fulfilment of an obligation may be 'impossible' in an uncontroversial sense (it is impossible for me to feed all the hungry people in the world, for example), it may be 'impossible' in at least two equivocal senses. The first derives from moral priorities. If I say to my student, 'I can't help you today because I have to take my daughter to the hospital', I mean, not that it is *impossible* for me to help him, but that my obligation to my daughter has, in the circumstances, *moral priority*. The second equivocal meaning of 'impossibility' derives from non-moral costs. If I were more like Mother Theresa than I am, I would help more needy people than I do. It is not obviously 'impossible' for me to emulate Mother Theresa, but it would be extremely costly for me to do so, and it is hardly an abuse of language to say that it is psychologically impossible. Arguments from 'impossibility' may be difficult to distinguish from more or less dubious *excuses*. We have no obligation to do what we are not able to do. But we may have an obligation to become able to do more than we are able to do now. Thus, the apparently straightforward ability principle of moral obligation conceals some difficult questions of the limits of our obligations to help the needy.

A common argument against universalism, cosmopolitanism and interventionism is that would-be interveners do not know the needs of those whom their universalist principles require them to help, and that therefore their interventions are likely to be either futile or counterproductive. This is an *epistemological* objection to intervention. It assumes that individuals generally know their own needs best, and that their nearest and dearest know them better than 'outsiders' do. Miller believes that fellow nationals generally are better judges of needs than foreigners are. Since this argument is common, and has considerable merit, it is worth pointing out that it is not infrequently false and made in bad faith. It was, for example, commonly made to defend apartheid in South Africa against its foreign critics. There is a consensus now that outsiders knew enough about apartheid to make valid moral criticisms of it, and to take appropriate action. It is, nevertheless, valid and important to emphasize that we may easily mistake the needs of distant strangers, and we should be sensitive to this possibility. I call this *the knowledge principle*. This principle states that we should take reasonable steps to understand the needs of those we may think ourselves obliged to help, and that it is easier to understand the needs of those similar to ourselves than those who are different. The knowledge principle does not subvert universalist or cosmopolitan obligations, however, or, as Miller believes, support the strong priority of obligations to fellow nationals, for two reasons. The first is that, especially in cases of extreme need or injustice, it may be quite easy to acquire sufficient knowledge for appropriate action. I don't need to know much about Rwanda to give generously to Oxfam. The second reason is that we may have an obligation to acquire the necessary knowledge. It has often been said, in relation to the question as to how much ordinary Germans knew about the Holocaust, that they knew enough to know that it would be imprudent to know more. This obligation to know more may be a core obligation in the universalist project to improve our *ability* to help those in extreme need.

The ability and the knowledge principles both refer to properties of putative obligation-bearers. The third principle governing the ethical division of labour refers to a particular *relation* between obligation-bearers and potential beneficiaries of the fulfilment of their obligations. It is plausible to suggest that we have some moral responsibility for the known and foreseeable *consequences* of our actions, and special obligations to those who have been harmed by what we have done or are vulnerable to future harm from what we propose to do.[22] This *vulnerability principle* might suggest that we give some priority to our nearest and dearest on the ground that they are more vulnerable to our actions than distant strangers are. However, although the consequences of our actions for distant strangers may often be extremely indirect, those consequences may also be catastrophic. For example, citizens of rich states support (not least, by paying taxes to) governments that have influence over the policies of the International Monetary Fund. The IMF has, through its structural adjustment programmes, caused a great deal of misery. Thus, some of the neediest people in the world are indirectly vulnerable to our actions. It is not clear what obligations, if any, follow for us from this. Perhaps to learn more about the IMF. Perhaps to support well-informed non-governmental organizations seeking to reform the IMF. Miller himself acknowledges that there may be structural–causal links between us and the world's poorest that give rise to some obligations on our part. There is at least a *prima facie* case that they give rise to a stronger universalist obligation than he endorses.

The right to freedom of association presents a challenge to the universalist, for there is a *universal* right to freedom of association (according to liberal universalists) but associations necessarily give rise to *special* obligations that may compete with universal obligations. Do I spend the weekend raising money for my cycling club or for Amnesty International? We should note that the universal right to freedom of association is not plausibly absolute, and that all associations are not good. The right to freedom of association does not legitimate the Mafia. Brian Barry has rightly pointed out that some associations may be exclusionary and distribute social benefits in ways that are unjust.[23] While the universalist right to freedom of association might properly be limited by universalist considerations, we should also note that particularist sentiments and special obligations may have *instrumental* value as means to universalist ends. In the Holocaust, rescuers of Jews were often motivated and assisted by their membership of particular associations and communities.[24] Associational commitments also enter the practical reason of universalist ethics as *conditions* of action. Universalists must pursue their goals in an actual world that includes associations of various kinds as important components. Associational life is therefore both a universal value and a condition for the implementation of other universal values. *Pace* Miller, universalists can value special relations and many of their concomitant obligations because they are necessary to the universalist conception of the human life of dignity and freedom.

The ability, knowledge and vulnerability principles can all be formulated in a way that supports a fairly strong obligation to needy strangers. The association principle provides a rival to universalist obligations, but not necessarily a deadly rival. On this account, it is clear that we have to balance our special and our universal obligations. But how? Barry suggests, plausibly, that the answer must recognize the right of everyone to a free, dignified and worthwhile personal life, while imposing on those who have more than that to help those who have less than that to achieve it.[25] This solution allows some recognition of limited altruism, but puts it under more pressure than Hume did. It allows a place for 'natural sentiments' of personal life as well as sentiments of cosmopolitan sympathy, but judges sentiments at the bar of need, vulnerability and justice. It recognizes that 'common-sense morality' and 'natural sentiments' are subject to manipulation and the play of power, and are therefore an inadequate basis for a conception of justice.

The Humean theory of limited altruism is attractive because it appears to be grounded in a reality that it would be foolish to deny. This 'reality' is, however, neither as fixed nor as narrow as Hume or Miller have assumed. The theory also suffers from a fact/value problem: the argument from supposed psychological realities to ethical values requires more argument than appeal to supposedly stubborn facts. On Miller's own account universalist, humanitarian sentiments can be powerful. Given the well-established fact that sentiments and altruism are variable, there is a strong case against making the move from fact to value too swiftly. Limited altruism ought to be regarded as a difficult obstacle to adequate moral action, and not as grounding an ethical ideal. Miller accepts that limited altruism and humanitarian sentiment are facts of human psychology. Since local sentiments are constituents of universal human nature, universalist ethics should show them a degree of respect. Since supra-local and transnational sympathies are also constituents of contemporary ethical sensibility, they merit a larger place in political ethics than ethical particularists allow them. Under contemporary conditions, limited altruism is simply not enough altruism. Changing this for the better will not be easy, but one contribution that moral philosophy can make is to show that philosophical theories that defend limited altruism are inadequate to the contemporary tasks of philosophy.[26] Arguments that more-than-limited altruism is *dangerous* can be countered by the careful formulation of universalism, and by pointing out the achievements of altruism.[27] Fortunately, rescuers of Jews from the Nazis were not much inhibited by the fact that they were ignorant of the intricacies of Jewish culture, and that therefore their interventions might be counterproductive.

The Humean moral character is not wholly unattractive. It is generous in a limited way. It is 'serviceable' and 'useful' within its narrow sphere. It is a small morality, which may do quite well in everyday life, but is not up to the grand occasion. It would probably be overwhelmed by the Holocaust. It is true that the rescuers of Jews commonly saw themselves as, and indeed in many respects were, 'ordinary people' with an ordinary, unheroic morality.[28] They were, however, able to transcend the limits of narrow altruism. Limited altruism is too limited because it may exclude those in most need. Norman Geras has rightly pointed out that the Jewish victims of the Holocaust may well have been the beneficiaries of limited altruism, but that was insufficient to save them.[29] Theories of 'limited obligation', such as that of Fishkin,[30] often emphasize the intolerable cost to the obligation-bearer if we abandon the principle of limited sacrifice. They emphasize less the intolerable cost to innocent victims of persecution, oppression and injustice of applying the more comfortable Humean standard. The hard truth is that the plain injustices of the contemporary world can be remedied only by considerable sacrifice by the well-off, although, if our political culture favoured even very slightly more sacrifice than we make now, considerable improvements would be possible. It is well known, for example, that very small cuts in arms expenditure can fund very beneficial improvements in health care for very poor people.

Miller argues for the 'communitarian' view that identity is closely associated with ethical motivation, and that, consequently, we will, and should, normally prefer our nearest and dearest to distant strangers. We know that the kind of altruism shown by the rescuers of Jews during the Holocaust is extremely rare.[31] However, the kind of altruistic universalism that motivated them does seem generally to have constituted in part their *identities*. Research on rescuers suggests that good people come from good families and good communities.[32] Miller's nationalism can be reconciled with the universalism of Holocaust rescuers when the national culture itself has a universalist component, as in the case of the Danish rescue of the Jews.[33] Rescuers of Jews in the Holocaust typically thought of them as fellow citizens or as human beings. For some, it was not a question of (explicit or conscious) reasons, still less of religion, philosophy or ideology:

> I cannot give you any reasons. It was not a question of reasoning. Let's put it this way. There were people in need and we helped them ... People always ask how we started, but we didn't start. It started. And it started very gradually. We never gave it much thought.[34]

The same, apparently unreflecting, rescuer reported that her mother told her that she had no right to engage in rescue activity, because her first responsibility was for the safety of her own children. She told her mother that it was more important for her children to have parents who had done what they felt they had to do, even if it cost them their lives.[35] This misses the point that they might have been risking *their children's* lives, but it illustrates well how altruism and universalism can be central to identity and obligation.

Samuel and Pearl Oliner conclude their study of 'the altruistic personality' by emphasizing the 'communitarian' character of altruistic behaviour. This leads them to distinguish between *altruism* and *autonomy*. Liberals usually value 'autonomy'. But the concept of 'autonomy' can have at least two distinct meanings that are relevant here. The first meaning has been well defined by Gerald Dworkin:

> [A]utonomy is conceived of as a second-order capacity of persons to reflect critically upon their first-order preferences, desires, wishes, and so forth and the capacity to accept or attempt to change these in light of higher-order preferences and values. By exercising such a capacity, persons define their nature, give meaning and coherence to their lives, and take responsibility for the kind of person they are.[36]

Such a person might become a heroic rescuer, or at least a decent person, but not necessarily so. This definition gives no content to 'autonomy', and thereby is neutral with respect to the preferences, values, nature and meaning of autonomous persons. Autonomous persons, by this definition, *could* be Nazis. Dworkin cites, as an example of someone who failed to act according to his principles, rightly, Huck Finn, who, 'knowing' that slavery was right, and believing that he ought not to help Jim to escape, 'was willing to sacrifice his integrity in favour of his humanitarian impulses'.[37] The Oliners' rescuers did not generally feel any contradiction between their principles and their impulses, but did act on impulse, and therefore not 'autonomously' in Dworkin's sense.

The second conception of 'autonomy' is the Kantian one, which shares with Dworkin's the idea of second-order reflection, but adds the conception of the rational will which accords with the requirements of the categorical imperative. Lindley summarizes the Kantian view thus:

> According to what I have called the Kantian view, to be fully autonomous is equivalent to being a fully rational agent. To be a fully rational agent is to be motivated by purely rational principles, which are untainted by particular inclinations or interests. Such purity requires that one act only on principles one is prepared to universalise in a strong sense. This in turn requires that one treat all human beings never simply as means to ends, but as ends in themselves (because it is impossible for a creature with a will to regard itself simply as a means to an end).[38]

The Oliners argue that, in cultures that value individualism and rationality, a morality rooted in autonomy is highly valued. Those who behave in accordance with commendable ethical standards, but who do so in compliance with social norms or standards set by those who are close to them, or because of empathy with others, are thought to be in some way morally deficient. Empirically, few individuals behave virtuously because of autonomous reflection on abstract principles. Yet advocates of autonomy recommend it as the most morally admirable style. The Oliners even suggest that, paradoxically, the value of rational autonomy may derive from a Romantic conception of the lone hero, as in the movie *High Noon* or Ibsen's play *An Enemy of the People*. The Oliners call this view 'dispiriting', for, if the future well-being of humankind is dependent on a few heroes of autonomy, its future is bleak indeed.[39] This argument conflates the motivation and justification of action. Identification with our nearest and dearest and empathy with others may best motivate altruistic action, although the former often does not, but the downgrading of autonomy disables us from judging which actions we ought to commend.

Conclusions

The problem that I have addressed is that common-sense morality endorses limited altruism, while limited altruism is insufficient to solve the kind of urgent moral problems raised by reflection on the Holocaust and subsequent moral disasters. We have strong obligations to our nearest and dearest, but we have stronger obligations to distant strangers than we commonly acknowledge. The principle of 'common humanity' that Miller recognizes as having moral force entails that the extreme needs of strangers impose obligations on us. The fear of some philosophers that a needs-led theory of obligation would lead to excessive demands is met by the principle of ability, although we have seen that this principle is rather indeterminate. We ought also to take seriously the epistemological case for non-intervention, but we ought also to recognize its limits and its dangers. The case for limited altruism is weakened further by the principle that we are responsible for our actions and thus for remedying their harmful consequences. The consequences of our actions are extremely complex, and extremely difficult to identify with confidence, but the interconnectedness of the fates of the rich and powerful with those of the poor and powerless is sufficient to ground a rather strong transnational obligation of aid and rescue.

There is a strong universalist case for ethical particularism. The philosopher who sacrificed her daughter's birthday for a 'higher' cause could make us morally uncomfortable. The Holocaust rescuer who sought to set a moral example to her children was, however, also surely an admirable parent. Limited altruism is morally wrong if it excludes some human beings altogether from the universe of moral obligation. Unlimited universalism, on the other hand, can be morally dangerous. Moral theory seems to stop at this point. The evil in the world is powerful. The altruistic impulse, in contrast, is weak. Moral philosophers should at least refrain from commending our moral weakness. 'Could (and should) do better' must be the verdict on our altruism.

Notes

1.   A. Gewirth (1988), 'Ethical universalism and particularism', *Journal of Philosophy* **85**, pp. 283–302; D. Miller (1995), *On Nationality*, Oxford: Clarendon Press, pp. 49–80. The term 'ethical particularism' is commonly used in moral philosophy to refer to the claim that there are no valid general moral principles. That claim is not the subject of the present enquiry, which is concerned with the relative merits of two rival moral theories, both of which are general in scope.
2.   H. Steiner (1994), *An Essay on Rights*, Oxford: Blackwell, p. 262 – emphasis in original.
3.   J. Locke (1970), *Two Treatises of Government*, Cambridge: Cambridge University Press, paragraph 14.
4.   J. Donnelly (1989), *Universal Human Rights in Theory and Practice*, Ithaca, NY: Cornell University Press, p. 12.
5.   O. O'Neill (2000), *Bounds of Justice*, Cambridge: Cambridge University Press, p. 188.
6.   Miller, *On Nationality*, pp. 53–5.
7.   I. Brownlie (ed.) (1992), *Basic Documents on Human Rights*, Oxford: Clarendon Press, 3rd edn, pp. 22–4.
8.   Miller, *On Nationality*, p. 50.
9.   J.S. Fishkin (1982), *The Limits of Obligation*, New Haven, CT: Yale University Press.
10. B. Barry (1995), *Justice as Impartiality*, Oxford: Clarendon Press, p. 205.
11. Miller, *On Nationality*, pp. 51–65.
12. Ibid., p. 64.
13. Ibid., p. 80.
14. Ibid., p. 58, footnote 11 – emphasis mine.
15. Ibid., pp. 73–80.
16. M. Walzer (1977), *Just and Unjust Wars: A Moral Argument with Historical Illustrations*, Harmondsworth: Penguin Books, p. 107.
17. S.P. Oliner and P.M. Oliner (1988), *The Altruistic Personality: Rescuers of Jews in Nazi Europe*, New York, NY: The Free Press.
18. Locke, *Two Treatises*, paragraph 6.
19. Miller, *On Nationality*, pp. 81–118.
20. Ibid., p. 49 – emphasis mine.
21. Oliner and Oliner, *Altruistic Personality*.
22. O'Neill, *Bounds of Justice*, p. 187; R. Goodin (1985), *Protecting the Vulnerable*, Chicago, IL: University of Chicago Press, p. 118; Miller, *On Nationality*, p. 51, footnote 2.

23. Barry, *Justice as Impartiality*, pp. 15–17, 211–13.
24. Oliner and Oliner, *Altruistic Personality*, p. 125.
25. Barry, *Justice as Impartiality*, pp. 206–7, 230.
26. N. Geras (1998), *The Contract of Mutual Indifference: Political Philosophy after the Holocaust*, London: Verso.
27. Oliner and Oliner, *Altruistic Personality*.
28. Ibid.
29. Geras, *Contract of Mutual Indifference*, pp. 33–4.
30. Fishkin, *Limits of Obligation*.
31. Oliner and Oliner, *Altruistic Personality*, p. 2.
32. Ibid.; N. Tec (1986), *When Light Pierced the Darkness: Christian Rescue of Jews in Nazi-Occupied Poland*, New York, NY: Oxford University Press; P. Hallie (1979), *Lest Innocent Blood Be Shed: The Story of the Village of Le Chambon and how Goodness Happened There*, New York, NY: Harper Torchbooks.
33. Oliner and Oliner, *Altruistic Personality*, p. 204; L. Yahil (1969), *The Rescue of Danish Jewry: Test of a Democracy*, Philadelphia, PA: The Jewish Publication Society of America.
34. Dutch rescuer quoted at Oliner and Oliner, *Altruistic Personality*, p. 216.
35. Ibid., p. 217.
36. G. Dworkin (1988), *The Theory and Practice of Autonomy*, Cambridge: Cambridge University Press, p. 20.
37. Ibid., p. 41.
38. R. Lindley (1986), *Autonomy*, Basingstoke: Macmillan, p. 20.
39. Oliner and Oliner, *Altruistic Personality*, pp. 255–7.

Chapter 10

Harming Some to Save Others from the Nazis

Frances M. Kamm

Recent philosophical discussion of when it is permissible to harm some in order to help others and when it is permissible to collaborate with evil may help us to morally evaluate the behavior of some who collaborated with the Nazis. I have in mind those who tried to reduce the total amount of harm the Nazis did by themselves helping to produce lesser evil.

Harming some to save others raises very basic questions: why is it morally preferable that we save a group containing the greater number of people where we face a conflict between saving this group and another group with fewer people? Are there characteristics that distinguish people (such as age or health) that should play a role in our deciding whose life to save? Recent philosophical discussion of these issues is also, I believe, relevant to the evaluation of decisions made by those who collaborated with Nazis in order to save lives.

In this essay, I shall not survey in detail recent philosophical discussions of permissible harm, collaboration, and principles for saving lives.[1] Rather, I shall briefly characterize what have been central areas of concern for nonconsequentialists (sometimes also called deontologists). Act consequentialists think that we may always do what is necessary to produce the best outcome. By contrast, nonconsequentialists argue (often from judgments about individual cases) that there are distinctions among the *ways* in which we bring about an outcome, and these may be important for whether it is permissible to act. In Section II, I make use of nonconsequentialist analyses to show how we might argue for the permissibility or impermissibility of certain types of acts that collaborators may have undertaken.

I

Consider two groups of people, one larger than the other, where there are no morally relevant differences between the people. We face the choice of whom to save, and whom to let die. Why does the fact that we would save a greater number of people give us reason to abandon a smaller number of other people rather than save them (or give each group an equal chance to be saved)? One argument might be that we thereby produce a greater good without abandoning anyone who would be worse off than any individual we wind up saving would have been. Some have argued that in conflicts like this, it is worse for the greater number if they die, but better for the lesser number, and there is no impartial point of view from which to judge that we produce a greater good if more are saved. However, the following Aggregative Argument suggests that this view is flawed: (1) using Pareto optimality, we see that it is better if both B and C are saved than if only B is saved – even though it is not better for B, it is better for C and not worse for B. (2) It is better to a still greater degree, if B, C and D are saved. Our judgment that the world is better to a greater degree, although it is also only better for one additional person, by comparison to what is true if B and C are saved, is made from a point of view outside that of any person (this goes beyond Pareto optimality). (3) A world in which A dies and B survives is just as bad as a world in which B dies and A survives. This is true, from an impartial point of view, even though the worlds are not equally preferred by A and B. (4) Given (3), we can substitute A for B on the right side of the moral equation in (1) and get that it is better if B and C are saved than if only A is saved.

Although it would be better if B and C are saved than if A is, that does not necessarily mean that it is right for us to save B and C rather than A. A nonconsequentialist says that we cannot automatically assume it is morally permissible to maximize the good, for this may violate justice or fairness. Some might claim that if we save B and C on the basis of (4), we abandon A to save the greater number without giving her a chance and this is unfair.

But is it really wrong to produce the best outcome in this case? The argument I prefer for the conclusion that it is not wrong does not appeal to the greater good we would produce. It considers what we owe to each individual person. I call it the Balancing Argument.[2] The Balancing Argument claims that in a conflict, what we owe is that each person on one side should have her interests balanced against those of one person on the opposing side; those that are not balanced out in the larger group help determine that the larger group should be saved. If we instead toss a coin between one person and any number on the other side, giving each person an equal chance, we would behave no differently than if it were a contest between one and one. If the presence of each additional person would make no difference, this seems to deny the equal significance of each person.

Sometimes, however, there may be differences in the individual characteristics of persons that are morally relevant to deciding whom to save. Here are two possibilities: (1) one person has lived a full life already, the other is quite young and would die not having had anywhere near as much a good life as the other has already had. (2) One person if saved will live a long time (or has a high probability of this), the other person will not live long anyway.

Now consider the additional element of *killing* some rather than merely letting them die to save others. There are many possible scenarios in which the issue of killing some to help others survive may arise. Here are some: (1) we would have to kill some innocent, nonthreatening people who would die anyway soon in order to save a greater number from dying natural deaths or being killed. Bernard Williams's much-discussed case of Jim and the Indians is of this type, since Jim must kill one of the twenty Indians who would otherwise be killed in order to save the nineteen others.[3] (2) We would have to kill some people who we are not sure will die soon anyway, in order to save a greater number from dying natural deaths or being killed. (In one case in this category, *each* person we would kill had a *higher* probability of being killed if we did nothing, though it is possible that the person we kill would not actually have been killed if we did nothing.) (3) We would have to kill innocent, nonthreatening people who we are sure would otherwise not die soon, in order to save a greater number of people from natural death or being killed. This bystander category could be divided into two subclasses: (a) we must redirect a threat from the greater number to the lesser number, or redirect the greater number away from a threat, and this results in the lesser number being threatened. The most-discussed version of this class is the Trolley Problem: a runaway trolley is headed toward killing five people and we can redirect it to a track where we foresee that one person will be killed.[4] Even many nonconsequentialists believe redirection is permissible. (b) Alternatively, we may save the greater number from a threat by doing something that kills the smaller number in some way other than described in (a). The most-discussed version of this case is known as Transplant: we must kill someone to get his organs in order to save five other people from organ failure. Nonconsequentialists, at least, believe it is impermissible to kill in Transplant. Much effort has been spent in trying to explain why killing could be permissible in Trolley but not in Transplant.

Killing in these types of scenarios need not involve collaborating with any evil persons who are responsible for the original threat to the greater number. There might not even be any evil persons responsible for the initial threat, only a natural disaster. Or, if there are such persons, we might just know of their threat and have to decide on our own without collaborating with them whether it is permissible for us to save the greater number. However, we could also imagine variants on all these cases in which we must collaborate (that is, engage in jointly intended coordination) with the evil people who began threats, in order to save the greater number.

II[5]

Consider the hypothetical case of someone who stayed in Germany when he, as a non-Jewish German, was free to leave, and undertook the construction of death camps. He did this only because he thought (assume correctly) that he would cause fewer deaths than his substitute.[6] On the other hand, we have Jews in the Judenrat, the Jewish community's governing bodies during the war, whose members were assigned by the Nazis to select people to be taken either to work or to concentration camps. It is said (suppose correctly) that at least some members of the Judenrat selected for the Nazis in the belief that they would thereby cause less suffering and damage overall than if the Nazis did the task themselves. I shall refer to these as the Selectors.

There are, of course, many differences between these cases. One is that the Selectors were themselves already, and likely to be further, victims of the Nazis. This might mean that if the Selectors' behavior was wrong, they are partially excused by duress. But we should be clear about the exact nature of the duress. It is possible that they would be harmed sooner if they did not do the selections, but they would not be set free for selecting. So what they stood to lose comparatively by not cooperating with the Germans was not so great. However, they may not have known this. In addition, their lives were constantly in jeopardy just as Jews, and a state of misery and panic can affect judgment.

On the other hand, whether the acts of the German and the Selectors were correct or incorrect, only the person – probably the German – who did *not* act from duress could claim that he acted solely for the good of others. Additionally, the Selectors, unlike the German, would be harming their *fellow* victims. This is a complex issue. It is obviously related to the problem of the black overseer and the peculiar satisfaction members of an evil system may take when they divide a subjugated group and turn some victims against others. But I shall put this issue to one side here.

Both the German and Judenrat cases differ from a case like Jim and the Indians. In the latter, we can be sure that a greater evil will come about (including the very person we harm) if we do not produce the lesser evil. In the former, we cannot be sure that the Nazis would themselves do as great an evil if the German and the Selectors did not collaborate. For example, it is said that in Denmark, when Danes refused to help select Jews, the Nazis simply did not proceed with their plans for harming Jews.[7] Another real-world factor is the possibility that collaborators help increase the total evil done by freeing up evil people to engage in yet *other* bad acts.[8] But suppose we could be sure that in the absence of our collaborators, the Nazis would have proceeded to do greater evil and our collaborators did not increase total evil.

One of the most important distinctions between the Selectors and both the imagined German and Jim is the way in which the outcome is better than it would otherwise be. Fewer people are killed in Jim's case, and I have stipulated fewer killed in the German's case. But the Selectors may not have been in a position to reduce the *number killed*, only the *number who died*. For example, they are said to have selected those (for example old, sick, very young) who would not have survived long anyway in the ghetto, perhaps even without being killed. So they selected those to be killed and tried thereby to save the lives of those who could survive in the ghetto (for example healthy workers) who might otherwise have been killed. The number killed would then be constant, but more overall would survive. Perhaps Selectors may even have known that they could not reduce either the number killed *or* the number who died, for eventually even the ones who lived longer in the ghetto would die there. If this were so, in selecting they would only be trying to increase time lived before death.

Would it have been a fundamental moral mistake to select for concentration camp on the basis of such characteristics as age (that is, to select someone who has already had more life than someone else) or expected outcome (that is, to select someone who would have *less* time alive if she were *not* selected than someone else would have if he were not selected)? Some of these choices seem not unlike choices we might be asked to make in distributing a scarce, life-saving health resource, thereby determining who lives and who dies. In the latter case, I do not think it is always immoral to select on these grounds. We might save the young rather than the old (other things equal) because it is morally more valuable to give life-years to someone who has had fewer life-years so far. Indeed, this could be true even if the younger person will not thereby have as many additional years as an old person would if he were saved. Expected additional length of life in itself, however, can be a factor of moral importance. If a young person will die in a few months if saved, it might be right to save a sixty-year-old who would live for fifteen years instead.

Still, the context of sending someone to be killed (rather than not be saved by a medical procedure) may make choices on these grounds seem more morally dubious. This is because killing will deprive someone of what he is *equally entitled to keep*, that is, whatever period of life he would have if not interfered with. Certainly, we should raise a moral objection to killing the old who have not much time left to live in order to prevent killings of young people who will then have long lives. This is consistent with the permissibility of providing scarce medical resources to the young who will then live long, rather than providing the elderly with the extra years they would not have without our help. Nevertheless, I believe this objection to using such characteristics as age and expected life-years gained as grounds for selection is misguided. It is true that in the Selector case, each victim will be deprived of life to which he is entitled when he is killed. But *if* and when it is permissible to decide who will be wronged in this way, it will be permissible to use the same characteristics for selection as we could permissibly use in distributing a scarce drug. Hence, the crucial question is whether and when it is permissible to help choose at all who will be wronged.

Using differential, morally relevant characteristics to select among victims may also be shown to be permissible by considering the various *different* things Selectors did. I have said that they decided who would go to the Nazis. However, they may have selected in the first instance who would *not go* (for example, because their skills were necessary in the ghetto). If this is so, then they are distributing a scarce benefit (for example work passes) with foresight to the fact that those who do not get this benefit are subject to the Nazis' own selection mechanisms. In distributing this scarce benefit, I believe they may permissibly make use of such criteria as might be used in a very different context where injustice will not be the ultimate cause of the death of those not saved.[9]

If there are no morally relevant differences between people, it is permissible for the Selectors to give work passes to some, using a random decision technique.

Let us abstract from the issues of uncertainty about whether a greater evil will occur if one does not act and differential characteristics among people who need to be saved. Assume a case in which one knows that a smaller number will be killed if one acts as Selector, and one also knows that all individuals among whom one selects have the same morally relevant characteristics. It is still true that we cannot be sure that if the German and Judenrat act, the lesser number who will be killed are selected from only those who would have been killed anyway, as is true in Jim's case. Does this threaten to make these cases more like the Bystander cases? Suppose that if the Selectors act, some people will be killed who would not otherwise have been killed if the Nazis had selected more people. May we not conceive of this on the model of the redirection of threat cases: either the Nazis select and kill M–Z or Selectors *redirect the Nazis* who are the threats to A–G? Redirecting a threat from harming a greater number to a lesser number of people who were not originally under any threat – even if a villain started the threat to the greater number and even when redirecting amounts to oneself being a killer – is commonly recognized as morally permissible.[10] Although the usual threat that is redirected is a mechanical device, not an agent who is yet to act, I believe agents may be redirected as well. This point *also* highlights the fact that Jim or the redirector of a mechanical device would kill someone; the Selectors *do not do the actual killing*, the Nazis do. Of course, in the Judenrat case, we are considering how there is collaboration. If Selectors' collaboration took the form of redirection of a human being who will kill, it should *not* be morally impermissible just because it involves such redirection. The objection would have to be to collaboration *per se*.

Perhaps, however, the Selectors' case was somewhat different from a redirection of threat case. Suppose the Nazis had not yet selected people they would kill, but had the Selectors do so in the first instance. Suppose, further, that this meant there was not *re*direction, but only direction of a threat. This is not a crucial difference. For suppose a villain has a trolley threat stationed at a cross point and you know he *will shortly direct it* to some large, not-yet-identified group of people. You are able to direct this stationary trolley in a direction where you know it will kill a small group who would not be part of the would-be larger group. It seems to me that it is equally permissible to direct to them as to redirect to them and for the same reason. But what is the reason for the permissibility of these acts?

This is a complicated issue at the heart of what distinguishes Trolley from Transplant. All I can hope to do here is state (in an oversimplified form and without defense) what I believe is the reason.[11] Harming some who would not have been under a threat in order to help others is permissible when either the greater good (of, for example, a greater number removed from a threat) itself causes the lesser evil (in this case, harm to the lesser number), or means that have the greater good as their *noncausal* flip side cause the lesser evil. (Call this a principle of permissible bad – PPB.) When we send a threat to A, the noncausal flip side of this is its not being sent to B and C. (By contrast, if we were to push A in the way of the threat and that diverted it from B and C, the threat's being away from B and C would be a causal consequence of a lesser evil (understood as 'involving someone against his will in a way we know will lead to significant harm to him').)

However, there is another truly significant problem with applying the redirection of threat analysis to what Selectors did. In most redirection cases, the involvement of the Bystander is not causally necessary in order for the greater number to be saved; it is merely a foreseen effect. However, if the Selectors redirect (or direct) Nazis, it is only if the Nazis get the people to whom they are directed that they will not be back for those the Selectors are trying to save. Therefore, at the very least, the Selectors would redirect *because* they believe those people to whom they direct Nazis will become victims of the Nazis. Does this make their redirection impermissible?

Interestingly, there is a version of the Trolley case known as the Loop case,[12] which also involves acting because we know the bystander will die. The trolley is headed toward killing five. We can redirect, but only toward a track that loops back to the five anyway. Because there is a bystander on that track, his being hit stops the trolley from looping. We would not bother to turn the trolley unless we expected the bystander to be hit, since we causally require the effects of his being hit. I believe turning on the condition that someone will be hit is permissible in the Loop case. The PPB, which I described above, would have to be revised to allow this; it can be revised in keeping with its spirit once we see two points. First, we require harm to Bystanders in order to *sustain* the greater good of five free of the threat that faced them originally, which we have managed to achieve in getting the trolley away. Second, we do nothing to harm the Bystander besides what is necessary to get the trolley away from the five. That is, we do not aim to establish the connection between what we do and harm to the Bystander; we merely take advantage of its being there. If this were similarly all the Selectors did when they make the occurrence of harm to others a condition of their action, they would also act permissibly, I think.

But Selectors may have been prepared to do more. For suppose those to whom the Nazis were redirected tried to escape. If they escaped, the monster would go back to devour the greater number. If Selectors were prepared to interfere with the escape, if they were prepared to do what was necessary to see to it the Nazis were successful in devouring the smaller number, I believe their behavior would not be justified by any principle that justified redirection. (Similarly, someone who gave the trolley an extra push not necessary for getting it away from the greater number, so that it would hit the Bystander, would not be justified by whatever principle permits redirection in the Loop case.)

But now we come to a deeper objection to the analogy with redirecting threats. It might be argued that the Selectors were not directing or redirecting the threat; rather they were moving around victims to be confronted by a steady threat. That is, they were not sending the Nazis to one group of people rather than another; they were sending one group of people rather than another to the Nazis. But, in some cases, it can be permissible to send one group of people to a threat in order to save others. For example, suppose a trolley threat is coming at a great number who are seated on a swivel table and we cannot redirect the trolley. It is permissible to turn the table thereby moving the greater number away from the threat, even if this moves a different but smaller number of people on the other side of the table into the threat. (I call this the Lazy Susan case.) Here the good of the greater number being removed from the threat itself causes the presentation of the lesser number before the threat, so it satisfies the PPB. (An even simpler case involves permissible ducking, that is, a large number of people who stand in front of a smaller group of people are made to duck and the smaller number then face the threat. Here too a greater good leads to the lesser evil.[13])

However, there are types of cases in which introducing a Bystander who is not otherwise threatened to a threat in order to save a greater number from the threat is not permissible, according to the PPB. For example, suppose a Monster will go to A and C, but if we throw B in front of it, this will stop the threat from reaching A and C. In this case, A and C are not saved just in (that is, as a noncausal flip side of) sending in B (our means to saving them). (This *would* occur if we sent in A rather than sent in B and C.) Instead, they are saved as a further causal effect of sending B in since sending him in causes the Monster to stop.

But the model closest to what some Selectors may have done *is* sending B to the Nazis rather than sending A and C. Here, as I see it, the greater good – A and C away from the threat – is the noncausal flip side of sending B in. They send in B as the alternative to sending in A and C; they do not send in B as a means (in the sense of a causal link) to saving A and C.[14]

We are not out of the woods yet, however. For, sending some people or others to a threat of death is not something anyone usually has the authority to do. (Generals in an army have the authority.) Whence could the Selectors have gotten the authority over persons such that they could appropriately have either sent in A, C, or B? Here is one part of this question: sending in B would have as its flip side the greater good of A and C *not* being sent, only if a given Selector were refraining from sending in A and C instead. But how did the Selector permissibly get into the position of having that alternative of sending A and C to the Nazis? The answer to this part of the question is that if these are the people the Nazis would have killed anyway, there may be nothing wrong with the Selector's exercising authority over them in order to save lives. The second part of the question is the real problem: how did the Selector get authority over B, whom (we are assuming) would not have been killed? When the Selector delivers up B to the Nazis instead of A and C, he will have to try, at minimum, to prevent A's escape. This was something we said no principle justifying redirection would let him do. Redirection of a threat and even movement of persons into a threat in ways said to be permissible do not require the same authority over that person. The problem for delivery arises, in part, because we are selecting a person, rather than an alternative route along which a threat will go.

To make this clearer, consider two analogies involving the trolley. (1) The trolley headed to five will stop if I step in to make the *choice* between sending it in the direction in which it will hit the five or the other direction where it will hit one. If I do not make the choice, the trolley starts up again to the five. This is like the case where I find the trolley that will soon go to the five but is now at the cross point (p. 160). It is as permissible for me to direct to the one when I have a choice between directing to one or five as when I had no choice whether to *direct to* the five (in the ordinary Trolley case). (2) The trolley headed to the five will stop if I step in to make the choice between sending the five *into* the trolley (with an impact that will kill them) or sending some bystander into the trolley (with an impact that kills him). If I do not make the choice, the trolley starts up again against the five. We can, I think, see how it might be permissible for me to send the five who will die anyway, if this helped other people. But it is impermissible to take a bystander instead of the five and send him at the trolley, even if the five's being saved is noncausally related to the means of saving them. This is because taking control of a person without his permission, especially when this will lead to harm to him, is wrong itself (unlike turning a trolley). So it involves a bad means and the fact that the good is the noncausal flip side of it is irrelevant to the permissibility of action.

I conclude that principles that justify direction or redirection of threats do not justify Selectors who delivered up some who would not be killed in order to prevent a greater number of others from being killed.[15] What might justify this behavior is showing that the Selectors had authority to control those whom they delivered up.

To do this, it might help to now reintroduce a consideration from which we abstracted in the last subsection: probably no one could know who would be selected by the Nazis and *there was no class of people known not to be in danger of the Nazis*. If each person would be uncertain if he would be selected by the Nazis, it could be in each person's interest *ex ante* to have a smaller number die. That is, each person's chances *ex ante* of dying might be reduced.[16] If it were, perhaps this could help account for the authority of the Selectors to deliver up people. But my description of the facts is not quite accurate. If it were known that Selectors would first send to die the old or sick or very young, then it does not reduce these people's chances of dying *ex ante* for Selectors to choose. It may actually increase their chances of dying or how soon they will die. Even if their fate is not made worse to a great degree, we still cannot say that *ex ante* it would be in *everyone's* interest (or at least not against anyone's interest) to have the Selectors choose. The interests of some would be sacrificed for the sake of others.

If this sacrifice were minimal, however, it might be argued that the Selectors get their authority to deliver up people because delivering makes little difference in outcome to those to whom it is done and it produces much good to others. Here the crucial factor to remember is that they are not delivering up people who really are Bystanders and would go on living unharmed for a long time. Furthermore, in the Selector case, even at the time someone is selected to be sent to the Nazis, it is not known if he would have avoided (or will avoid) this fate if the Selectors had not acted. This would be true even if, in fact, people die who would not otherwise have died. In this way, the case differs from other cases where each person's *ex ante* probability of dying is lower if someone will be selected for death, such as certain versions of the Transplant case where everyone in a society would lower his probability of death if we had a policy of killing someone for his organs. For in this Transplant case, at the time the one person is to be killed, we know he would have avoided death from organ failure and will be able to live on if not killed, as it is only the ones who turn out to be healthy that are sacrificed. (I do not assume that the *ex ante* self-interest of each can justify anything done to the persons. For example, I do not think it justifies delivering up someone to be killed in the Transplant case.)

It may be, therefore, that we can justify even the Selectors' delivering people to the Nazis.

How might the fact of collaboration itself bear on the permissibility or impermissibility either of selecting or actually killing? Collaboration has negative aspects, for example dealing with evil people. Yet, I wish to argue, it sometimes not only reduces harm but also keeps moral discredit where it belongs and preserves a certain sort of purity in an agent. When we realize this, we see that it sometimes releases us to do what we should otherwise not do quite so easily.

Strictly speaking, both the German and the Selectors would be considered collaborators, since they worked with the Nazis. But I am concerned that how they entered into work with Nazis may be morally significant. In the Judenrat case, the

Nazis arguably gave the Selectors an opportunity to do something rather than have Nazis do it. Sometimes they gave them an order, but when they did not, they offered them the opportunity to select, though perhaps they never intended that it lead to fewer deaths. Nevertheless, if the selection was more favorable if the Selectors did it, then even though the Nazis were not responsible for intentionally 'offering a better outcome,' they made an offer that leads to a better outcome.

In the German case, the Nazis (it is assumed) made no *offer* that if he did something, the Nazis would not do worse. He simply believed (we assume) that he would cause fewer deaths and he therefore initiated the collaboration with the Nazis that involved him in causing deaths. I believe there may be a morally significant difference between (1) cases where one takes up an offer or acts on an order, and (2) cases where one either initiates an offer or (sometimes) acts on one's own to produce less evil than would otherwise be produced.

Suppose one takes up an offer to do an act that already has certain characteristics in favor of doing it; for example, it gives everyone a greater chance of survival. Then, I believe, full moral responsibility and accountability for any negative consequences of one's act will belong to the evil persons who would otherwise have done worse. Here is one way of understanding why this is so: when one does such an act in response to an offer or order, one makes oneself the Agent (note the capital 'A') of evil persons. By Agent, I mean someone chosen by the evil persons to carry out their will, as a lawyer who is hired to evict tenants is the Agent of his employer. (This is distinct from being an agent [note lowercase 'a'] in the sense of anyone who performs an act.) One is morally responsible for one's choice to become an Agent, but the person for whom one acts becomes morally responsible for the negative consequences of one's act, at least if one's act is within certain bounds. (If one kills an innocent bystander who had no chance of being killed by Nazis to save a greater number from Nazis, the absence of factors speaking in favor of the permissibility of this act makes responsibility for the death remain with the person who causes the death. This is true of those who do immoral acts and cannot be excused because they 'only followed orders.')

The fact that moral responsibility for the lesser number of deaths lies with the evil persons has at least two implications: (1) the evil persons get moral responsibility for unjust deaths, not just moral responsibility for creating circumstances where others face the choice of having to kill to save a greater number. Hence, they can be punished for murders. (2) Often, when one does what is overall the right act, negative aspects of the act, which are overridden by the positive characteristics, nevertheless remain. One can have responsibility for those negatives and for trying to compensate for them. Hence, even though one is 'morally pure' in the sense that one did the right act, one's purity is diminished as an agent in the sense that one is responsible for the negative aspects. (A fairly innocuous example of this is when one breaks a promise to someone in order to save a life instead, and then one still owes an apology or compensation to the first party.) But if it is permissible to act as an Agent, one retains even this aspect of one's moral purity, since responsibility for negative aspects of one's act lies with the evil persons.

By contrast, suppose one initiates an offer to the evil persons or one acts on one's own to kill a fewer number before the evil persons act to kill a greater number. Even if one's act is permissible – and I do not want to deny that it might be permissible, for example, to deliberately kill one of those who would otherwise die anyway as a result of the Nazis' acts – I believe moral responsibility for the negative consequences of one's act is either shared with the evil people (in the case where one's offer is accepted by the Nazis) or remains one's own (where one acts independently). When one acts independently, the most obvious reason why this is so is that the evil people do not license one's act. In the case where one initiates a plan with evil people, I believe responsibility is not totally transferred to the evil persons, because one acts (in proposing the plan) before evil persons have done all that they can do that is sufficient to bring about the deaths.[17]

I believe it is understandable if an agent prefers to act if there will be a transfer of full moral responsibility for the negative aspects of his act to the evil persons. If this is so, members of the Judenrat should have felt morally freer to collaborate than the German.[18] This is not to deny that the Nazis share responsibility for the deaths the German causes; after all, he works for them and does what they want. It is just that the German also would have moral responsibility for the negative consequences of his acts. He could not have correctly told himself that if he did what would lead to people being killed, the negative consequences of these acts were only being added to the moral account of the Nazis as they would if one were an Agent. I have not, of course, claimed that this is a decisive reason for not acting. But if there is a bias of the sort I have described in favor of not acting when moral responsibility for negative consequences cannot be completely located in the villain, then this is one reason, from the German's point of view, to think his actions would be more morally problematic than those of the Judenrat who were Selectors.

Conclusion

I have argued that some ways Selectors may have used of saving a greater number by not helping or even by harming a smaller number are permissible. These are: (1) giving work passes to some, even if all cannot have them, (2) redirecting the Nazis to a smaller number, even because they know they will harm them. Some other ways are at least harder to justify. These include sending people to the Nazis to save a greater number.

In focusing on these issues, I have not meant to imply that saving lives even by permissible means should have been the paramount motivation of victims of Nazi injustice. Waging counterwar on the unjust may have been preferable, whether it saved lives or not. Doing this would raise a whole different set of moral issues, and in conclusion, I shall just consider some of them.

When one is attacked, self-defense is commonly thought to be permissible. But what if we know in advance that one cannot successfully defend oneself against an enemy? That is, one may succeed in harming the one who is attacking to some degree, but not sufficiently to avoid death oneself. Is it no longer permissible to attack the unjust aggressors? No, since one may be saving others who would also be attacked by the aggressors. What if there is no hope of life for oneself or even others? May one give up hope of successfully stopping an aggressor and just act to inflict as much damage on the aggressor as one can? Peter Graham believes that such action is permissible, and I agree with him.[19] But how can one justify acts that one would permissibly do in self-defense but without any hope of defending self or others? Do the acts become punishment undertaken without legally instituted investigation of guilt and innocence? Unlike punishment, however, the act of aggression is still going on. This, I believe, leaves the aggressor open to attacks on him, even when one knows they will not succeed in stopping the damage he does or will do.[20]

Notes

1.   For lengthy discussion, see my *Morality, Mortality, Vols 1 and 2* (New York: Oxford University Press, 1993, 1996). For shorter discussions, see my 'Nonconsequentialism,' *Blackwell's Guide to Ethical Theory*, ed. H. LaFollette (Oxford: Blackwell, 2000); 'Toward the Essence of Nonconsequentialism,' in *Fact and Value: Essays on Ethics and Metaphysics for Judith Jarvis Thomson*, ed. A. Byrne and R. Wedgwood (Cambridge, MA: MIT Press, 2001); and 'Responsibility and Collaboration,' *Philosophy & Public Affairs* (Summer 1999), pp. 197–202.

2.   I first presented it in 'Equal Treatment and Equal Chances,' *Philosophy & Public Affairs* (Spring 1985), pp. 177–94.

3.   See J.J.C. Smart and B. Williams, *Utilitarianism: For and Against* (Cambridge: Cambridge University Press, 1973), p. 98.

4.   This case was introduced by Philippa Foot in 'The Problem of Abortion and the Doctrine of Double Effect,' reprinted in her *Virtue and Vices* (Berkeley, CA: University of California Press; Oxford: Blackwell, 1978).

5.   This section borrows heavily from 'Responsibility and Collaboration.' However, it also attempts to revise aspects of that article.

6.   I discuss the hypothetical case here because I am not sure there really was anyone like this, although I believe Albert Speer (Hitler's architect) may have conceived of himself in this way.

7.   I am grateful to Susan Wolf for this information.

8.   I owe this point to Richard Arneson.

9.   There is an additional problem that arises when differences between people that are in question bear only on the *instrumental* role they have. For example, suppose we must choose whether to save a doctor who can save other lives or someone who will live as long and is the same age but will not save others. In medical contexts, such as distributing a scarce organ for transplantation, if our duty is the proper distribution of organs and not maximizing lives saved overall, a candidate's being a doctor should not make a difference. (This is so, even if no other doctor can substitute for her in saving other lives.) However, if the Judenrat's duty was simply to maximize lives saved (without acting immorally), saving the doctor seems to be a means to their fulfilling their duty. (Similarly, suppose our duty is just to properly distribute a scarce drug. One of the potential recipients, but not another, can go on to deliver the drug to more people we cannot get to, once he is saved. I believe we may take this as a reason to save him.) See *Morality, Mortality, Vol. 1*, where I first discussed such a distinction between cases.

10.   I have discussed these issues in *Morality, Mortality, Vol. 1*.

11.   I have dealt with this issue in detail in *Morality, Mortality, Vol. 2* and more recently in 'Toward the Essence of Nonconsequentialism.'

12. Invented by Judith Thomson.

13. However, a smaller number may also duck, even if this leaves a larger number under threat. This is because ducking involves someone terminating the assistance (in shielding from a threat) that he is providing to someone behind him, assistance to which that person has no right.

14. It is a mistake in considering this issue to treat the paperwork representation of what a Selector would do as governed by the same moral principles as apply to actual treatment of people. Consider three possible types of paperwork, where 'A,' 'B' and 'C' are letters representing three different people. (1) 'A' and 'C' are on a written list and then someone writes in 'B' ahead of them. (2) 'A' and 'C' are at the top of a list, with 'B' next. Someone crosses the first two out, and so 'B' is at the top of the list. (3) 'A' and 'C' are alone on a list; someone crosses them out and puts in 'B.' There need not be any moral difference in what one may do based on which list one starts with and what one does to it.

15. More should be said about the problem of sending someone into the threat. Return to the Lazy Susan example. I said it was permissible to turn the table to remove the greater number from the threat, even though this pushes the smaller number into the threat. But it matters how we do this. If I have to take hold of the table (not owned by anyone) or take hold of the five I will save, this is permissible. But what if I must take hold of the one (I will push into the threat) in order to move the table? This seems impermissible. Similarly, if that one person owns the swivel table, taking hold is a violation of the person's property when this will lead to something very bad for him.

16. If we know the Selectors will pick the old and sick to go to the Nazis, but the Nazis would have taken these anyway, the arrangement is at least no worse for them than it would otherwise have been.

17. In fact, I think that the first explanation can be subsumed under the second. For more detailed discussion of this issue, see 'Responsibility and Collaboration.' I would now revise and add to certain arguments in that article. For these reasons, see the article (revised) in my collection, *Toward the Essence of Nonconsequentialism and Other Essays in Moral Theory* (forthcoming).

18. I am not, however, claiming that they had a duty to do so, as my remarks in the conclusion should make clear.

19. It is he who raised for me (in conversation) the issues of what one may do in cases where one knows self-defense will not succeed as defense.

20. I thank Prof. Doris Bergan for information about the Judenrat.

References

Foot, Philippa (1978), 'The Problem of Abortion and the Doctrine of Double Effect,' reprinted in *Virtue and Vices*, Berkeley, CA: University of California Press; Oxford: Blackwell.

Kamm, F.M. (1985), 'Equal Treatment and Equal Chances,' *Philosophy & Public Affairs*, Spring, pp. 177–94.

Kamm, F.M. (1993), *Morality, Mortality, Vol. 1: Death and Whom to Save From It*, New York: Oxford University Press.

Kamm, F.M. (1996), *Morality, Mortality, Vol. 2: Rights, Duties and Status*, New York: Oxford University Press.

Kamm, F.M. (2000), 'Nonconsequentialism,' in *Blackwell's Guide to Ethical Theory*, ed. H. LaFollette, Oxford: Blackwell.

Kamm, F.M. (1999), 'Responsibility and Collaboration,' *Philosophy & Public Affairs*,

Summer, pp. 197–202; also, revised in F.M. Kamm (forthcoming), *Toward the Essence of Nonconsequentialism and Other Essays in Moral Theory*.

Kamm, F.M. (2001), 'Toward the Essence of Nonconsequentialism,' in *Fact and Value: Essays on Ethics and Metaphysics for Judith Jarvis Thomson*, ed. A. Byrne and R. Wedgwood, Cambridge, MA: MIT Press.

Smart, J.J.C. and B. Williams (1973), *Utilitarianism: For and Against*, Cambridge: Cambridge University Press.

Chapter 11

Tragic Decisions: Removing Jewish Children from their Christian Guardians in Postwar Europe

Daniel Statman*

When Jewish parents faced the Nazi occupation in Europe, they first did all they could to protect their children by trying to retain some measure of normalcy; they continued to feed and educate them in the hope that somehow the hard times would pass. But the closer the instruments of the 'Final Solution' drew, the more evident it became that the dangers of starvation, disease and deportation were too imminent and serious to ignore and that the chances of the children surviving if they stayed with their parents were close to nil. Acknowledging this terrible reality, some parents looked for shelters in which to place their children in an attempt to avert their otherwise inevitable fate. Often they turned to non-Jewish friends and asked them to take care of the child. At times, they simply left the child – if young enough – on the doorstep of a monastery or of a non-Jewish family, or sent him or her out of the ghetto with no definite address, in the hope that the child would find some mercy and humanity. At other times, the Gentile caretakers were approached by third parties or themselves volunteered to risk their lives and the lives of their families to shelter one or more Jewish children.[1] Needless to say, such options of rescue were extremely rare and were available to a very limited number of Jews. Most Jews had no non-Jewish friends or connections, or, at any rate, had no practical way of getting to them. For the million and a half Jewish children who perished in the Holocaust no shelter was found, no solace from suffering, no escape from cruelty and murder.

The exact number of Jewish children saved by non-Jewish families and institutions is unknown.[2] On the basis of research published recently, I would estimate that their number in the whole of Europe did not exceed several thousands. In almost all cases, the parents of these Jewish children did not survive to reclaim their children. Nor did other close relatives, and even when they did so and wanted to find the children, they often had no idea of who had survived or no information about the whereabouts of relatives hidden by Gentiles. Yet, by the end of the war, it became known that a few thousand Jewish children had found shelter in non-Jewish institutions and families, and various Jewish organizations took upon themselves the task of finding these children, of 'rescuing'[3] them, and placing them in a Jewish environment, in Israel (then Palestine) and in other countries.

Was this project morally justified? It is easy to see the *prima facie* reasons against it. These children had already undergone one traumatic separation when they were handed over by their parents to these non-Jewish caretakers, and a second separation would double the psychological trauma. Moreover, the non-Jewish caretakers had acted out of genuine humanity and compassion when they risked their lives and the lives of their loved ones to rescue these children, as the Nazis punished by death any attempt to help Jews.[4] Surely these good souls deserved some consideration. From the point of view of many of these Jewish children, the non-Jewish families were *their* families. How could anybody who cared about these children wish to remove them from these families and send them to orphanages and programs in other countries, to become part of a world that at the time of their removal was so alien to them?

At first sight, this seems just another instance of the well-known problem regarding the best interests of the child, a problem extensively discussed in legal and other literature.[5] But I believe that, from a philosophical point of view, the issue is more interesting and complex. What makes it so interesting and challenging is the fact that, unlike typical predicaments of this sort, here it was not only the interests of the parents (or other close relatives) that needed to be weighed against those of the child, but also those of the Jewish people, arguably represented by the organizations active in rescuing the children.[6] Thus one central issue here seems to be the nature and normative status of *collective entities*. On the face of it, if no such entities exist, or if, in any case, no sense can be made of the idea of group rights or entitlements, then the claim of the above organizations over the children is groundless.

The other philosophical issue which is of special interest here is that of *identity*. The children under discussion were born Jewish, but brought up as non-Jewish by their adopting parents. Many of them, who were babies or toddlers when separated from their biological parents, were totally ignorant of their Jewish roots, an ignorance which played a crucial role in keeping them alive. So according to their own self-perception, they were not Jewish. Often they were not Jewish in the eyes of the surrounding Gentile population either, not even in the eyes of (step-)siblings. Thus, we may well ask, *were* they Jewish? Can their removal from Gentile homes to Jewish institutions be considered as returning them to where they, in some significant sense, *really belonged*? Can we make sense of the claim that Jewish children (= children with Jewish 'roots') who grew up as Catholic-Polish, for example, were not really Catholic (by religion) or Polish (by nationality), because they were Jewish?

The third issue I'll be discussing is the normative status of the parents' desires *vis-à-vis* their child once they (the parents) died or were involuntarily separated from their offspring. Hardly anybody disputes the convention that parents are entitled to decide what education their child should receive, which, in effect, means an entitlement to bring up their child to be in many central respects like *them*. Society is not supposed to intervene in this education even if such intervention could be considered to be in the best interests of the child. Does this hold true only when the parents are alive or do their wishes and dreams *vis-à-vis* their child's education and identity carry moral weight even when they are dead? Most of the

Jewish parents probably wouldn't have wanted their children to grow up as Gentiles if they (the parents) had known they would not survive the war. What weight should we assign to their wishes in determining the children's fate after the Holocaust?

Before turning to discuss these questions, I wish to make two clarifications. First, my focus here is on cases in which the job of locating the children and removing them was conducted by Jewish organizations, not by relatives. Second, I am referring to cases in which the children were young enough to have their fate decided by others. Save for exceptional circumstances, if a seventeen-year-old Jewish boy said he preferred to stay with the non-Jewish family that had sheltered him during the war, he ought not to have been (and probably could not have been) forced to leave them.[7]

Like all philosophical discussions, the discussion below tends to be cold and universalistic, thereby veiling the depth of tragedy involved in the cases under discussion. I know of no way to avoid these characteristics of philosophical discussion but only to remind myself and the readers that the problem I attempt to deal with was anything but cold. In the course of working on this essay I read and heard many stories which were deeply moving and often heart-breaking. I feel I owe some kind of an apology to these child survivors, as well as to their generous and brave Gentile caretakers, for turning their tragic stories into an object of abstract philosophical enquiry.

To the best of my knowledge, this is the first philosophical discussion of the topic. Though a huge body of literature exists on child custody in general, none refers to the special question of who should have gotten custody over the Jewish children in the cases under discussion. One or two writers do mention these cases, but do not go into any serious discussion of them.[8] What literature about child custody does teach us, however, and what seems a good point of departure, is the importance of considering the 'best interests of the child.' As removing a child from his or her home is usually harmful to the child and hence against the child's best interests, there seems to be a strong *prima facie* reason against the project of rescuing the children under discussion from Gentile homes. The *onus*, so it seems, lies on those who want to justify the project.

How can one justify removing a child from home? One line of argument is to show that ultimately, in the long run, such removal serves the best interests of the child, or, at least, does not make the child worse off in comparison to her prospects if left where she is. A different line of argument rejects the idea that the child's interests are the only ones that count and relies on other kinds of considerations to justify the removal of the child, for instance the interests of the parents. This second line of argument does not ignore the interests of the child, but insists that the interests of others also need to be accounted for, and sometimes the latter override the former.

Accordingly, the discussion will proceed as follows. Section 1 deals with arguments concerning the removal of the children from the point of view of the best interests of the children. I seek to show that, ultimately, such removal was for the good of the children, or, at least, that, overall, it caused them no significant harm. In Section 2, I present and defend arguments for the removal of the children based on considerations other than the best interests of the children. These two kinds of arguments reinforce each other and, if successful, establish the conclusion that the project of relocating the Jewish children after the Holocaust was justified.

1. The Best Interests of the Child

Many legal and moral discussions on child custody take it for granted that custody ought to be determined by the best interests of the child. Any other approach is seen as sacrificing the interests of the child for those of the parents, the nation, the state, or some other powerful entity. The child is supposedly treated then not as an end, but merely as a means towards the gratification of the parents, the honor of the nation or the power of the state. The child's rights are violated and his or her personhood denied.

But what *are* the best interests of a child? Answering this question requires no less than a full account of what the best interests of an *adult* are, since, after all, childhood is only a relatively short period on the way to adulthood. The best interests of the child are those whose fulfillment makes him or her better off (or best off, if that makes any sense) as an adult. What, then, makes one better off as an adult? We can immediately see how difficult it is to answer this question. First, there are problems concerning *value*. Is the poor peasant in China worse off than the rich lawyer in Tokyo? The former surely makes less money than the latter, but would one say that, therefore, he leads a worse, or less worthy, or less happy, life? And would anybody argue that, therefore, it is in a Chinese child's best interests to be brought up in urban Tokyo rather than in rural China? Second, there are problems concerning *knowledge*. To determine that some option is in the child's best interests, we need to know what other options exist and what the possible outcomes of each option are. But such knowledge of the future is not available to us. Hence, as Elster has argued at length,[9] the standard of the best interests of the child is hopelessly indeterminate. On Susan Wolfson's view, this indeterminacy has led to so much disagreement as 'to render the standard itself meaningless,' a 'virtually empty vessel.'[10] This indeterminacy explains how the standard under discussion has been and is still used to support the social and cultural *status quo*, as argued by many writers.[11] If the courts don't like the parents' lifestyle, or their sexual preferences, they can always try to rely on the notion of the child's best interests to deny them custody over their child.[12]

Yet, even if we are at a loss to determine what the *best* interests of the child are, can't we at least determine what is *bad* (or *worse*) for the child? If a father sexually abuses his daughter, we are on firm ground when we argue that removing her from his custody is in her best interest. Below a minimal threshold, comparative statements about the best interests of an individual do seem to make sense. As with other evaluative judgements, it is easier to identify evil than good, easier to know what's bad for one than to know what's good for one. In custody cases, this principle seems to offer rather limited assistance, since most parents pass the above threshold in a way that prevents us from saying that granting them custody would definitely be *bad* for the child. Yet, in the present context, the idea of not *harming* the child might help, as, in regular circumstances, removing a child from his or her parents does seem to be extremely harmful and traumatic to the child. Hence, there seems to be a strong *prima facie* reason against removing the Jewish children from their Gentile parents.

1.1 How Traumatic was the Removal of the Children from their Gentile Parents?

I will not deny that a presumption against removing the children, based on the above consideration, exists. But I do wish to deny the strength of this presumption, particularly the view that it is so strong as to trump almost any other consideration.

The view that separation at a young age is traumatic and causes significant mental damage both in the short and in the long run is usually connected to the psychological work of John Bowlby and to what is known as 'attachment theory.'[13] The basic idea of the theory is that the success of primary attachment is crucial to the mental health of the individual. If children suffer various kinds of parental deprivation, or if they are separated from their parents, they suffer from distress and personality disturbances, including anger, anxiety, depression and emotional detachment. In most cases, the object of attachment is the biological parent, but it is not necessarily so. An adopting parent who raises a child from infancy can be just as good as a biological one in providing for the psychological needs of the child. The crucial thing is that the child has at least one adult with whom he or she can create an enduring, trustworthy, emotional bond.

If indeed early attachment is so important for future healthy development, then, in disputes over child custody we usually ought to leave the children where they are, to spare them the pain and mental damage of separation. Thus, there is a strong presumption in favor of the *status quo*; wherever the child is, it is in his or her best interests to remain there. In the present context, this view, of course, implies that the Jewish children should have been left with their Gentile parents.

Such views, however, about the conditions for healthy development are not accepted by all psychologists. In particular, it has been argued that children are more adaptable to changes than allowed by attachment theory, including changes in the identity of their caretakers.[14] Relying on various studies in this direction, Arlene Skolnick argues as follows:

> Perhaps the most controversial aspect of attachment theory concerns the impact of early relationships on later developments ... Some children manage to overcome adversity and loss, others do poorly in life after promising beginnings. These more recent views are more optimistic than the older assumption that children who experience early insecurity are doomed to later difficulties.[15]

If these more recent views are sound, then short of extreme conditions, the loss or separation from a mother or psychological parent may not be a direct cause of later disturbances. Rather 'it may act more like a vulnerability factor, a psychological weak spot, which may make the person more susceptible to later losses.'[16]

To illustrate these doubts about the harm of separation, Skolnick refers to the well-known case of Baby Jessica. Jessica was born to Cara Clausen who decided shortly after the birth to give her up for adoption. She signed the adoption papers with the man she had named as the father and Jessica was adopted by Jan and

Roberta DeBoer. Three weeks later Cara Clausen changed her mind and claimed she had named the wrong man. She told her ex-boyfriend that he was the father and the couple married. They then started a long legal struggle to get back their biological daughter, at the end of which the Michigan Supreme Court ruled in their favor and ordered that Jessica be removed from her adopting parents back to her biological ones.[17] The scene of Jessica being taken from the couple that had raised her as their child since shortly after birth was shown on television across the country and aroused intense feelings. Many felt that the separation was cruel both for Jessica and for the DeBoers and that the court's decision was against the best interests of the child.

But, as Skolnick reports, a few months after the separation, a television program presented an interview with the biological parents and with their daughter. The impression a viewer would get was that this was a normal happy child in a normal happy family. At least on the surface, no lasting trauma seemed to have affected Jessica (by then renamed Anna). Was there, however, any deep post-traumatic damage *under* the surface? To this Skolnick replies:

> We don't know. It's possible that the first three years of her life made her a resilient child who could bounce back from trauma, or that the removal of a child from one set of loving parents to another is not as upsetting as the other kinds of separations that have been observed. On the other hand ... children who have been exposed to traumatic events ... may also seem to be 'normal,' only to show the effects of trauma years afterward.[18]

On a more mundane level, these hesitations about the psychological damage of separation seem to be consistent with the personal experience of many parents. Parents often undergo the unpleasant experience of handing over a crying child to a nanny, a babysitter, or some other caretaker. The first day of school or of kindergarten is full of heart-breaking scenes of this sort, and young parents seeing their first child cry this way and stretch out his hands for succour often feel guilty for what they are doing to the child. But, as most of us learn, these separations are far less cruel than they seem, and in most cases the children adjust very well to the new environment and the new caretakers. Usually the weeping ends very quickly and, by the time the parent gets into his or her car, the child is content and happy in his new environment. Temporal separation for a few hours or a few days is, of course, not the same as permanent separation, but, nevertheless, we might learn from these instances that the weeping and agony at the time of separation is not necessarily a predictor of long-term pain and agony.

That children have a remarkable ability to adjust to painful changes is also evident from cases of divorce. To be sure, in some cases, the separation brought by divorce has serious psychological results for the children. But, in many cases, the damage does not seem so bad and at times the separation seems to leave no negative effects at all. The divorce rate in the West in the last decades has become very high, which means that many children have undergone painful separations from a parent. All of us know examples of such situations. But only a small percentage of the children can be said to be mentally less healthy than their friends. This common-sense view is confirmed by scientific evidence, as shown by Stewart et al.:

Although the experience [of divorce] may have been traumatic in a few cases, mostly it was not … The children generally showed improved adjustment over time and did not seem to suffer extreme psychological or behavioral disruption.[19]

Once again, divorce is not exactly the same as the cases under discussion. In divorce, the child stays with at least one of the parents, often remains at home, in most cases goes on seeing the other parent, and goes on living with (or, at least, meeting) the other siblings, while in the cases under discussion, the Jewish children were separated from both their (Gentile) parents as well as from their (step-) siblings, and moved to a different environment altogether. Still, there is enough in common to make the comparison interesting. In both cases, children are forced to undergo a painful change that has to do with partial or full separation from beloved people. And, in both cases, one would expect that this change would cause severe psychological damage to the children,[20] which we now have reason to doubt.

Maybe we can go one step further and learn another lesson from the comparison with divorce. There is, no doubt, a high likelihood that divorce would psychologically damage the children, either severely or moderately. Except for rather extreme circumstances, it is in the children's best interests that the parents do *not* separate, but instead make a much greater effort to stick together.[21] But very rarely would we morally condemn couples who decide to divorce, and never would we legally ban the divorce on such grounds. The expected psychological damage to the children is not thought to carry too much moral weight, and probably not thought to be too traumatic in any case. If that is so, then maybe a similar (though weaker) conclusion can be deduced regarding the Jewish children under discussion, namely, that the trauma of separation was not so damaging in the long run and that, at any rate, it could be overridden by other considerations.

Let me sum up the argument of this section. Removing a child from his or her home seems so traumatic as to almost silence any other consideration. Regarding the present problem this view would imply that, as a rule, the Jewish children should not have been removed from their Gentile families. The purpose of this section was to start challenging and undermining this view. I argued that, contrary to both popular conceptions and some psychological theories, separation from their parents (biological or adoptive) does not necessarily cause long-term psychological damage to children. Had we really believed in such damage, we would have been far more critical (that is, *morally* critical) of couples getting divorced. That we are not so critical expresses a common belief that either the damage of separation is not so grave, or that, at any rate, the interests of the children can be overridden by those of the parents. To oppose the removal of the Jewish children fiercely on moral grounds is thus inconsistent with the common, lenient (if not encouraging) attitude toward divorce.

The conclusion of this argument is, of course, not that we should be indifferent to removing children from their parents, but that the reason against doing so is not as powerful as we might have thought at the outset. Thus, though I concede that there still exists a presumption against removing the Jewish children from their foster homes, the presumption has gotten weaker, and therefore weaker reasons will suffice to override it. In the next sections, I seek to develop such reasons. Some have to do with the interests of the children and they will be discussed in Sections 1.2 and

1.3, while others have to do with the interests of the parents and of the people, and they will be discussed in Section 2.

1.2 Connecting to One's Roots

Most of the children we are dealing with had no recollection of their biological parents or of their Jewish background and if they did, it faded during the years. As mentioned earlier, such ignorance of their Jewish origins was crucial for the children's survival. Yet, once the war was over and such ignorance was no longer a necessary means for survival, we may well ask could the Jewish origins of these children have been concealed from them for ever? *Ought* they to have been so concealed?

I believe the answer to both questions is negative. First, in many cases, there were Gentile relatives, friends, or neighbors who knew about the Jewish children, and one can assume that such secrets could not be hidden for ever even if that were the intention of the (Gentile) parents. Second, as often the case with adopted children, there was likely to be a perception of physical dissimilarity between the Jewish child and the Gentile parents and siblings, which would eventually make outsiders think 'Hey, this child just can't be their son' and make the child himself suspect that the people he knew as parents were not his 'real' parents. Even more so if the child had a 'Jewish look,' which would not only indicate lack of genetic relation but also raise for the child the possibility of Jewish origin.[22] Hence, in those rare cases in which hiding the Jewish origins was practically possible, it must have involved serious self-deception and denial which would probably have had their own damaging effects.

Yet, even if the origins of these children could be hidden, I submit that they ought not to have been. Adoptive parents have a duty to tell their adopted children the truth about themselves, just as they have a duty to tell their biological children the truth about events and biographies relevant to them. The duty to tell the truth is not an absolute one, but one needs a good reason to justify not doing so. Adopted children would normally be furious if they found out that they were deliberately and knowingly deceived about who their real, that is, biological, parents were. So, to conclude this point, after the war the Gentile parents ought to have revealed to their Jewish child the true facts about her tragic biography, and if they didn't do so, often the child would anyway have discovered the story by herself (or alternatively live a life of denial and self-deception).

The argument I would like to present now is that the capacity to connect to one's roots contributes to one's quality of life. We know this from scientific as well as from popular literature (and movies) about adopted children who searched for their biological parents. According to studies of such cases, all the children who had completed a part of the search for a blood relative indicated that the post-search changes 'marked considerable improvement in their lives.' Among other things they referred to

> Significant changes in self-esteem, self-confidence, and assertiveness ... Many mentioned feeling 'connected,' 'grounded,' or 'belonging' in a way they had never experienced before. Another grouping of responses referred to a sense of 'validation,' feeling 'real,'

and 'authentic'; peace of mind and a sense of calmness was mentioned by several, as was a greater ability to handle and express emotions. Several respondents made extensive references to the effectiveness of the search in breaking an impasse in their development as persons.[23]

Such responses to the results of the search were not confined to children who for some reason were dissatisfied with their adoptive parents. According to Bertocci and Schechter, the same terms – feeling 'connected,' or feeling 'whole' – were used, regardless of how the adoption experience was evaluated. Not knowing one's 'roots,' that is, one's biological parents and family, often entails a diminished sense of identity and a sense of incompleteness. Reconnecting to them makes one feel whole, integrated, authentic, and, generally speaking, improves one's life. David Archard also suggested that

> It could well be that one's genetic nature is crucial to one's sense of identity. Or even, simply, that a sense of affinity, given by biological relations, exerts a very real influence on people's discovery of their 'self.' [24]

If all this is true, we could assume that, in the case of the Jewish children too, connecting them to their Jewish roots by removing them to a Jewish environment was – in many cases – essential for granting them a better sense of belonging, identity and completeness than they would have had if they had stayed in their non-Jewish families. In this sense, the removal can be said to have been good for the children.[25]

It is telling to note in this context the recent phenomenon of young Poles of Jewish origins who discovered those origins and decided to return to their Jewishness in various ways. This phenomenon was the topic of a television documentary program entitled *The Secret*, shown on Israel's Channel 8 on 27 August 2001.[26] The program tells the story of Poles who had been raised as Catholics but found out that their parents, or at least one of them, were Jews, whose families had perished in the Holocaust. This revelation encouraged them to search for details about their Jewish families, to study Judaism, and in some cases to adopt a religious Jewish way of life. Such stories show the incredible influence the discovery of genetic origins can exert on people's perception of their true 'self.' Indeed, Emunah Nachmany-Gafny reports on many requests to her and to other individuals and organizations by Poles asking for help in finding their Jewish relatives in Israel and in other countries. In her view, expressed in the concluding lines of her study,[27] the importance of 'roots' for one's sense of identity is the main reason for saying that the project of removing the Jewish children was justified.

Is it rational to assign such importance to one's biological origins? Is it rational for a happy, adopted child to feel incomplete just because he doesn't know his biological parents? We should be cautious about the use of the notion of rationality here. From a Stoic point of view, it is surely irrational to care about one's genetic roots, but it is just as irrational to care about one's adoptive parents and about family and friends in general. So that concept of rationality would not be of much help here.[28] A more helpful sense of rationality here would be what suits one's nature, or what contributes to one's well-being. Thus understood, the questions posed above amount to asking whether connecting to one's genetic roots is really necessary for leading a 'full' and meaningful life. If it is, then it is rational to seek such a connection and regret its absence. If it's not, it is irrational to do so.

The search of adopted children for their biological parents and family and the search of second-generation clandestine Jews in Poland for their Jewish roots seem to indicate that people do have a genuine interest in connecting to their origins. Against this, it has been argued that the value assigned to one's genetic nature is a mere cultural construct which does not express a truly human need. Skolnick refers in this context to 'new biologism,' the view that 'the essence of a person is rooted in the primordial differences of gender, race, ethnicity, genes,'[29] and argues that this view is part of a culture that emphasizes that 'identity and belonging are defined in biological terms.'[30] In other cultures, identity is defined (or could be defined) in other ways, implying that nobody would be worse off for not knowing his or her genetic roots. Hence, to conclude this objection, the need of the Jewish children to connect to their Jewishness was not genuine; therefore, in this respect, their removal from the Gentile environment cannot be said to have been for their good.

The question of whether some needs are a matter of nature or of culture and of the significance of this distinction is an old one and discussing it lies beyond the scope of this essay. For the argument of the present section, it suffices to make the following remarks. First, whether natural or cultural, the data about adopted children indicate a strong interest in connecting to the genetic family and a significant improvement in the quality of life for those who did so. This part of the essay focuses on the interests of the children as they actually were, namely on what would have made them better off or worse off given the interests and preferences they had. That different cultures have, or might have, a different view about what constitutes identity is irrelevant to determining the factors influencing the sense of identity in *our* culture and the effects of these factors on the well-being of the individual. Thus, if we care about adopted children's subjective well-being, we will let them connect to their genetic roots, regardless of whether the importance of such a connection is natural or cultural.

Second, it seems to me that there are good reasons to think that the search for one's 'roots' is not as contingent as the objection above suggests. According to one study, 60 percent of the adopted children searching for their biological families indicated that lack of perceived similarities had been a significant factor in their sense of frustration, embarrassment and insecurity. Though the nature of these dissimilarities might differ across cultures, some, such as the color of one's skin, are so visible and manifest that they will be experienced as troubling everywhere. The reason is that self-esteem is tightly connected to a sense of belonging and of being included in the relevant social group. When one senses oneself as deeply different, one's social status is perceived as insecure and a feeling of exclusion is likely to develop.[31] The relation between humiliation, fall in self-esteem, and sense of social exclusion has been established in various studies, as I have argued elsewhere.[32]

That one's *sense* of identity has to do with awareness of one's genetic nature is also supported by some philosophical views on the nature of personal identity. According to Bernard Williams, what determines personal identity is what he terms

'The Zygotic Principle,' according to which 'a possibility in which a given human being, A, features is one that preserves the identity of the zygote from which A developed.'[33] Why is the zygote so essential in determining identity? Because it helps give substance to the distinction between possible different life stories of two individuals and possible different life stories of the same individual. Had Dan grown up in the UK instead of in Israel, he would have been a very different person, but this would still be a possible life story of Dan, while if Dan's brother, Bob, had grown up in Israel instead of in the UK where he actually grew up, his life would have been very similar to that of Dan, but still it would be a possible life story of Bob, not of Dan. This interest we have in distinguishing between different life stories explains the importance of the zygote as the point from which the story begins. Before the existence of the zygote, no individual exists, and once the zygote does exist, the story begins. Endless paths are open to the individual who develops out of the zygote, and all mark possible stories of *this* individual. If, then, the notion of a life story is so central in understanding the *concept* of personal identity, and if such understanding grants a central role to one's genetic nature, that is, one's original zygote, it is no wonder that one's *sense* of identity depends on connecting to one's life story and ultimately to one's genetic nature.

It is not only one's genetic origins that one wishes to discover to get a rich and integrated sense of identity, but also one's membership in various groups. Writers on groups have emphasized that, while with some groups, such as the local tennis club, membership is voluntary, with other groups it is different. As Margalit and Raz put it, in these groups 'membership is a matter of belonging, not of achievement ... Qualification for membership is usually determined by nonvoluntary criteria.'[34] Membership in a nation is a paradigmatic case of such nonvoluntary belonging, hence getting in touch with one's national roots can enrich or make one's sense of identity more complete. The good of such a connection, of establishing a sense of belonging, is not without qualifications. If the relevant group is immoral, or if connecting to it might damage the individual's life in some respect, then there are good reasons for not doing so. Still, in regular circumstances, one's sense of identity will be positively enriched by connecting to the national and other groups of which one is a member.

To a degree, such enrichment can be gained by the mere *knowledge* of one's roots. Yet I am assuming that knowledge coupled with real, that is, social connection, might be even more conducive to a sense of wholeness and integrity.

In concluding this section, let me make several clarifications about the nature and limits of the argument put forward. First, the general aim of this part of the essay is to evaluate the removal of children from their Gentile foster homes from the point of view of the best interests of the children. To do so, we must look at possible disadvantages the children would have suffered had they stayed in the Gentile homes, and possible gains in the removal. The suggestion made in this section was that one such possible disadvantage is a damaged sense of identity that would result from growing up in a non-Jewish environment. This possible injured sense of identity is definitely not something that all children would have suffered from, nor would it necessarily be an unbearable one. Still, for many of them, it does seem to constitute a reason for bringing them back – for their own good – to the Jewish community.[35]

Second, as pointed out to me by Eve Garrard, the ideal of complete integration and belongingness seems to be beyond human achievement, at least in industrial societies. All of us, or at least most of us, have diverse and multiple identities such that we never really 'belong' wherever we live. This fundamental incompleteness of modern human existence seems to weaken my argument, for, if nobody can achieve a sense of wholeness, there is not much point in moving people around with this aim in mind. But a sense of wholeness, like most good things, is not a matter of all or nothing, but a matter of degree. Surely some people suffer from it more than others and, in many cases, the suffering can be alleviated by having them connected more significantly to basic elements in their identity. I am not suggesting that the Jewish children under discussion gained a perfect sense of wholeness by being removed to a Jewish environment, only that they gained a better one than they would have had had they stayed in the Gentile environment.

Finally, I should recapitulate that the argument made here does not rely on metaphysical claims regarding the nature of groups or of personal identity, but on psychological claims regarding the source of one's *sense* of identity and the importance of this sense for the well-being of the individual. I shall return to discuss this issue from the metaphysical angle in Section 2.3.

1.3 Retroactive Justification

Many, probably most, of the Jewish children were upset when they had to leave their Gentile homes and move to a new life under the supervision of Jewish organizations and institutions. Yet, more than fifty years later, it is hard to find even one who regrets the move. Quite the contrary. Most are explicitly grateful for having been removed from the Gentile homes and for having had the kind of lives they had.[36] Doesn't this retroactive assessment provide a decisive argument for justifying the removal (once again: from the point of view of the children's good)?

Some would say 'No.' For them, to show that one is justified in doing *a* is to show that at the time of decision one has, overall, better reasons for doing *a* than for abstaining from doing *a*. If this condition is not fulfilled and the agent, nevertheless, does *a*, then the agent is *un*justified in doing so, even if, in retrospect, the agent or somebody else judges the act as justified. If I bet on the slowest horse in the race simply because I'm too lazy to enquire about the horses and riders participating, then I'd be behaving stupidly and irresponsibly, even if, by a miracle, this horse ends up winning and I gain a million dollars. Similarly, if I release my son from his safety belt, I am risking his life and thus behaving in an unjustified manner, and this assessment would remain true even if the fact that the child was not buckled in his seat happened to save his life in a car accident (for example by enabling him to escape from the burning car). Hence, to return to the present issue, the fact that, in retrospect, the removal of the children seems to have been good for them provides no basis for saying that the removal project was justified. It might still have been morally unjustified to remove the children from the Gentile families.

In his seminal paper on moral luck and in a later postscript to it, Bernard Williams has shown how this concept of justification is motivated by a desire to make essential parts of our lives immune to luck.[37] The desire is most familiar in the moral sphere, especially in the Kantian tradition, according to which the goodness of an act does not depend on its contingent results. In Kant's famous words:

> Even if it should happen that, by a particularly unfortunate fate … this [good] will should be wholly lacking in power to accomplish its purpose … it would still sparkle like a jewel in its own right, as something that had its full worth in itself. Usefulness or fruitfulness can neither diminish nor augment this worth.[38]

This Kantian conception, argues Williams, 'links, and affects, a range of notions: morality rationality, justification, and ultimate or supreme value.'[39] Indeed, notwithstanding its title, most of his paper is not about morality, but about rational justification, in particular about the reflective self-justification of one's own actions. Williams's main idea is that good deliberation does not make one immune to self-criticism if, in retrospect, it turns out that the decision led to disastrous outcomes. Similarly, bad deliberation does not block the way for retroactive justification if a seemingly wrong decision turns out to have led to great results. Rational justification, whether moral, prudential or other, is (also) a matter of luck.

If Williams is right in his view, as I believe he is, then the above objection can be ignored, and the argument set out above reestablished as follows: at the time of the decision to launch the project of removing the Jewish children, the decision-makers did not have enough resources to guarantee that they were doing the right thing. Like all decisions, certainly significant ones, only the future could determine whether the project could be ultimately justified or not, a justification which would depend on whether the project succeeded or failed.[40] If we evaluate success or failure in terms of subjective well-being, we are on firm ground to argue that the way the lives of these children turned out retroactively justifies the decision to remove them from the Gentile homes.

Yet, at this stage, readers might feel that I have played some trick on them. To be sure, the Jews under discussion were happy and proud to have led a Jewish life, but that's just because they were brought up as Jews and lived in a Jewish environment from a young age. Had they stayed with their Gentile families and spent all their years as Polish Catholics, they would also have been happy and proud to have led the lives they did. To put it in general terms: the preferences and desires of an adult individual are determined by early decisions made by him or her and by others, so that the late retroactive assessment of life is conditioned by these early decisions. This means that, except for rare cases, we cannot rely on predictions regarding later approval to justify one decision over another.

A similar argument is made by Jon Elster in his attempt to show the indeterminacy of the principle that custody cases should be determined by the best interests of the child. To rely on the child's preferences at the time of decision would be problematic, he argues, as the child 'can be expected to have large gaps in his preference ordering.'[41] To make an informed choice on behalf of the child would almost inescapably engage in objectionable paternalism. Would it help to instruct the judge to make a decision of which the child would approve later, assuming such a prediction to be possible? To this Elster rightly answers, that since the later preferences would depend largely on the decision made, 'the instruction might not discriminate sufficiently between the options.'[42]

Back to our present problem, then. As retroactive evaluation of the children's whole lives depends on the decision – *any* decision – made for them in their childhood, it could not have been a basis for preferring one decision over the other. Suppose in 1946, we are hesitating about whether or not the best interests of some child, Joseph, entail that we should remove him from his Gentile home. And suppose we gain divine insight into the future and know for sure that if Joseph grows up as a religious Jew in an Israeli kibbutz, he'll be very grateful for our action. But we also have this miraculous knowledge about other possible routes Joseph might take and in many of them he will also feel grateful for the kind of life we gave him as a Catholic priest, as a proud farmer, and so on. Hence, satisfaction with the life a person actually leads does not in any way show that life was better for him than other possible lives he could have had, had his parents, caretakers, state officials, or religious leaders, chosen differently.

But what exactly follows from this argument? True, retroactive satisfaction with the removal of these children does not prove that life as Jews was *better* for the children than life as non-Jews. They would probably have been (retroactively) satisfied with the latter life too.[43] But it, at least, shows that life as Jews was not *worse* for them than other alternatives. Comparing possible (or real) life stories is a classic case of comparing incommensurable options.[44] It is really hard to see how, in terms of the best interests of the child, one can compare his or her possible life as a Jewish-American citizen in New York to the same individual's possible life as a Catholic-Polish citizen in Warsaw. At the very least, the impossibility of making helpful comparisons here means that no option can be said to be better than the other. But if that's the case, then the presumption against removing the children is *weakened*, as we cannot say that removing them was to create a worse life for them than leaving them where they were.

Furthermore, the retroactive approval of their removal provides some support for the assumption that the removal did not have such a traumatic effect on their lives. If the removal had caused severe and lasting psychological damage, it would have affected the children's lives in such a way that they could not look back with content. Of course, the damage might have been repressed and denied, and might have caused unnoticed psychological injury. But we'd need more evidence to show that this was the case. If, on the conscious level, these people were happy with their lives, maybe the lesson to draw (which is not a novel one) is that repression and denial can be very helpful devices in coping with unpleasant experiences, without leaving too painful bruises in the psyche.

Finally, contrary to what is implied by the above objection, it is definitely not the case that, in retrospect, everybody is happy with his or her lot and approves of the decisions – of parents, courts or teachers – that shaped their actual lives. A good example directly relevant to the present case is that of Bruna Vasconselos. Bruna was born in Brazil in 1986 and kidnapped by her nanny when she was four months old. She was later sold through an adoption agency to the Turgeman couple in Israel who adopted her, named her Caroline, and raised her with care and love. Two years later the biological parents found out that their daughter was in Israel and claimed her back. The case reached the Supreme Court of Israel, which decided in favor of the Brazilian parents, on the basis of what the court called 'the cry of blood.'[45] In his decision, the deputy president of the Supreme Court, Menachem Elon, mentioned the struggle to remove the Jewish children after the Holocaust as a reason why the court ought to be sympathetic to the desire of Bruna's parents to get their daughter back. Many in Israel cried with the Turgemans when their daughter was taken away from them, yet hoped with them that she would, at least, be happy back in Brazil. Unfortunately she was not. Her biological father, who had already been separated from the mother before the trial, left home shortly after their return to Brazil and did not meet his child again until recently. Bruna became pregnant out of wedlock before she had reached her fourteenth year and gave birth to a boy, Daniel. Her mother refused to let them stay at home and they are now staying with the grandmother in very harsh, poor conditions. Bruna says she does not remember her Israeli parents, but she knows they are wonderful people and is sure that, had she stayed with them, her life would have been much better.[46] Thus, in the case of Bruna, retroactive assessment provides a good reason to think that returning her to the biological parents was not the right thing to do (in terms of the best interests of the child). That very few (if any) of the Jewish children think that they would have been better off had they stayed with their Gentile families is thus not insignificant.

2. The Interests of Others

For those who believe that the child's interests are the only legitimate consideration in deciding custody cases, our discussion could come to an end at this point. But I doubt if anybody holds such an extreme view. Suppose we are 100 percent sure that some newborn baby B would be much better off if raised by some adoptive couple than if raised by its biological family (even after considering the possible unfortunate effects of being adopted). Very few would allow that, in such a case, the child be removed from its biological parents and given for adoption. Notwithstanding the importance of caring for the child, the child is not the only player in the game to merit our care and attention.

The idea of taking a baby from its biological parents and giving it for adoption might seem far-fetched and imaginary. But the opposite situation, which points to the same conclusion, is quite familiar, namely, a case where a child is raised happily by non-biological parents, and then returned to the biological ones. I have already mentioned above the cases of Baby Jessica and of Bruna Vasconselos. The essential point about such cases is the basis on which the decision was determined. It was not decided that the child should be returned to her biological parents because the court was convinced that the child would be better off with her biological parents, but rather the basis for the decision was the fact that *they were her parents*. In order to get custody over a child, beyond establishing a rather low threshold of parental capability, all one needs to demonstrate is that one is the parent (assuming, of course, that there was no consent to adoption and so on).

Needless to say, the fact that the child's good is not the only consideration in disputes over custody does not mean that it has no or low value. It does, however, mean that the door is open for other interests to be considered and balanced against those of the child. In the words of Jon Elster, 'children do have a need for special protection, but their interests do not lexicographically dominate those of all other parties.'[47] Let us turn, then, to look at these other interests.[48]

2.1 The Biological Parents

In almost all cases, the biological parents of the Jewish children under discussion did not survive. The conflict, therefore, was not between the interests (or rights) of the adoptive parents and those of the biological ones, as in the cases of Baby Jessica and Bruna Vasconselos. Nevertheless, the Jewish parents must have had wishes *vis-à-vis* their children. Though they were not in a position to leave clear instructions as to what should be done with the children if they (the parents) did not survive, we can speculate about what they *would* have said had they been presented with two fundamental options, namely, for the child to be raised as a Catholic in a Polish family, or for the child to be raised as a Jew. Though I can offer no direct evidence for my own speculation, I am sure that most of the parents would opt for the latter option.[49]

This speculation might be strengthened by the fact that Jewish children who grew up in a non-Jewish environment, in Poland for instance, were in real danger of becoming anti-Semitic, just like their counterparts in that environment.[50] Indeed strong fear of and hatred towards Jews and Judaism already existed among some of the young children under discussion. Some hated the Jews because they believed that Jews crucified Jesus, and some sincerely believed the Jews used Christian blood to bake unleavened bread at Passover. A girl removed from Poland to a Jewish institute in Lyon wrote the following letter to her former Christian family:

> Dear Aunt, why did you hand me to these Jewish murderers, bandits? It would have been better had you handed me to the Germans ... The Germans have killed too few of them ... They [the Jews] are sure that they are taking us to terrible Palestine. When we crossed the Czech border, I started crying. They said: *Oy Vey*, you'll go back to the *goyim* [Gentiles], because they don't say 'Polish,' only '*goyim*.' I answered them: You sick Jews, I wish the Germans had killed you.[51]

It seems to me reasonable to assume that Jewish parents who had suffered so badly from anti-Semitism in the 1940s would not have wanted to take the chance that their children adopt such views,[52] and, hence, would have preferred them to be removed from their Gentile homes to a Jewish environment.[53]

Let's assume, then, that the parents had to make a choice between three options: (a) that their child stays with them and dies; (b) that the child is rescued by Christians and then raised as Christian; (c) that the child is rescued by Christians but after the war returns to a Jewish environment. I contend that almost all Jewish parents would have preferred options (b–c) over option (a),[54] and – more important for the present argument – most would have preferred option (c) over option (b). The philosophical question now is, does such hypothetical preference carry any moral weight? It is one thing to compromise about the interests of the child for the sake of what the (biological) parents *actually* wish, for example to grant them the autonomy to send the child to what we take to be an awful school. It is quite a different thing to compromise about the child's interests for the sake of what the parents *would have* wished. Or is it? There seem to be two issues here. The first concerns the hypothetical nature of the wish, the second the fact that its subject is no longer alive. As for the distinction between actual and hypothetical here, it does not seem to carry too much weight. In contract law, in the absence of explicit utterances, it is common to rely on what the parties would have consented to had they been asked. So in the present case too, in the absence of explicit statements, it is reasonable to rely on what the parents would have said had they been asked. How we would gain knowledge into such preferences is a different problem, but there is no reason to think that an explicit statement is the only way to do so. The parents' attitude to their Jewish identity, as expressed in a multitude of ways in their lives, is a good enough reason to guess what their preferences would be with respect to the present dilemma.

Having established the preference of the parents, the second issue concerns the moral relevance of this preference given that the parents are no longer alive. Why care about what the parents would have wished for their child if the parents are dead, and thus cannot be harmed by what is done to their child? Yet, most of us believe that wills ought to be respected even though their subjects will never know if they are not and, more generally, that one can suffer all kinds of misfortunes after death.[55] As Nagel explains, the misfortune that befalls an agent need not coincide in time with the agent's life, just as it need not coincide with her spatial location. One can be harmed by events far from one in place, and, similarly, one can be harmed by events far from one in time.[56] That one knows and feels the pain of an evil can make the evil even worse, as noted rightly by Hanfling,[57] though its very existence does not depend on such experiences. Hence, *if* a person has a right that her preference be taken into account in some matter, this right does not simply evaporate once she is dead. Back to our problem: *qua* parents, the Jewish parents had a right that their preferences as to how their offspring ought to be brought up be heard. If I am right, in most cases, their preferences would have been in favor of a Jewish upbringing. If so, then, although the parents were dead at the time of the decision, their interests constituted a good reason in favor of removing the children.

Note that for the sake of this argument it makes no difference why (biological) parents have the power to determine their children's lives; that is, why the parents' preferences *vis-à-vis* their children constitute moral reasons for treating the children in various ways. If parents (usually the father in this context) *own* their children, then surely they should have a say about what should be done with the children, just as they have a say in disposing of any other property they own. But very few philosophers hold such a view nowadays.[58] If parents earn the right to rear the children by committing themselves to taking care of them, then, again, once they have thus committed themselves, their preferences about the children's future ought to be respected. But if this is the model for the parent–child relationship, then it seems to imply that, in the case under discussion, the Gentile parents have priority, since they risked their lives to save the children. Let us, then, turn to discuss their status.

2.2 The Gentile Parents

Probably everybody would agree that sperm donors have no rights *vis-à-vis* the child who is born of their donation. Sheer genetic parenthood is insufficient to grant parental rights. It is not necessary either, as evident from the parental rights we grant adoptive parents. As indicated at the end of the previous section, what is essential for parenthood in the relevant moral and legal sense is an actual commitment to take care of the child, to be responsible for him or her, in short, to treat the child *as* one's son or daughter. This is how David Archard summarizes his view on this:

> Biological parenthood is the existence of a blood tie between begetter and offspring. Moral parenthood is the giving to a child a continuous care, concern and affection with the purpose of helping to secure for it the best possible upbringing … Biological parenthood does not guarantee moral parenthood … It is rather that those who undertake to discharge the duty to give children the best possible upbringing thereby acquire the right to rear.[59]

This sounds a plausible enough view of (moral) parenthood. What follows from it regarding the problem at hand, however, is unclear. On the one hand, those who undertook the duty to care for the Jewish children and who risked their lives for their sake were the Gentile parents.[60] Hence, according to Archard's view, these parents acquired the right to rear, hence they had the right to determine whether the children grow up with them or be removed to a Jewish environment. Yet, on the other hand, the Jewish parents, too, had undertaken the duty to care for their (biological) children. They did their best to care for them in their early years, and their handing them to Gentile caretakers was a clear demonstration of their care and love, their attempt to save the lives of their children at all costs. Thus, on the above view, they too had acquired the right to rear, hence their interests *vis-à-vis* the children also ought to be respected.

If moral parenthood were determined by genetic parenthood, then every child could have only two parents, one supplying the sperm, the other supplying the egg. (Things might change with human cloning.) But if it is determined by a commitment to care, children might have fewer or more than two parents: 'Moral parenthood is not restricted to any particular familial form. It is consistent with natural, adoptive, foster or multiple parents, as well as a children's residential institution.'[61] Our tragic cases are ones of *successive parents*: first, the Jewish genetic parents, then the Gentile ones and later the Jewish adoptive family or the relevant Jewish institution. As all of them undertook the duty to care for the children, they all seem to have acquired some right to rear the children, or at least have some say in decisions concerning their lives.

In the case of successive parents, none willingly giving up his or her parental status, how can we balance the possibly conflicting interests of the parents? There is no clear criterion here. The answer would depend on various factors, including the length of time the child spent with each parent, the depth of the commitment to care for it and the nature of the relationship with the child. If these various factors are more or less equal, I would suggest that the interests of the genetic parents be given some priority, as part of a general presumption in favor of genetic parents.[62]

Moreover, a significant difference exists between our cases and regular cases of adoption (where there are also successive parents). In adoption, the genetic parents give up their right to rear and transfer it to another couple, thereby making their wishes *vis-à-vis* the child morally irrelevant in determining its future, while, in the cases under discussion, the Jewish parents did not wish to give up their parenthood when they handed their child to the Gentile caretaker. They hoped that, after the war, they, or some relative, would return and take the child. This is supported by the fact that, in most cases, the Jewish parents shared the secret with some other person, in the hope that if they did not survive, there would be somebody else who would know where the child was hidden and who could take custody of him or her. In some cases, the children themselves were given names and addresses to turn to after the war if the parents did not survive.[63] Even in hopeless situations, people tend to believe that somehow they, or their dear ones, will survive. Probably most of the Jewish parents who parted from their children in the horrendous circumstances they faced believed and hoped that one day, either they, or some relative, would survive to reclaim the child.[64]

Even more relevant to the present argument is that this view of the Jewish parents regarding the temporary nature of the 'adoption' of their children was implicitly accepted by many of the Gentile parents too. This, I believe, is evident from the fact that most of the Gentile parents handed the children to the various Jewish agents *voluntarily*. Only in a small minority of the cases were they forced to do so by threats, deceit, legal measures, or, in very rare cases, actual kidnapping. In the majority of cases, the Gentile parents were persuaded by the arguments presented to them by the Jewish agents, and were no doubt encouraged by the increasing sums of money they were offered.[65] It would be a total misconception to deduce from the fact that the Gentile parents demanded increasing sums of money for the children that they treated these children as commodities, that they didn't genuinely care for them. We have unequivocal evidence that they truly cared about the children throughout the war as well as feeling genuine sadness and depression when they had to part from them. What can be deduced from these facts is that, deep in their hearts, many of the Gentile parents too saw their custodianship over the children as temporary. With regard to genetic parents, it is hard to imagine considerations that could persuade them to willingly give up their children. The same holds true for adoptive parents, though in their case maybe such considerations are slightly more imaginable. That most of the Gentile parents in the cases under discussion were persuaded to do so indicates that their perception of their relationship with the Jewish children was different from the common perception of both genetic and adoptive parents towards their children. It is a praiseworthy perception, as – if my former arguments are sound – it reflects an adequate understanding of the unique nature of the 'deposit' with which they had been entrusted. It also seems to confirm the view that the status of the Gentile parents *vis-à-vis* the Jewish children they had sheltered was weaker than that of the Jewish parents and, hence, one that had to give way in case of conflict.

In concluding this section, I would like to reemphasize the extraordinary character of many of the Gentile parents at the price of slightly weakening the position developed above. The behavior of these people was not only morally acceptable, not only a question of 'doing what any decent human being would do' when they gave shelter to the Jewish children. The Gentile caregivers behaved like moral saints, acting well beyond the call of duty, risking their own lives and the lives of their families. Such saints deserve special consideration, and to denigrate them in any way is particularly troubling. I concede this is a powerful reason for not removing the children, yet I believe that it does not override the other reasons mentioned above. That most of these saints agreed to release the Jewish children they had sheltered attests their recognition that their taking them in did not grant them final custody over the children. The saintliness of their acts cannot void the significance of this recognition.

2.3 The Jewish People

As I said at the outset, and as became evident in the course of the discussion, the problem at hand bears many similarities to other problems concerning custody of children, in cases of divorce, adoption and so on. Yet the present problem also has some unique aspects, most notably the fact that the claimant for the children was often not a family relative (not even a remote one), but various organizations that saw themselves, and were seen by others,[66] as acting on behalf of the Jewish people. Thus understood, the conflict involved not only the interests of individuals (the children, the adoptive and the biological parents), but also those of a *collective* entity, that is, the Jewish people. That being the case, the reasonableness of the claim to remove the children would seem to depend, at least partially, on whether or not an entity like the Jewish people can be said to exist or to have rights. If it can, then it is capable of making all kinds of demands, including demands of the kind discussed here. If it cannot, then the Jewish organizations appear to have had no standing *vis-à-vis* the children and, hence, no right to claim them 'back.'[67]

Yet, surely, this is a rather superficial way of introducing the dilemma. Nobody would deny that collective entities like nations, states, companies, or social classes can be said to act or to have interests ('The Palestinian people has an interest in developing Palestinian culture'; 'The United States has declared war against terrorism'; 'Microsoft is concerned about its future'). The philosophical debate is about the *nature* of such entities, their acts and their normative status. In particular, the debate is about whether collective entities can be said to act and have moral status above and beyond that of the individuals who constitute it at any given time, or whether all claims about collectives must be reduced to claims about individuals. In the present context, the question is: whose interests (or rights) were competing with those of the Gentile parents (and possibly of the children), those of the Jewish *people*, or those of (some? all?) *individual* Jews?

The idea that collectives can act and have rights above the acts and rights of individuals sounds to many people metaphysically dubious and paradoxical. I cannot enter into this large and complex discussion here, though I do wish to say something toward the dismissal of this air of paradox. Opponents of collectives assume that the acts, rights and obligations of collectives must be reduced to the acts, rights and obligations of individuals. They probably rely on some general view about the explanatory power of reduction.[68] Yet, as argued by Tännsjö, 'if we want reduction, why stop at individual actions? Why not go, say, for sociobiological explanations of social phenomena?'[69] Since we *are* ready to stop (for many purposes) at individuals, in spite of the fact that we could further reduce them, we should also be ready to stop (for other purposes) at other entities – such as nations – even if they, too, are susceptible to further reduction. The naturalness of individual existence, argues Noam Zohar, is 'more apparent than real ... Change and reconstitution over time are the fate not only of nations but also of persons, and critical reflection reveals the difficulties in positing a unified and constant "individual person."'[70] If, nevertheless, we do not give up talk about individuals, we must not shy away from talk about collectives either and should not view it with such suspicion.

Having said that, I think that we do not need to decide about the existence of collectives in order to answer the question under discussion. Writers on collective rights have often made a distinction between collective rights that can be reduced to individual rights and those that cannot. To say that Moslems have a right to pray to Allah is to say that each individual Moslem has such a right. But to say that Moslems have a right to political control over the holy places in Saudi Arabia cannot be reduced to saying that each Moslem has such a right. A right for national self-determination is of course of the second type: it is *nations* that have such a right, not any individual.[71] Thus, rights exist, such as the right for self-determination, or the right for preferential treatment, that must be understood as rights of *groups*, rather than as aggregate rights of many individuals. That it makes sense to talk about rights of groups, or of collectives, seems to be accepted by most writers in the field,[72] notwithstanding disagreements about the nature of and the basis for such rights.

But, as argued by Vinit Haksar, even in the case of irreducible collective rights, 'the ultimate justification could be in terms of the interests of individuals.'[73] The bearer of the right for self-determination is a nation, but the justification for it, that is, the justification for the duties imposed upon others, is grounded in the interests of individual members of the nation. Similarly, to use another of Haksar's examples, it is a group, not its individual members, that might have a right to a certain quota of the relevant jobs, though the justification for giving certain disadvantaged groups quotas lies in the promotion of the interests of their members. This view is entitled by Michael Hartney 'value individualism,' which is defined as follows: 'Only the lives of individual human beings have ultimate value, and collective entities derive their value from their contribution to the lives of individual human beings.'[74] It is contrasted with 'value collectivism,' according to which a collective entity can have value independently of its contribution to the lives of individual human beings.[75]

Suppose now that the Jewish people did have a (*prima facie*) right to remove the children from their Gentile homes and bring them up as Jews. Could this right be reducible to the right of each individual Jew to do so, like the right to raise one's own children as Jews, or the right to eat *kosher* food? That would sound rather odd. While eating *kosher* food might be viewed as a right for any individual Jew, this could not be said about removing the children. Surely not every Jew had a right to removing the children under discussion from their Gentile homes.

Thus, assuming that the Jewish people had a right to remove the children, it was an irreducible collective one. As explained above, this still leaves us with two ways of justifying this right: one in terms of the interests of the collective itself ('value collectivism'), the other in terms of the interests of its individual members ('value individualism'). But first we must ask, individual or collective, *what* interests were there to be protected by the removal? Why would the Jewish people, or individual Jews, have an interest in removing the children from their Gentile parents?

Think of the following case. Suppose some extreme missionary Catholic group kidnaps a four-month-old Jewish boy, baptizes him and sends him to some remote monastery to be brought up as a Christian. The entire Jewish world protests and demands that the child be returned to his home. What interests of the Jewish people are hurt by the kidnapping, or by the fact that the child is not returned home? One answer might be the survival of the group. If Jewish children are kidnapped and brought up as non-Jews, then the existence of the Jewish people is threatened. The fewer Jews there are, the weaker the Jewish collective. But the protest would be loud even if only one Jewish child were kidnapped, an act which, by itself, would definitely not threaten the very existence of the Jewish people. Hence, the explanation seems to do with the troubling *message* of such an act, that is, that Jews are weak, vulnerable, and incapable of protecting their children. Such a message both undermines the Jews' sense of honor and self-respect, and also fosters fear and uncertainty regarding the security and future of the Jewish people. In these senses, attacks against individual members of a group are quite similar to minor bodily assaults on one individual. The injury caused by such assaults is not to be measured merely by the bodily harm, but by the message conveyed by it and by the psychological (and social) results that tend to follow. Such a kidnapping has a significant *symbolic* meaning which would explain the rage and protest of the Jewish people in this imaginary scenario and their attempts to make the kidnappers return the child.

For the sake of argument, I have assumed that the kidnapped child is happy and content in this monastery, and have argued that, nevertheless, the Jewish people have a right to claim him back. Of course, if the child is unhappy there, an even stronger reason exists for the claim, and deep interest in the good of the child comes into play. To be a member of a collective is to feel solidarity with other members and to care about their good more than about the good of non-members. It is to have an interest in promoting the welfare of other members of the collective and in reducing their pain and misery.

But can this child be said to be a member of the Jewish collective? For all *he* knows – assuming he is kept in that monastery for several years – he is Christian. In what sense are we justified in saying that he is Jewish nevertheless? I mentioned earlier Margalit and Raz's claim that membership in collectives is not a voluntary matter, nor one of achievement, but a matter of belonging. Essential to this belonging is a mutual recognition of one as member. Other conditions underlie such recognition, such as birth, but none suffices by itself for membership, unless supplemented by mutual recognition. In the imagined case under discussion, the boy was *born* as Jewish and definitely recognized as such by his family and everybody else who knew him. The kidnappers too acknowledged his Jewishness; that was precisely why they kidnapped him. Even if he grew up all his life as Christian, it would make perfect sense if some priests were to refer to him behind his back as 'the Jew,' and if, upon revealing his true biography at the age of seventy, he himself said, 'Wow, so I am a Jew.' This would not be a mere subjective feeling, nor a matter of identifying with the Jewish people. What he would be discovering in this imaginary scenario is a true fact about himself, namely, his belonging – in some sense – to the Jewish people.

Let us return now to the issue of removing the Jewish children. Not removing the children would not have caused anything close to a threat to the existence of the Jewish people. Still, the Jewish people did have an interest in removing the children because of the symbolic meaning of doing so (and the symbolic meaning of *not* having done so), particularly after the Holocaust. By bringing these children back to a Jewish environment, their survival was to be made meaningful to the Jewish people and to the world at large. After having lost a third of its members, the Jewish people had a strong interest in recovering and getting back on its feet. Removing the children was instrumental in sending forth and encouraging a message of survival, rebirth and hope. It also expressed the Jewish people's renewed ability to take care of its members and to fight for them, an ability which had been crushed during the Holocaust. This expression too was instrumental in assuring its members, as well as non-Jews, of the worth of the Jewish people.

Given this understanding of the relevant interests, for the sake of the present issue, I see no need to decide between value individualism and value collectivism. If we adopt the latter, then clearly the Jewish people, *qua* collective, had an interest in encouraging the above messages and in caring about the thousands of its members who were handed over to non-Jewish guardians under terrible circumstances. If we adopt the former, then plainly it was in the interest of individual Jews, too, to advance these goals. The above messages and the welfare of the Jewish children were collective goods that they had an interest in promoting.

But there was another message to be sent through the removal of the children, a message that had meaning not only for Jews but for humankind in general. This is the message that power ought not to prevail. In most cases, the children under discussion would have been brought up as Jews by their parents, had the latter not been forced by the most dreadful and cruel circumstances to seek shelter for their children in non-Jewish homes. That a person voluntarily chooses to exit from his or her community – be it nation, religion or culture – might be regrettable for other members, but, surely, the decision must be respected by anybody with even minimum respect for human autonomy. But if a person is forced to exit, it is important to undo the consequences of force, thereby proclaiming a universal message against violence and terror.

Finally, from the Nazi point of view, the best 'solution' for the 'Jewish problem' was the death of the Jews. But if this could not be achieved for some reason, surely they would concede and accept a 'second-best' solution, namely, the complete destruction of Jewish identity. In the Nazi evil mind, this would at least partially reduce, and in the course of time eliminate, the poisonous influences of Jewish blood. From this point of view, the Nazis would have viewed the Christianization of the Jewish children as at least partial success of their Satanic plan. And that is precisely why the children ought to have been removed from their Christian homes, namely, in order not to let evil prevail, not to let the Nazi ideology triumph.

Liberals are often suspicious about collective rights because of the threat such rights pose to the rights of individuals. In the present case, one could worry about the Jewish children being viewed as mere instruments for the benefit of the people.[76] Yet I believe this suspicion is warranted only when collective rights are granted privileged status as reasons for action, not if they are regarded as one kind of reason among others, as they were here. For anyone who concedes that the interests of individuals in general, and children in particular, might be overridden by other considerations, there is nothing unreasonable or even surprising about this conclusion. As David Archard correctly explains, we ought not to accept the idea of a sharp contrast between an extreme individualism which leaves no room for collective considerations and an extreme, Platonic-like collectivism, that leaves no room for the individual.[77]

3. Summary and Conclusions

Moral dilemmas are situations in which, though there might be a right answer to the question of what, all things considered, the agents ought to do, they must still incur an irreparable moral loss and, hence, they cannot escape feelings of guilt and remorse.[78] The problem at hand definitely belongs to this category. In most cases, the removal of the children was unfair to the Gentile parents and often must have caused them deep pain. In some cases, it also caused damage to the children, an additional hurt to the scars they were already carrying with them from the time of the forced separation from their parents and family. But not removing the children would have also claimed its (moral) price. It would have been unfair to the (biological) parents, it would have ignored the interests of the Jewish people and, in some cases, would have been bad for the children too. There was no 'clean' solution to the problem at hand.

Nevertheless, in spite of the moral cost involved in it, I think the project was justified. Let me try to tie together the various threads of the argument that lead to this conclusion. In the first section, I discussed various considerations from the point of view of the best interests of the child. My aim was to weaken the presumption that removing the children was traumatic, causing everlasting damage to the children. I relied on psychological literature that casts doubt on the traumatic effect of early separations, and points to the remarkable ability of children to adapt to new circumstances and new frameworks. I also referred to research on children of divorced parents, showing that divorce does not cause extreme psychological or behavioral disruption and that, over time, adaptation to the new situation improves. At any rate, very few people would suggest banning divorce because of the psychological injury caused to the children, and most people would find it inappropriate even to condemn the parents for this reason on moral grounds.

I then argued that, generally speaking, it is better for people to live where they 'belong,' in terms of the relevant nation, race or culture. Here I relied on literature about adopted children and their search for their roots, as well as on the voyages of second- or third-generation hidden Jews in Poland back to their Jewishness.

Finally, to reinforce these two lines of argument, I mentioned the fact that the great majority of children retroactively approved of the removal in their adulthood. Had the removal caused such severe and enduring psychological effects, it should have damaged the children's lives in a way that would make such positive assessment impossible. That it is possible shows that the trauma of the removal was not so crushing to them or, in any case, that it was (partially) compensated for by a feeling of connection to their roots and of living among their own.

The first section of the essay might have been sufficient to establish that the removal was morally legitimate. But, in disputes about child custody, it is never only the interests of the child that matter. There are also the interests of the parents and even those of the public.[79] So in the present case too, we had to continue and discuss the interests of others, which was the aim of the second section. I started with the interests of the biological parents. I tried to show (a) that their preferences for their children had moral weight, and (b) that, in most cases, the parents would have supported the removal of the children from the Gentile families. I then turned to the Gentile parents and argued that their preferences definitely carried moral weight, but that when balanced against the preferences of the biological parents, in most cases, the latter prevail. I relied on a general presumption in favor of biological parenthood and also on the fact that most Gentile parents were not forced to agree to the removal, hence their doing so expressed their tacit understanding that the children were put in their custody only temporarily. Finally, I argued that the Jewish people can be said to have had an interest in removing the children, mainly as a symbolic way of affirming its existence after the Holocaust and of spreading a message of survival, hope, and resistance to evil.

The bottom line, therefore, is that the project was morally justified. Of course, this conclusion has exceptions, cases where the price of removing the child turned out to be too high for him or her. In these cases, the Jewish organizations, acting out of good will, added unnecessary distress to lives which had already experienced so much pain. That the Jewish people had to face such tragic dilemmas and that it must have erred in deciding some of them is yet a further painful consequence of the Holocaust.

Notes

* For helpful comments on earlier drafts, I am greatly indebted to Shulamit Almog, Eve Garrard, Emunah Nachmany-Gafny and Saul Smilansky. Special thanks to Eve Garrard for her constant encouragement in the writing of this essay.

1. For the historical facts relevant to this topic, I will be relying primarily on a recent dissertation by Emunah Nachmany-Gafny, *The Removal of Jewish Children from Gentile Families in Poland in the Immediate Post Holocaust Years*, Bar-Ilan University, Israel, 2000 (in Hebrew – English version forthcoming by Yad Vashem, Jerusalem), and also on Nachum Bogner, *At the Mercy of Strangers: The Rescue of Jewish Children with Assumed Identities in Poland*, Jerusalem: Yad Vashem, 2001 (in Hebrew). I wish to thank Emunah Nachmany-Gafny for kindly providing me with a copy of her study while it was still under review and for patiently clarifying many crucial points in conversation.
2. I shall refer to them throughout the essay as 'the Jewish children.' I refer to the Gentile rescuers as 'caretakers,' or simply as 'the Gentile parents.'
3. To 'save,' to 'rescue,' or to 'redeem' were some of the terms used by these organizations to describe their activities. I will use the neutral term 'to remove,' in order not to beg the question in favor of the project under discussion.

4. For the heroic dedication of the Gentile parents, see, for example, Nachmany-Gafny, *Removal of Jewish Children*, pp. 34–5, and Bogner, *At the Mercy of Strangers*, pp. 72–8. That the caretakers were moved by humanity and mercy does not mean that such moral emotions were the only source of motivation for their deeds. At times other motives existed too, such as having another pair of hands to help on the farm, or converting the Jewish child to Christianity. The desire to convert the children to Christianity was especially relevant with regard to children hidden in monasteries. See Bogner, p. 286.
5. See, for instance, Laura M. Purdy, *In Their Best Interest?*, Ithaca, NY: Cornell University Press, 1992; Michael Freeman and Philip Veerman (eds), *The Ideologies of Children's Rights*, The Netherlands: Martinus Nijhoff, 1992; Jon Elster, *Solomonic Judgements: Studies in the Limitations of Rationality*, New York: Cambridge University Press, 1989, pp. 134–9.
6. The involvement of relatives was often problematic in the rescue efforts; see Nachmany-Gafny, *Removal of Jewish Children*, p. 169.
7. Some indeed chose to do so, see Nachmany-Gafny, *Removal of Jewish Children*, pp. 162–4.
8. See Arlene Skolnick, 'Solomon's Children,' in M.A. Mason, A. Skolnick and S.D. Sugerman (eds), *All Our Families: New Policies for a New Century*, New York: Oxford University Press, 1998, p. 238 (on political refugees who have to flee their country, leave their baby with neighbors and come back ten years later to claim it) and p. 245 (on a child of Holocaust survivors raised by another family as an exception to the rule formulated by Goldstein et al. that children ought to be left with their adoptive parents).
9. Elster, *Solomonic Judgements*.
10. Susan Wolfson, 'Children's Rights: the Theoretical Underpinning of the "Best Interests of the Child,"' in Freeman and Veerman, *Ideologies of Children's Rights*, p. 7.
11. See especially Janet Dolgin, *Defining the Family: Law, Technology, and Reproduction in an Uneasy Age*, New York: New York University Press, 1997, who shows at length how the idea of the best interests of the child 'has supported society's continuing nostalgia for the way families were thought once to have been.' Her main concern is to show how this nostalgia underlies much of the opposition to new methods of reproduction and new forms of family.
12. See, for instance, the Virginia Supreme Court decision in *Bottoms v. Bottoms*, in 1995, granting custody of a young boy to the grandmother rather than to the mother, essentially on the grounds that the child's best interests would not be served by residence with his lesbian mother. Referred to by Dolgin, *Defining the Family*, p. 220.
13. See John Bowlby's three-volume *Attachment and Loss*, London: Hogarth Press, 1965, 1973 and 1980.
14. For some of the critical, 'revisionist' views, see the references mentioned by David Archard, *Children: Rights and Childhood*, London: Routledge, 1993, p. 174, n. 7, esp. A.B. and C.B. Clarke (eds), *Early Experience: Myth and Evidence*, Harmondsworth, UK: Penguin, 1972.
15. Skolnick, 'Solomon's Children,' p. 249.
16. Ibid., p. 246.
17. 442 Mich. 648; 502 N.W. 2d 649; 1993 Mich. LEXIS 1659.
18. Skolnick, 'Solomon's Children,' p. 251.
19. A.J. Stewart, A.P. Copeland, N.L. Chester, J.E. Malley and N.B. Barenbaum, *Separating Together: How Divorce Transforms Families*, New York: The Guilford Press, 1997, p. 90.
20. My concern with long-term psychological damage does not deny the pain of separation as harm in itself, regardless of such damage. Yet, if only short-term pain is involved, pain which is soon forgotten and which leaves no scars, the onus on those removing the children is much lighter.

21. It might be relevant to note that the overwhelming majority of children in divorced families say that they would have preferred the unhappy marriage to the divorce. Quoted by Elster, *Solomonic Judgements*, p. 124, n. 3.
22. Personally, as I grew up in Israel, I find it almost impossible to identify Jews from non-Jews just by their physical appearance. But I know that Jews who live for long enough among non-Jews are pretty good at doing so, and (unfortunately in most cases) non-Jews are rather good at it too. I was recently told by a non-Jewish philosopher that, due to the way he looks and talks, he had been often taken to be Jewish and more than once was beaten because of this false identification.
23. Marshall D. Schechter and Doris Bertocci, 'The Meaning of the Search,' in David Brodzinsky and Marshall Schechter (eds), *The Psychology of Adoption*, New York: Oxford University Press, 1990, p. 71.
24. Archard, *Children*, p. 104.
25. Like most arguments of this essay, I'm assuming that this argument holds true for most children, though not for all of them. *If* revealing to the children their Jewishness had caused severe pain and instability and *if* it could have been concealed from them successfully, then obviously they would have felt no lack in 'wholeness' or 'authenticity' growing up as Catholic Poles.
26. See also 'The New Jews,' *Ha'aretz*, 17 August 2001, Supplement, pp. 60–65 (in Hebrew).
27. Nachmany-Gafny, *Removal of Jewish Children*.
28. For a deep moral criticism of the Stoic ideal, see George Harris, *Dignity and Vulnerability*, Berkeley: University of California Press, 1996.
29. Skolnick, 'Solomon's Children,' p. 240.
30. Ibid., p. 241.
31. This seems to establish an argument against cross-cultural adoption, an issue being hotly disputed in the UK in recent years. But it is only a *prima facie* reason against such adoption, which can be rebutted by stronger ones. As, in most cases, the alternative to cross-cultural adoption is institutional care, it is almost always better for the child to be adopted – at the risk of suffering from some feelings of exclusion and so on – than to be left in some institution.
32. Daniel Statman, 'Humiliation, Dignity and Self-Respect,' *Philosophical Psychology* **13** (2000), section IV ('humiliation and the fear of exclusion'). Apparently, the sense of security gained by inclusion in a social group that one usually gets from one's (biological or adoptive) parents is not strong enough to make one immune to painful messages of exclusion coming from larger social circles.
33. Bernard Williams, *Making Sense of Humanity and Other Philosophical Papers*, Cambridge: Cambridge University Press, 1995, p. 224.
34. Avishai Margalit and Joseph Raz, 'National Self-Determination,' *Journal of Philosophy* **87** (1990), pp. 439–61.
35. Michael Hartney objects to the view 'that ceasing to belong to the community one was born into would have disastrous effects on one's "identity" and would leave one an impoverished individual.' In his opinion, such a thesis is 'surely false,' as it flies in the face of the fact that many people experience the change to the new culture as liberating and as making them better off ('Some Confusions Concerning Collective Rights,' in James Grawford (ed.), *The Rights of Peoples*, New York: Oxford University Press, 1987, p. 297). But the thesis under discussion does not argue that exiting from one's community always has 'disastrous' effects on one's identity, only that, in typical cases, and other things being equal, it has some negative effect of this kind. That this is so is confirmed by the experience of millions of immigrants all over the world who might be happy with their immigration for all kinds of reasons, but still regret it because of its effects on their sense of identity and belonging.

36. I am relying here on conversations with Nachmany-Gafny, who has interviewed dozens of survivors about their experiences and feelings.
37. Both papers, 'Moral Luck,' and 'Postscript,' appear in D. Statman (ed.), *Moral Luck*, Albany, NY: SUNY Press, 1993, chs 2 and 14, respectively.
38. *Foundations of the Metaphysics of Morals*, 1st section, 3rd paragraph.
39. Williams, 'Moral Luck,' p. 36.
40. More accurately, according to Williams there are two kinds of failure, 'intrinsic' and 'extrinsic,' and only the former is relevant to proving the project *un*justified. In the celebrated example of Gauguin, who deserted his family to paint in Tahiti, an extrinsic failure would be getting injured in a road accident on the way to Tahiti, while an intrinsic failure would be a failure in his artistic enterprise.
41. Elster, *Solomonic Judgements*, p. 136.
42. Ibid., p. 137.
43. At the end of 2001, Emunah Nachmany-Gafny launched a quantitative research in Poland to examine precisely this point, namely, to see how Jewish children who, for various reasons, were not removed from their Gentile families retroactively assess their lives. This is the first empirical study of the topic, and it is hoped it will shed light on the possibility of making meaningful comparisons between the lives of children who were removed and those who were not.
44. See, for instance, Joseph Raz, *The Morality of Freedom*, Oxford: Oxford University Press, 1986, ch. 13, esp. the example of the choice between a career in law and a career as a clarinettist. I'm not arguing that different life stories can never be compared. Surely it is better to live with non-abusive parents than with abusive ones. That incommensurability does not necessarily exclude comparability is a central point in chapter three of my *Moral Dilemmas*, Amsterdam: Rodopi, 1995.
45. *Vasconselos v. Turgeman* (1988) 45(ii) P.D. 626.
46. Bruna was interviewed by an Israeli journalist who visited her in Brazil. See Uri Misgav and Hillit Yanay, 'Remember Bruna–Caroline?', Magazine *HA'IR*, Tel-Aviv, 2 August 2001, pp. 46–51 (in Hebrew).
47. Elster, *Solomonic Judgements*, p. 127.
48. One kind of arguments for removing the children that will not be discussed here are religious ones. These can be of two main kinds: arguments claiming that for the sake of the children they ought to be raised as Jews (for example because otherwise their souls would be ruined); and arguments claiming that such rescue was a religious duty incumbent upon the parents. To properly evaluate such arguments, much needs to be said about the role of religious arguments in moral and political debate, a topic that goes beyond the scope of the present essay. See, just as a start, A. Sagi and D. Statman, *Religion and Morality*, Amsterdam: Rodopi, 1995.
49. Indeed those executing the project expressed their feeling that they were carrying out the parents' will. See Nachmany-Gafny, *Removal of Jewish Children*, pp. 99, 125, 251.
50. Anti-Semitism was deeply rooted in Polish culture and expressed itself in numerous ways during the Holocaust. It has received new attention recently following the revelations about the massacre in Jedwabne. See Jan Gross, *Neighbours: The Destruction of the Jewish Community in Jedwabne, Poland*, Princeton, NJ: Princeton University Press, 2000. According to Gross, the massacre of the 1,600 Jews of Jedwabne was not carried out by the Germans, but by the Polish neighbors of the victims. After the war, such pogroms flared up again against survivors of the camps who tried to return to their homes. More relevant to the present study: in most cases, it was a Polish informer who told the Nazis about Jewish children hidden in the neighborhood or in the village, thereby leading to the death of the children together with their guardians. See Bogner, *At the Mercy of Strangers*, p. 45.

51. Nachmany-Gafny, *Removal of Jewish Children*, p. 237. As a policy, the organizations that dealt with these children did not forward the letters to the Gentile families, to expedite the children's adjustment to their new environment. So quite a number of such letters remained in the archives and are a good source of information.

52. For Jewish children becoming anti-Semitic in their Gentile families, see also Bogner, *At the Mercy of Strangers*, p. 72. Bogner tells the story of a Jewish girl hidden by the former housemaid of her parents. The girl, Martha, celebrated with her friends in the street the news about the final destruction of the Warsaw ghetto. When she returned home joyfully, her Catholic rescuer beat her up and said to her: 'In the street you may behave like everybody else. But in this home remember that the Jews are good people.'

53. The fear that the Jewish children, victims of anti-Semitism, would become anti-Semitic themselves was an explicit motive of many Jewish agents active in the removal project. See Nachmany-Gafny, *Removal of Jewish Children*, p. 251.

54. Some orthodox parents might have preferred their child to die than to risk having him or her brought up as a Christian, or even living temporarily in what they perceived as an idolatrous environment. Whether or not Jews ought to let their children die, or, to take a more extreme position, ought to actually kill them in order to save them from converting to Christianity, is an issue under dispute in Jewish law. The dispute arose in Europe during the period of the Crusades, when Jews at times killed their own children and then killed themselves to prevent forced conversion. On this tragic chapter in Jewish history, see Israel Jacob Yuval, *Two Nations in Your Womb: Perceptions of Jews and Christians*, Tel Aviv: Am Oved Publishers, 2000 (in Hebrew), ch. 4.

55. Cf. Aristotle, *Nicomachean Ethics*, bk 1, chs 10–11.

56. Thomas Nagel, 'Death,' in *Mortal Questions*, Cambridge: Cambridge University Press, 1979, p. 6.

57. Oswald Hanfling, *The Quest for Meaning*, Oxford: Blackwell, 1987, p. 67: 'If there are unexperienced evils, they are not *as bad* as those within our experience.'

58. An exception is Jan Narveson, *The Libertarian Idea*, Philadelphia, PA: Temple University Press, 1988, pp. 269–74. For a rejection of the ownership model, see, for example, Archard, *Children*, ch. 8.

59. Archard, *Children*, p. 109.

60. Those who agreed to take care of the children only for money tried to get rid of the risky deposit sooner or later. See Nachmany-Gafny, *Removal of Jewish Children*, p. 28.

61. Archard, *Children*, p. 109.

62. For such a presumption, cf. ibid., p. 104.

63. Nachmany-Gafny, *Removal of Jewish Children*, p. 24, n. 67 tells the story of a girl whose mother asked her to learn by heart two addresses in Canada and in New York before handing her to the Polish caretakers, then asked her to forget the addresses and her Jewishness, telling her that her life depended on it.

64. Whether handing over the Jewish children was intended for good or only for a limited period was a question discussed by a Polish court in 1946. The Foxbergs handed their daughter to a Gentile family. The parents were killed during the war, but an aunt survived and claimed the girl. In the trial, the lawyer representing the aunt argued that no parent gives away his or her child as a gift and when Foxberg handed the girl to the non-Jewish family, he surely believed that one day he would get her back. See Nachmany-Gafny, *Removal of Jewish Children*, p. 194.

65. In the months immediately following the end of the war, on their own initiative, some Polish guardians brought the Jewish children they had sheltered to Jewish organizations and asked for no compensation. Only later, when it became known that these organizations were willing to pay for the children, did the Polish caretakers ask for money. See Bogner, *At the Mercy of Strangers*, p. 198.

66. Even legally, these organizations were allowed to appear in court (at least in Poland) as representing the interests of the Jewish people.

67. The Holocaust has been a focus of many discussions regarding collective rights, responsibilities and emotions. Regarding the Jews, it has been disputed whether, as a people, they have a collective right to demand compensation from the Nazis. Regarding the Germans, whether they bear collective responsibility for what the Nazis did, whether they have an obligation to the victims and whether they should feel collective shame or collective remorse have been recurring topics. The literature on these questions is extensive. See recently Aleksander Jokić (ed.), *War Crimes and Collective Wrongdoing*, Oxford: Blackwell, 2001.

68. See, for example, Jon Elster, *Making Sense of Marx*, Cambridge: Cambridge University Press, 1985, p. 5, quoted by Torbjörn Tännsjö, 'Methodological Individualism,' *Inquiry* **33** (1990), p. 73.

69. Tännsjö, 'Methodological Individualism.' Tännsjö's paper is a strong attack on methodological individualism and concludes by suggesting that, in our best explanations of some social phenomena, we may well need to have recourse to collective entities.

70. Noam Zohar, 'Collective War and Individual Ethics,' *Political Theory* **21** (1993), p. 617. Zohar claims to be relying on the works of Eddy Zemach and Derek Parfit.

71. See Raz, *Morality of Freedom*, pp. 207–8 and Vinit Haksar, 'Collective Rights and the Value of Groups,' *Inquiry* **41** (1998), p. 31.

72. Here are some references: David Makinson, 'Rights of Peoples: Point of View of a Logician,' in James Grawford (ed.), *The Rights of Peoples*, New York: Oxford University Press, 1987, p. 83 ('There is no self-contradiction in the very idea of rights or obligations attaching to an abstract or collective bearer, such as a people … Neither the step to the collective, nor the step to the abstract character of the bearer is in itself incoherent'); Raz, *Morality of Freedom*, pp. 207–9; Virginia Held, *Rights and Goods*, Chicago: University of Chicago Press, 1984, p. 255; R.W. Brimlow, 'On Groups, Group Action and Preferential Treatment,' *Journal of Philosophical Research* **21** (1996), pp. 341–76.

73. Haksar, 'Collective Rights', p. 31.

74. Raz expresses a strong version of value individualism when he says that 'rights, even collective rights, can only be there if they serve the interests of individuals. In that sense, collective interests are a mere *façon de parler*' (*Morality of Freedom*, p. 208).

75. Hartney, 'Some Confusions,' p. 297.

76. Such a concern was voiced by those carrying out the project of removing the children. One said he felt at times that he was 'stealing the child from his parents and making him a child of the public,' see Nachmany-Gafny, *Removal of Jewish Children*, p. 241. But most of the time they believed that the removal was not only in the interests of the Jewish people, but would work out for the personal good of the children too.

77. Archard, *Children*, ch. 13, especially pp. 164–5.

78. I defend this conception of dilemmas in *Moral Dilemmas*. This is a kind of a middle-ground position between those who argue that in dilemmas no right answer as to what ought to be done exists and those who argue that if such an answer exists, the dilemma is unreal.

79. For the claim that public interest can override the best interests of the child, see Elster, *Solomonic Judgements*, pp. 148–50. Sometimes there is a general moral principle that is thought to override the interests of the child, as in the following case. A married, forty-year-old man, whose wife could not conceive, seduced his fifteen-year-old neighbor with the intention of raising the baby that would be born out of the relationship. When the baby was born, the girl immediately gave up her parental rights and the biological father demanded that he and his wife get custody over the child. The case reached the

Supreme Court of Israel that decided against the biological father. Most of the judges argued that, in the circumstances, letting the child grow up with his biological father (and his wife) would run against the child's best interests, hence he would be better off with adoptive parents. But one judge, Justice Heshin, argued convincingly that there was no serious basis to thinking that the child would be better off with some adoptive parent than with his biological father. The real basis for not letting the father have the child, he argued, was the principle that evildoers ought not to be allowed to benefit from their evil deeds. See 3798/94, P.D. 20 (3) 133.

Chapter 12

Forgiving the Unforgivable?

Laurence Thomas

The Nazi: Mr Adolph Paul-Damascus (b. 1920)

Mr Paul-Damascus was a Nazi in Adolf Hitler's army. Serving with pleasure, he was responsible for several hundred Jews being deported to their deaths, knowing full well that the trains were carrying the Jews to the death camps, Auschwitz or Treblinka (say). He was as proud of his atrocious deeds as any Nazi.

But the war ended; and Mr Paul-Damascus went into hiding in South America, where he took on an entirely new identity. He then emigrated to the US, where he began working in the steel industry, amassing an absolute fortune. But by the late 1950s he was truly pained by and remorseful for the wrong that he had done. Mr Paul-Damascus anonymously devoted all his fortune to Jewish charities.

He lived as a mere pauper, and the millions upon millions of dollars that he made each year went to Jewish charities; and upon his death, billions of dollars would go to Jewish charities. All his past donations were anonymous; and his bequest to Jewish charities would be anonymous as well.

And this is how Mr Paul-Damascus lived until 1998. The fiftieth Anniversary of the State of Israel moved him beyond words; and at the age of 78, he turned himself in to the Israeli Court. This he did not have to do. He would never have been caught. So fear of being apprehended was not his motivation for so behaving. Mr Paul-Damascus lived a life of extraordinary contrition.

No one quite knows what rid Mr Paul-Damascus of his anti-Semitism. Some say he became a Christian; others say that he found out that his father was a Jew. Still others say that in South America he was often mistaken for a Jew, and that it was being the object of such vile anti-Semitism that brought home to him the wickedness of his ways. But one thing is clear: Paul-Damascus had a genuine change of heart.

Should Adolph Paul-Damascus be forgiven?

Many argue that he should not be forgiven, because he was motivated simply by guilt to donate anonymously all his wealth to Jewish charities. But a wise Jew by the name of Solomon made a very poignant observation. Refusing to state publicly whether Mr Paul-Damascus should be forgiven, Solomon asked whether we are better or lesser human beings if we discredit Paul-Damascus's post-Nazi life in the name of his having being consumed by feelings of guilt. Others cried out that Paul-

Damascus's money wouldn't bring a single Jew back to life. To this Solomon retorted: nor will Paul-Damascus's death. Solomon is serving as the lawyer for Mr Adolph Paul-Damascus.

It has become virtually an article of faith, at least among a great many Jews, that no Nazi war criminal should ever be forgiven, no matter what the individual went on to do. And this point is finessed by the commonplace observation that only those who have been wronged can forgive those who committed the wrong in question. In the harrowing words of Jankélévitch: forgiveness died in the death camps. This observation, of course, is intended to put an end to the very discussion by ruling out of order on conceptual grounds the issue of forgiving a Nazi war criminal. But this conceptual move may not quite work.

If the Israeli Supreme Court or the International Court of Justice has the authority to punish or to pardon such a person, then absent other considerations the question of whether a Nazi could be forgiven has not been for ever rendered out of order on conceptual grounds. We could quibble over what exactly a court is doing if it pardons a war criminal; and we could note the formal differences between a pardon issued by a government (or court of law) and forgiveness offered by an individual. But one thing is certain: if a court could ever be justified in pardoning a war criminal, this would be close enough to forgiving the person to raise the specter of forgiveness itself. What is more, we can ask what reasons could there be – what reasons could anyone have – for forgiving such a person. It makes sense to say, and it is significant to say, that 'Your parents would have reason to be proud of you if they were alive.' Accordingly, it could be true that if so-and-so had not died from cardiac arrest, then she would have good reasons to forgive her assailant. And if such a claim were true, that would surely be significant. That is, then, we can ask whether a person is forgivable, that is, worthy of forgiveness, even if strictly speaking those who could in fact forgive him are no longer around to do so. And this is particularly relevant when it comes to war crimes, precisely because war crimes are aimed not at individuals as such, but at individuals as members of this or that community of people. (Interestingly, some war crime acts can be directed towards some members of a given community and not others, the rape of women being a case in point.) Whether a war criminal is worthy of forgiveness is certainly relevant to a community that has been the object of war crimes.

Quite related here is the following point. Whether strictly speaking a wrongdoer can be forgiven by those around, it is nonetheless possible for those around to have a moral attitude of exclusion or inclusion towards that person, or an unfavorable or favorable moral attitude towards that person. Thus, as the member of a once-targeted community, it can be disingenuous to say 'It is not my place to forgive,' all the while holding the most hostile of attitudes towards a person who has changed mightily, as if the fact that one is not in the position to forgive not only licensed the hostility but excluded taking into account any reasons for having a less hostile attitude towards the person. Sentiments of ill-will or good-will are options even if, strictly speaking, forgiveness is not.

My aim in this paper is to examine the view that a Nazi war criminal could never be worthy of forgiveness – not just any Nazi war criminal, but one like Adolph Paul-

Damascus. On the prevailing view, forgiving any Nazi war criminal, or judging him forgivable, is a despicable thing to do. I want to see whether this view can withstand critical scrutiny. In particular, I want to consider whether we can have it both ways. That is, can we insist that Adolph Paul-Damascus should not be forgiven, all the while accepting and being moved by the plea for forgiveness that the bishops of France and, indeed, the Catholic Church itself, made to the Jewish people? Many arguments against forgiveness focus upon the fact of irreplaceable loss; whereas the focus should be upon the transgressor's sincerity of contrition. Or so I shall argue. For the moment, let me just observe that during World War II many parents lost their sons who fought for the Allies. Surely, the loss was no less irreplaceable. As we shall see, the problem with forgiving Adolph Paul-Damascus is that there is a sense in which he had too much luck.

Significantly, the issue that I am raising in this paper should not be confused with a fundamentally different one, namely whether a person like Paul-Damascus should be shown mercy. As we shall see below (Section 2), it is possible to forgive without showing mercy, and conversely.

By way of a question, a final introductory remark. Could a person rejoice in Paul-Damascus's change of heart and all the good that he went on to do and yet not forgive him, as opposed to recognizing that Paul-Damascus is worthy of forgiveness? This question has to be answered affirmatively. If anything is clear, it is that for independent reasons we cannot always overcome the scars of life. Hence, overcoming forgiveness can be strictly a psychological matter and not a moral one, meaning that although all the conditions for forgiveness are judged as having been met, the person is psychologically unable to do so. To be sure, an individual may be self-deceived about this. Or, a person may avail himself of this line so as to put an end to the moral discussion of the matter. In a different direction, however, there could be considerations of moral decency, whatever one suspects might be the truth of the matter, that counsel against questioning a person who asserts that she or he is psychologically unable to forgive. I do not address these very important matters in this paper.

1. Forgetting and Forgiving

At the outset, a clarification is in order. In Micah 7, we find the following words:

> Who is a God like unto thee, that pardoneth iniquity, and passeth by the transgression of the remnant of his heritage? he retaineth not his anger forever, because he delighteth in mercy. He will turn again, he will have compassion upon us; he will subdue our iniquities; and thou wilt cast all their sins into the depths of the sea. (vv. 18–19)

This passage, which has given rise to the expression 'sea of forgetfulness,' has inclined many to think that genuine forgiveness entails forgetting. Yet as others have duly noted, forgetting the horrific wrong that has been done not only seems psychologically impossible; it also seems woefully inappropriate. In some instances, prudence alone would counsel against forgetting. And when it comes to the Shoah, Elie Wiesel and others have made 'Never Forget' one of its rallying cries.

Significantly, though, Wiesel makes it clear that for him these words stand as a plea for all human beings to be vigilant against the occurrence of horrific injustices. In his acceptance speech for the Nobel Prize, Wiesel claimed:

> I struggle against forgetfulness and lying. To forget is to choose to be complicit ... The world knew [that Hitler was trying to exterminate the Jews] and remained silent. That is why I have vowed never to be silent when human beings are either persecuted or humiliated. I will always take a position, because neutrality serves the oppressor and not his victim.[1]

Without getting involved in biblical exegesis, I shall adopt Jeffrie Murphy's view that forgiveness involves forswearing resentment;[2] and I shall understand doing so to entail the complete absence of any delight whatsoever in making the transgressor suffer on account of the wrong that one has suffered. Nor is there any desire continually to remind the wrongdoer of the wrong that she or he committed. This is compatible with allowing that a forgiven wrongdoer be punished. It is also compatible with there being good reasons for not forgetting that someone has transgressed in certain ways even if the person has been forgiven. An example of this latter sort might be the following.

Suppose that during his childhood a man had been sexually abused by his father. The father eventually acknowledges this and begs his son for forgiveness. The son might have the wherewithal to do this, especially if he learns that his father had been systematically abused sexually. Yet, the son might make it a point never to let his own children be alone around his father. Although he has forgiven his father, the son does not forget, and he has good reason for not forgetting. Nonetheless, the reason why he will not let his children be alone with his father has nothing whatsoever to do with trying to make his father suffer for the pain that he (the son) went through. Quite the contrary: he regularly has his father over for dinner, and he regularly takes his children over to see their grandfather. Indeed, the son acknowledges the good things that his father did in other respects. Thanks to his father, he never wanted for material things and he was able to attend an Ivy League university, as well as spend several years traveling abroad. All the same, the son has a very good reason to bear in mind that his father has a certain kind of moral weakness. In fact, it would be utterly irresponsible for the son to forget. In not forgetting, the son's aim is not to keep the father continually reminded of the wrong that he did. Nor, in not letting his children be alone with their grandfather, is the son's aim in any way to keep hurting his father. Rather, the son's aim is simply to protect his children, to keep them from ever being a victim of child sexual abuse. Surely this is a laudable reason for not forgetting the wrong that someone has done if ever there could be one.

Not to forgive, then, is not to forget in a particular kind of way, where continually holding resentment against the wrongdoer is taken as justified in and of itself. Other benefits may come of doing so. Perhaps other lives will be spared suffering. However, these benefits are ancillary at best; and are not seen as relevant to one's continually holding resentment against the wrongdoer. If one is justified in continually holding resentment, then not forgiving does not constitute holding a grudge; whereas if one is not justified, then to continue harboring resentment does constitute holding a grudge (with perhaps the exception of the person who is psychologically unable to forgive, though the wrongdoer is judged worthy of forgiveness). The grudge holder delights in taking pleasure in his resentment and wants there to be nothing that would give him a reason to be less resentful; whereas having good reasons not to forgive is perfectly compatible with wishing that the person would come to be worthy of forgiveness. It seems clear, then, that harboring a grudge surely veers in the direction of being a vice. By this line of reasoning, we can see that God does not hold a grudge against sinners. Even if some souls should end up in hell, God takes no delight in there being unrepentant sinners.

Presumably, Jews are not interested in simply holding a grudge against Nazi war criminals. Rather, the point is that there is something about the very nature of what was done that makes forgiving these war criminals inappropriate as a matter of principle. Why? Because it is not just murders that Nazi war criminals committed, but murders with a certain insidiousness. The most manipulative and deceptive practices imaginable were employed in order to kill Jews, requiring that every ounce of human decency be surmounted.

Owing to the attempt by the Turks to exterminate the Armenians and then the attempt by the Nazis to exterminate the Jews, an entirely new category of immoral behavior was introduced, namely: crimes against humanity.[3] With crimes against humanity, we have an indifference to the humanity of an entire people, and not just indifference to the humanity of a specific person. Indifference to the humanity of an entire people would seem to reach a level of callousness that embodies the very essence of evil itself, because nothing can make sense of wanting to kill an entire people – to eliminate them from the face of the earth – simply on account of who they are; whereas we can understand all too well anger and rage towards a particular person for certain offenses (such as the killing of a loved one) even if it is wrong to act out these sentiments. Had Hitler been simply interested in ridding Germany of its Jews, this would not have particularly distinguished him from other leaders in history who sought to remove certain others from their territory. However, Hitler sought to rid the earth of its Jews; and this radically changed for the worse the moral nature of the scope of his aim. Perhaps, then, the general point among Jews is that it is crimes against humanity (the attempt at the genocide of Jews, in this case) that are by their very nature unforgivable.

One needs to proceed cautiously, though. It is not a conceptual truth that a crime against humanity is unforgivable. To show that a wrong constitutes an unimaginable, unspeakable wrong is one thing; to show that such a wrong is, on that account alone, unforgivable is quite another. What follows, if anything, in this regard is that the bar of forgiveness rises to heights hitherto unimaginable, from which it does not at all follow that this level is unreachable in principle.

2. Forgiveness: A Brief Topology

As I have already noted, Murphy defines forgiveness as forswearing resentment. Just so, we may usefully distinguish three notions of forgiveness.

First, Christ is reported to have said that the number of times one should forgive a person is seventy times seven. While one may debate whether this means that one should forgive no matter what, the spirit of the point certainly seems to be that generally speaking forgiving is a good independent of how the person forgiven may be affected.

Perhaps this is because it is only in forgiving that we exhibit a strength of character that is not otherwise exhibited. One way to live in the shadow of evil is to hold on to the wrongs that one has suffered. By forgiving, one rises above the experiences of having been wronged. Forgiving enables us to keep at the forefront of our lives the good of which human beings are capable, whereas not forgiving keeps at the forefront the evil of which human beings are capable. Or, perhaps the idea is that none of us is perfect. And just as this or that person has wronged us, there is simply no doubt whatsoever that we have wronged or will wrong others. The mistake of wronging others is an unfortunate part of the fabric of humanity. Alas, it is often possible to wrong people, by unwittingly offending them for example, without even being aware that we have done so. Thus, persons exhibit considerable arrogance in thinking that they will never stand in need of forgiveness from others; accordingly, in being willing to forgive another, persons exhibit an appropriate measure of humility with respect to the flaws, seen or unseen, of their own character. The text commonly referred to as the Lord's Prayer suggests this line of thought: 'Forgive us our debts as we forgive our debtors ... For if ye forgive men their trespasses. Your heavenly Father will forgive you' (Matthew 6:12, 14).

We might bring these two views together as follows. Although it is a characteristic feature of human beings that we all make mistakes, and do what is wrong, it is true nonetheless that each human being is capable of enormous goodness. Without ignoring the human capacity for wrongdoing, forgiveness keeps in place a vision of the human capacity for doing what is good. Let us call forgiveness of this sort humanitarian forgiveness, because forgiveness here is essentially tied to a certain conception of human beings and much less to what the wrongdoer does afterwards. In particular, humanitarian forgiveness does not in any way require a contrite apology on the part of the wrongdoer or that the wrongdoer makes restitution.[4]

While humanitarian forgiveness is perhaps most closely associated with Christianity, it should be mentioned that Judaism can also be seen as embracing this form of forgiveness, or something close to it. In the book of Proverbs, written by the Jewish icon King Solomon, we find the following passage: 'If thine enemy be hungry, give him bread to eat; if he be thirsty give him water to drink. For thou shall heap coals of fire upon his head, and the Lord shall reward thee' (25:21–22).

In any event, on the humanitarian view of forgiveness, it is not so much that persons are worthy of forgiveness, about which I shall say more later, as it is that there is something wrong in not forgiving others, whether they apologize or not, since committing wrongdoing is a part of the human condition. With respect to the topic at hand, namely forgiveness and the Shoah, this is an extremely acute point because, as both Thomas Nagel and Margaret Urban Walker have observed, the reason why most of us have not committed Nazi-like behavior against some group or the other is owing not so much to strength of character on our part as to the simple reality that we have been fortunate enough not to have lived in a society with such a despicable moral climate. Raised in a despicable moral climate, most of us would unthinkingly commit the unspeakable. This point by Nagel and Walker is roundly confirmed by Jonathan Glover's recent book *Humanity: A Moral History of the Twentieth Century.*[5]

Many would insist that the account of humanitarian forgiveness offered is unacceptable. They would insist that even humanitarian forgiveness is appropriate only if the transgressor has acknowledged and expressed sorrow for his wrongdoing, maintaining that there is something fulsome rather than virtuous about forgiving the person who shows no remorse at all for the wrong that she or he has done. Perhaps. What should be noted, though, is that humanitarian forgiveness does not require that the transgressor be trusted again. Humanitarian forgiveness is perfectly compatible with never interacting with the wrongdoer again.

Let me at this juncture briefly distinguish between mercy and forgiveness. Clearly, one can show mercy by way of forgiveness. However, one need not; for even humanitarian forgiveness is compatible with insisting that a person pay the moral debt that she or he owes on account of the wrong done. To forgive is to forswear resentment. It is not, on that account alone, to revoke punishment or any other form of moral debt. By contrast, one can show mercy where no wrong has been committed. Minimally, mercy is the enforcement of a less stringent set of standards or demands than one is entitled to enforce; and while this may be in connection with wrongdoing against others, this need not be the case. The Bible (such as Proverbs 14:21; Daniel 4:27), for example, occasionally speaks of being merciful to the poor. It is not so much that the poor have wronged others, as it is that they have not always measured up. In forgiving, that is, forswearing resentment, a person may also set aside requirements of punishment, which accounts for the affinity between forgiveness and mercy. However, it does not follow, as a matter of logic, that punishment or repayment must be set aside.

Second, taking the wrongdoer back as a member of good standing in the community is yet another form of forgiveness. I shall refer to this conception as restoration forgiveness. The good here consists in the restoration of mutual bonds of trust. Typically restoration forgiveness is ineluctably tied to the transgressor having, at the very least, acknowledged, shown sufficient contrition, and sincerely apologized for the wrong that she committed. In some cases the transgressor might be expected to make amends or a suitable gesture in that direction. But, of course, there are wrongs for which amends are not possible. Nothing brings back a life. Nothing restores the damage that a child has suffered who has been systematically abused sexually by a loved one. Yet even where amends are not possible, acknowledgement on the part of the transgressor along with extraordinary contrition and sorrow are. Unlike humanitarian forgiveness, restoration forgiveness is quite explicitly something of which a person can be either worthy or unworthy. Restoration forgiveness seems to be utterly out of the question for the person who shows no contrition whatsoever for the wrong that she did. And certainly not if the person were to insist that she would act in the exact same manner if she had it to do all over again. Interestingly, then, restoration forgiveness would not seem to be the kind of forgiveness that either Solomon had in mind when he spoke of feeding one's enemy or Jesus when he spoke of forgiving a person 490 times or loving one's enemy.

Third, there is also the view that forgiving others for the wrongs that one has suffered at their hands is simply the best way to get on with one's own life. Following Howard McGary,[6] I shall refer to this view as self-interested forgiveness. One may think of self-interested forgiveness as taking the insight of humanitarian forgiveness and merely applying it relentlessly to one's own life: nothing is gained by dwelling upon one's misfortunes. In fact, much is lost. And it is irrelevant that the misfortunes turn out to be due to the wrongdoings of others. What is more, there is the poignant point that in not forgiving the wrongdoer, that person scores a double victory: first the harm of the wrong itself and then the harm that comes from our preoccupation with it. Self-interested forgiveness involves a good, namely that one is better able to live one's life with the appropriate richness and meaning if one puts the wrong entirely behind one. Significantly, this line of thought does not in any way diminish the wrong that one has suffered. It allows that what happened to one is just as horrible as one has made it out to be. Rather, it merely insists that forgiving is in one's interest because it will facilitate getting on with one's life. One might argue that there is not much difference between self-interested forgiveness and what we refer to nowadays as 'letting go,' which may raise questions regarding the propriety of the term forgiveness, particularly since there is a multitude of ways in which a person may bring it about that she or he simply 'lets go.' That said, it should be noted that a self-interested conception of forgiveness is compatible with strength of character. After all, doing what is in one's own best interest often requires considerable self-discipline. As McGary conceives of it, this conception of forgiveness is not about resorting to brainwashing techniques, but finding the wherewithal to put behind one the wrong that one has been dealt. So both McGary and Murphy agree that how a person forswears resentment is relevant to whether we have forgiveness or not, although it is not clear whether Murphy would accept McGary's self-interested conception of forgiveness.

When all is said and done, it must be acknowledged that surely sometimes 'letting go' is really the best thing that a person could do for her- or himself, regardless of whatever other considerations could be marshaled in favor of doing so. Or, as may be more likely the case, the most personally persuasive argument for putting a wrong behind one may be none other than the fact that failing to do so is very much to one's detriment. And when this is the case, it may not matter if strictly speaking what we have is forgiveness or not. It should nonetheless be noted that self-interested forgiveness has one thing in common with humanitarian forgiveness, namely that neither requires trusting the wrongdoer again. And to those who think that forgiveness necessarily requires some remorse, the account of self-interested forgiveness makes the significant point that holding out for remorse may turn out to do the very person wronged more harm than good. Without denying that remorse on the part of the wrongdoer would be a good thing, the account merely points out that not forgiving until remorse is forthcoming may simply not be in the victim's interest.

Although these three notions of forgiveness are conceptually independent of one another, they are formally compatible with one another. Or more precisely, in the wake of humanitarian forgiveness either self-interested forgiveness or restoration forgiveness or both could follow. That is, a person whose forgiveness is motivated entirely by humanitarian considerations could nonetheless enjoy the benefits of either of the other two notions of forgiveness. Likewise, a person whose forgiving is motivated entirely by self-interested considerations could enjoy the good of restoration forgiveness and conversely. By contrast, if a person's forgiving of another is motivated entirely by either self-interested or restoration considerations, then the individual cannot exhibit humanitarian forgiveness.

Now it might be thought that humanitarian forgiveness must entail restoration forgiveness, otherwise we do not have genuine forgiveness. But not so. Suppose that Lani Schmitt was an unfaithful wife. She had a one-night stand; this event rendered her pregnant; and she decided to keep the child. The husband, let us imagine, had been in the hospital for six months, so it is out of the question that he might have fathered the child. Now, suppose that the husband, Floris, wants a divorce because he is absolutely devastated by it all. He may forgive her and yet want a divorce. The husband holds merely that Lani, in deciding to have this 'love-child,' has embarked upon a course of life of which he does not want to be a part. His concern in getting a divorce is not to destroy either her reputation or financial standing, but simply to disentangle himself from her life. To this end, they agree on a most amicable means for dividing things, and the husband then moves to another part of Europe and launches a new career. Lani's name comes up frequently in his business meetings; and he always speaks highly of her. In fact, when it is learned by someone that they were once married, this comes as quite a surprise. Moreover, when Floris learns that Lani is marrying Jacov, he (the former husband) is truly happy for the both of them. He does not think that Jacov is making a mistake because Lani is a person of low moral character. Quite the contrary: the former husband is very confident that she will never be unfaithful to Jacov. There can be no doubt whatsoever that the former husband has forgiven her, although he insisted upon the dissolution of their marriage. Just so, we do not have restoration forgiveness here.

Humanitarian and not restoration forgiveness? It might seem, with the Lani Schmitt story, that surely we have the latter. Perhaps things are too amicable, as I have told the story. Let us understand, though, that Lani Schmitt definitely wanted to stay in the marriage and that it is Floris who insisted upon the divorce. He is not willing to trust her in his life again, although he can say that she is trustworthy. He is not friends with her; nor does he want to be. And make no mistake: it is Floris's relocating that made it possible for him to gain sufficient emotional distance from what happened. Most people so betrayed do not get to start a new life elsewhere. What is more, we all know intellectually that a single act of infidelity does not entail that a person is morally bankrupt. Just so, such behavior generally wounds us for ever. Floris's behavior and manner merely reflect the first truth, whereas most of us are sufficiently wounded that we cannot bring ourselves to acknowledge that truth about the person.

The above discussion of Floris sheds some light on why humanitarian forgiveness is often thought, albeit mistakenly, to require restoration forgiveness. It perhaps happens often enough that when a person claims to have forgiven an individual but refuses to restore the individual to the community that the person is in fact holding a grudge against the individual. Generally, when a person holds a grudge against an individual, then the actual wrong which that individual committed is accorded a relevance that is out of all proportion to the reality of things. The grudge holder typically looks for reasons to discount the individual's character. Thus, in our example, suppose that Floris thought it obvious that Lani's single instance of unfaithfulness to him is a very good sign that she could not be trusted in matters of finances; and he took every opportunity available to him in order to raise doubts about her character in this regard. Needless to say, this would be a case of his holding a grudge against his former wife; for we know that sexual infidelity, as such, let alone a single instance of it, has nothing whatsoever to do with financial competence. Likewise, if Floris were to make a point of trying to convince Jacov that Lani's single instance of infidelity shows her to be of despicable moral character. Clearly, though, this is not at all the case in the story that I have told regarding the former husband. Hence, we can see that humanitarian forgiveness, not holding a grudge, and not restoring a person to the community are not just all formally compatible; all three can be simultaneously realized in practice.

It might also be thought that if a person is worthy of forgiveness, then he is entitled to it. But this line of reasoning is also mistaken. There are lots of things that a person morally ought to do on behalf of others which cannot be explicated in terms of others being entitled to have such things done for them. Or, to put the point another way, a person can be morally indecent without violating anyone's rights. Most significantly, a person can be morally indecent in insisting on what she or he in fact has an unquestionable right to. Here is a simple example.

Suppose that José, a man of more than sufficient means, lends Imani $100, which Imani promises to pay in full two weeks later. In the meantime, Imani learns that his daughter will be inducted into the International Honor Society for undergraduate majors in biology; and he would like to purchase for her the induction robe that the inductees wear, which costs $100. Imani explains this to José and asks José if he could have an additional two weeks to pay him. Certainly, Imani has no right against José that José should give him an additional two weeks to repay the $100. Yet, if anything is clear, it is clear that José should give Imani the additional two weeks that he has requested for repaying the loan. This is because José has no need of the money and Imani obviously has a very good reason for requesting the extension. José ought to do for Imani what Imani is not in any way entitled to José's doing for him. It would in fact be utterly mean of José not to do so. Although Imani is eminently worthy of this kindness on José's part, it is true nonetheless that he, Imani, is not in any way entitled to it. We can be worthy of that to which we are not entitled. There can be moral reasons for acting on behalf of another, without that person being entitled to such behavior. If restoration forgiveness is understood in this way, then there is no tension at all between the views that a person cannot be entitled to restoration forgiveness, yet it can be wrong – even deeply insensitive – not to forgive, because the person is worthy of it.

That said, let me be clear that the general premise here is not that one always does what is wrong in not giving a person that of which he is worthy, but to which he does not have an entitlement right. If José had decided to take an extraordinary vacation that depleted his funds, Imani would still be worthy of an extension.

3. Time's Arrow: Forgiveness and Contrition

The saying is that time heals all wounds. This is probably false. All the same, time is surely a relevant factor in our coming to forgive another. It is important to understand why.

Both McGary and Murphy make the extremely important point that forgiveness seems entirely inappropriate immediately after one has suffered an egregious wrong. Surely there is something right about this. The very idea of immediately forgiving the murder of one's child seems repugnant beyond words, whatever one's conception of forgiveness might be. But why is that if forgiveness is a virtue? The answer in part lies with the fact that forgiveness is unlike other virtues in that by definition it is a response to the agent who has willfully performed a wrong to one; and the proper psychological response should never be that of having a favorable attitude toward one's wrongdoer with respect to the wrong done to one, but rather an unfavorable one. This is just a simple psychological point regarding how persons act towards an outcome judged to be unfavorable with respect to their lives, namely that human beings are not pleased about the occurrence of unfavorable outcomes (taken in and of themselves). If, for instance, a person from North America had been eagerly planning to witness the light display at the Eiffel Tower to usher in the year 2000 and the trip had to be canceled owing to extraordinarily violent weather, it would make no sense at all if the person were nonetheless pleased about this outcome (taken in and of itself). And if the person showed any delight at all over this, we would think that something was amiss with the person's psychological make-up. To be sure, we would expect the person to get on with his life and, naturally enough, to put this behind him. Still, if he were not sad upon learning that the trip would not take place something would be amiss, however wonderful his life might be otherwise. This has to do with what we might call the psychological saliency of the moment. If our traveler is at the airport hoping to make the trip and, as it happens, the trip is canceled, then what is certainly quite psychologically salient at that moment is just the fact that the trip has been canceled. If six months later this cancelation were to remain psychologically salient, that would portend considerable stagnation in his life.

Returning to forgiveness, when a person has been wronged by someone, this is what has become psychologically salient at the moment. What is more, this is what we would expect of a psychologically healthy individual, just as we would expect the cancelation of the trip to be psychologically salient for our traveler. Accordingly, just as the psychological saliency of the trip's cancelation makes being immediately happy not a viable option for our traveler, the psychological saliency of having just been wronged makes immediate forgiveness not a viable option for the person who has been transgressed. Or so it is in the typical case of wrongdoing.

Jesus is reported to have asked for the forgiveness of those who were crucifying him even as he was in agony on the cross. A very similar claim is made on behalf of some of his followers, some of whom welcomed death. In these cases, the person in question fervently believed that either the redemption of others or his own redemption was necessarily secured by virtue of the wrong that he was suffering at the hands of others. This, as it were, takes the sting out of the psychological saliency of being wronged. Thus, the wrongs suffered in these cases are quite different from the wrongs that people typically suffer. This is because nothing redemptive is thought to be inexorably tied to being an object of the wrong in question, in the way that Christ's suffering is understood to have been. Hence, there is nothing to take the sting out of the psychological saliency of being wronged.

Now, there is another way in which time is relevant to diminishing the psychological saliency of having been wronged. I shall call this the base-line of recovery consideration. It is not possible to predict how a wrong – even a serious wrong – will impact upon a victim's life. Some individuals are utterly derailed by a serious wrong done to them; whereas others rebound from such a wrong in absolutely stunning ways. But it generally takes time before it is clear as to what the impact will be. Suppose that two people, Marc and Jamilla, are wrongfully dismissed from their equally high-paying jobs with a computer firm. Marc goes into a deep depression, loses his home, and his marriage fails. Fifteen years later, he is living on the streets as a 'rag man.' Not so for Jamilla. She establishes her own business; and fifteen years later that business turns out to be an extraordinary success – so much so that she is able to buy the firm for which she once worked. Both have been wronged and equally so. Yet, whereas Marc has never recovered from the wrong done to him, and so has remained for ever below the base-line of recovery, Jamilla has far exceeded the base-line of recovery, surpassing whatever expectations she might have had with her former employment. It would not be at all surprising if Marc were bitter over what happened to him. His not being able to forgive the person who wrongfully dismissed him would at the very least be quite understandable. By contrast, if Jamilla were bitter towards the person who wronged her – supposing he is still with the computer firm – this would be rather surprising. Indeed, if at this point she went after her old boss, just for the sake of doing so, her behavior would be more properly characterized as vengeance rather than justice delayed.

As is clear, what is absolutely relevant in Jamilla's case is not just that time has passed, since the same has happened with Marc also, but that she has done so well in spite of the wrong that her former boss did to her. Yet, it is not just the fact that she has done so well. For suppose that upon being dismissed by her boss at the computer firm, she had been immediately hired as a CEO at ten times her former salary. Once more, she has far exceeded the base-line of recovery. Notwithstanding this incredible good fortune, though, we might yet expect her to be more than a little angry over the wrong that had been done to her. In view of having just been wronged, certainly her good fortune would not, in and of itself, constitute a reason to forgive her former computer boss.

In fact, I have not argued at all that good fortune constitutes a reason for forgiving. Rather, I have argued that good fortune, as determined by the base-line of recovery, serves to diminish the psychological saliency of the wrong done to one. However, as the example of Jamilla shows, not even good fortune does so all at once.

Perhaps nothing better illustrates the importance of the passing of time with regard to forgiveness than the fact that it is only with the passing of time that certain acts of repentance seem credible. Some wrongful behavior is owing to a weakness

of the moment or a confusion of thought or some such thing. The be
keeping with the person's character, and so does not reveal the
someone of low moral character. By contrast, some wrongful beh
the very essence of a person's character. This is what a person does if ne ...
kind of character. What is more, some wrongdoing may reveal enormous
deliberation, determination and defiance of moral decency. It is not possible that the
person could have just accidentally committed the wrong in question. With wrongs
of this latter type, it is implausible to think that the wrongdoer could have a change
of heart shortly after having committed the wrong in question. Why this is so shall
become clear in the discussion that follows.

In 1963, the late Governor George Wallace stood in a schoolhouse door in
defiance of integration at the University of Alabama.[7] If, just a week later, he had
claimed a change of heart this would have been rightly greeted with complete
incredulity. Why? Because a person that is strongly committed to racial inequality
does not just have a change of heart in the absence of an extraordinarily riveting
experience. Wallace did not just happen along as the National Guard was trying to
integrate the University of Alabama; rather, he made a point of going to the
university in order to defy them. Recall that Saul of Tarsus on his way to Damascus
to persecute Christians does not simply change his mind; rather, he has an
extraordinarily riveting experience. The biblical story recounts that he was knocked
off his horse and chastened by none other than Jesus himself. Although Wallace did
not have a Paul-like moment, it is clear that, over the course of the two decades that
followed his defiant stance, he had a genuine change of heart. Some think that this
change of heart was brought on by the 1972 would-be assassin whose bullet left
Wallace paralyzed. In any case, many were persuaded of his change. Quite
significantly, many blacks of Alabama were. And thus with their support, he was
elected in 1982 to a fourth term as governor of Alabama. Still, the man who came
to recant his racist views and to be accepted by blacks as a friend would, with good
reason, not have been believed in 1963 if he had recanted his racist views just after
having defiantly stood in the door of the schoolhouse in opposition to integration.

Amazingly, what we have in this instance is not just humanitarian forgiveness on
the part of the blacks of Alabama, but restoration forgiveness. For in electing him to
the governorship, they trusted him as chief officer of the state to be properly
responsive to their interests.

In 1997, the bishops of France issued a Declaration of Repentance in France's
leading and prestigious newspaper, *Le Monde*. The bishops apologized for their
silence – the 'morbid silence' of which Wiesel spoke. This is the 'morbid silence'
that bespoke a complete complicity with Hitler's view that the world would be
better off without Jews – a people who were seen by many as having committed
deicide and, therefore, deserving of some form of divine punishment. This was not
a silence born of fear or confusion. It was a willful silence, tied to a massive
ideological framework,[8] that expressed approbation of what was being done, though
perhaps with the relief that the real dirty work – namely the actual killing of Jews –
was being done by Hitler. For in the words of John-Paul II, this 'morbid silence' was
born of certain

erroneous and unjust interpretations of the New Testament concerning the Jewish people

and their supposed culpability [for the death of Christ] that had enjoyed acceptance for far
too long which gave rise to sentiments of hostility towards the Jewish people.

These interpretations of the New Testament have been entirely and definitely rejected.[9]

Accordingly, had the bishops of France issued a Declaration of Repentance in
1950 this would have been seen as merely a mockery of justice – adding an insult
to injury. There would have been no reason – no series of events that would have
made it plausible – to think that in the few intervening years the ideological
framework that had given rise to that silence had somehow been dismantled or even
rattled. But not so, however, in 1997. Starting with Vatican II, especially, the
Catholic Church made a concerted effort to distance itself from its earlier
conception of Jews as a morally bankrupt people, referring to them, instead, as the
elder brothers of the Christian people. Rather than continuing to look with disdain
upon Jews for failing to become Christians, the Catholic Church began to
acknowledge its indebtedness to them. Like a glacier moving to the ocean, the
Catholic Church had changed its course bit by bit, resulting in an entirely different
direction in the end. And it is precisely this change of course at the very center of
power in the Catholic Church that made it possible for the Declaration of
Repentance issued by the bishops of France to be taken by Jews as a genuine act of
contrition.

On 23 March 2000, Pope John-Paul II stood in Yad Vashem and begged for
forgiveness from the Jewish people. The Catholic Church had indeed become a
different institution.

A significant change of heart (for the better in this case) typically takes time
because it involves a change in a complex nexus of beliefs which have to be
unraveled and replaced. One does not just stop believing that a given group of
people is inferior, but that belief regarding this group is replaced by another belief.
What is more, the belief that a group of people is inferior involves a complex set of
beliefs about the nature of that inferiority, its manifestations, false positives (that is,
instances where a member of the inferior group does not appear inferior), and the
appropriate responses to both the displays of inferiority and the members of the
group in general. Thus, the Catholic Church did not simply desist in its claim that
Jews were a morally corrupt people for failing to believe in Christ as the Messiah,
but it replaced that belief with the view of Jews as the elder brothers of the Christian
people. Given its own interpretation of Christianity, the Catholic Church could not
simply ignore Jews. It needed a way to accord standing to the Jewish people, all the
while gesturing towards an acceptance of the difference between Judaism and
Christianity. The language of brothers allows for both unity and independence of
thought.

Of course, what is equally relevant to a change of heart for the better is an
acknowledgement that one has done wrong. The Catholic Church did not simply
cease advocating its negative conception of Jews, but it acknowledged that it had
advanced such a conception of Jews and it acknowledged the wrong of this.

I began this section by talking about the psychological saliency of being
wronged. While I did not make the point explicitly, it stands to reason that the
greater the wrong, the greater the psychological saliency. If while walking together
both Jacques and Jorn were victims of an armed robbery, but Jorn was brutally

beaten, we expect the psychological saliency of being wronged to be greater for Jorn than for Jacques. And the greater the psychological saliency of the wrong, the more time it might take for the saliency of the wrong to diminish. So much seems obvious, at least intuitively. But the surprise seems to be this: the more heinous a wrongdoing turns out to be, and so the more the wrong reflects a depraved moral character, then the more time is needed before we are able to believe that the transgressor is capable of genuine contrition. This means that accepting an immediate apology for heinous behavior is completely out of the question, because the apology from the wrongdoer could not be credible. A weak moment of character might very well explain why someone stole a candy bar; it will certainly not explain why someone tortured a child.

This last point holds even if the wrong itself stands as a powerful catalyst for a change for the better on the part of the wrongdoer. Typically, the victim still needs to experience this change. Or so it is unless there is some powerful event that enables the victim to compensate for not experiencing such a change on the part of the wrongdoer. Notice that in the change from Saul to Paul, where he is sent to abide with Ananias for a time, Ananias's worry is that this is precisely the man that used to harm 'the saints of Jerusalem.' And the text reads that Ananias is informed by the Lord himself that '[Paul] is a chosen vessel unto me [the Lord], to bear my name before the Gentiles' (Acts 9:15). There was no time for Ananias to experience Saul as Paul; and a vision directly from the Lord enables Ananias to traverse the psychological gulf between the persona of Saul and the persona of Paul.

4. Adolph Paul-Damascus

Can we have it both ways? On the one hand, can we accept and admire the Catholic Church – the bishops of France and Pope John-Paul II – for acknowledging the immoral role which it played during the Holocaust and then begging the Jewish people for forgiveness? On the other, can we insist that a person like Adolph Paul-Damascus must not be forgiven, under any circumstances whatsoever? First of all, it must be remembered, as was just noted (Section 3), that the silence of the Catholic Church was born of a deep ideological framework that expressed approbation for what Hitler was doing to the Jews. Second, whether or not an act and an omission which has the very same consequences are morally equivalent, it is clear that an omission is nonetheless wrong (even if less wrong than the outright act itself) if that omission is born of the desire to see the other harmed. And in the case at hand, we have not just a wrong but a grave wrong. It is an indisputable fact that the behavior of both, the deportation of the Jews by Paul-Damascus and the 'morbid silence' on the part of the Catholic Church, issued from the very same morally bankrupt vision of the Jews.

The fact that Paul-Damascus is directly responsible for sending Jews to their death, whereas the Catholic Church, as it were, watched in silence, perhaps thinking the outcome appropriate, is a difference that does not give us a substantial moral difference with respect to forgiving one and not the other.[10] To see the point in a different context, suppose that a Ku Klux Klansman murdered my child, and my law-abiding neighbor, seeing the murder take place, simply chose not to get involved in any way. Many years later, it might very well be easier to forgive the Klansman who repented and went on to live a life of great contrition than my neighbor. (Legally, of course, this is another matter entirely.) Despicable people behave despicably. But how does one trust a supposedly decent person who behaves in an utterly despicable manner (and so not in any way out of fear for his well-being) by simply doing nothing at all about the horror taking place before his very eyes? I should never want to see that person again. And heaven forbid if this neighbor were ever to say to me 'Well, you know, LT, it is that repentant Klansman who murdered your child. Why are you so vexed with me who never laid a hand upon your darling child?' The fact that it is my child hardly explains all of the example's moral force. For if it were another person's child instead, my first thought would certainly not be that at least my child is safe with the neighbor.

Now, there are important moral differences, to be sure, between the Catholic Church and Adolph Paul-Damascus. To begin with, the Church is an institution, whereas Paul-Damascus is a person. What is more, John-Paul II did not himself stand in silence as Jews were being killed. Quite the contrary, he actually aided Jews. Likewise, the Declaration of Repentance was issued by the bishops of France, most of whom did not themselves participate in the 'morbid silence' of the Vichy era. Indeed, for the most part those who were silent are now dead. If we attach great weight to these differences, then we effectively render otiose the very acts that are regarded as marvelous acts of contrition. After all, although one can be extremely sad over (sorry about) someone else's loss, one cannot be contrite about that loss if one had nothing whatsoever to do with its coming about. This is so even if the loss was caused by a family member. Thus, the statement by Jankélévitch, given at the outset of this paper, proves to be a double-edge sword. Just as it is true that the dead cannot forgive, it is equally true that the dead cannot seek forgiveness.

However, in their 1997 Declaration of Repentance, the bishops of France were very clear: 'We confess our faults … We seek God's forgiveness; and we beseech the Jewish people to hear our words of repentance.' Likewise, Pope John-Paul II was equally clear: 'The Catholic Church wishes to express her profound pain in the face of the weaknesses of her sons and daughters of every age. This is an act of repentance … ' It is incontrovertible that both statements are to be understood as a confession of the wrongs committed by the Catholic Church understood as an institution, and a request by the Church as an institution to be forgiven for those wrongs. What is more, the world perceived things in this way. On behalf of the institution, men of character confessed the faults of the Catholic Church and sought forgiveness from the Jewish people for them. No one – absolutely no one – took either the bishops or the Pope to be seeking personal forgiveness. What is more, the sincerity of these words of contrition is hardly in doubt.

I shall not here attempt to offer an account of institutions.[11] Interestingly, the most significant difference with regard to the difference between institutions and individuals, especially as it pertains to the Catholic Church, is that it is not clear what it would mean to punish the Church for its wrongdoing during the Shoah. Nor, for that matter, is it clear the Church could do anything analogous to turning itself in to the authorities. I shall come back to this momentarily. What I want to draw attention to, now, is the incontrovertible fact that the contrition displayed, the requests for forgiveness made, and the response of others, including many, many Jews, were all *as if* the Catholic Church itself had moral agency. A philosophical account may show us that it is a mistake to respond here *as if* the Catholic Church had moral agency. However, it seems rather unlikely that at the phenomenological level we could actually respond otherwise. Between Pope Pius XII and Pope John-Paul II, what we have is not just two very different popes, but an unequivocal change in the Catholic Church regarding its attitude towards Jews, a change that had its origins in the work of Pope John XXIII.[12] No one could have foreseen that the papacy of John-Paul II, building upon the work of Pope John XXIII and Pope Paul VI, would have brought about such a dramatic and official change on the part of the Catholic Church with regard to its attitude towards Jews. If, in 1950, anyone would have said to Jews that one day the Catholic Church would apologize for its behavior during the Holocaust, this would have been greeted with utter incredulity.

Likewise, no one could have foreseen that a man called Adolph Paul-Damascus would one day not only come to have great contrition for what he did to the Jews, as a member of Hitler's army, but that he would in fact freely and anonymously give to Jewish causes the considerable fortune that he had amassed. Thus in a manner quite analogous to the transition of the Church: no one could have foreseen that this very man would one day become a person of considerable moral character. To be sure, his evil past will always haunt him. This poignant truth, however, should not be confused with the false thesis, namely that his evil past for ever renders him an evil person. Notice that the Church, too, will always be haunted by its past.

At this juncture, let me return to a point mentioned in the introduction. The most formidable obstacle to forgiveness should not be that there has been an irreplaceable loss (as such), but rather our doubts regarding the sincerity of the wrongdoer's contrition. Irreplaceable losses can happen in many ways. As we know, during World War II many parents lost their sons in battle – sons who fought on the morally right side. Yet, we do not expect these parents to bemoan continually the loss of their sons. Significantly, we expect these parents to take comfort in the fact that their sons died for a just cause. But surely this is not because – surely no one would dare suggest it – the lives of these young men were less irreplaceable than the lives of victims of the Shoah. And while it may be true that some of these young men willingly fought the good fight, this truth does not change the fact that their deaths constitute an irreplaceable loss. If a mother and father failed to grieve profoundly the loss of their son because, after all, he willingly chose to fight the good fight, that would be absolutely incomprehensible to us, however much pride they might have in the courage that he displayed. Quite significantly, what has most embittered parents who have lost a son in battle is not so much the death of their son, but the failure of the government to recognize in the proper way that death. Time and time again, what most concerns us in the face of the death of a loved one is that others show the appropriate moral response – one which will vary according to context and the actors involved.

Of course, when the death is owing to a wrongdoing – heinous murder, in particular – on the part of another, the only appropriate moral response on that person's part is deep, deep contrition. It is poignantly true, to be sure, that no amount of contrition will bring back a life. But does it follow from this that, in the case of heinous willful murder, it is for ever appropriate to reject contrition out of hand? For reasons that were advanced in Section 3, immediate contrition can be generally rejected out of hand, since not enough time will have passed for there to have been a change in the structure of the murderer's moral character. This truth, though, should not be confused with a different claim, namely that never enough time could pass for there to be a sufficient change in the structure of a murderer's moral character.

In the case of heinous murder, what is needed is not just contrition, but contrition continuously and freely lived. That is, we need to see that the person has, as it were, willingly taken on the pain that he has caused others by his heinous act of murder. He is not just moved when he sees the anguish that he has caused the dead person's loved ones and friends. Rather, owing to his own assessment of things, he is distraught because it disgusts him that this wrongdoing is attributable to him. And though he is free to do otherwise, he seeks by word and deed to dissociate himself from this horrendous deed of his past – not by denying it, but by forging a path of behavior that is as incompatible as any could be with his past wrongful behavior. With deep sensitivity to the wrong that he has done, he freely chooses to live in ways that will insure that his future self could never commit the horrendous wrong committed by his past self. So far so good, except that one is inclined to say that such a person cannot have it both ways: if he is genuinely contrite, then he should freely choose to turn himself in to the proper authorities; and the fact that he does not freely make this choice suffices to show that he is not that contrite after all. Yet, if the person turns himself in to the authorities, the opportunity for contrition freely lived will be foreclosed if the heinous murderer is executed. And with prison walls, it is not so much that a person could not be genuinely contrite as it is that the circumstances for the appearance of contrition are notoriously overdetermined. For the heinous murderer who does not turn himself in, a pall of doubt is initially cast over the sincerity of his contrition in virtue of this fact alone, whatever else he might do.

It is here that we get a most interesting difference between the institution of the Catholic Church and Adolph Paul-Damascus. The Catholic Church did not go into hiding; and the possibility of its turning itself in to an authority did not exist.[13] Nor, again, is it clear what it would have meant to punish the Church. To be sure, the Vatican is a sovereign state of considerable influence; and there can be formal diplomatic ties between it and other states. All the same, because it is essentially a spiritual state, the Vatican is clearly in many respects a state quite unlike other states. Accordingly, there are moral obstacles to destroying the Vatican that no modern state would wish to engage.[14] No doubt this is part of the explanation for why there does not seem to be the thought that the Church should in some way be punished for the wrongs that it committed during the Shoah.

Ironically, then, what seems to call into question the sincerity of Adolph Paul-Damascus's contrition arises in large measure from just that fact that he is not an institution, and so did not do what, as an individual, he could have done, and should perhaps have immediately done, namely turned himself in. But we need to proceed cautiously here.

First of all, it need not be true that the only appropriate response for a wrongdoer is to turn himself in. When it comes to the Shoah, the subject-matter has come to be so emotionally charged that such a thought almost seems blasphemous. But as is brilliantly illustrated by Bernhard Schlink in his Holocaust novel *The Reader* (which is about a male adolescent who discovers that the woman with whom he had a six-month affair during his youth was a war criminal),[15] there are human complexities that defy simple patterns. In the case of Paul-Damascus, it is very easy to think that surely he deserved to die. However, even this seemingly simple but weighty moral judgment is not without complexity. For suppose that he had killed himself, *à la* Judas, leaving a note as to why he did so. Surely many would be dissatisfied with this, though they have just what they want, namely his death, born of his having a deep sense of wrong that he had wrought. On the basis of what, though, would there be this dissatisfaction, given that he killed himself owing to a profound sense of guilt? This question is particularly poignant, since the three monotheistic traditions hold that a person commits a greater harm, from the standpoint of divine judgment, in killing himself than in submitting to punishment by death.

In any case, even if it is true that Paul-Damascus's failure to turn himself in initially casts some doubt upon the sincerity of his contrition, it does not follow from this that we thereby have in perpetuity a reason to doubt his contrition. From the fact that one initially had reason to doubt a person's sincerity, it surely does not follow that, thereby, one always has a reason to do so. That, obviously, depends on what else the person goes on to do. The admitted and deplorable wrong of not turning himself in does not thereby taint all else that Adolph Paul-Damascus went on to do, freely and anonymously, on behalf of Jews.

Besides, as I have told the story, precisely what Paul-Damascus did go on to do was turn himself in. And arguably, we could not have any better evidence of Paul-Damascus's genuine contrition than the very fact that he turned himself in so very many years later after having lived the life that he lived. Whereas many similarly situated would have perhaps thought that they had somehow earned the right to put their hideous past entirely behind them, this is not the case with Adolph Paul-Damascus. In turning himself in, though, what he presents for examination is not just his atrocious life as a Nazi, but his entire life; and those who should judge him are not entitled to pick and choose which aspect of his life they will take into consideration. And there is a level of moral goodness, about which I shall speak shortly, which requires that they consider his entire life as it pertains to his character.

In a very nearly perfect world, there would be no crimes against humanity of which the Shoah counts as perhaps a paradigm example. However, in the face of such crimes having been committed, in the next-best world perhaps it would be possible to apprehend immediately each and every criminal when the stench of their wrongful behavior is fresh and they have had no time to present us with reasons for thinking that there was anything redeemable about their character. The issue of forgiveness would simply not arise. It is perhaps an indication of just how wicked Hitlerian Nazis were that none like Adolph Paul-Damascus appears to have been found.[16] And with each passing day, it seems most unlikely that fate will hand us an Adolph Paul-Damascus. The point, though, is that just as Paul-Damascus is so clearly not an instantiation of the first world, he is just as clearly not an instantiation of the second one either.

What is more, it will not do to discount the good that he went on to do on behalf of Jews on the grounds that this is what any Nazi might have done if only he had fifty years to get his life in order. For one thing, there is no reason whatsoever to believe that this is what any Nazi might have done; and for another, it is a fact of inestimable importance that this is what Paul-Damascus actually did. While we know that any Nazi *could* have become a contrite person of moral character of the order of Adolph Paul-Damascus, what we most certainly do not know is that any Nazi *would* have become such a person, even if he had wanted to. Why? Because with the utmost sincerity, any Nazi could have started down the moral path of contrition and upright behavior only to find himself conquered by unsavory desires, including the very Nazism he wanted to reject. With Paul-Damascus, we have a completed moral project, if you will. That others might have done like him had they not been apprehended is irrelevant in terms of acknowledging what he has done and giving him credit for it, just as it is irrelevant to our high esteem of Raoul Wallenberg that others might have done what he did.

Now, it was presumably a matter of luck that Paul-Damascus was never caught.[17] It was not, though, a matter of luck that he anonymously donated millions of dollars to Jewish charities and that his entire fortune would anonymously be bequeathed to such institutions. Nor was it a matter of luck that he turned himself in. These were acts of extraordinary strength of character. And it would be a mistake to think that the luck he had in not being caught negates these subsequent acts of character on his part. No viable moral theory will permit such a thing. And this brings me to what I believe is at the heart of the matter concerning Adolph Paul-Damascus. For in a way that I shall now try to show, there is a sense in which Paul-Damascus was too lucky.

What is troubling about Paul-Damascus is not that one doubts his contrition. Nor, therefore, is it that one doubts that he is a changed person. Rather, the problem is that he has deprived all those who opposed the evil of Hitler, Jews in particular, of the opportunity to *express moral outrage*, which is not to be confused with punishment. Parents, for example, may express moral outrage over what a child has done, without necessarily being moved to punish the child. Indeed, their expression of moral outrage may so humiliate and shame the child, that there is no need for punishment. And, of course, they will certainly forgive the child for what he has done. In fact, there may be times when the expression of moral outrage is in order and punishment out of order. Thus, for the gifted sixteen-year-old female college student who is about to graduate summa cum laude, her parents might express great moral outrage over her becoming pregnant. Punishing her, though, could be just plain silly, depending upon what that would involve.

The expression of moral outrage, like feelings of resentment, is also characteristic of having self-respect when wronged – a point of tremendous importance to the accounts of forgiveness advanced by McGary and Murphy. The outrage exposes the wrongdoer to the reality of his actions from another perspective. Intuitively, it is the difference between suffering a wrong at the hands of another and having the wrongdoer be made to witness the harm that he has caused in one's humanity from a context where one is not at his mercy. In and of itself, moral outrage seeks neither revenge nor punishment. Instead, it aims to pique the moral sensibilities of the wrongdoer. What is more, expressing moral outrage is not in any way incompatible with the wish to forgive the wrongdoer. Quite the contrary, it would seem to play a central role in leading up to restoration forgiveness; for surely the person who is to be forgiven should have a full appreciation of the wrong that he has done; otherwise, restoration forgiveness misfires. A full expression of moral outrage allows for proper forgiveness and underwrites the integrity of the person wronged. Persons who can forgive without expressing moral outrage, but with their integrity intact, are indeed saints.

Lest there be any confusion here, expressing moral outrage is certainly compatible with (having good reasons for) not forgiving a person. Forgiving the unrepentant wrongdoer may be out of order regardless of how much moral outrage has been expressed. I have merely wanted to underscore the fact that seeking to express moral outrage is fundamentally distinct from the desire either to punish or to seek revenge. When, in certain instances, the expression of moral outrage occasions sufficient humility, shame and remorse, then the desire for revenge or punishment may never materialize or be extinguished if it does.

With Paul-Damascus, there has been no occasion to look this past wrongdoer in the face – Adolph Paul-Damascus the deporter – and to let him see the anger, the hurt and the disgust people share on account of what he has done. He has deprived the moral community of the opportunity for moral outrage because expressing moral outrage, at this point in time, is inappropriate to the moral character that is quintessential to the kind of person that Adolph Paul-Damascus now is. In religion, his case is essentially tantamount to a horrendous wrongdoer who, as a result of genuine contrition, has been given a divine pardon, where that pardon is made public to all; and then the individual is anointed and sent on a heavenly mission, which of course is the story of Saul of Tarsus in the New Testament. In an instance such as this, those wronged must, for all practical purposes, simply put aside their anger and resentment. To be sure, we do not have divine intervention in the case of Adolph Paul-Damascus. However, we have no less of a dramatic change in moral character. And that is the point.

The problem, then, with Adolph Paul-Damascus is that from the standpoint of experiencing moral outrage he was indeed too lucky. For he was never made to bear witness to the wrong that he did when, from the standpoint of moral character, he was someone who identified with those heinous acts. Accordingly, people are right in thinking that there is something out of order in just letting him go. But the problem, I suggest, is not that he isn't worthy of forgiveness. After all, human beings are worthy of forgiveness provided that over time they have lived a life of sufficient contrition; and a human being will not get more worthy of forgiveness than Paul-Damascus. Forgiveness does not require that what was lost be restored. Besides, the wrong of the Shoah, and its just characterization as an unspeakable evil, consists not merely in the fact that innocent lives were lost, but that it was an affront to all Jewish people, and to humankind. Adolph Paul-Damascus has restored the fault in the moral line caused by his ignoble deeds. At any rate, my point here is that if one grants these considerations for the sake of argument, there is still something left unanswered. That something is moral outrage. It is a profound truth about the importance of human beings affirming their humanity that, in face of past heinous wrongful behavior, not even an impeccable moral character on the transgressor's part from henceforth renders otiose moral outrage towards her or him.

5. Forgiveness, Justice and Righteousness

I hold that Adolph Paul-Damascus is worthy of forgiveness – indeed, restoration forgiveness. (Or, in any case, he is worthy of being re-accepted as an upstanding member of the moral community.) I have not claimed that he is entitled to it. Nor have I claimed that it would be wrong not to forgive him. It will be recalled that, in the discussion of José and Imani, I specifically noted that one does not necessarily do what is wrong in failing to give a person that of which he is worthy, but to which he has no entitlement claim. This way of viewing forgiveness is very much in keeping with the idea that forgiveness is a moral gift, as I believe it is.

But any gift, of which the recipient may be worthy or unworthy, may be given or withheld with moral wisdom or the lack thereof.[18] And forgiveness is certainly not the exception. Clearly, where forgiveness is warranted, moral wisdom may counsel only humanitarian forgiveness rather than restoration forgiveness (or some limited form of this), as we saw in our discussion of the son with his children and their grandfather. And even humanitarian forgiveness alone may take several forms. Significantly, though, moral wisdom may counsel forgiveness though our hearts cry out for blood. Forgiveness, then, may be very much like the case of José with respect to Imani. Forgiveness is the morally decent thing to do, though there is no right to be forgiven that appears on the moral landscape. And just as we may think of José as being a less admirable person for refusing to give Imani a few extra weeks to repay the loan, we can think of a person as being less admirable for refusing to forgive someone who by word and deed has shown profound contrition. This would have been undoubtedly the case with Nelson Mandela and Archbishop Desmond Tutu, though there is no gainsaying the evil that they endured under the regime of apartheid.

A no-doubt surprising claim is that justice, like love or rage, can be blind. But blind to what? One such thing is righteousness.

Righteousness is the exemplification of the highest level of moral goodness for its very own sake, where this issues from an utterly firm trait of character. And while an act that goes beyond the call of duty may be a righteous act, this need not be so. Not all acts of supererogation are righteous and not all righteous acts are supererogatory. A person may on a whim perform an act that goes beyond the call of duty, even regretting it later. This is not righteousness. To be sure, an act of supererogation may exhibit righteousness, as presumably Mother Teresa's life beautifully illustrated. The point, though, is that such an act need not. Purity of motives is so important to the idea of righteousness that people who give all to save their family are rarely, on that account alone, referred to as righteous. On the other side, a person who adheres to a deep moral principle at great costs to himself may exemplify righteousness, although others are not made better off on account of it. A case in point might be the early Christians of Rome who suffered being thrown to the lions rather than renouncing their belief in Christianity. This was not an act of supererogation on their part; other Christians were not made better off as a result of such high moral stances. What is more, whereas an act of righteousness requires purity of motives, an act of justice does not. A person can begrudgingly act in a just manner (that is, do what is just), whereas a person cannot begrudgingly act in a righteous manner.

Interestingly, a person may exhibit righteousness in one aspect of her or his life and not another. Thus, Oscar Schindler is considered to be a righteous gentile for his efforts in saving the lives of 1,100 Jews or so. Yet, as the saying goes, Schindler was no saint otherwise, which made his unshakable commitment (once in place) to saving the lives of Jews all the more remarkable. All of this, however, simply points to what we already know, namely that no human being is wholly righteous.

At any rate, a consideration that I should like to bring out is that it is possible that justice is served but righteousness disserved. The three monotheistic religions presuppose not only that the Supreme Being is just, but that He is also righteous. That is, He exhibits a level of moral goodness and purity of heart that is not captured by justice alone. Go and aspire to be righteous – as opposed to just – is the demand that each religion makes of its adherents. Justice is not the zenith of moral goodness; righteousness is. The just person can come across as greedy or callous or indifferent.[19] But not the righteous person. And while justice may never require great sacrifices of us, righteousness can. This is why it is fitting to think of Mother Teresa or Nelson Mandela or Oscar Schindler or Raoul Wallenberg not only as just individuals, but also as righteous individuals. For the moral goodness that each exhibited in a certain morally significant context far exceeded the demands which justice could have made of them. Significantly, Mandela's righteousness is inextricably tied to his marvelous spirit of forgiveness for the hatred of the apartheid of the (old) South Africa – which for more than twenty years he had experienced first hand as a prisoner.[20]

Accordingly, from the standpoint of moral goodness, it is possible that righteousness could counsel forgiveness, whereas justice does not. This is precisely how each of the monotheistic religions characterizes its Supreme Being: one who offers forgiveness (and mercy) when he could have demanded justice. And most significantly, it is never supposed that the Supreme Being exhibits weakness of any kind in showing forgiveness (or mercy). Righteousness and only righteousness. What is more, when done in the right way, at the right time, and to the right person, forgiveness may allow for the teaching of a moral lesson that could not otherwise be taught.

From the standpoint of righteousness, it is not clear there is any act the very nature of which makes it unforgivable. That is, it is not clear that there is any act which is intrinsically unforgivable. Rather, there are acts which if performed tell us an awful lot about the kind of individual the agent is now and is likely to be in the future. The serial killer can only be understood as an individual who has a deep, deep indifference to human life, as opposed to an individual who became overly agitated and acted out of character in killing someone. Accordingly, a repentant serial killer seems to be an utter unlikelihood. Thus, it is plausible to hold that if a person is a serial killer he is highly likely to be unrepentant; and, needless to say, an unrepentant serial killer is unforgivable if anyone is. In this case, though, what is unforgivable is not being a serial killer but being an unrepentant serial killer. If contrary to all reasonable expectations, a serial killer were to become exceedingly contrite and, over time, to live a life of utter contrition, it is not at all obvious that in principle he cannot be forgiven owing to his past. It will be true, to be sure, that no amount of contrition or good deeds will bring back the lives that he has taken. However, as I have repeatedly noted, the point of forgiveness is not to restore that which was lost. Those whose have engaged systematically in deeds of wickedness rarely become individuals who are profoundly contrite over their wrongful deeds. On the one hand, though, this does not show that it is impossible for that to happen. On the other, there is no obligation in any way to wait and see if contrition will be forthcoming.

Does a son do what is wrong in forgiving his father for the sexual abuse, if the father were sufficiently repentant? Or in the case of a serial killer, suppose that such a person went on to do extraordinary missionary work even while serving a sentence of life in prison. Do family members do what is wrong in forgiving such a serial killer since, contrary to what anyone would have ever imagined, he went on to live this life of extraordinary contrition? In either of these cases, do we have some sort of moral insensibility to the wrong that was done? Do we have some defect in reasoning? I do not see that either of these questions has to be answered positively. The person(s) in question may be unable to forgive or unwilling to forgive. But this is fundamentally different from its being the case that forgiving constitutes a defect in reasoning or a display of moral insensibility to the wrong done.

Returning, then, to Adolph Paul-Damascus: to cry out for his punishment in the name of justice would be to treat his life as if it were just like the lives of other Nazis who remained for ever indifferent to the wrong they did – Himmler or Goebbels or Bormann. Yet, precisely what is true, at this point in time, is that he is not just like any other Nazi. He is, rather, a repentant Nazi who has – and as deliberately and as willfully as any human being could under the circumstances – lived a life of extraordinary contrition. He is worthy of restoration forgiveness (or at least re-acceptance as a member of full standing in the moral community). Certainly, no Holocaust survivor who would forgive can be accused of being morally insensitive to the facts of Paul-Damascus's life.

Justice, alone, may entitle us to focus simply upon the wrongs that Paul-Damascus committed. Righteousness, however, may counsel us to cast our net of moral reflection much wider. What is more, it is disingenuous to hide behind the view that forgiveness, by its very nature, is a sign of weakness or a way of condoning what was done. None of the monotheistic traditions attribute either view to divine forgiveness. Nor, again, will it do to insist that forgiveness constitutes ignoring the wrong that a person has done. This, too, has no basis in any of the monotheistic traditions; and it is utterly incompatible with the idea of restoration forgiveness. The desire to treat Paul-Damascus as a scapegoat would be perfectly understandable. Just so, this would not be the right thing to do. This last consideration no doubt points to why forgiveness is a hard virtue; for it involves surmounting hostile feelings towards another that, at the outset, one was justified in coming to have. And understandably, these feelings are just that much more acute

when they are owing to an immoral act that resulted in an irreplaceable l(
It might be claimed that the death of Paul-Damascus would result in
cosmic justice with respect to an evil of the enormity of the Shoah. Here, S(
retort in the story that I recounted at the outset is very instructive. Had Paul-
Damascus been caught hiding in South America during the 1950s, there can be little
doubt that justice would be best served by his death. But why, at this point in time,
would cosmic justice be best served by his death rather than by his continuing to
live a life of extraordinary contrition? Why would one not want to have such an
extraordinary living example?

Justice allows us to fix our gaze entirely upon the past; righteousness counsels
that, under the circumstances, the pain of the past not be allowed to have the last
word. Like all the other virtues, the virtue of forgiveness cannot be one that is
exercised only when it pleases us. Unlike the other virtues, the most admirable
exercises of the virtue of forgiveness are most likely to go beyond justice and
exemplify righteousness.

Still, although I have claimed that Adolph Paul-Damascus is worthy of
restoration forgiveness, I have not claimed that he is entitled to it. Instead, I have
argued in this section that there is a level of moral goodness to be addressed, namely
righteousness, that cannot be subsumed under considerations of justice alone. I have
suggested that in judging Paul-Damascus the standard of righteousness should be
employed. As always, we may choose not to be righteous. And sometimes we can
have a good reason for so choosing. Had Wallenberg chosen not to risk his life in
order to save Jews, surely no one could have blamed him. In the case of Adolph
Paul-Damascus, there could very well be a good reason not to exhibit righteousness
towards him. Perhaps this is psychologically impossible for some. But, alas, a good
reason for not doing so will not be that justice is the only measure of moral goodness
available to us. And that is very much moral food for moral thought.

Drawing upon Moses Maimonides' remarks regarding perfect repentance,[21]
suppose that before the Israeli Court Adolph Paul-Damascus's final remarks before
the jury convenes are as follows:

> According to Jewish tradition, the miracle of Hanukkah is that Jews survived when by all
> accounts they should have perished. Bearing this thought firmly in mind, your honor, it
> seems to me that on any reasonable account the survival of the Jewish people after the
> atrociousness of the Holocaust might very well be seen as Hanukkah Two. And I have
> devoted my entire post-Nazi life, your honor, to paying homage to this richness of the
> Jewish people. I am not worthy to be a Jew. But if in the very bowels of hell I can testify
> to their greatness, that shall be good enough for me.

6. Conclusion

This essay has been an intellectual exercise. Fortunately, it has not been a trivial
one. While clearly there has never been a Nazi war criminal like Adolph Paul-
Damascus, I have tried, in the concluding remarks which I have attributed to him,
to paint a picture of an extraordinary transformation: from an evil person to a
righteous person. No good could possibly come of punishing him in any way. Even

if justice were served, surely righteousness would not be. This intellectual exercise puts into sharp relief the moral distance a Nazi would have to travel in order to be worthy of forgiveness. Most importantly, what we have learned is not that being a Nazi war criminal is intrinsically unforgivable, but the quite different truth that no such person has ever lived a life that would make her or him even remotely a candidate for forgiveness. Obviously, nothing like a definitive argument has been presented to show that Paul-Damascus should be forgiven. But it is important to bear in mind that none could be entitled to forgiveness – not because no person like Paul-Damascus could be worthy of forgiveness, but because forgiveness, on my view, is properly understood as a moral gift. At its best, forgiveness is a moral gift of righteousness rather than justice. And this turns out to be particularly significant from the standpoint of moral education. For as a moral ideal, and for the good of society as well, it may not be enough that we teach our children of the importance of justice; it may be that we kindle their souls with a higher moral ideal, namely that of righteousness itself. After all, without the mortals here and there whom we would call righteous, there is a moral good that we would not know, and our lives would be so very much less rich on that account.

Righteousness, like justice, does not require that we ignore the evil that we see, let alone cater to it. Rather, it requires that in our staunch opposition to evil, in all its many forms, we nonetheless keep alive the hope of redemption.[22] Justice, by contrast, does not; and that is one reason why righteousness constitutes a higher form of moral goodness than does justice.[23] Alas, in relentlessly pursuing justice, it may sometimes turn out that we get that to which we are entitled even as we morally shortchange ourselves nonetheless.

Notes

1.   *Discours d'Oslo*, Paris: Bernard Grasset, 1987.
2.   'Forgiveness and Resentment,' in Jeffrie G. Murphy and Jean Hampton, *Forgiveness and Mercy*, New York: Cambridge University Press, 1988. In the same work, see also Jean Hampton's 'Forgiveness, Resentment and Hatred.' How one forswears the resentment is a fundamentally important issue. I do not offer an account of this important issue. See, also, Martha Nussbaum, *The Fragility of Goodness*, New York: Cambridge University Press, 1986. In ways that are perhaps different from what Nussbaum had in mind, this essay underscores the importance of imagination in defining the parameters of forgiveness.
3.   Alain Renaut, 'Le Crime contre l'Humanité, le Droit humanitaire et la Shoah,' *Philosophie*, Numéro 67 (2000), writes 'À partir de la Shoah … En toute rigueur historique, c'est sans doute pour la première fois en 1915 que la notion de "crime contre l'humanité" apparut expressément, après le massacre des Arméniens par les Turcks – la France, la Grande-Bretagne et la Russie publiant, le 18 mai 1915, une déclaration qui dénounce les "nouveaux crimes de la Turquie contre l'humanité et la civilisation".' I have followed Renaut in my characterization of crimes against humanity.
4.   See Hampton's introductory remarks, 'Forgiveness and Christianity,' in *Forgiveness and Mercy*. She talks about the challenge of forgiving someone who had seriously wronged her family without saying a word about the wrongdoer apologizing. I take her to be endorsing humanitarian forgiveness.

5. New Haven: Yale University Press, 1999; Thomas Nagel, *Equality and Partiality*, New York: Oxford University Press, 1992; and Margaret Urban Walker, 'Moral Luck and the Virtues of Impure Agency,' *Metaphysics* **22** (1991). See, also, Stanley Milgram, *Obedience to Authority*, New York: Harper & Row, 1974 and, of course, Daniel Jonah Goldhagen, *Hitler's Willing Executioners: Ordinary Germans and the Holocaust*, New York: Alfred A. Knopf, 1996.
6. 'Forgiveness,' *American Philosophical Quarterly* **26** (1989).
7. I am indebted here to Dan T. Carter, *The Politics of Rage: George Wallace, the Origins of the New Conservatism, and the Transformation of American Politics*, New Orleans: Louisiana State University Press, 2000.
8. For two reasons, this claim is perhaps difficult to appreciate nowadays. One is that Christianity and Catholicism are no longer synonymous as they were during Christianity's history up to the Protestant Reformation. The other is that religious tolerance is one of the marks of contemporary modern societies. But not so in times past. During Christianity's ascendancy during the Middle Ages, the Catholic Church did not abide religious tolerance; and, in particular, it often sustained an extremely hostile attitude toward the Jews. The reason for this is that, at the time, the Jews continued to present a challenge to the doctrine of Christianity, owing to Christianity's historical moorings in Judaism. As Blaise Pascal wrote: 'If the Jews had been converted by Jesus Christ, we would no longer have any suspicious testimony from them. And if they had all been exterminated, we would not have to worry about their testimony at all' (*Pensées*, Series XXIV, my translation). This line of thought is masterfully developed by Bernard Blumenkranz, *Juifs et Chrétiens dans Le Monde Occidental: 430–1096*, Paris: Imprimatur National, 1960. On the one hand, Christianity has held that Jews were special because, after all, without Judaism there would have been no Christianity. On the other, it has held that Jews were more than a little stubborn in failing to see what by their own biblical texts must be true, namely that Jesus is the Messiah. Accordingly, during the Middle Ages, the Church often regarded the Jews as a wicked people. See Joshua Trachtenberg, *The Devil and the Jews: The Conception of the Medieval Jew*, Philadelphia, PA: The Jewish Publication Society, 1988. Anti-Jewish tales often took the form of a Jew acting in a hostile manner toward an innocent child reflecting in some extraordinary way the miracle of Jesus – this rather than being properly moved by what had transpired. Still, the Catholic Church vacillated between caring for the Jews in order to convert them and punishing them for not having converted. For an extraordinary history of this love–hate relationship in Rome, see Emmanuel Robocanchi, *Le Saint-Siege et les Juifs: Le Ghetto à Rome*, Paris: Librairie de Firmin-Didot, 1891.

    I have chosen the expression 'willful silence' because it seems best to capture the moral reality of the moment. According to James Carroll, *Constantine's Sword: The Church and the Jews*, New York: Houghton Mifflin Company, 2001, who also has much that is illuminating to say about Rome's treatment of Jews (pp. 364–7; 376–8), no Catholic Nazi was ever excommunicated – not Hitler; not Himmler. And in 1949, Pope Pius XII summarily excommunicated all Communists throughout the world without any thought to what might happen to Catholics behind what was then called the Iron Curtain (p. 437). Yet, his utter silence with respect to the Jewish genocide was deafening (pp. 524–5 and p. 686, n.11). He could have done something, even something symbolic, even something that would not have accomplished anything. If a 40-ton truck falls on a mother's child, covering its body entirely, we would expect her to try to do something even if what she does is to no avail. We would not be impressed with her inaction on the grounds that there is nothing that she could do. It is a deep feature about caring that we often try to relieve the suffering of a loved one, though it is obvious that trying is to no avail. The silence of Pope Pius XII should come as no surprise if we bear in mind that he was Cardinal Eugenio

Pacelli and, as cardinal, negotiated most of the agreements with Hitler that led in Germany to 'the complete withdrawal from politics of all Catholics *as Catholics*' (p. 499).

9. John-Paul II, 'Nous Nous Souvenons: Une Réflexion sur la Shoah' (1998). This document was ten years in the making. See, also, Pope Paul VI's *Nostra Aetate*, 'Judaism' (28 October 1965). In this document, we find the following remarks: 'True, the Jewish authorities and those who followed their lead pressed for the death of Christ; still, what happened in His passion cannot be charged against all the Jews, without distinction, then alive, nor against the Jews of today' (Section 4, para. 7). Here, the Church has formally repudiated the charge of deicide that it had made against the Jews. According to Michel Remaud, this text constitutes the very first time that the Church had formally recognized Judaism as being on an independent theological plane that merited respect. See his *Chrétiens et Juifs entre le passé et l'avenir*, Bruxelles: Éditions Lessius, 2000, pp. 13, 21.

10. I am drawing here upon James Rachel's famous essay 'Active and Passive Euthanasia,' *New England Journal of Medicine* (1975), No. 292.

11. For a very sensitive discussion of this matter, see Peter A. French, 'The Corporation as a Moral Person,' *American Philosophical Quarterly* **16** (1979).

12. It is perhaps arguable that this change had its origins in the work of Pope Pius XI – not Pius XII – who in August 1938 on the eve of World War II issued an extraordinary document, 'Humani Generis Unitas,' condemning racism of all forms, racism against blacks as it was practiced in the United States during this period as well as the racism that goes by the name anti-Semitism. It is Pope Pius XII, acceding to the papacy in 1939, who adopted a rigorous attitude of silence in the name of neutrality in the hopes of being able to play a key role in matters of arbitration. Whatever his motivations, it was an attitude that was far too reminiscent of the Church's negative view of Jews that his predecessor had sought to correct. Pope John XXIII picked up where Pope Pius XI had left off.

13. Although the Church could not have turned itself in, the depth of its contrition has been measured in other ways. And there have been problems. For example, the Church's wish to canonize Pope Pius XII has for the reason indicated in notes 10 and 12 above not sat well with Jews. This wish has troubled some Catholics as well. Jews have also noted a certain play on words, in particular the distinction between 'the Church' and the 'sons and daughters of the Church.' The first refers to the 'bride of Christ' who cannot err; the second refers to individual members of the Catholic Church who can err in their ways. By this line of reasoning, the Church did not do, and could not have done, anything wrong during the Holocaust, although some of its members did. Accordingly, the Church is not apologizing for what *it* did, because it can do no wrong, but only for the wrong that some of its members did. To many Jews, this appears to be a sleight of hand. So while the sincerity of John-Paul's contrition has seemed beyond doubt and the changes in the Catholic Church brought about under his leadership are unquestionably real and significant enough, it has nonetheless seemed to some Jews that the Catholic Church yet has some distance to travel in completely apologizing. I am indebted here to 'Réponse au document du Vatican,' by La Comité international de Liaison entre juifs et catholiques,' in *Judaïsme, anti-judaïsme et christianisme*, Colloque de l'Université de Fribourg, 16–20 mars 1998, Paris: Éditions Saint-Augustin, 2000. The response is to Pope John-Paul II's 'Nous Nous Souvenons' cited in note 9 above. Still, it will be noted, there is not the thought that as a matter of principle the Church could not be forgiven. On the Church's sincerity, see Carroll's searching remarks, *Constantine's Sword*, ch. 60.

14. I am much indebted here to David Alvarez and Robert A. Graham, S.J., *Nothing Sacred: Nazi Espionage Against the Vatican. 1939–1945*, London, Frank Cass Publishers, 1997.

15. New York: Vintage Books, 1999. For a while, it has been fashionable to talk about

understanding others whose experiences of suffering differ from our own. I tried to speak to this in an article entitled 'Moral Deference.' This was first published in *The Philosophical Forum* **24** (1992–93); and then reprinted with substantial revisions in Cynthia Willet (ed.), *Theorizing Multiculturalism*, Malden, MA: Blackwell Publishers, 1998. It seems to me that the idea of moral deference can be extended to those who, having performed egregious wrongs, genuinely seek forgiveness. Perhaps most of us do not want to know what that is like. Here I owe much to Terri Aronowitz's searching arguments.

16. In his important work, *The Nazi Doctors*, New York: Basic Books, 1986, Peter Jay Lifton records the case of a Dr Ernst B. who was acquitted at the Nuremberg trials thanks to the testimonies of former prisoners of Auschwitz. This Dr Ernst B., though, whom survivors referred to as a 'Human being in S.S. uniform,' also defended Josef Mengele as a decent and admirable person, claiming to be entirely unaware of his vicious experiments with twins.

17. I am deeply indebted here to Walker's essay cited in note 5 above. The subject of moral luck has attracted much attention, following the publication of the seminal essays of Williams and Nagel on the subject. These have been handily collected in Daniel Statman *Moral Luck*, Albany, NY: State University of New York Press, 1993.

18. I am indebted here to Jacques Ricot, *Peut-On Tout Pardonner?*, Paris, Éditions Pleins-Feux, 1999 and to Vladimir Jankélévitch, *Le Pardon*, Paris: Éditions Montaigne, 1967. As a religious notion in the monotheistic traditions, God's forgiveness can only be seen as a moral gift of which human beings can never be worthy because of His complete holiness. And our secular conception has not fully escaped its religious moorings, except that humans (lacking in complete holiness) can be worthy of one another's forgiveness. Here I follow Monique Canto-Sperber, *L'inquiétude morale et la vie humaine*, Paris: Presses Universitaires de France, 2001, pp. 43–9. Considerations of space, though, prevent me from offering an account of the idea of a moral gift. A woman who bears a child, when owing to medical complications doing so puts her life at great risk, offers that child a moral gift, even as she also does what might be considered supererogatory. She is not just being kind. Yet, a moral gift need not be supererogatory at all, as with forgiveness. Nor do all acts of kindness constitute a moral gift, as when I offer to attend to my neighbor's mail during her vacation. See, also, the remarks in the text below concerning righteousness.

19. As Brian Barry has so eloquently argued regarding justice in 'And Who Is My Neighbor?,' *The Yale Law Journal* **88** (1979). A person can be perfectly within her moral and legal rights, Barry observes, and yet be open to moral condemnation for her or his behavior (p. 641).

It would perhaps be remiss of me if I did not say a word about Norman G. Finkelstein's book, *The Holocaust Industry: Reflections on the Exploitation of Jewish Suffering*, New York: Verso, 2000, though doing so seems to be a matter of treading very treacherous waters. For one, no two people seem to have read the same book that bears the title; and, for another, Finkelstein has, to put it mildly, utterly enraged many Jews. His style of writing does not always serve him well. Moreover, some of his criticisms of Elie Wiesel seem to be awfully gratuitous and get in the way of the argument. At any rate, the distinction that I have drawn in the text between justice and righteousness is one that he could very much have put to good use; and is applicable to any people that has endured vicious injustices. It is a simple fact that insisting on justice may be counterproductive to realizing the greater moral good, as Archbishop Tutu was at pains to point out with respect to South Africa (see note 20 below). It is most unfortunate that victims of injustices (for example blacks, Jews, Native Americans) have come to use the charge of *x*-ism (racism, anti-Semitism, and so on) as a way of silencing legitimate discussion. For once a person is called an *x*-ist, there is very little that the individual can say or do in order to diffuse the charge. The liberal and unreflective use of the charge of *x*-ism is tantamount to crying wolf. And as everyone knows, the gain is not without a very serious drawback, to wit: the utter loss of credibility. I have explored some of these matters in "'The Matrices of Malevolent Ideologies: Blacks and Jews,' *Social Identities* **2** (1976).

20. See Archbishop Desmond Tutu's *No Future Without Forgiveness*, New York: Doubleday, 2000. In ch. 11, Tutu directly addresses the topic of forgiving a Nazi, and recounts the criticism that he received for suggesting this possibility, being called, among other things, a 'black Nazi.' If anything is clear, it is that South Africa would not have survived apartheid had forgiveness or reconciliation not been pursued by Mandela and Tutu. Our admiration of them is but a sham if we ignore this reality in their lives; for their greatness is inseparable from the fact that they were able to forgive. The relentless pursuit of justice, instead, albeit ever so understandable, would have detracted mightily from their moral stature. Yet, there are problems with the blanket forgiveness that Tutu called for; and I want to be clear that the view which I have defended calls for no such thing. Still, there is an insight here that is applicable to the Shoah. Certainly, Finkelstein's argument (note 19 above) would have been better served had he cast it in these terms.

21. In *The Book of Knowledge*, Section 5, ch. ii, Maimonides claims that we have perfect repentance when the repentant refrains from wrongdoing not by reason of fear or physical incapacity, but owing to his very act of repentance itself. Maimonides' example is that of a man who sins on account of a woman.

22. Whilst the term 'redemption' has become intimately associated with Christianity, the idea of redemption is at the very core of Jewish thought, as expressed in the writings of Moses Maimonides in *Thirteen Principles and the Resurrection of the Dead*. For an extraordinarily illuminating discussion of the difference between Judaism and Christianity with regard to redemption, see Avital Wohlman, *Maimonïde and Thomas d'Aquin: Un Dialogue Impossible*, Suisse: Éditions Universitaires de Fribourg, 1995.

23. In writing this paper, I am indebted to many. First, a number of students who challenged my argument. Foremost among these is Daniel Hoff. The idea of moral outrage was introduced to speak to many of his concerns. Others include Jason Tanenbaum, Nathan Federman, Jeffrey Adelson, Adam Schechter and Joshua Sandels. At the professional level, I wish to thank, in addition to the editors, Simone Bateman, David Benatar, Jay Garfield, Jeffrie Murphy, Terrence McConnell, Jennifer Parkhurst, Elizabeth Spelman and Alasdair MacIntyre (who has helped me with so much that I have written) for both searching and encouraging comments upon various drafts. The Thomas More Institute (Montreal) hosted a reading of this essay, much to my benefit; and Thomas Nagel graciously read the penultimate draft and discussed it with me at length. To my knowledge, Martin Golding is the first philosopher to address directly the topic of forgiveness and the Shoah. His ideas have meant a great deal to me.

Chapter 13

Forgiveness and the Holocaust

Eve Garrard

Forgiveness is not, perhaps, the most important issue that confronts us when we consider the Holocaust. But still, it is one of the moral questions that arises out of that great catastrophe. Should we forgive its perpetrators? Do we have reason to forgive them? Whether or not the Holocaust was unique, it certainly was not unique in being evil, so any answer we find to this question may help us understand the state of play with regard to the perpetrators of other great evils. Furthermore, finding out whether we have reason to forgive the Holocaust perpetrators may also reveal something about the nature of what was done and those who did it, thus furthering at least by a little our understanding of the nature of evil. And of course it will reveal something about forgiveness itself, something about its limits. So there are several considerations which make this investigation worthwhile.

On the face of it, the answer to the question 'Do we have reason to forgive the perpetrators of the Holocaust?' seems to be: no. What possible reason could there be to forgive such people, given what they did? Although there has not been very much direct treatment of the Holocaust in analytic moral philosophy, the Nazis appear again and again as examples or touchstones in the construction of moral theories. This (entirely legitimate) use of them does, however, have the result that they acquire a kind of symbolic status, so that it is easy to think of them just under the description 'a limit case of evil'. We need to bear in mind that these were people who were not very long ago up to their necks in blood, who not only killed millions of innocents but also devised endless agonizing tortures to inflict on them. We need to remember this when we ask if we have reason to forgive the perpetrators of the Holocaust, because *that* is what we would be forgiving. And that is why it is plausible to claim that the default position on the question is: no, so that the onus is on the forgiver to show how there can possibly be a reason to forgive the willing devisers of such a drowning tide of atrocity.

We cannot, at least in a secular context, help ourselves to the principle that we ought always to forgive evildoers. If that principle holds, then there is no need for a special argument about the perpetrators of the Holocaust, since they are paradigmatic cases of evildoers. But they seem so plausible a counter-example to the principle that they function as a test for it, so we cannot judge the status of the principle until we have established the moral state of play in just this case. However, we do not have to suppose that a reason for forgiving the perpetrators must amount to a *requirement* to forgive them (as stated in the purported principle); it would be enough if we could find a consideration in favour of forgiveness which is capable of being an all-things-considered reason in at least some cases. The rest of this paper is devoted to the search for such a reason.

We need to start by looking at the possibility that there is a moral *prohibition* on forgiveness in this kind of case, because if there is, then any reason which might exist in favour of forgiveness will always be overridden. So in Section 1, I will consider the claims that are made by those who strongly object to forgiveness, particularly since these include the views of some of the survivors and their relatives, who have a special claim on our attention on this issue.[1] If it can be shown that there is no prohibition on forgiveness, then it is at least morally permissible. But that does not amount to the claim that we have a reason to forgive. More is needed to establish that stronger claim, which will be examined in Section 2.

1. Arguments against Forgiveness

What considerations are appealed to by those who say we should not forgive? The reasons offered seem to divide into two main groups: first, what we might call the metaphysical objections to forgiveness of the Holocaust, claiming that we *cannot* forgive the perpetrators; and second, what are primarily moral objections to forgiveness, claiming that we *ought not* to forgive them.

Metaphysical Objections to Forgiveness

The first claim is that only the victims can forgive the perpetrators, and most of the victims are dead. There can be no third-party forgiveness; any such pseudo-forgiveness cannot replace or substitute for that of the victims.

There are two possible rejoinders to this claim. On the one hand, doubt can be cast on the (admittedly widespread) view that there can be no third-party forgiveness. We certainly seem prepared to countenance third-party *refusals* to forgive. Suppose one person harms a second. A friend of the second person can say: '*She* may have forgiven him, but I'll never forgive him for the harm he's done to her.' We do not regard this as incoherent; we do not respond by saying: 'You couldn't forgive him anyway, even if you wanted to, since you're not the victim.' And if we accept the legitimacy of third-party refusals to forgive, it seems plausible to suppose that third parties are at least sometimes able to forgive. The friend can come to say: '*She* forgave him quickly, but it took *me* much longer to forgive him for the harm he did to her. But in the end, I managed it.' This does not seem any more incoherent than the original third-party refusal to forgive.

But in any case, it seems possible that the whole issue of third-party forgiveness can be sidestepped in the case of the Holocaust. After the war ended, some of the principal perpetrators were charged with having committed crimes against humanity. Hannah Arendt's formulation of this is particularly perspicuous: 'The Nazis committed a crime against humanity on the body of the Jews.'[2] The actions which constituted crimes against humanity were not *additional* to the actions which constituted crimes against the Jews and others; crimes against humanity are not to be construed on the model of collateral damage. Rather they should be construed as having been constituted by the crimes against more circumscribed groups: in harming the Jews, Gypsies and others, in the way and to the extent that they did, the Nazis committed crimes against humanity. If this is so, then all of us, all of humanity, are victims of the Nazis, though not of course to anything like the same extent as the primary victims, the ones who suffered directly at their hands. So our forgiveness, were it to be forthcoming, would not be third-party forgiveness.

None the less, those who insist that our forgiveness cannot replace that of the victims who died are correct. Nothing can substitute for that. But this is just a particular case of the quite general and uncontentious principle that if an agent wrongs more than one victim then he needs forgiveness from more than one person if he is to be fully forgiven. The Nazis can never be fully forgiven (at least, not from a secular viewpoint) since most of their primary victims are dead. Their forgiveness would have been far more important than ours, and ours cannot substitute for theirs. But it does not follow that there is nothing we have to forgive the perpetrators for, or that we cannot forgive them. So the possibility of there being a reason to forgive the perpetrators of the Holocaust cannot be dismissed purely on the grounds of this first metaphysical objection.

The second objection claims that forgiveness is impossible without repentance, and most of the Nazis never genuinely repented. It seems all too likely that the second part of this claim is true. But the first clause, that forgiveness is impossible without repentance, is much more dubious. Certainly there are some elements in Western culture which present forgiveness independent of repentance, unconditional forgiveness, as a high ideal to be aimed at. In the biblical story of the prodigal son, the father forgives him before ever hearing his words of repentance. (Most of us are aware that any sneaking sympathy we feel for the begrudging brother who doesn't want to forgive runs against the moral current of the story.) A recent example of unconditional forgiveness is that of Gordon Wilson at the Enniskillen bombing in Northern Ireland. As he lay in the rubble of the bomb explosion beside his dying daughter, he forgave the terrorists who had injured him and killed her. There was no question of repentance here; he could not have known, perhaps would never know, whether or not they came to repent their actions.

Some people might argue (indeed some *have* argued) that Wilson should not have been so ready to forgive his daughter's murderers. But this objection, even if it can be justified, is clearly a *moral* objection. It is just irrelevant to the metaphysical claim that forgiveness is impossible without repentance. (Indeed it seems to presuppose the falsehood of the metaphysical claim. There is no point in telling someone that he ought not to do something which it is metaphysically impossible for him or anyone else to perform.)

The third metaphysical objection to forgiveness claims that the Holocaust was too great a crime to be forgiven; its perpetrators are beyond ordinary guilt, and hence are beyond forgiveness. Taking the second clause first, we can perhaps agree that the perpetrators are beyond ordinary guilt, since what they did was certainly beyond ordinary wrongdoing. How far, and in what way, beyond is a very difficult question to answer, bordering as it does on the issue of the purported uniqueness of this moral catastrophe. But however that issue is to be resolved, it does not seem likely that the resolution will conclude that the perpetrators are guiltless. Beyond ordinary guilt there lies, for all we can see, extraordinary guilt, which does not by itself seem to entail unforgiveability. A further argument is needed to demonstrate that. And the first clause of this objection does not provide such an argument. What it does is claim that the Holocaust was too great a crime to be forgiven. By itself, this begs the question at issue; in asking whether we have reason to forgive the perpetrators, we are in part asking whether crimes of such great magnitude can be forgiven. The bare assertion that they cannot does not provide us with a reason for believing that they cannot.

The final metaphysical objection that I will consider arises out of the widely held view that there is something about what was done in the Holocaust that eludes our understanding – a mystery at the heart of evil, inaccessible to rational investigation. And if we cannot fully understand what was done, so the objection goes, how can we forgive it?[3]

I do not doubt that there is something incomprehensible about the Holocaust, though it is not easy to say exactly what it is. And there is no doubt that it is harder to understand than less appalling wrongdoings. But first, it was carried out by evildoers who were human agents like the rest of us, and what they did was part of the human repertoire of action. We should not be too ready to see their actions as beyond human understanding, unless we want to give up on the project of understanding ourselves. And second, there is something difficult to understand about *all* wrongdoing. How is it possible to choose the worse in preference to the better? If the explanation is our ignorance, then how can we be blamed? These extremely familiar problems in moral psychology do not incline us to think that all wrongdoing is unforgiveable. So it's not clear that our incomprehension of aspects of the Holocaust by itself rules out forgiveness. As the more ordinary cases show, we do not have to have complete understanding of an action in order to forgive it.

So far, the arguments seem to suggest that there is no legitimate metaphysical block on forgiveness. But there might still be an ethical barrier – it might be morally prohibited. So let us now turn to the moral arguments against forgiveness.

Moral Objections to Forgiveness

I start with what seems to be the least plausible of the moral objections, the claim that forgiveness will encourage future perpetrators in their misdeeds, so it should be withheld on essentially consequentialist grounds. This is an empirical claim, and we lack the evidence by which it could be established one way or the other. But it does seem fairly implausible. The threat of future *punishment* might be deterrent, but can we suppose that future genocidal tyrants will stay their hands for fear of not being forgiven should they ultimately lose power? Such people, such regimes, do not generally plan on losing power. Nor is the forgiveness of their despised victims or hated adversaries likely to appear morally significant to them. In the absence of substantial empirical evidence, this objection seems to rest on what is ultimately a piece of wishful thinking about perpetrators' psychology – on the belief that deep down inside, they see their actions, and their victims, as we do, and hence will care, as we would, about not obtaining forgiveness for their misdeeds. This is not a convincing account of the motivational state of evildoers.[4]

It might be argued that forgiveness of the perpetrators, while irrelevant to the conduct of future perpetrators of comparable magnitude, might none the less give encouragement to lesser wrongdoers. They might think that if major perpetrators can be forgiven, then so can lesser ones. And this might encourage them in their wrongdoing. Perhaps it might. But this argument is too strong. Forgiveness of ordinary wrongdoers may encourage future (comparably ordinary) wrongdoers, but that is not generally taken as a clinching reason to withhold forgiveness. If it were, there would be very little scope for forgiveness at all. So the fact that forgiving major perpetrators might encourage (ordinary) wrongdoers does not show that forgiveness of these major perpetrators is morally impermissible.

A more persuasive moral objection to forgiveness is the claim that the perpetrators should be punished, not forgiven. As a claim about desert, this is of course correct, at least for those who subscribe to some broadly retributivist theory of punishment.[5] No one could plausibly claim that the perpetrators *deserve* to be forgiven. But then, neither do many ordinary wrongdoers; this is not generally taken as an insuperable barrier to forgiveness. We can have reason to forgive even people who do not deserve it. So the fact that the Nazis do not deserve to be forgiven does not by itself show that we ought not to do so. And nor does the fact that they do deserve to be punished, since forgiveness and punishment are not incompatible. A wrongdoer who has undergone the just punishment for his actions may then be forgiven by his victim, or he may not be – the two issues are independent. A victim may fully forgive her tormentor, and yet still insist that he be punished, perhaps for deterrent reasons, or perhaps because sadly it is what he needs if he is ever to fully realize the gravity of what he has done. So the claim about punishment, even if true, does not constitute a successful objection to forgiveness.

Similar considerations seem to apply to the next objection, which asserts that it is wrong to excuse or forget the evil done to the primary victims; we should never neglect or deny the horror of their sufferings. So it is wrong to forgive the perpetrators.[6]

Certainly it is wrong of us to excuse or in any way deny the evil which was done. But this is not a reason for withholding forgiveness. For not only is forgiveness compatible with not excusing and not denying; it actually *requires* these things. To excuse an agent is to say that she is not to blame for doing the wrongful action. But if she is not to blame, then she is not a candidate for forgiveness at all – there is nothing to forgive. And although forgiveness may lead to forgetting, it does not require it – who could require of the victims' relatives that they forget how, say, their loved children died? But it is not impossible that one who remembers may also forgive. What makes forgiveness so difficult is precisely that it requires us to recognize the full horror of what was done, and then to forgive those very actions. Ignoring, denying or forgetting amount to evasion, not forgiveness.

A quite different kind of objection to forgiveness is the claim that it involves a morally obnoxious motivation. On this view, those who are anxious to forgive the perpetrators of the Holocaust are motivated by considerations that are self-indulgent and ultimately self-serving. They wish to see themselves, and be seen by others, as generous, tolerant, understanding, liberal, sensitive to the difficulties and complexities of the human condition.[7] They secretly admire their own fine feelings. Forgiving, for them, is a form of vanity.

This objection is, of course, *ad hominem*, though not necessarily to be dismissed on those grounds. We are, after all, inclined to feel that forgiveness driven solely by such motives would be morally objectionable. And there can be little doubt that such motives are sometimes in play (among other less disreputable ones) in those who favour forgiveness. The real problem with this objection is that it is too strong. If the presence of morally disreputable motivations counts as an objection to forgiveness, then it will count as an objection to the refusal to forgive as well. For there can be just as little doubt that those who refuse to forgive may sometimes do so because they wish to see themselves, and have others see them, as morally upright, unyielding in their rejection of evil, uncompromising in their solidarity with the victims, untainted by any sympathy with wrongdoing or wimpish tolerance of the intolerable. In short, their refusal to forgive is driven by vanity.[8]

The trouble with the *ad hominem* objection is that it is as damaging to the case against forgiveness as to the case for it. The insistence on purity of motivation for morally permissible actions always leaves the moral terrain devastated, since it is so rarely to be found.

The final moral objection which I want to consider is the view that forgiveness is wrong because it harms the victims. How can we countenance something which harms those who have already been so desperately harmed, in order to do something which helps those who so profoundly do not deserve it? This claim, if true, is forceful. But it is hard to see how exactly forgiveness does harm the victims, since it involves no ignoring, forgetting, denying or excusing of the wrong done, in all its horror. What does the putative harm consist in?

One possible answer is simply this: the harm consists in the fact that it would make the victims, or their relatives (who are also victims of another kind) distressed.[9] Of course, this certainly would be important. But part of the point of this investigation is to see whether they need be distressed – whether, that is, there are any *grounds* for such distress. Even if there are not, the fact (if it is a fact) that they would be distressed would remain morally significant. But a reason provided by a groundless distress in the victims would not carry as much weight as a grounded one, and so far such grounds remain unclear.

The moral objections to forgiveness seem no more successful than the metaphysical ones, largely because they involve a misunderstanding of what forgiveness is. So let us turn briefly to the nature of forgiveness. What does forgiveness actually amount to? Contrary to some quite common assumptions, forgiveness does not amount to forgetting or ignoring or denying or excusing what was done by the perpetrators; indeed such things are incompatible with forgiveness.[10] It does require the overcoming of resentment and hatred towards the perpetrator,[11] but this is not on its own sufficient for forgiveness. A victim may feel that resentment is beneath him, that the perpetrator does not even warrant the amount of attention involved in resentment, and so may cease to feel it, out of contempt for the evildoer and his deeds. This is indeed a way of overcoming resentment, and it may sometimes be justified, but it certainly does not amount to forgiveness.

What is required for forgiveness, as well as the absence of resentment, seems to be the adoption of a particular attitude towards the perpetrator, an attitude which can be broadly described as wishing him well. What the well-being of a perpetrator actually amounts to might easily involve his punishment, and his recognition of the terrible nature of his acts. (Here I am supposing that a person's well-being is not just a matter of her happiness, or her preference-satisfaction, but rather of the realization in her life of genuine values, including of course moral ones.[12]) In forgiving another, we no longer desire his downfall, nor even feel indifferent to what becomes of him, but instead want him to flourish, to have a worthwhile life – again, on a moralized understanding of what a worthwhile life amounts to. We might, in some moods, sum up the forgiver's attitude towards the perpetrator as the adoption of a *loving stance*.

On this construal of forgiveness, the objections canvassed so far do not seem to succeed. It does not seem to be morally prohibited. But is there anything actually to be said in favour of it? Do we have any positive reason to forgive these perpetrators?

2. Reasons for Forgiveness

First, I want to exclude from the discussion a certain kind of reason, one example of which is this: forgiveness is good for the forgiver – it releases her from the corrosions of resentment and hatred. The difference between this kind of reason and the kind I do want to discuss involves a distinction to be found throughout the class of reasons, but it is remarkably difficult to characterize this distinction at the general level,[13] so I will confine myself to distinguishing between reasons which are focused on the forgiver, and reasons which are focused on the perpetrator and his actions. That forgiveness is good for the forgiver, if true, is a reason focused primarily on the forgiver, and does not seem to derive directly from features of the perpetrator or his actions. Hence it is not likely to reveal anything about the nature and status of the evildoer. I am going to confine myself to considering reasons which do seem to stem from the nature of the perpetrator or of what he has done.

Some classic reasons for forgiveness in lesser cases of wrongdoing are considerations such as: the wrongdoer has repented, he understands how wrong his actions were, he asks to be forgiven. These, however, seem inadequate in the case we are considering. If you have killed and tortured thousands of innocents, then seeing that this was profoundly wrong of you, and being truly sorry that you did it, does not seem to count for much against the horror of what was done. (As a matter of fact, evildoing on the scale of the Holocaust is not necessary to provoke these dismissive thoughts – some people feel them about those who sexually abuse and murder children, such as the Moors murderer Myra Hindley. I do not intend to imply that people are right to feel this; only that we have here a response that may seem appropriate for the perpetrators of the Holocaust.) Some evildoing is so great that later repentance just seems irrelevant – there are some moral journeys from which there is no returning down the repentance route. And of course most of the major perpetrators of the Holocaust showed little sign of any such repentance.

Where else might we look for reasons to forgive? Two aspects of the perpetrators seem possible sources of such reasons: first, their status as autonomous rational agents, and second, their status as our fellow human beings.

Let us start with autonomous agency. This is normally thought to demand respect: we ought to show respect for persons, because they are autonomous rational agents, able to make their own moral choices. But the problem here is obvious: certainly the perpetrators of the Holocaust were autonomous agents (that's why they are blameworthy), but who can respect the *use* to which they put their capacity to make their own autonomous choices? Their practical reasoning was so distorted that no grounds remain, it might be claimed, for respecting that capacity in them. Hence there is nothing there which could possibly generate a reason to forgive.

This argument seems too sweeping, in that respect for persons does seem to do some residual work in generating reasons to treat perpetrators in some ways rather than others. What else can explain the quite widespread feeling that it would be wrong to punish these men by, for example, torturing them to death? I do not think it can plausibly be said that that punishment would be disproportionate to their crimes (indeed it is hard to think of *any* punishment that would be disproportionate to those crimes), and in that sense they certainly would deserve it. And the claim that we should not do this because it would degrade *us* is only convincing if there is something else objectionable about such a punishment – how could it be degrading to us if there is nothing wrong with it? It looks as if respect for persons is present here, and giving us a reason to act. But that does not show that it constitutes or generates a reason to *forgive*. Why should we take a benevolent stance to people who used their capacity for moral choice in so distorted and horrifying a way?

Tracy Govier, in her paper 'Forgiveness and the Unforgivable',[14] does offer an argument for forgiveness deriving from autonomous rational agency. She claims that we ought to forgive (at least where there has been repentance) out of recognition of the human capacity for moral choice and change. Respect for the human worth and dignity founded in that capacity, so she argues, gives us reason to overcome hatred of the perpetrators, and regard them once again as members of the moral community.[15] But even if Govier is right in thinking that respect for the capacity for moral choice and change gives us reason to regard the perpetrators as members of the moral community, this does not by itself amount to a reason to forgive them. Forgiving someone certainly involves regarding them as a member of the moral community, but then so does refusing to forgive them. Contrast this with our attitude towards those whom we do unequivocally regard as outside the moral community. We do not withhold forgiveness from animals, we do not feel indignation or resentment at their behaviour, and this is because they really are not members of the moral community. But perpetrators who are responsible for their actions, and hence are proper objects of blame, and who can appropriately be regarded as objects of resentment and hatred, *are* members of the moral community. Admittedly, they're not members in *good standing*, but then, how could they be, considering what they have done? An answer to that question is needed to identify a reason to forgive, but nothing in Govier's comments about respect for autonomous agency provides this answer.

So I turn now to the other feature of perpetrators, the fact that they are our fellow human beings. Whatever moral work is done by this consideration is effected, I think, mainly by the idea of fellowship, since the other morally relevant features of human beings generally boil down to aspects of personhood, which we have already discussed and found wanting. So the hope here is that the fact that perpetrators are our fellows, that is, 'one of us', will yield a reason to forgive them.

The claim that someone is 'one of us', given as a reason for action, has had something of a bad press. Notoriously, Mrs Thatcher is said to have asked 'Is he one of us?' when considering someone for one of the governmental posts which were in her gift.[16] Our concern about this is mainly because of the potential for unjust exclusiveness – we worry about those who are not 'one of us' losing out unfairly. But with respect to the forgiveness issue, the 'us' in question is the whole of the human race – no one is left over to be excluded, except the animals, and they are not candidates for forgiveness at all. So the exclusionist worries do not apply here.

How might the thought that someone is 'one of us' be seen as a reason to forgive him for his wrongdoing? We are all used to the idea that the relationships in which we stand to other people can generate reasons to treat them in special ways – for example, the doctor has a duty to help her patients that others may not have, or may not have so strongly, since they do not stand in the doctor–patient relationship to that person. Now let us consider a central case of such a relationship, which is also one in which people can count as 'one of us', namely the family. The fact that someone is a member of the family generates all sorts of reasons for treating her in some ways rather than others – consider, for example, whom we buy birthday or Christmas presents for. And among these reasons are, I think, reasons to forgive. Suppose some loved member of your family – a brother, say – has done some truly dreadful thing to you; the sort of thing that if a friend did it, you would never speak to them again for the rest of your life. But you love your brother, and you eventually forgive him. If someone asked 'Why did you forgive him, after he'd treated you so terribly?' you might say, 'Well, he's my brother, after all.' In saying this, you can be citing a recognizable, adequate reason for forgiveness.

Can we look to the fact that the evildoer is a fellow member of the human race, and in that way 'one of us', to provide us with an analogous reason to forgive? One obvious objection at once arises: family relationships are close, warm and intimate, and hence apt for generating reasons such as a reason to forgive. But the relationship in which I stand to one who, like me, is a member of the human race is very tenuous indeed. Most of the time it makes absolutely no difference to my actions or feelings at all. And perhaps things have to be like this, given human psychology and the sheer numbers constituting the human race. Most of the time there is no possible way in which I could feel anything at all about most of the humans with whom I share the world. Hence, so the objection goes, this relationship isn't substantial enough to yield a reason to forgive.

Now all of the premises in this objection are true, as far as I can see. But that does not make the objection conclusive. In the context of horrific evildoing, the vanishingly weak bonds which attach us to the rest of the human race seem in fact to thicken and gain strength. Take, for example, the idea of *crimes against humanity*. As we have already noted, this does not involve activities over and above what is directly done to the specific groups who are the victims in such cases. Rather, we regard such treatment of the victims, such crimes against them, as crimes against all of us. What harms them, harms us all – not as collateral damage or because of some chain of cause and effect, but because we are in some way, due to our common human nature, implicated in their suffering. We should note here that it is not purely the *suffering* of the victims that generates this response in us, since we do not have it for animals, whose treatment by humans has often been indescribably horrific. But however seriously we take the maltreatment of animals, we do not feel inclined to regard it as a crime against *ourselves*, a crime against humanity. What makes the mass torturing and killing of innocent people capable of being a crime against humanity is that the victims are human, are like us.

So the relationship of fellow human being seems, at least where there has been terrible wrongdoing, to be strong enough to generate a sense of a shared condition, in which the harms and injustices done to some are done in some sense to us all. And this certainly generates reasons to act, for example to pursue the alleged perpetrators of crimes against humanity through the international courts. And furthermore, we should notice that crimes against humanity are not the only way in which the relationship of fellow human being seems to lay claims on us. Consider how much the advertising of the major international charities lays stress not just on the suffering of those for whom our help is solicited, but also on how like us they are. And this is of course quite correct – other human beings *are* like us; we share a common human nature.

This common nature is what grounds the responses we've been discussing so far, responses which we might describe as expressions of *human solidarity*. In solidarity, we are concerned for the well-being of the other, on the basis of a shared nature and condition. And this solidarity provides us with reasons to act in various ways, and sometimes we *do* act in the appropriate ways – we do charge people with having committed crimes against humanity, we do sometimes give money to charity to help our fellow humans, we do sometimes help these humans directly ourselves, at risk to ourselves, when their needs are desperate, just because we see them as fellow humans in need.[17]

But of course we also share a common human nature with the perpetrators. Does this provide the basis for any kind of solidarity with them? The very idea of solidarity with perpetrators sounds morally *appalling*, mainly I think because it sounds like an endorsement of their deeds and values. But in solidarity with a group, we want their well-being, which may not be the same as wanting for them what they want for themselves. We don't have to construe people's well-being in terms of the satisfaction of their desires, since people sometimes desire things that are not at all conducive to their well-being. Rather, we should construe it in terms of the realization of genuine values in their lives. Wanting the well-being of a perpetrator will probably amount to wanting his repentance and reform, which will generally be the very converse of what he wants for himself. Put this way, the thought of solidarity with perpetrators doesn't sound quite so objectionable.

It might perhaps be argued that we do not in fact share a common nature with evildoers – just because they are evil and we are not. (The very idea of a determinate human nature used to be generally unpopular, with anthropology and sociology laying emphasis upon the extreme plasticity of human behaviour. But in recent years there has been a marked change, with both empirical and philosophical research now countenancing appeal to a distinctive human nature.[18]) However, the evidence of the blood-soaked twentieth century alone strongly suggests that human nature is morally mixed, not in the sense that some of us are almost entirely good, and some entirely evil, but rather in the sense that most if not all of us are capable of both good and evil. Some of the most striking evidence from the Holocaust is of how very *ordinary* many of the killers and torturers were; not dedicated SS men, but ordinary men who had no particular career stake in what they were doing, nor an obsessional ideological history.[19] Killing and torturing turned out not to be so very hard for them to do, and many enjoyed it. This is a recurrent aspect of human nature, as events other than the Holocaust have amply demonstrated. (Solzhenitsyn writing on the Soviet Gulag camps emphasizes this point.) So the perpetrators do share a common human nature with us; we share, to some unknown extent, their capacity for evil.[20]

Nor can it be said, as we were able to say of rational agency, that the perpetrators have hopelessly distorted the human nature which they share with us. Evildoing is not a distortion of human nature, in the way that it is a distortion of practical reasoning. Human nature just is whatever we humans are like – it does not have the strong kind of normativity that (practical) reason has. The Nazis may have been failures at practical reasoning, but they certainly were not failures at being human, in any other than a metaphorical sense. They were just as human as anyone else, just as human as the heroes and saints who protected some (few) of their victims. So we cannot distance ourselves from them, *qua* human beings, by appealing to the idea of distortion.

It might be thought that people whose moral perceptions are at all in good shape would be disinclined, or even psychologically incapable, of feeling anything like solidarity with perpetrators. But there is a common, though somewhat neglected, feature of our moral experience which suggests that we do, in fact, feel something rather like solidarity with wrongdoers, though admittedly it does not present itself in quite that way. This is the phenomenon which we might call *vicarious shame*, that is, shame felt by one person for the wrongdoing of another. A classic statement of it is to be found in Robert Nozick's essay on the Holocaust, in which he says:

> Like a relative shaming a family, the Germans, our human relatives, have shamed us all. They have ruined all our reputations, not as individuals – they have ruined the reputation of the human family. Although we are not all responsible for what those who acted and stood by did, we are all stained.[21]

Here we find the suggestion that we are all inextricably implicated in, and shamed by, the deeds of our fellow human beings the perpetrators, even though we do not endorse them and are not responsible for them.

The phenomenon of vicarious shame is actually not at all uncommon, and by no means confined to extreme contexts. A common case of it can be found in the reactions of those travelling abroad who see some of their co-nationals behaving disgracefully (as drunken louts and vandals, say). They feel ashamed, even though they are not responsible for what their co-nationals do. An even more domestic example is provided by the spectacle of a mother, perhaps in the supermarket, who treats her child horribly – unkindly, unfairly, maybe even cruelly. Most of us have witnessed such things. And many of us feel not only concern and pity and perhaps outrage for the child, but also a horrible embarrassment – we don't know where to look in the face of such dreadful behaviour towards an innocent child. It is hard to see how to describe this embarrassment except in terms of felt shame – shame at the disgraceful behaviour of the perpetrator. This shame cannot be explained solely in terms of the ineffectiveness of our will in preventing the action, because in some cases at least, we may have rightly decided that we should not prevent the action, even if we were in a position to do so. We might, for example, think that respect for the autonomy of the mother precludes our intervening, as long as no law is being broken, and as long as the child is not being physically harmed. But we can still feel embarrassment and shame in the presence of this wrongdoing.

It is worth noting that vicarious shame is completely unnecessary if the focus of our concern is purely the victims. It is in our horror and outrage that we feel for, and reject, the harm done to the victims. We reject the perpetrator's actions, for the sake of the victims. Vicarious shame adds nothing to this. In our experience of vicarious shame, what we actually feel for, and reject, is the harm the perpetrator does to *himself*, partly perhaps because we feel our common humanity implicates us in his evildoing. And we wish, both for ourselves and for him, that he should not harm (that is, debase and degrade) himself and us in this way. We wish that he was not the kind of person who commits such deeds, not only for the victims' sake, but also for his.

What is the relation between vicarious shame and the perpetrators' own state of mind? It is tempting to think that this is a case of empathy, of the kind normally felt in solidarity with the victims. But that would be a mistake. The various forms which empathy can take involve feelings which in some way echo or share what the other feels.[22] But the perpetrator feels anger, contempt, indifference to the suffering of others, exultation in his own will. We do not share these feelings in vicarious shame. Strangely, what is felt in vicarious shame is much more like *sympathy*, construed as a response of concern about some impending harm to the other.

Vicarious shame involves a rejection of the harm done to the perpetrator by himself, and a desire for him to be different and better, all based on a recognition of our common human nature. Given how solidarity has been characterized earlier, this can be seen as a specialized form of it. We are concerned about the harm the perpetrator is doing to himself and wish that harm to be averted.

Of course, vicarious shame is something we experience intermittently, and in between its episodes we are likely to feel nothing but contempt or resentment or hate for the perpetrator. None the less, while we are experiencing vicarious shame we do seem to feel concern for the terrible debased condition which the perpetrator has got himself into. Indeed, if the resentment and hatred can be overcome, we seem to have in vicarious shame at least some of the psychological materials out of which forgiveness might be constructed.

I am not, however, arguing that in vicarious shame, and the experience of being both implicated in the evildoer's actions and concerned for the harm he does to himself, we find a reason for forgiveness.[23] I am only arguing that the phenomenon of vicarious shame suggests that the relationship of fellow human being in which we stand to the perpetrators is morally rich enough, significant enough, to generate a reason to forgive them. I do not regard this as a strong argument in favour of forgiving major perpetrators, but nor does it seem to be entirely negligible. We used to capture the central idea here by saying that all men are brothers, and should act accordingly. Now, of course, we very rightly want to point out that some of them are sisters too. But the point remains the same: if my sister becomes a monster of iniquity, there is still a reason for me to forgive her – she is, after all, my sister. It may not, of course, be a very strong reason, but even a weak reason is still a reason.

I will close by trying to meet some objections that can be raised to the treatment of vicarious shame as a morally serious phenomenon. First, it might be said that in fact it is just a lightly disguised version of a much less mysterious response, namely a prudential concern that we may be tarred with the same brush as the perpetrator, that others may regard us as sharing his terrible nature and habits. Or perhaps vicarious shame is a mask for another, again less mysterious, attitude: perhaps what we really feel is a weak sense of guilt, because we have not done enough to prevent the evildoing, or perhaps have even sympathized with or connived at it in some way ourselves. Finally, it may be suggested that vicarious shame is a kind of luxury emotion, felt by anxious liberals in their protected ivory towers, which would not survive the rigours of the harsher moral climate in which most people have to live.

Of course we do sometimes feel these other responses, sometimes for good reason. But the prudential worry is unlikely to be found in the group least able to be tarred with the same brush as the perpetrators, namely the victims. And similarly a worry about whether we have really been conniving with the evildoers is unlikely to be found among those who can be expected to be least in sympathy with them; again, the victims. And lastly, luxury emotions cannot plausibly be attributed to those living in the most extreme and terrible of conditions, such as the Nazi concentration camps. So all three objections would be undermined by cases of vicarious shame among the victims themselves. And we do find these cases (though they are not of course called by that name). One such case is given us by Primo Levi, who survived Auschwitz, and has written unforgettably about it. In describing the feelings of the concentration camp victims as they witnessed or underwent the torments inflicted on them, Levi says this:

> It was not possible for us, nor did we want, to become islands – the just among us, neither more or less numerous than in any other human group, felt remorse, shame and pain for the misdeeds that others and not they had committed, and in which they felt involved, because they sensed that what had happened around them in their presence, and in them, was irrevocable. It would never again be able to be cleansed; it would prove that man, the human species – we, in short – were potentially able to construct an infinite enormity of pain.[24]

Even in the depths of those hells, some of the innocent victims felt implicated, tainted, in virtue of their common humanity, by what the perpetrators alone had done. Given its source, this seems to be evidence that the bonds of common humanity are strong enough to make the crimes of the perpetrators shame and contaminate all the rest of us, even the victims. If so, then there is some reason to think that the relationship between fellow human beings may be significant enough to generate a reason to forgive even those who, in their slaughter of the innocents, have degraded and debased all those who share their common humanity – that is, all of us.

Notes

1. Here I will be drawing mainly on the discussions provided by the commentators in Simon Wiesenthal's *The Sunflower: on the possibilities and limits of forgiveness*, New York: Schocken Books, 1997, and also on Jean Amery's *At the Mind's Limits*, translated by Sidney and Stella Rosenfeld, New York: Schocken Books, 1990.
2. H. Arendt (1963), *Eichmann in Jerusalem: a report on the banality of evil*, London: Faber.
3. See H. Arendt (1958), *The Human Condition*, Chicago: University of Chicago Press. I am grateful to Garrath Williams for discussion of this objection.
4. For a fuller discussion of the motivation of evil agents, see E. Garrard (1998), 'The Nature of Evil', *Philosophical Explorations* **1**, January, pp. 43–60.
5. Those who are committed to a purely consequentialist theory of punishment are less likely to raise this objection. But they might raise a parallel one: that the outcomes will be better for all of us if the perpetrators are not forgiven. But this is likely to amount to a claim about deterrence, which has already been dealt with.
6. This may be Primo Levi's view. In *The Drowned and the Saved* he says: 'I am not inclined to forgive because I know no human act that can erase a crime.' I am uncertain whether his focus here is on the need for punishment or on the inexcusability of the crimes. See P. Levi (1988), *The Drowned and the Saved*, London: Michael Joseph, p. 110.
7. See Amery, *At the Mind's Limits*, pp. 65, 67.
8. I do not, of course, intend to imply that these are the only motives for wanting to withhold forgiveness. Amery himself is the most obvious counter-example. But sometimes these less reputable motives are present in non-forgivers.
9. See Amery's reference to loneliness in *At the Mind's Limits*, p. 70. I am grateful to Norman Geras for pressing this point on me.
10. I am grateful to David McNaughton for extensive discussion of this topic.
11. See J.G. Murphy and J. Hampton (1988), *Forgiveness and Mercy*, Cambridge: Cambridge University Press.
12. Here I am appealing to an objective list theory of individual well-being, and a moralized one at that. See Brad Hooker (1996) in R. Crisp (ed.), *How should One Live?*, Oxford: Clarendon Press. I do not think that Hooker's tentative conclusion against a moralized list theory of individual welfare applies to objectivist versions of the theory.
13. One way of characterizing it, which I owe to Robert Dunn, is as the difference between *attitude-focused* and *object-focused* reasons.
14. T. Govier (1999), 'Forgiveness and the Unforgivable', *American Philosophical Quarterly* **36**, January, pp. 59–75.
15. See also M. Holmgren (1994), 'Forgiveness and the Intrinsic Value of Persons', *American Philosophical Quarterly* **30**, pp. 331–40; P. Benn (1996), 'Forgiveness and Loyalty', *Philosophy* **71**, pp. 369–84.
16. See Hugo Young (1989), *One of Us: a biography of Margaret Thatcher*, London: Macmillan.
17. See the activities of rescuers during the Nazi era documented in K.R. Monroe et al. (1990), 'Altruism and the Theory of Rational Action: Rescuers of Jews in Nazi Europe', *Ethics* **101**; N. Tec (1986), *When Light Pierced the Darkness: Christian Rescue of Jews in Nazi-occupied Poland*, New York: Oxford University Press.
18. Cf. D.E. Brown (1991), *Human Universals*, New York: McGraw-Hill, in anthropology; J. Barkow, L. Cosmides and J. Tooby (1992), *The Adapted Mind: evolutionary psychology and the generation of culture*, Oxford: Oxford University Press, in evolutionary psychology; N. Geras (1983), *Marx and Human Nature: refutation of a legend*, London: Verso, in political philosophy.

19. See C. Browning (1992), *Ordinary Men: Reserve Battalion 101 and the Final Solution in Poland*, New York: HarperCollins; D. Goldhagen (1996), *Hitler's Willing Executioners: Ordinary Germans and the Holocaust*, London: Little, Brown and Co.
20. I do not wish to suggest that this shared capacity for evil means that we are all equally to blame. This generally turns out to mean that no one is really to blame. Manifestations of the capacity for evil are what matter for blameworthiness, not mere possession of it.
21. R. Nozick (1990), *The Examined Life*, New York: Touchstone, p. 238.
22. See the extremely useful taxonomy of these psychological states in S. Darwall (1998), 'Empathy, Sympathy, Care', *Philosophical Studies* **89**, pp. 261–82.
23. This may indeed be true, but I do not currently see how to show that it is.
24. Levi, *The Drowned and the Saved*, p. 66.

Chapter 14

The Holocaust and the Possibility of Art

Oliver Leaman

One of the most quoted statements of Adorno is one which he did not actually make. He is often credited with having said 'No poetry after Auschwitz', but this is not what he said precisely. A slogan of that brevity is not characteristic of Adorno. He actually wrote 'To write a poem after Auschwitz is an act of barbarism.'[1] This indicated his view, which we shall discuss here, that the Holocaust was a break in human history, so that the ordinary aesthetic concepts and approaches which previously had force no longer work. This slogan was challenged by many writers in both the Jewish and non-Jewish worlds, and a characteristic response is that of Gunter Grass, who acknowledged his membership of the Auschwitz generation, albeit not as a criminal but in the camp of the criminals, but who set out to refute Adorno by writing poetry.[2] I was previously rather critical of this claim by Adorno, and of the idea that the Holocaust constitutes a radical break with the past,[3] but I should like to defend the claim now and see whether we can make more of it than immediately seems to be the case.

There is a lot of controversy about whether the Holocaust represents a unique event in human history, a controversy which can become rather mawkish, as when individuals who have had unfortunate experiences compete with each other as to who has suffered most. There is an amusing British television sketch in which a variety of people describe their hard childhoods, the penultimate complainant claiming that all he had to live in when he was a child was a box. This is met by the last speaker saying with mock wonder 'You had a box!' The point of this sketch is not to poke fun at people who had difficult experiences in the past, but more to doubt the point of comparing such experiences in a useful way. Certainly there are cases where comparison is sensible. Some people are a little unwell while others are very unwell, and it is entirely appropriate for the latter to complain more than the former. But in cases where an attempt has been made to wipe out an ethnic community, cases which sadly are far from rare, it is difficult to see how to assess comparative suffering and disaster. One could look to numbers killed, or at the numbers as a proportion of the whole group, and on these calculations the murder of the Jews would be an unusually severe event as compared with the attempted destruction of many other ethnic groups. Yet even if this is true it is difficult to see it as essentially different from other attempts at genocide, and despite what Hitler said about the Armenians, other genocides are well remembered and continue to haunt the countries from which the murderers came. On the other hand, some such evil events are not really properly acknowledged. It is sometimes argued that the large-scale death of African Americans and Native Americans during the period of slavery and colonization, and their subsequent impoverishment, criminalization and contemporary high morbidity represent a holocaust greater than the murder of the Jews (I was present at a plenary session of a conference in the United States where this was said[4]). We might criticize this claim, but the whole structure of this discussion is rather distasteful. What the African Americans who said this meant is that the suffering of their community requires some public acknowledgement, no less than that of the Jews, and who could deny that every community should be given a voice? Unfortunately it often seems that only a limited amount of suffering can be allowed to have taken place, so that one community's suffering is in some way at the expense of another group. This is the sort of rhetorical confusion into which we descend once we start thinking of a holocaust as unique.

It might seem that if the Holocaust was not a unique event, then the idea that there could be no poetry after it loses all plausibility. Let us examine this in more detail. First, I do not think that it is poetry which is at issue here, but culture in general. What Adorno does not mean is that culture can no longer work because the generally optimistic assumptions on which it is based no longer apply. That is, there is a general view often loosely held that culture makes us 'better' as moral beings, so that we improve morally as we advance culturally. As Rilke puts it in *Archäischer Torso Apollos*, 'du müsst dein Leben ändern'.[5] Yet we know that some of the worst murderers of the Holocaust were highly cultured individuals, who saw no contradiction between killing innocent people during the day and playing Beethoven on their piano during the evening, and indeed there is no contradiction between these two activities. The idea that culture makes it impossible for us to behave badly, or even less likely, is naive and there is no evidence that Adorno used it.

As a factual claim Adorno's statement is obviously false. That is, there has been lots of culture since the Holocaust, and indeed there was culture within the Holocaust itself, even within Auschwitz. Some of it has had the Holocaust as its subject. Some has ignored it, or appeared to ignore it, and one of the notable features of Adorno's claim is that it appears to be very Eurocentric. The progress of culture in other parts of the world, for which the Holocaust is a little-noticed event in a far-off land, has proceeded apace without any problems. Of course, Asia and Africa have had their own ethnic disasters to discuss, and sometimes their artists have and sometimes they have not. Adorno is implying that European culture is really the basis of all culture, but there is certainly more to culture than Kultur, despite what Adorno's experience of life in the United States suggested.

Adorno's claim is not really a claim, it is an exhortation. It is a demand that those who would otherwise participate in cultural work take notice of the Holocaust and what the Holocaust means. But why? What is so compelling about that event which makes it obligatory on artists to take note of it, and even to question their whole activity as a result? A plausible suggestion is that the Holocaust led to an entirely new way of using language and other cultural instruments. This is because the event was of such a magnitude that it changed for ever the relationship which human beings have with each other and with the ways in which they represent each other.

But this does not seem to be the case. The language does not seem to have changed. People who were born before the Holocaust have no difficulty in understanding what is said or written after the Holocaust. Language does of course change over time, and one needs to be sensitive to that change if one is to understand fully what is said. The claim is not that language has changed, though, but rather that the underlying presuppositions on which that language is based are no longer as they were, and so the language has in fact radically altered. What are these presuppositions? They are not presumably that art changes life, which we know after the Holocaust is not the case. In any case, it is difficult to see why it might be thought that this was a presupposition of our use of language, since it is both naive and hardly plausible except as an expression of faith.

What is at issue here are the ways in which people treat each other. We know from our personal experience how shocked we can be when a friend turns on us and is hostile or even violent. We know in abstract that people can be wicked, but often when we actually experience this sort of behaviour we are literally struck dumb, because the whole basis of our relationship with a particular person now requires examination. How much more is this the case, one might ask, when a complete civilization turns against one of its constituents, systematically robs and persecutes it, and then takes every care to exterminate every aspect of it. We can in retrospect produce theories which make this sort of behaviour comprehensible objectively, but at the subjective level it is very difficult to understand how it could happen. The difficulty does not lie in the scientific understanding, although that is hard enough, but in coming to terms with the ability of such a large-scale instance of treachery, of cruelty and hatred which seems to be so total. Again, if we refer back to the case where we discover that a particular individual harbours huge feelings of hostility to us, for no apparent reason, we are shocked and then look around at everyone else we know and wonder what they think of us. It changes our ideas of our links with each other, and perhaps it is on those links that our language rests. After all, language is an effect of the relationships between people, and if those relationships change, then the 'old' language may no longer work properly.

This thesis seems to be too strong. Is it really plausible, for example, that our referring expressions no longer have purchase when the links between people have changed radically? Surely we all know what we mean by 'dog' however suspicious we may become of our neighbours. But art, and poetry in particular, is far more than just descriptive. It is not dogs which have changed but the relationships which exist between people, and those relationships do enter into the warp and woof of poetry and other forms of culture.

Yet very few commentators apart from Adorno seem to have noticed that such a radical change has occurred after the Holocaust as compared with before. Many poets find the Holocaust a constantly fascinating subject for their work, and they seem to be writing the same sort of poems as before the Holocaust, albeit perhaps with a grimmer subject-matter. The fascinating conjecture which Adorno raises is that the meaning of what artists do is different but not in a way which anyone notices. That is, in fact the language has changed, but its users do not notice that change. This idea has a respectable history in the history of ideas. When Nietzsche referred to the death of God he did not mean that no one believed in God any more, nor that no one referred to the deity. He meant that the easy acceptance of God was no longer feasible in modern society, and so the meaning of the term had irretrievably changed. Some people may think that God is not dead, in just the same way that some people think that Elvis Presley is not dead, but even those who proclaim his continuing existence in fact base their lives on his death. This is because the role of God in modern culture is no longer equivalent to the role of an active participant, and so the culture regards him as dead.[6] Now, this is not the place to consider the merits of this particular thesis, but we need here to acknowledge the possibility which the thesis suggests, that a radical change can come about in human thought without our noticing it. This can certainly happen in individual human relationships, where one participant carries on as though nothing important was different, but we know that the whole basis of their relationship is now very different. While for outside observers the change is obvious, to the participants it is often far from obvious, and the question arises as to whether the Holocaust has actually changed radically the nature of the relationship which we have with our language and our culture, but in a way which has remained imperceptible to most of us.

It would not be inappropriate to ask what sort of criteria would be crucial to resolving this issue. For example, when we think of the claim that God is dead, we need to ask how we would determine that this is in fact true as a report on contemporary cultural life. We would look at what people say and write, how we lead our lives, and we would look for some strong evidence that religion plays an important part in our lives. If we discover that religion really has little to do with our lives, perhaps as a report on what we do as compared with what we say, then the claim that God is dead has some justification. It would be difficult to argue this for Adorno's claim, since what we have after the Holocaust is really very much the same sort of cultural work as before. We could say that despite appearance it was really very different, but we would need some evidence for such a claim. We could imagine what that evidence would be. For example, it might be that the familiar phrases of language which before the Holocaust had a particular resonance no longer 'worked' after the Holocaust, or it might be that certain words had changed their meaning. The point is that we could detect such changes, perhaps not immediately, but there would certainly be some evidence of their having taken place, and we could then provide some grounding for the idea that the language had radically altered. Certainly some words and phrases have been infected by the Nazi times; for example, it is difficult to use the expression which hung over Auschwitz, 'Arbeit macht frei', without being ironic, but is this a problem which affects the whole of the language? And in any case which language are we referring to here, language in general or the German language in particular?

If the answer is language in general then we have the difficulty of acknowledging the Eurocentric flavour of the claim, but perhaps this is not so fatal after all. Perhaps the claim is that once we acknowledge that human beings are capable of acting as they did in the Holocaust, this demonstrates that humanity as a whole is incapable of holding on to the notion of a stable concept of who they are and what limits exist for the scope of their actions. After all, the Germans during the Nazi times merely represent one of the highest-developed forms of human civilization, so that if they could end up doing what they did, anyone could. So if Adorno's claim is to be interesting it must refer to language as such.

Thus far we have looked at some ways of supporting the claim, and rejected them. Let us see if we can construct a more successful argument out of the nature of language itself. Language is more than just a syntax; it rests, as Wittgenstein puts it, on agreement in opinions, on a common form of life. Language is part of our social network, and if that social network collapses, language will also be affected. Now, at a superficial level that appears not to be the case. For example, those few Jews who survived in Nazi Germany by pretending to be non-Jews[7] were using the German language to get over the meanings which they wished to get over, albeit these were not their real opinions. They knew what the language meant; had they not they would not have survived, and although they had a different understanding of many of the principal phrases in that language they still knew what they meant.

At a deeper level, though, the situation is not so clear. Because society had essentially been revealed to be a shallow institution, an institution which could sanction murder on the scale of the Holocaust, the language which is linked to society can no longer be taken seriously. Only an ironic use of that language is feasible. That is, although one may use the language in a perfectly straightforward sense, one has to stand back from it and observe it from outside, as it were, since it is no longer possible to feel at home inside it. If one does feel at home in it, then this is a case of 'Glücklich ist, wer vergisst, was doch nicht zu ändern ist' (He is fortunate who forgets what cannot be changed), as in the words of the Strauss operetta, which hardly represents a thoughtful attitude to the Holocaust.

This brings in the interesting question of how one should commemorate an event like the Holocaust. In the Jewish Bible there is an important passage which is traditionally read in synagogues at the start of the month of Adar, the month of Purim, the commemoration of the escape of the Jews from destruction at the hands of Haman in Persia. The passage refers to the treachery of Amalek, who attacked the rear of the Israelites on their escape from Egypt, doing so when they were already in a weak condition and the weakest part of the group.[8] There is a story that all the major enemies of the Jews are descended from Amalek, including Haman and Hitler! What this biblical passage suggests appears paradoxical: it recommends remembering and never forgetting what Amalek did and yet at the same time blotting out his name. These appear to be contrary instructions; how can one at the same time both remember and blot out someone's name? It might be that what is meant here is that a balance should be struck between acknowledging the significance of the crime while not allowing the criminal to dominate one's life. This is sensible, since if the criminal does have such an effect on one that it is impossible to escape his influence, then the crime becomes insurmountable. In a letter after World War II Hannah Arendt refers to this when she comments on the accused at the Nuremburg trials looking smug, because they knew that nothing could be done to them which would be at all proportionate to what they had done. Yet in any disaster it is important for the psychological survival of the innocent that they do not constantly refer to the disaster. Jewish history has been such a grim sequence of disasters that it could easily have transformed the religion into a gloomy commemoration of things going wrong. Yet Judaism is not like that, and indeed the traditional prayer which is said by mourners, the *kaddish*, does not even mention death but is rather a celebration of life.

This all militates against the view that the Holocaust was of such significance that our language no longer works. It also suggests that it can hardly be that the significance of the event means that we cannot discuss it aesthetically or in any other way, since if that were the case we could not commemorate it. What Adorno is stressing is that the event is of such significance that it cannot (yet?) be pigeonholed away along with other apparently similar events and brought out occasionally to be dusted off and examined. Yet we know that if we constantly harp on this event we are unlikely to survive it psychologically, and it is surely not appropriate to allow such memory to destroy spiritually those of us who were not destroyed physically. This seems to be what Adorno is demanding when he rejects the possibility of art after Auschwitz, as though even that form of catharsis is no longer feasible. Yet the ability to describe and discuss a tragedy is a very important way in which we as human beings can try to put it within some wider context and go beyond it; it may not be that we can do this through great art if we are not especially skilled or creative, yet there seems no good reason for ruling it out altogether.

We see here the motive for Adorno's claim that the Holocaust is an event which it is important that we do not 'get beyond'. We should not get beyond it because it is still so fresh in our minds, or certainly was in his shortly after the ending of World War II. Perhaps one day we shall be able to file it away and categorize it with the other disasters in human history which have occurred in the more distant past, but it would not be right to think of doing this right now. Yet all remembering must come to an end at some stage. In the poem of Abraham Shlonsky:

> I have taken this oath: to remember everything
> To remember and to forget nothing
> To forget nothing until ten generations have passed
> Until all the grief and all the pain have gone.[9]

What is interesting about this passage is the acknowledgement that a time comes when it is appropriate to think of the suffering attached to a memory coming to an end. That is not to say that the memory itself comes to an end; that can continue to be alive if it is incorporated within some cultural context, and religions are excellent at doing this. Religions have rules and procedures which help us regulate our mourning and prevent it from overwhelming us. Adorno seems sceptical about this, but presumably this is not unconnected with his general commitment to secularism. He is sceptical of the capacity of religion to embody the suffering of the Holocaust acceptably within a ritual. Perhaps he is right to be sceptical, but it is worth noting that this is an activity which religions are skilled at carrying out, a function which it is difficult, although certainly not impossible, to replicate otherwise.

One is reminded here of a claim which is often made in the United States that too much emphasis is put on the Holocaust if this is the only or main source of Jewish identity. In a situation where many Jews are without strong or any religious belief, it is only their identification with each other because they know that they too would have suffered had they fallen into the hands of the Nazis that establishes them as

Jews. The Holocaust then comes to have huge significance, since it actually constitutes a principle of identity. From a religious point of view this led Emil Fackenheim to talk of the 614th commandment, not to hand any posthumous victories to Hitler, by which he means that the Jewish people should not be assimilated or disappear in the benign atmosphere of modern Western society. Some Jewish thinkers interpret the Holocaust as *kiddush ha-shem*, as deaths not in vain but carried out to sanctify the divine name, and this is certainly a possible response, albeit a difficult one given the scale of the murder and its success in wiping out large and important religious communities. Adorno completely rejects this possibility in his claim, finding no logic in the event at all, and since the Holocaust is regarded as completely inexplicable, there is no way of representing it aesthetically, nor is there any way of representing anything aesthetically any more. In Schiller's words:

Nichts Heiliges ist mehr, es lösen
sich alle Bande frommer Scheu;
Der Gute räumt den Platz dem Bösen,
und alle Laster werden frei.[10]

(There is nothing holy any longer
all the bonds of pious reverence are loosening
The good individual gives up his place for the bad
and all vices are set free.)

Readers will be aware of the irony of what has just been written, since it is an excellent evocation of the events of the Holocaust, and yet it is an aesthetic evocation, something which Adorno denies is possible. The fact that it was written before the Holocaust is irrelevant, since we are using that passage to bring to our minds an aspect of the Nazi times. It works as a description of the times since it is written in such a way as to resonate with a whole range of different periods and events, as is the case with works of art in general, and so it appears that poetry before Auschwitz may be used to deal with aspects of the Holocaust experience.

Adorno's claim, which I have been examining as though it is meant to be declarative, is of course really imperative. He is saying that we should not think that after the Holocaust we can do art in the ways in which we could do it before. But even that claim seems to be exaggerated, since if pre-Holocaust verse seems to work after the event then it suggests that there is no general problem with representing that period aesthetically. We have already mentioned the possibility that we do not notice that the familiar poetry no longer works, but we found it difficult to assess evidence for that conclusion. Although we have not examined post-Holocaust art there is surely no reason to think that it cannot work in confronting the Holocaust. We may agree with Adorno that there are enormous problems in putting the Holocaust in any sort of theological context which would help us understand it, but surely it is the role of art to represent the unrepresentable, to express the inexpressible. Adorno is far too pessimistic in thinking that the Holocaust demands an entirely different approach to art. We have argued here that it is not to disparage the Holocaust to try to link it with other disasters and to deal with it in just the same way that one deals with similar (albeit less extreme) events. It is only such an approach that allows us to deal with it at all and overcome it, in so far as this is possible. And surely it is possible, if we embody our response to it in art, not to mention the tried and tested route of religion.

When we talk with bereaved people we often expect them to end their mourning at some socially acceptable stage, and psychologists tend to claim that failure to do so is an indication of an unhealthy response to loss. Indeed, we see the Victorian era in Britain as a time when mourning was turned into something of an art form, and yet it is worth noting that Queen Victoria was frequently criticized for her prolonged mourning for Prince Albert. She extended the mourning period in a way which was felt to be exaggerated and artificial. I have argued that there is no 'normal' period of mourning or 'appropriate' reaction to loss, although we can certainly appreciate that some reactions are likely to be more effective in helping the mourner come to terms with her loss than others.[11] It is true that the rites of passage and rituals of mourning have as their end the return of the mourner to ordinary society and the psychological and social overcoming of the loss. If there were no ways of resolving grief, it would literally overwhelm us and make it impossible for social life to continue. This is acknowledged in many of the rituals which religions provide to deal with death, and in particular Judaism responds to the death of an individual with the *kaddish*, a prayer that is really a celebration of life.

The implication of this part of the discussion is that Adorno is really making too much of what should be, eventually, overcome. He is perhaps illustrating the critique which Hegel provided of Judaism where he suggests that it has such a distant notion of God that Versöhnung, reconciliation between the divine and the human, is ruled out from the beginning. Hence the suffering which emerged in the Holocaust is something which Judaism is systematically incapable of resolving.[12]

This is not the place to try to resolve these involved issues, but they clearly affect Adorno's statement. Although we have not been able to find any good arguments for thinking that the fact of the Holocaust makes art inconceivable, we have acknowledged that his claim does point to something very important, namely, that our response to a tragedy is not necessarily going to be limited to particular rules of social engagement. Indeed, our response could be that the tragedy is so all-encompassing that it makes any aesthetic response vacuous. This pessimism about the scope for art to deal with disaster is unjustified, and yet it does raise an interesting question. Is there anything which is so totally evil that we cannot think of an aesthetic response to it being possible? One is tempted to reply in the negative, and yet this persistent faith in the ability of art to help us represent and respond to disaster may be a sign of a facile confidence in our ability to stretch art further than it will really go. There is no reason to think that art can deal with absolutely anything. 'No poetry after Auschwitz' is a slogan which alerts us to this difficulty.

Notes

1. T. Adorno, *Minima Moralia*, in P. Kiedaisch (ed.), *Lyrik nach Auschwitz? Adorno und die Dichter*, Ditzingen: Reclam, 1995, p. 5.
2. G. Grass, *Schreiben nach Auschwitz*, 1995, in trans. K. Winston with A. Wensgner (1990), G. Grass, *Two States – One Nation*, Harcourt Brace Jovanovich, p. 102.
3. O. Leaman (1995), *Evil and Suffering in Jewish Philosophy*, Cambridge: Cambridge

University Press; also (1999), 'Time, Modernity, and Destructive Habits of Thought', *Canadian Journal of Philosophy*, Supp. Vol. 25 (1999), pp. 127–46.

4. This claim was made during a plenary session at a conference on Gendered Violence UK, 30–31 March 2001, University of Kentucky.
5. This theme of the salvific effect of art runs through Rilke's work and was very influential in the German-speaking world.
6. See the relevant entries in G. Howarth and O. Leaman (eds) (2001), *Encyclopedia of Death and Dying*, New York: Routledge.
7. M. Roseman (2000), *A Past in Hiding*, New York: Henry Holt.
8. Deuteronomy 25:17–18.
9. A. Shlonsky (1967), *Abraham Shlonsky: Yalkut Shirim*, ed. A.B. Yafeh, Tel Aviv: Yachdav.
10. Schiller, *Das Lied von der Glocke/The Song of the Bell*.
11. O. Leaman (1995), *Death and Loss*, London: Cassell.
12. 'Evil and Suffering', in ibid., pp. 185–219. For some attempted strategies to discuss the Holocaust within Jewish philosophy, see 'The Holocaust', in D. Frank, O. Leaman and C. Manekin (eds) (2000), *Jewish Philosophy Reader*, New York: Routledge, pp. 538–51, and also the chapter by Steven Katz in D. Frank and O. Leaman (1997), *History of Jewish Philosophy*, New York: Routledge.

Chapter 15

The Holocaust in American Life as a Moral Text

Lawrence Blum

Whitwell, Tennessee, is a small town, almost entirely white, Christian and fundamentalist, with no Jews. In the late 1990s, in response to a new curriculum on the Holocaust, a class of eighth graders (thirteen-year-olds) decided to collect six million paper clips, representing the Jews killed in the Holocaust, and make them into a sculpture.[1] The Whitwell 'paper clip project,' as it came to be known, exemplifies the sort of penetration of the Holocaust into American consciousness which Peter Novick attempts to account for – and about which he expresses a good deal of dismay – in his important book, *The Holocaust in American Life*.[2]

The Nazis' partially successful attempt to exterminate the Jews of Europe – an event widely referred to as 'the Holocaust' – has come to serve as a symbol of absolute moral evil and horror. Virtually every American can identify the Holocaust, at least in its main outline, while ignorance of salient facts about American history is widespread.[3] Many Americans, especially Jews, regard this as unremarkable; the Holocaust is worthy of any attention it is given, so its salience is no cause for wonder or explanation.

Novick attempts to dislodge this sense of inevitability about 'Holocaust-consciousness' in the contemporary United States. He traces American awareness of the Holocaust from the 1940s to the late 1990s. Through meticulous scholarship and plausible, if sometimes somewhat speculative, historical supposition, Novick paints a picture of social, cultural and political factors that account for the new visibility and previous invisibility of the Holocaust.

Novick argues that it was not until the 1960s that 'the Holocaust' emerged into consciousness as a distinctive event, separate in historical and moral character from other Nazi atrocities. In the period following the war, Novick argues, Jews were not generally singled out for specific attention as Nazi victims.[4] During the war, fears of anti-Semitism (which was quite pronounced in the prewar and war years) plus pessimism that anything could be done short of winning the war as quickly as possible inhibited Jewish organizations from calling attention to the specifically Jewish dimensions of Nazi atrocities.[5] Furthermore, the onset of the cold war severely dampened American receptivity to German crimes. The new enemy was the Soviet Union; the Germans were allies. Even the war itself came to be reframed as part of a struggle against 'totalitarianism,' a concept that embraced Nazism and Soviet communism equally. Refugees from communism became the favored victims, and Jews' fears of being associated with communism – especially intensified by the Rosenberg spy trials in 1953 – made it difficult for American Jews to depart publicly from the cold war consensus and call attention to German crimes against Jews during the war.[6] The bombing of Hiroshima was an atrocity of more ongoing concern, both because Americans perpetrated it and because of the fear of nuclear attack against the US.

The idea of the Holocaust as an event of transcendent significance was not in evidence:

> In the first postwar years, the Holocaust was viewed, by Jews as well as Americans in general, as part of history. It was an event that had taken place there and not here; it was an aspect of a period – the era of fascism – that was now ended; it had been the result of a particular constellation of forces.[7]

Although Novick fully recognizes the distinctiveness of Jewish victimization by the Nazis, he decries a Jewish overpossessiveness about the Holocaust in recent decades, and clearly thinks there is a salutary lesson in remembering an era in which Nazi crimes were viewed in a less particularistic, more universalist manner.

In a different vein, the 'upbeat' mood of the postwar years encouraged a focus on optimistic hopes for the future, not appalling memories of the past. Anti-Semitism had discouraged Jews from calling attention to themselves, but, ironically, the growing acceptance of Jews as Americans through the 1950s encouraged an assimilationist consciousness among Jews that had the same result.

All this changed in the 1960s.[8] The 1961 trial (in Israel) of Adolf Eichmann, charged with administering 'The Final Solution,' brought the details of the Holocaust forcefully to public awareness. Then the 1967 Israeli-Arab War, and even more so the 1973 Yom Kippur War, seemed to emphasize Israeli vulnerability, and intensified a tendency to link the Holocaust to the plight of Israel, a link increasingly pressed by the Israeli government and pro-Israel lobbyists in the US.

Novick mentions later events and cultural factors that encouraged and solidified the salience of Holocaust-awareness in American, and especially American Jewish, consciousness – the TV mini-series *Holocaust* in 1978; a rising cachet, connected to multiculturalism, attached to 'victim identity' (when, in contrast to racial minority groups, Jews had little in their current circumstances to support this sense of victimhood); a desire for the clarity of good versus evil provided by the Holocaust, when other moral reference points were becoming uncertain; the weakening of traditional forces securing Jewish communal identity (anti-Semitism, religious belief and ritual observance), allowing the Holocaust to fill that breach; the opening in 1993 of the Holocaust Memorial Museum in Washington, which has become the best-attended museum in US history.

At one level, Novick's book is purely historical. But his argument is infused with moral import, both explicit and implicit. Three moral strands in Novick's book bear mentioning. Novick is particularly concerned to counter a 'moralized' account of the history of American Holocaust-consciousness, according to which its initial near-absence was caused by American (including American Jewish) guilt for having failed to take steps to stop the Holocaust (such as bombing railway lines to death camps) or to help Jewish refugees, and by survivors' repression of their traumatic experience. The eventual breaking through to consciousness, on this account, was due to getting past such barriers, and coming to recognize the genuine moral and historic importance of the Holocaust. Novick's counter-narrative involving more mundane, contingent, social and opportunistic factors is meant to undercut this moralized and psychological account. In addition, he attempts to demonstrate that there was little that the US, and American Jews, could have done to halt the Holocaust; so there was little reason for them to feel guilty.

A second moral strand is Novick's approval of some of the developments he details and disapproval of others. He is quite explicit about this, expressing in his Introduction skepticism 'that the prominent role the Holocaust has come to play both for American Jewry and American discourse is as desirable a development as most people seem to think it is.'[9] He disapproves of the centrality of Holocaust-consciousness to Jewish identity, seeing in that consciousness an intimate connection with an inward and politically rightward turn among Jews, an engagement in a morally revolting contest of sufferings, and a withdrawal of concern from the plight of more deprived groups. In Israel and the US, Holocaust-consciousness has provided a rationalization for supporting what Novick regards as deplorable and oppressive Israeli policies toward the Palestinians.[10] Independent of these effects, Novick also finds regrettable a Jewish communal self-definition in terms of suffering. (Interestingly, Novick provides no *alternative* basis for what he, or someone, might regard as a healthy form of Jewish identity.[11])

With regard to the more general salience of the Holocaust in American consciousness, Novick suggests that it has diverted public attention and concern from morally serious issues close to home, such as the plight of African Americans.[12] He avers that it enables a costless moral regret that does no one any good, yet yields the illusion of some sort of moral accomplishment.

The decrying of the salience of Holocaust-consciousness is tied in with the third, and most prominent, moral thread in Novick's book, one on which I will focus the remainder of this paper. That is his rejection of what he regards as the widespread idea that the Holocaust has vital moral lessons to teach with respect to the world we currently inhabit. Novick devotes an entire chapter – which he sardonically entitles, 'Never Again the Slaughter of the Albigensians' – to criticizing 'the lessons of the Holocaust,' and arguments to that end are peppered throughout the book.

The attack on Holocaust lessons is no mere moral add-on to Novick's historical argument. Novick states in his Introduction that the public rationale for confronting the Holocaust is 'that the Holocaust is the bearer of important lessons that we all ignore at our peril.'[13] That is, Novick sees the acceptance of Holocaust lessons as both a *rationale* for sustaining attention to the Holocaust, and also as perhaps a major prop in what *actually does* sustain it. If he can show that Americans have wildly overblown the lessons to be learned, this removes an important normative, and possibly empirical, prop of Holocaust-consciousness.

Novick's criticisms of 'Holocaust lessons' are quite distinct in spirit from those that imply a kind of sacralizing of the Holocaust, or seeing it as a kind of trans-historical event. For example, Berel Lang, criticizing his own title for a piece on 'lessons,' says that the title is offensive because it implies that the enormity of the Holocaust should be viewed as a school for study, as if together with the horror of that event, we ought also ... to observe it with a detached and calculating eye that looks ahead to future contingencies and opportunities in our own lives and in those of others.[14]

By contrast, for Novick one should be able to contemplate the Holocaust from a distance and with a historian's detachment.

In response both to Lang's remarks and to Novick, I would suggest that one should not contemplate any horror with a view *simply* to what it can teach us about how to deal with our current dilemmas. However, this is as true of the murder of a single innocent as of genocides such as the Holocaust, the Rwandan, the Armenian, and so on. Each atrocity should be appreciated in its distinctiveness and particularity, and accorded the moral attention and moral response it deserves; but, contrary to Novick, I also see distinct value in attempting to mine these atrocities for moral lessons for our own times. (Lang agrees, answering his own criticism.)

However, Novick thinks there is not much, or much of use, to be learned from the Holocaust. I find in Novick at least ten distinct criticisms of the 'lessons of the Holocaust,' and will discuss all but the last two:

1. People take from the Holocaust moral stances that they already hold, rather than actually learning those lessons from an encounter with the Holocaust.
2. For various reasons, the Holocaust has little to teach us that is applicable to our current situation; we can best learn the lessons we need from other sources.
3. Much more urgent moral tasks (racial injustice, world hunger) face American society than taking up a morally appropriate stance toward the Holocaust.
4. Some prominent alleged lessons about the Holocaust itself (for example the culpability of 'bystanders,' the culpability of the US government for not taking action during the war to bomb rail lines to death camps) are not well founded.
5. The American public and government have failed to apply obvious lessons of the Holocaust to comparable atrocities (Bosnia, Rwanda, Cambodia) since that time.
6. The Americanization of the Holocaust has led to strained or banal views about the significance of the Holocaust for Americans (for example, that the US stands for values that are the precise opposite of those of Nazism, or that American commemoration of the Holocaust is particularly appropriate because of American failure to do more to stop the Holocaust or to rescue Jews).
7. Advocates of the importance of a confrontation with the Holocaust often swing inconsistently between claiming that the Holocaust is unique – a claim that is politically reprehensible, as well as counterproductive to any use of the Holocaust for the purposes of moral education – and that it is the repository of universal lessons.
8. The Holocaust is invoked in moral contexts (sometimes, as in 7 above, by claiming that the Holocaust is unique) in such a way as to render any other atrocity virtually trivial by comparison.
9. At the same time, the constant invocation of the Holocaust in relation to other allegedly morally objectionable phenomena has served to trivialize the Holocaust itself.
10. Looking to historical events for moral lessons tends to distort our understanding of history, encouraging oversimplification.

The Uniqueness Controversy

I begin with the related criticisms 7 and 8, which raise issues familiar in philosophical writing on the Holocaust. Novick is right to note the tension between claiming that the Holocaust is unique, and that there are lessons to be learned from it. Lessons require points of comparison. If we are to learn that the bureaucracy of a modern state can be put in service to mass murder, in order to prevent such a thing happening again, we must believe that it is at least possible for modern states other than Germany to do so as well, whether or not any have actually done so. If we are to learn from the Holocaust the horrors to which blind obedience to authority can lead, such blind obedience must exist, or be possible, outside the Nazi context. If the Holocaust were 'unique,' in the sense that nothing could properly be compared with it, these comparisons could not be drawn. This seems an elementary point, but Novick is correct to claim that both views are frequently expressed in American discourse about the Holocaust without a sense of their inherent tension if not outright contradiction.

In addition to this point, Novick is particularly disturbed by the claim of uniqueness, or, more precisely, by the way that claim has been parlayed in discourse about the Holocaust and other atrocities. In one sense, Novick notes, claiming the uniqueness of any historical event is vacuous; no two historical events are exactly alike. On the other hand, every historical event shares some features with other events while being distinctive in other ways. In this sense *no* historical event, including the Holocaust, is unique. One can, however, set up a particular criterion as one's definition of uniqueness, and show that the Holocaust is unique by that criterion – say, a combination of the use of modern technology and an avowed intention on the part of the state to murder every individual of a particular ethnic group. But the choice of that criterion of uniqueness, if not entirely arbitrary, can hardly be vindicated as the only plausible candidate.

So the claim of uniqueness is somewhat arbitrary, but Novick is particularly concerned with its practical effect. 'The assertion that the Holocaust is unique ... is, in practice, deeply offensive. What else can it possibly mean except "your catastrophe, unlike ours, is ordinary."'[15] This claim is what Novick means by criticism 8, that the Holocaust is invoked in such a way as to imply that other atrocities are almost trivial by comparison.

Proponents of the 'uniqueness thesis' are often sensitive to the concern Novick raises. For example, Alan Rosenbaum, in his preface to the collection *Is the Holocaust Unique? Perspectives on Comparative Genocide*, cautions that any warranted claim to uniqueness must not 'diminish or still the certain moral authority that must be accorded to other groups whose members have also been forced to endure unspeakable atrocities during their history.'[16] And Steven Katz, perhaps the most prominent uniqueness theorist, says 'In arguing for the uniqueness of the Holocaust, I am *not* making a *moral* claim' – not saying that it was more evil than other atrocities (slavery, devastation of Native American communities, murder of Armenians by Turks).[17]

Novick regards such disavowals as disingenuous, or at best naive, because these claims take place in a context in which invidious comparisons are being made.

Katz's further argument would seem to exemplify Novick's point. Katz says that by uniqueness he is referring to the fact that never before has a state set out, as a matter of intentional principle, to 'annihilate physically every man, woman, and child belonging to a specific people.'[18] Katz can hardly deny that he has chosen a morally infused criterion of uniqueness; the intention to wipe out an entire people is surely a particularly evil one. It is not as if Katz picked a criterion of uniqueness that could be regarded as historically interesting, but of uncertain moral import – such as the use of modern technology in the service of genocidal policies.[19] Katz thus seems disingenuous, or at least confused, when he says that his uniqueness assertion is not meant as a 'moral claim.'

Rosenbaum's (qualified) sympathy with the uniqueness hypothesis reveals different concerns. He says,

> Is it inevitable as many people today fear, that the attenuating hold [the Holocaust] has on our generation will gradually yield to a more generalized noting that the Holocaust was merely only one of many significant horrors that occurred in this century's most horrific conflict?[20]

That is, Rosenbaum appears to think that the assertion of uniqueness is the only alternative to minimizing some of the distinctive, and morally pertinent, features of the Holocaust among other Nazi crimes (and, perhaps he means to imply, among other twentieth-century atrocities as well). But the Holocaust has some historical and moral features that distinguish it from other Nazi crimes (and from other atrocities as well) – although this is also true of each particular atrocity. (This is the trivial meaning of 'uniqueness'.) To recognize the Holocaust's distinctiveness, and to accord it the moral attention it warrants, it is not necessary to see the Holocaust as, in some total way, 'unique.' Moreover, as Berel Lang notes, the moral horror of the Holocaust would not in the least be diminished if events exemplifying the features thought by Katz or Rosenbaum to constitute that uniqueness were to be repeated in the future.[21]

Although his claim that invoking the Holocaust has the effect of demoting moral concern about other atrocities seems intuitively plausible, Novick actually provides little empirical support for it. Indeed, it is equally plausible to think that, in public contexts (in contrast to scholarly contexts, as above, in which detailed comparisons are drawn), invoking the Holocaust has the effect of calling attention to atrocities that many will regard as somewhat comparable. In fact Novick provides instances of this latter effect, as we will discuss in the next section. It is probably safe to say that instances of both the demoting and the calling attention can be found.

Criteria for Moral Analogies to the Holocaust

Regarding criticism 1, Novick cites several contexts in which the lessons of the Holocaust have been invoked to support a moral stance whose sources clearly lie elsewhere – opposition to 'big government,' environmentalism, animal rights, gun control, and (the most enthusiastic constituency of lessons of the Holocaust) opposition to abortion (spoken of as 'the American Holocaust').[22] Yet Novick recognizes, albeit hesitantly and ambivalently, that this fact does not invalidate a claim that something is a valid or authentic lesson of the Holocaust.[23] We are still left with the question of what makes something an authentic moral lesson of the Holocaust. However, Novick is extremely reluctant to concede that one can produce criteria for the validity or invalidity of moral lessons. The analogy between the Holocaust and whatever it is being analogized to (abortion, harm to the environment) must, he says, simply 'click.' If it does, one cannot persuade that individual to abandon the analogy; if it does not, one cannot get him or her to see it.[24] At the end of the chapter on lessons, Novick doubts, as if in conclusion, that useful, much less redemptive, lessons can be learned from the Holocaust.[25]

However, the view that there are no general, non-subjective, criteria for validity of moral analogies is at odds with the implications of Novick's criticism 5 – that there are, indeed, lessons to be learned from the Holocaust, important ones too, but that relevant parties (such as Western governments) continually fail to heed them. Novick devotes much attention to the Serbian attack on Bosnian Muslims following the break-up of the former Yugoslavia, with the use of concentration camps, the language and motivation of 'ethnic cleansing,' and other features strongly analogous to the Nazi treatment of the Jews.[26] He also cites the 1994 Rwandan genocide as meeting 'just about every imaginable criterion' for being a holocaust.[27] Novick notes that prominent Jewish organizations called for action to halt the atrocities in Bosnia, citing the Holocaust as a source of their moral concern.[28] Moreover, the opening of the Washington Holocaust Museum coincided with the debate concerning Bosnia, and Novick cites several prominent Jews who opined that failure to act in Bosnia would render the ceremonies opening the Museum an empty gesture.[29]

Novick clearly regards opposition to the Serbian ethnic cleansing of Bosnian Muslims as a plausible and legitimate lesson of the Holocaust. His historically reasonable observation that the American failure to act on it – he acerbically remarks, '"the lessons of Vietnam" easily trumped "the lessons of the Holocaust"'[30] – serves only to reinforce this plausibility.

If Bosnia contains a legitimate lesson from the Holocaust, there must be some moral guideline that renders it so. Before examining what such guidelines might be, let me clarify what Novick is talking about when he speaks of lessons of the Holocaust. He has primarily two categories in mind. One is a particular event in the present (or, in any case, subsequent to the Holocaust), a stance toward which is implied by analogy to the Holocaust – attempting to stop ethnic cleansing in Bosnia, for example. A second is a standing public issue with a moral dimension – abortion, the environment, execution by gas – an appropriate moral stand on which the Holocaust is alleged to provide guidance.

Novick is interested in these two categories because he is concerned with the public functions of the Holocaust in the United States – how the Holocaust has been used to influence policy on moral issues facing American society. He is therefore less interested in a third category of item often discussed in terms of 'lessons of the Holocaust' – general morally significant historical truths to be gleaned from the Holocaust but not directly applicable to distinct events and public issues. Berel Lang provides a thoughtful discussion of such lessons in 'Afterword: Lessons to Learn, or What Future for the Holocaust?'[31] Some of his examples of lessons are that the intention to commit genocide might develop incrementally rather than being fully formed at the outset; that since the Holocaust happened once, something like it can happen again; that with respect to genocide there are no legitimate bystanders.

Novick does, in passing, remark on some lessons of this sort – a reminder of the presence of evil in the world, or that science and technology are not necessarily benevolent, or disabusing us of Enlightenment illusions about the 'perfectability of man.'[32] Novick is, however, skeptical of the *value* of such lessons: either they are empty, or we already know them and do not need to learn them from the Holocaust (criticism 2). 'Most Americans are bombarded with crime in the streets, terrorist bombings, and so know there is evil.'

This is a weak argument. For one thing, the sort of evil involved in ordinary, even violent, crime is not of the magnitude or character of the wholesale intentional slaughter of an ethnic group. More significantly, these deeper truths about bystanders, evil and so on, can be understood at a more or a less profound level, and the Holocaust can be a source of the former. Indeed, somewhat inconsistently, later in the chapter Novick acknowledges a useful Holocaust lesson of this sort that he does regard as salutary – that barbarous deeds can be perpetrated by 'advanced' peoples, not only those seen in the West as more primitive and less 'cultured.'[33]

So Novick finds himself occasionally, grudgingly and inconsistently, conceding the legitimacy of some lessons to be learned from the Holocaust. He does not want to explore how one might go about discerning the significant truths to be so garnered, because it seems to him that to do so would provide a reason why one might think it important for the Holocaust to be a significant moral reference point for Americans. His 'take no prisoners' approach to the latter issue ill suits his nuanced historical account. He could have argued that Americans have misused the Holocaust, have accorded it too much importance, and even have failed to make use of the lessons there to be gotten, without having to take the extreme and implausible position that (inconsistently) guides his discussion – that there are no important lessons to be gleaned from the Holocaust.

Guidelines for Holocaust Analogies

To answer Novick's claim that we have no basis for assessing proposed analogies to the Holocaust, I would like to propose some such guidelines. Even if in only a provisional and tentative way, I hope they will suggest the feasibility of an enterprise that Novick rejects, even if he implicitly relies on it in some of his examples. The general idea is that awareness of the Holocaust will sensitize to and elicit appropriate moral concern toward that which is (validly) analogized to it.

Two somewhat distinct directions suggest themselves. One is to require that the analogized phenomenon be, in some overall sense, comparable to the Holocaust. The second is a much more minimal standard, that requires only that the analogized phenomenon share some important morally significant feature with the Holocaust taken in its historical specificity.

The Holocaust-based curriculum provided by the organization Facing History and Ourselves ('Facing History') is a good illustration of the latter approach. In use since the late 1970s, Facing History teachers have taught hundreds of thousands of secondary school children important lessons about prejudice, hatred, the need to stand up against injustice and persecution, the costs of violence, and the need for civic participation. Moving back and forth in time between the Nazi era and contemporary society, Facing History continually encourages students to draw on morally pertinent dimensions of the Holocaust to make connections to their own lives and societies. To give one concrete example, students in a junior high class (12–13-year-olds) studied the Holocaust and focused on 'bystanders,' emphasizing the moral cost of inaction. At the time that they were engaged in this unit of study, some youngsters from a nearby school gay-baited and then assaulted a female classmate who was holding hands with another girl. During a discussion of this incident, which was widely reported in the local papers, the Facing History students decided they should respond to this hate-based outrage. They planned and executed an elaborate protest on the Underground, where the assault had taken place. It is clear that their study of bystanders in the Holocaust, and of the costs of hatred, had helped these students to focus their moral attention in a productive and impressive way.[34]

In one respect, Novick would presumably approve of Facing History's approach. He worries about a moral tunnel vision that can be promoted by a too Jewish-centered take on the crimes of Nazism. He would approve of a form of Holocaust-awareness that was less parochial, and that linked to other non-Jewish social injustices.

On the other hand, a central part of Novick's criticism 2 is that the Holocaust is so extreme an example of a moral horror that the sorts of moral dimensions taken up by Facing History in application to contemporary American life – bystanders, prejudice, conformity and so on – are not well learned about from a study of the Holocaust. As Novick says,

> I have, in this chapter, expressed doubts about the usefulness of the Holocaust as a bearer of lessons. In large part these doubts are based on the Holocaust's extremity, which on the one hand makes its practical lessons of little applicability to everyday life.[35]

Novick is right that, for example, incidents such as the gay-baiting just mentioned do not, in the contemporary US, carry 'seeds of a Holocaust,' and forms of racial prejudice, suppression of political dissent, and public indifference to injustice in the contemporary US are not wrong and morally troubling because left unchecked they threaten to lead to a holocaust.[36] They are simply wrong in their own right, and Facing History does not imply otherwise. But Novick's reservations on this matter here implicitly point to an important cautionary guideline regarding the 'shared morally significant feature' approach practiced by Facing History – moral ills shared between the Holocaust and other entirely disanalogous situations must be given their appropriate moral due in their particular social and historical context, which are likely to be entirely different from Nazi Germany. In the contemporary United States, incidents embodying such features – an anti-Semitic defacing of a Jewish synagogue, for example – are extremely unlikely to have anything like a 'holocaustal' significance. But such incidents are still quite morally troubling in their own right.

Thus, the 'morally significant feature' approach allows for a fairly wide range of moral lessons of the Holocaust, but limits the place of the Holocaust in teaching about them. The Holocaust supplies the source of these lessons; but the lessons themselves cannot legitimately draw on the distinctive moral horror of the Holocaust itself.

The second approach to analogies to the Holocaust is quite different. It requires that the event or circumstance analogized be of sufficient moral gravity, in some overall sense, to say that the Holocaust is analogous to it; the Holocaust then becomes an appropriate source of moral recognition of the event in question. For example, several years ago, in Texas, a black man, James Byrd, was brutally murdered in an appalling instance of racial hatred, by being tied to the back of a truck and dragged through town. Revulsion at this racist murder was widespread in the United States. Racial hatred is a morally significant dimension of the Holocaust, and this incident could profitably be studied under the 'shared moral feature' approach. However, it does not, I suggest, rise to the level of moral gravity – it is simply on too small a scale – to be analogized to the Holocaust in an overall way.

The 'sufficient moral gravity' condition is met, I suggest, by a range of large-scale human atrocities committed by states. I would include, for example (though I do not rest my case on the inclusion of any particular one of these), the Bosnian, Armenian and Rwandan genocides, slavery in the United States, the American bombing of Hiroshima and Nagasaki, the starvation and killing of a million and a half Cambodians by the Khmer Rouge, Stalin's starving of many millions of peasants in the early 1930s, the decimation of Native Americans in the United States, the Indonesian treatment of the East Timorese. The intuition operating here is that these atrocities are of sufficient scale and dreadfulness that the moral horror of the Holocaust should be permitted to direct appropriate moral attention to them; and, in addition, that comparisons of the two atrocities can be profitably undertaken in a spirit of dispassionate enquiry that will illuminate both the moral and historical character of each in its particularity.[37]

This 'sufficient moral gravity' criterion is admittedly quite ill defined; I would be loath to define how 'massive' the scale needed to be to meet the criterion. It does *not*, however, require rough moral *equivalence* to the Holocaust. In part, as mentioned in our 'uniqueness' discussion, this is because the meaningfulness of asserting such equivalence is in question. And in part it is because the attempt to establish such equivalences is fraught with moral perils. But the idea is that some atrocities are so appalling that they cross into something like a distinct moral terrain, occupied by the Holocaust, and that establishing their further equivalence to the Holocaust is unnecessary (as well as problematic). Take the Rwandan genocide of 1994, for example, which Novick is correct to say bears, among genocides, perhaps the closest resemblance to the Holocaust. This atrocity involved the mass slaughter of an ethnically identified people (the Tutsis, as well as many politically moderate Hutus) on the part of a state, with an intention to destroy every member of that group within the borders of the state. Is this genocide morally equivalent to the Holocaust? In about one hundred days, between five hundred and eight hundred thousand people were murdered (at a rate that surpassed the mass killing in the Holocaust), while six million were murdered in the Holocaust.[38] Although there is no uniform agreement that 'numbers matter' when it comes to morality, it is at least *plausible* to regard this numerical difference as involving some moral significance. If so, it will be impossible to gain agreement that the Rwandan genocide and the Holocaust are roughly morally equivalent.

I am guided by the overall standard that every atrocity deserves its appropriate form of moral attention; that attention should not be demoted or curtailed by the thought, 'Atrocity X is not as bad as atrocity Y.' Yet when the Holocaust is utilized to generate that appropriate attention to other atrocities, that is all to the good.

Remember that the proposed criterion is not of 'rough moral equivalence.' I am skeptical that such a concept could meaningfully be applied; and I agree with Novick that it is generally morally distasteful and unproductive to do so. Nor am I taking a stand on the vexing and contested issue of how, and in what ways, similar and different each of the 'candidate atrocities' is to the Holocaust. I have selected atrocities which have in fact been compared to the Holocaust. Some of these comparisons are made in the spirit criticized earlier (pp. 261–2) that, intended or not, has the effect of demoting the non-Holocaust atrocities. But in other cases – and here I may be in disagreement with Novick – the particular character of a given atrocity may well be helpfully brought out and highlighted by comparisons with the Holocaust.

Perhaps a consideration of the category of 'genocide' will help clarify my proposal here. In 1948, the United Nations declared genocide a crime under international law (in the Convention on the Prevention and Punishment of the Crime of Genocide), and the concept has subsequently garnered a good deal of political and scholarly attention. Leaving aside problems about the range of groups legitimately considered as targets under the concept of 'genocide' (for example whether to include politically defined groups, as the UN definition does not), all agree that the concept of genocide is meant to mark out a particularly atrocious and abominable form of crime, deserving of the severest condemnation by the international community, and, at least in theory, licensing activity across national boundaries to punish perpetrators of it. (In practice the United Nations has done little in this regard, although the trials in the past few years of alleged perpetrators in the Bosnian and Rwandan genocides are a sign of hope.)

At the same time, no one denies that atrocities short of genocide – such as the Chinese government's massacring approximately five thousand students in the protest in Tiananmen square in 1989, or 'ethnocide' (the destruction of a group's culture without the physical destruction of members of the group themselves) – deserve severe opprobrium and censure from the international community. But it is rightly felt that the concept of 'genocide' picks out a particularly horrific sort of mass atrocity deserving of a distinct form of opprobrium. Moreover, to count as a genocide, not all such atrocities need be thought of as equivalent in moral horror and reprehensibility (depending, for example, on the degree of premeditation, number of people killed, devotion to barring of escape, and so on[39]).

Similarly, I am suggesting that certain large-scale human atrocities are of 'sufficient moral gravity' to be candidates for analogy to the Holocaust, just as some atrocities deserve to be designated as 'genocides,' while others do not. But this does not mean that every sufficiently morally grave atrocity is *equal* in gravity to the

Holocaust, just as not every genocide is equally grave. Nor, obviously, does failure to meet the 'sufficient moral gravity' standard exclude a crime (such as the murder of James Byrd) from being horrific.[40]

So I have suggested two, not mutually exclusive, guidelines – the 'shared moral feature' and the 'sufficient moral gravity' approaches – for using the Holocaust as a source of 'moral lessons.' In this regard, I disagree with Novick's claim that this cannot, or should not, be done, and in doing so, I draw on some of Novick's own examples related to his different criticism 5 that Americans have failed to learn certain lessons of the Holocaust.

My defense of 'lessons of the Holocaust' so far still leaves in place part of Novick's criticism 2 – that the sort of lessons taught, say, by Facing History about prejudice, injustice and civic participation in the United States could be more profitably gleaned from other sources. To some degree, Facing History itself recognizes this. In its early years, its curriculum gave attention to the Turkish genocide of Armenians in 1915–23, in which (it is estimated) a million and a half Armenians were murdered. And in recent years, the organization has developed curricula focusing directly on African American issues, in recognition that such issues have special pertinence to American school children. The horrors of Cambodia, Rwanda and Bosnia surely deserve comparable attention in the study of mass atrocity, and issues of complicity, indifference, state-sponsored murder, resistance to authority, heroism in the face of appalling inhumanity, the involvement of official religious organizations, and other matters central to the Holocaust, could equally well be learned in these other contexts. In part (though only in part) because these atrocities are much more recent, there is nothing like the same level of documentation, personal testimony, and ethical and religious reflection on these events as there is with regard to the Holocaust.

In addition, however, one suspects another somewhat disturbing factor at play, that Novick mentions briefly, citing Phillip Lopate. Lopate has noted mass slaughters of Cambodians, Bengalis, Ibos (in Nigeria), Indonesian 'communists,' and others, and speculates,

> It is hard to escape the conclusion that, to us in North America, those piles of other victims are not as significant as Jewish corpses. Is it simply because they are Third World people – black, brown, and yellow-skinned?[41]

I fear that there is some truth to this, if we confine the point to the present and recent past. Although anti-Semitism has been 'the longest hatred,' in contemporary America, even in isolated Christian enclaves such as Whitwell, Tennessee, Jews are still, that is, have become, *white*; they are no longer the paradigm 'other,' as they were in Europe for centuries. I cannot help but look forward to the development of curricula and forms of public attention and recognition of these non-white victims of genocide and other mass atrocities, that would press white Americans to extend their empathy and understanding across America's long-intractable racial divide.

Problems with the Americanizing of the Holocaust

This brings us to two other of Novick's criticisms, 3 (more urgent tasks for Americans than Holocaust remembrance) and 6 (Americanization has led to strained links to Holocaust) (and 2 as well [sources other than the Holocaust provide the moral lessons contemporary Americans require]), relating to the American uses of the Holocaust. The salience of the Holocaust in American consciousness has had the effect of making it seem as if remembering the Holocaust, that is, remembering it in the morally appropriate way, is a vital task for Americans. The placement of the Holocaust Memorial Museum on the Washington Mall symbolizes this view. Imagine if, instead, a museum devoted to American slavery and segregation, or to the mistreatment of Native Americans by the US government and its people, were comparably prominent memorials in the nation's capital. How much more appropriate specifically to Americans would be such a public expression of the importance of coming to terms with the nation's historical mistreatment of African Americans and Native Americans.[42] (Perhaps the teachers in Whitwell, Tennessee, might go on to create a unit of study that encouraged their students to set out to collect paper clips for every African who died in the Middle Passage en route to slavery in the Americas.)

Admittedly, it is extremely unlikely that museums dedicated to slavery or the mistreatment of the American Indian would ever come to fruition with the widespread public and official support comparable to the Holocaust Museum, even if no Holocaust Museum had been built. Too many public figures, and many ordinary Americans, simply do not want to face these historical depradations with their continuing legacy of misfortune and injustice visited upon African Americans and Native Americans.[43] Indeed, in part because of that continuing legacy, African Americans and Native Americans are themselves ambivalent about memorials to their own past victimization.[44] To say this, however, is to vindicate Novick's very point. The reluctance to deal with America's own historical injustices is intimately tied to the very urgency of doing so. A main reason Americans have been willing to embrace the Holocaust Museum is precisely that, by contrast, the Holocaust is an atrocity for which Americans bear minimal responsibility.

In light of the relative remoteness of the Holocaust to specifically American history, national leaders have understandably felt compelled to link America to the Holocaust in explanation of American memorializing of the Holocaust in 'remembrance' days and the Museum. This explanation has gone in two quite different directions – one emphasizing American culpability in not doing more about the Holocaust at the time, the other emphasizing the 'un-American-ness' of the Holocaust. Novick is critical of both. He devotes a chapter to rebutting critics of American failure to bomb Auschwitz or rail lines to other death camps, of claims that anti-Semitism (rather than restrictionist sentiment more generally) lay behind not allowing more Jewish refugees to flee to the US, and other alleged failures to do more to rescue Jews (criticism 4).[45] I am insufficiently knowledgeable to assess these arguments, but it is striking that at the end of the chapter Novick concedes that

A much more energetic program of rescue on all fronts might have reduced the overall toll by perhaps 1 percent, conceivably 2 percent. Given the absolute numbers involved, this would have been a worthwhile achievement indeed.[46]

Novick is on stronger ground regarding criticism 6 – the strained or banal views about the Holocaust's importance for Americans. Even if Americans *could* have done somewhat more than they did to slow Hitler's genocide, their responsibility for this atrocity is still so much more minimal than their responsibility for their own history of mistreatment of African Americans and Native Americans.

The second public rationale for the prominence of American commemoration of the Holocaust – that America represents the mirror opposite of what Nazism stood for – is even more problematic. This rationale feeds an American triumphalism that acts as if the United States has already achieved the ideals of liberty, justice and equality that its national story valorizes. Witness the following official statement from the council charged with planning the Holocaust Memorial Museum:

> This Museum belongs at the center of American life because as a democratic civilization America is the enemy of racism and its ultimate expression, genocide. An event of universal significance, the Holocaust has special importance for Americans: in act and word the Nazis denied the deepest tenets of the American people.[47]

The idea that the United States has uniformly and unequivocally rejected racism is almost laughable, in light of the aforementioned legacy of racial slavery, segregation, and the racist mistreatment of Native Americans. Novick is right to worry that this particular dimension of the Americanization of the Holocaust feeds a lack of concern with urgent American injustices (criticism 3), implying that we have already transcended them.

Despite his irreverent and often sardonic tone, Novick occasionally acknowledges that he too contemplates the Holocaust with horror, awe, and a never-diminished sense that this is an event that can do no less than boggle the mind. Nor does Novick deny that Jews held a distinctive role in the outlook and genocidal policies of the Nazi state. Still, he is right, I believe, to decry common uses of the Holocaust that make it a sort of exclusive Jewish preserve, and that serve to divert attention from more urgent moral ills of our time, or past appalling sufferings of other peoples. In this light, I suggest a general guideline – that every atrocity be given its due, its appropriate form of moral attention and response, be that attempting to prevent mass slaughters that threaten or are in the process of being carried out, bringing perpetrators to justice, honoring the memory of the dead and the loss to the peoples involved, and teaching young people about these crimes. This standard can be used to assess whether, in whatever context, the Holocaust is being used to encourage, or to discourage, that appropriate attention; it can do both.

Novick is also on firm ground in pointing to some absurd, trivial and offensive uses of the Holocaust, as well as to some unfortunate aspects of the excessive Americanizing to which it has been subject. But I cannot follow him in his general attack on the idea that important lessons can be learned by studying the Holocaust – a position driven in part by his desire to undercut the legitimacy of the intensely

American appropriation of the Holocaust. Novick provides little support for this extreme position, and, indeed, takes stands inconsistent with it. As he rightly says, we should have learned from the Holocaust that a genocide was in the making in Bosnia and Rwanda; and that the risk of some American (and European) lives would have been justified in mitigating the horrors that took place in these nations. More generally, as Facing History and other Holocaust-based curricula suggest, it is possible to utilize the Holocaust for meaningful and important moral education on a range of issues. Peter Novick has provided us with a remarkable and essential disquisition on the post-Holocaust history of the Holocaust, one that is enriched by its moral concerns. It should spur us to deeper reflections on some of the most profound and intractable moral concerns of our time.

Notes

1. Dita Smith, 'A Measure of Hope: The Whitwell, Tenn., Holocaust Project Has Spread Far Beyond the Classroom,' *Washington Post*, 7 April 2001, p. C01.
2. Peter Novick (1999), *The Holocaust in American Life*, Boston: Houghton Mifflin.
3. Novick reports a summary of a series of polls taken in the early and mid 1990s, that 97 percent of those surveyed 'knew what the Holocaust was,' many more than knew what Pearl Harbor was, and even more than knew that the Soviet Union fought with the Allies in World War II. Ibid., p. 232.
4. Novick points out that the majority of prisoners liberated from Nazi concentration camps by American (as contrasted with Soviet) troops were not Jews. 'The best estimates are that Jews accounted for about one fifth of those liberated from concentrations camps in Germany by American troops.' Ibid., p. 65.
5. Ibid., pp. 41–4.
6. During this period, the Jews most visibly calling attention to the Holocaust were Jewish leftists, who emphasized the anti-fascist dimension of the struggle against Nazism. Ibid., p. 93. For a more detailed discussion of continuing struggles within the Jewish community over whether Holocaust-consciousness was to be given an anti-fascist and anti-racist direction, or (as Novick emphasizes) a more particularistic and politically conservative direction, see Michael E. Staub (1999), '"Negroes are not Jews": Race, Holocaust Consciousness, and the Rise of Jewish Neoconservatism,' *Radical History Review* **75** (Fall 1999), pp. 3–27.
7. Novick, *Holocaust in American Life*, pp. 177–8.
8. *The Diary of Anne Frank*, published in the US in 1952, made into a popular and prize-winning Broadway play in 1955, and a Hollywood film in 1959, is an only apparent counter-example to Novick's chronological account. *Diary* is not really about the Holocaust itself; the narrative takes place entirely in Amsterdam, omitting Anne's subsequent death in Bergen–Belsen. Moreover, especially the stage and screen versions downplayed the (in any case quite minor) Jewish elements in the diary and in Anne's self-identity, in favor of a more universal message (one very much supported and promoted by Otto Frank, the surviving member of the Frank family, who brought the diary to public attention), including the absurdly hopeful line from the diary, that closes both the play and the film: 'In spite of everything, I still believe that people are really good at heart.' Novick, pp. 117–20. On this issue, a fuller, quite helpful discussion is Hilene Flanzbaum (1999), 'Introduction' to her edited collection, *The Americanization of the Holocaust*, London: Johns Hopkins University Press, pp. 1–4.
9. Novick, *Holocaust in American Life*, p. 1.

10. Because Novick's primary focus is the United States, he gives much less attention to the uses of Holocaust-consciousness in Israel where, arguably, it has done a good deal more direct damage than in the US.

11. It is worth noting that Novick provides very little empirical substantiation for the factual claims on which many of these moral judgments are made. For example, he does not show, or really even attempt to show, that a focus on the Holocaust has served to render Jews more conservative; that conservative trend has affected all ethnic groups, and Novick provides no evidence that Jews as a group have moved further in a conservative direction than have any other ethnic group. Jews remain the only ethnic group besides African Americans that has consistently voted Democratic in national elections.

12. Novick, *Holocaust in American Life*, p. 14.

13. Ibid., p. 12.

14. Berel Lang (1999), 'Afterword: Lessons to Learn, or What Future for the Holocaust?', in his *The Future of the Holocaust: Between History and Memory*, Ithaca, NY: Cornell University Press, p. 174. Despite this cautionary note, Lang does in fact go on to derive some lessons from the Holocaust. See below, pp. 263–4.

15. Novick, p. 9.

16. Alan S. Rosenbaum (ed.) (2001), *Is the Holocaust Unique? Perspectives on Comparative Genocide*, 2nd edn, Oxford: Westview Press (from Introduction to the first edition), p. 3.

17. Steven T. Katz, 'The Uniqueness of the Holocaust: the Historical Dimension,' in ibid., p. 49.

18. Ibid. Novick cites this definition of Katz's on p. 196.

19. My own argument here implies, and I accept this implication, that the Holocaust can be spoken of as worse than other atrocities *in particular respects*, for example in involving a genocidal intention on the part of a state. This is not the same as saying that it is worse *all things considered*, a judgment that one should be less confident about making. But if I understand Novick correctly, he is not really denying that judgments of comparative moral horror can legitimately be made across atrocities, but that the public use of the 'uniqueness hypothesis' in our current circumstances is offensive.

20. Rosenbaum, *Is the Holocaust Unique?*, p. 2.

21. 'Nothing in the enormity of the Nazi genocide would change if that series of acts turned out to be the second, or fifth, instance of its kind.' Cited in Novick, p. 197.

22. Novick, pp. 242–3.

23. Novick says, 'Does the fact that these lessons didn't originate with the Holocaust mean that they aren't really lessons of the Holocaust, or at least not authentic ones? I don't think we should be in a hurry to say that.' Ibid., p. 242.

24. Novick, p. 243. Cf. 'I don't know of any criterion for the aptness of an analogy except the pragmatic one: does it or doesn't it click?' Ibid.

25. Ibid., p. 263.

26. Novick speaks of photographs of 'emaciated Bosnians peering out from behind barbed wire, pictures that might have been captioned "Buchenwald, 1945."' Ibid., p. 251.

27. Ibid., p. 250.

28. '"Stop the Death Camps," was the headline of an advertisement placed in the *New York Times* by three important American Jewish organizations.' Ibid., p. 251.

29. Ibid., p. 252.

30. Ibid., p. 253.

31. Lang, 'Afterword: Lessons to Learn,' pp. 175–93.

32. Novick, pp. 239–40.

33. Ibid., p. 262.

34. See account of this incident, 'Facing History Students Decide to "Stop Talking and Start Doing"', in *Facing History and Ourselves News*, spring 2000, p. 7.

35. Novick goes on to reiterate a different point, that I discussed earlier: 'on the other hand [it] makes anything to which it is compared look "not so bad".'

36. Novick is particularly derisive toward the version of this when anti-Semitism is involved: 'first stop, an anti-Semitic joke; last stop, Treblinka' (p. 178).

37. The comparisons are made, for example, in the collection George J. Andreopoulos (ed.) (1994), *Genocide: Conceptual and Historical Dimensions*, Philadelphia, PA: University of Pennsylvania Press; Rosenbaum, *Is the Holocaust Unique?*; and Laurence Mordekhai Thomas (1993), *Vessels of Evil: American Slavery and the Holocaust*, Philadelphia, PA: Temple University Press. We saw above, in the uniqueness discussion, that such comparisons are sometimes, even in the scholarly literature, made in a way that runs afoul of Novick's concern that the Holocaust not be used to demote in significance the atrocities compared to it. However, this is by no means always the case.

38. Account of Rwanda from Jeffrey Sharlet, 'Fierce Debate Divides Scholars of the 1994 Rwandan Genocide,' *Chronicle of Higher Education*, 3 August 2001, pp. A16–A19, and Philip Gourevitch (1997), *We Wish to Inform You That Tomorrow We Will be Killed with Our Families: Stories From Rwanda*, New York: Farrar, Straus, Giroux. The use of 'the six million' in reference to the Holocaust brings to the fore an assumption I have been making in referring to 'the Holocaust' – that that term refers specifically to the murder of Jews by the Nazis. Novick's book contains an excellent discussion (pp. 214–26) of the arbitrariness of this use of the term 'Holocaust.' He cites the other oft-employed figure of eleven million, itself a somewhat arbitrary figure, but one meant to encompass the range of non-Jewish victims of Nazism. I make no brief for my use of 'Holocaust' but mean only to be following what has become common usage, a usage that supplies the context for Novick's criticisms.

39. On possible criteria for degrees of moral culpability within genocides, see Israel Charny (1994), 'Toward a Generic Definition of Genocide,' in Andreopoulos, *Genocide*, p. 85.

40. The 'shared moral gravity' criterion is meant to be broader in its reach than 'genocide.' For example, it would include the bombing of Hiroshima and Nagasaki, and the treatment of Native Americans in the United States, neither of which seems to me usefully called 'genocide.' It is worth noting that the concept of 'genocide' has come to have such power as a term of shared condemnation that all sorts of crimes and (alleged) outrages have come to be called genocides (for example closing of synagogues in the Soviet Union; encouraging birth control and abortion among 'third world' peoples). This debasing of the term 'genocide' is parallel to the process Novick decries, although he does not exactly put it this way, of alleging a too broad range of alleged lessons to be drawn from the Holocaust (criticism 1).

41. Novick, p. 235. Fuller account in Phillip Lopate (1989), 'Resistance to the Holocaust,' *Tikkun* **4** (3), p. 58. Lopate goes on to suspect that both class and race factors are in play here. If Lopate is right about this, his point would probably not, however, have applied to the way the 'piles of corpses' were viewed in the first postwar photographs and accounts, when these Jewish bodies were not generally regarded as 'like us' by most Americans.

42. Between 1984 and 1994, several black organizations and individuals were instrumental in attempting to secure Congressional support for such a museum of African American life. Fath Davis Ruffins, 'Culture Wars Won and Lost, Part II: The National African-American Museum Project,' *Radical History Review* **70** (winter 1998), pp. 78–101.

43. The creation in the early 1980s of a national holiday commemorating Martin Luther King's birthday constituted a significant public recognition of African Americans. However, the public understanding of this national holiday has come to focus on King as a great national leader upholding American ideals of equality and justice, rather than on the actual (and continuing) racial injustices King's life was dedicated to eradicating. See Ruffins, 'Culture Wars', pp. 96–9.

44. Ibid.
45. Novick, 'The Abandonment of the Jews' (ch. 3), *Holocaust in American Life*, pp. 47–59.
46. Ibid., p. 58.
47. Quoted in: James E. Young, 'America's Holocaust: Memory and the Politics of Identity', in Helen Flanzbaum (ed.) (1999) *The Americanization of the Holocaust*, Baltimore: Johns Hopkins University Press, p. 73.

Index